SHELTER CITY

Shelter City

Protecting Citizens Against Air Raids

Koos Bosma

LHS

LANDSCAPE AND HERITAGE SERIES

AMSTERDAM UNIVERSITY PRESS

The publication of this book is made possible by grants from:

CLUE
RESEARCH INSTITUTE FOR THE HERITAGE AND HISTORY OF
CULTURAL LANDSCAPE AND URBAN ENVIRONMENT

Cultural Heritage Agency
Ministry of Education, Culture and Science

Translation: Vic Joseph

Illustration research: Koos Bosma
Photography 2004-2005: Anja de Jong
Bunker drawings: Cyane Conijn
Cartography: Bert Brouwenstijn

Cover illustration: Bill Brandt, Liverpool Street Underground Station, London, 12 November 1940.
Imperial War Museum.
Cover design and layout: Magenta Ontwerpers, Bussum

ISBN   978 90 8964 211 0
e-ISBN   978 90 4851 208 9 (pdf)
e-ISBN   978 90 4851 754 1 (ePub)
NUR   612/686

Contents

Foreword

Although cities and city dwellers are vulnerable to assaults on their biotope, however crude or sophisticated, they are resilient and not easily wiped from the map. The defensive reflex that has beset the Western world, including Europe, in recent years merits some critical scrutiny. Historically, it is by no means a unique phenomenon. We may view the current syndrome in the light of the earliest attempts at national risk management, namely the defensive measures taken against air raids, and when we do so, a striking continuity emerges. The present obsession with security is thus part of a tradition. One enduring constituent of this tradition is the recurrent portrayal of cities overwhelmed by man-made catastrophe in literature and art. In reality as well as in the imagination, every technological extension of our human powers contains within it an inherent potential for disaster. People have been weaving fantasies about assaults on cities and tall buildings from the moment the first flying machines took to the skies. Since the attacks on the Pentagon and the Twin Towers, the ideological, political, military and symbolic tensions between cities and buildings on the one hand, and aircraft and missiles on the other, have once more reached fever pitch. Another ingredient in the tradition is the enduring trauma of past aerial attacks on cities, including the bombardment of European cities during the Second World War, the nuclear annihilation of Hiroshima and Nagasaki, the bombing and napalm attacks in Vietnam, the devastation of Grozny from the air and the firing of Scud missiles on Israel.

Air raid protection is synonymous with an epoch – with a mentality, a political and administrative concept, and a diversity of technical and organizational measures to protect civilian populations against airborne assault. This epoch has apparently not yet ended. In 2000, when my research into the function and cultural significance of a German bunker in Utrecht expanded to include the air raid defence of Dutch civilians during the Second World War (a subject which to my astonishment has hitherto escaped systematic study), I imagined I was addressing a historical epoch with little if any contemporary relevance. The only topical thing about it seemed to be its bearing on whether the bunker should be preserved as a historical monument or demolished.

The worldwide shock and dismay resulting from the flames, dust and smoke of the collapsing World Trade Center towers in New York – mediocre architecture, but of great symbolic importance – led, in the Netherlands as elsewhere, to solemn declarations of determination to safeguard public security. There was little to go by but the yellowing pages of past scenarios. The foundations of today's disaster planning and risk management were laid in the 1930s and 1940s and were last updated during the Cold War. Despite major changes on the world scene, including new technologies, relatively recent threats such as international terrorism, and significantly modified military and strategic thinking, the notions of that period have not dated all that much. Present-day approaches to civilian defence, together with the associated planning, civil engineering and architectural typology, appear to be a continuation of theoretical concepts and practical experiments which were developed between the wars, and during the Second World War and the Cold War. The continuity is threefold in nature. Public fear is allayed by the rhetorical ingenuity with which the media presents technical novelties as averting impending doom when in reality nothing has changed. In Israel, for instance, anxiety about gas-armed missile attacks from Iraq was mollified by the launch of a new product: a plastic tent with a special air filtering system, as protection against the fallout from biological and chemical weapons.[1] There is also a regressive kind of continuity – a recapitulation of situations familiar to us from the past – as exemplified by the scenes of city-dwellers in Baghdad digging pits in their gardens to create shelter from bombs and rockets, and even donning second-hand World War II gas masks. A cruder example is the hideaway where Saddam Hussein was finally discovered, his underground lair linked to the outside air by a pitifully slender breathing tube. A third element of continuity, finally, is the ongoing technological race between bombs and missiles of increasing speed, precision, payload size and explosive force on the one hand, and the increasingly resistant defensive shields for vulnerable cities on the other.

ALS HET OM MENSCHENLEVENS GAAT...

2. "When it's a matter of life or death"

One rule of technology is that every new weapon elicits the development of corresponding defensive countermeasures, so the armament race has repercussions for urban planning, civil engineering and architecture. In 1933, the Netherlands hesitantly began constructing a parallel city as a protective measure against air raids, with architects and engineers playing an active part as in Britain and Germany. Following mobilisation, building activities accelerated. Then the Germans, who invaded Holland on 10 May 1940, took over the task of building that parallel universe. While the military sector of the occupying powers expanded their field of combat, in 1942 their civil counterparts embarked on a feverish campaign to build durable shelters in houses, public buildings and places of work, where the civilian population could take cover during air raids.

My research into the civilian aspect of bunkers and other forms of shelter in Dutch cities disclosed a common denominator to all the air raid protection schemes. In every city of any size, there emerged the social and physical contours of an alternative city, dedicated to protecting the civilian population against assault from the air. Henceforth, this book will use the term *Shelter City* to denote these hidden realms.

During the Second World War, city dwellers led a double life in a double city. Nowhere is their twofold existence, above ground and underground, so poignantly and impressively portrayed as in Bart Janssen's *De pijn die blijft. Ooggetuigenverslagen van het bombardement van Nijmegen 22 februari 1944* ("The Pain that Remains. Eyewitness Accounts of the Bombing of Nijmegen, 22 February 1944", 2005). The book not only documents the personal stories of those who died when Allied aircraft erroneously bombed the Dutch city of Nijmegen; it also reveals the effects of air raid warnings, the mutilation of both human bodies and the urban tissue by high-explosive and fragmentation bombs, the dedication and exertions of the personnel of the Shelter City, and – makeshift though they were – the day-to-day part played by domestic air raid shelters.

The duplicate city was never visible in its entirety; no synoptic view of it was possible. It is still very hard to gain an impression of the spatial elements and architecture of these warrens of air raid defences. Most of them were dismantled immediately after Liberation. A researcher must therefore attempt to reconstruct them as fully as possible and piece them together into a coherent pattern. A full study of Shelter City requires a special approach to its architectural history, one which endeavours to expose links between the ideology, urban culture, civil engineering and communications systems. It is not impossible to trace these links, as long as one sees the protection of city-dwellers against air raids as a planning task that combines social as well as spatial aspects.

A historical reconstruction of Shelter City, some remnants of which are still visible as vivid reminders while others survive only in a fragmentary form deeper beneath the surface, can perhaps best be characterized by a medical metaphor. The historian must conduct a full-body scan of the urban tissue in order to discern an image of the Shelter City.

It is worth digressing briefly here about one of the more prominent spatial elements of the Shelter City, the bunker. From July 1941, Germany adopted the military term *Bunker* to denote bomb-proof, gas-tight structures purpose-built for the civilian population (as opposed to the lesser air raid shelters that offered protection only against flying shrapnel, falling masonry and low concentrations of gas). The bunkers were introduced to the public as *Wehrhäuser* ('defensive houses') or *Luftschutzhäuser* ('air defence houses'). These names had an ideological motive: their homeliness invited associations with historical fortifications such as medieval city gates, and was intended to cultivate their popular acceptance. At first, the civic authorities also planned to embellish the architecture of the purpose-built shelters with historicizing allusions, but it soon became clear that the only completed structures would be the crude concrete monoliths we recognize as bunkers.

There were considerable differences between the civilian bunkers and those built for military use, such as the Westwall (or Siegfried Line, 1936-1940) and the Atlantic Wall (1942-1944). The military bunker complexes have already been the subject of extensive historical study and have been exhaustively documented. They were conceived for the conventional front line; the Atlantic Wall was a continuous structure intended to parry a seaborne invasion, while also providing rearward cover.[2] These bunkers were manned by fighting forces, and defence against air attacks played little part in their design.

The character and design of the military bunkers were matched to the anticipated war situation. Different requirements were imposed on their civilian counterparts, since the continuation of normal city life meant more than spending time cooped up in a fort. Even as early as 1939 and 1940, the German air defence ordinances place a non-military bunker in the same category as a house, a city hall or other public building: that of a *Sonderkonstruktion*, that is, "an independent structure erected near, adjacent to, or adjoining other buildings."[3] In terms of siting, an air raid shelter was thus like any other civilian structure, and merely required insertion into the urban context. The planning departments of the major German cities had some freedom in the design of a *Sonderkonstruktion*, and as the war progressed and the shortage of materials became increasingly acute, they opted for widespread standardization.

The bunker typology of the Atlantic Wall also betrayed a distinct tendency toward standardization, in a design that visually expressed both the function and the military hierarchy; other design priorities were compactness and decentralization. Civilian bunkers, on the other hand, sheltered not soldiers but members of the public of both sexes and all ages and social ranks. The bunker was a survival machine,[4] like the interior of a submarine or the pressure cabin of an aircraft, and this accounted for its half-hearted acceptance by both city dwellers and the civic authorities. As a survival machine, the bunker was a necessary evil, and there was no point spending too much effort on it, whether architecturally, programmatically or aesthetically. The agitated crowds of city-dwellers would be compressed *en masse* into gloomy square or rectangular boxes, where they were obliged to wait patiently until the bombs had finished their business, after which they could go outside and inspect the damage. Like a bizarre experiment of behavioural science, the civilian bunker combined the extremes of human fear, hope and claustrophobia. Life in Shelter City was like entering a vacuum; an eternal present or a moment outside time. The mood that prevailed in the bomb shelters was aptly characterized by the English novelist Elisabeth Bowen as follows: "The very temper of pleasures lay in the chanciness, in the canvas-like impermanence of their settings, in their being off-time."[5]

In this book, the concept of a bunker (civilian or otherwise) will be treated in a very broad sense, firstly as a survival machine that is more or less resistant to bomb shrapnel, gas or explosive forces, and secondly as a cultural, technological and architectural phenomenon whose prominence in the urban scene made it a significant formal constituent of Shelter City. They were a material component in a sophisticated social and spatial framework that included many other ingredients, such as sandbags, air raid sirens, blackout curtains, communication systems and food depots. The personnel of the shelters consisted of public works officials, police, firemen, medical personnel, volunteers, rescue teams, shelter staff, meal providers and air raid wardens. They had emergency plans that specified all kinds of special powers, regulations, protective clothing and equipment, such as gloves, goggles, rubber boots, helmets, lightweight and heavyweight chemical suits, fire extinguishers, respirators and gas masks. Their duties included keeping the public informed and holding courses to prepare them mentally for the rigours of air raids.

The aims of this book are threefold. First of all, it endeavours to present a comparative international perspective of the Shelter City phenomenon and an interpretation of the Dutch air raid protection measures. It then considers the physical and formal manifestation of Shelter City, for example through a historical reconstruction of it as realized in the Netherlands, including under the German occupying forces from 1942 to 1945. Finally, the book presents an analysis of Cold War thinking on defence against aerial threats.

For the first of these aims, the book reviews current knowledge on British and German civilian air raid defences (Chapters 2, 3 and 4). These chapters may be read separately, but together they form a context for a comparative analysis of the Dutch apparatus for air raid protection and emergency relief. British historians described their national air raid protection in great detail back in the 1950s and 1960s, while they still disposed over a considerable quantity of first-hand information. Inevitably, they reconstructed life underground from the standpoint of a victorious power, interpreting the behaviour of Londoners during the Blitz from a heroic viewpoint, rather than seeing it through a Machiavellian lens as a form of mass insanity. Their wish to portray a homogenous home front yielded a history peopled by brave soldiers with right on their side and resolute civilians. This victor's perspective raises several moral issues. For example, photographs showing corpses, body parts and maimed victims of the bombing were suppressed for decades so as to uphold the myth of British grit. But just how heroic was it to dispatch youngsters as message boys during the London Blitz, when their chance of arriving alive and well at their destination was so disproportionately small? The surge in looting and other crime in London was similarly underexposed, as was the way the sex trade shifted its field of operations underground along with the rest of the population. Another suppressed episode was the collapse of public morale in Liverpool following the Blitz on that city, when the army had to be brought in to restore order.[6]

German historical accounts of the impact of the Allied air offensive at street level were long non-existent; it is only in recent years that historians in Germany have broached the subject and discussed the human cost of the bombardments in detail[7] (the same is true of Belgium and France). British historians have widely expressed discomfort at this, as though it were an infringement of their intellectual territory. The civilian air raid defences in Germany have been analysed in a few general works, mainly in the 1990s and especially with regard to their ideological aspects, the communication systems, the strategies of attack and defence, and life in the bunkers.

The second aim of this book includes an interpretation of the Dutch air raid protection system and its significance for the construction of Shelter City. For the first time, the legal framework of the Dutch air raid protection system (1936) and its practical implementation in various Dutch cities are analysed and compared with those in the surrounding countries (Chapter 2). On a basis of literature and archive research, I proceed to examine the emergence of Shelter City in the Netherlands before and during the German occupation. The widely held picture of Dutch air raid precautions had little heroic about it from the outset. This reputation was partly a product of the subordinate position of the urban air raid protection services to the occupying authorities, and of the amateurishness and ineffectiveness of the personnel of Shelter City. But it was above all due to the low public confidence in successive regimes and in their ability or willingness to set up a genuine air raid defence system. The measures taken at the *moment suprême*, during the bombardment of Dutch cities – relief plans, the establishment of municipal air raid defence services and the building of private and public bomb shelters – receives attention in Chapter 5. The postwar concept of civil defence, with its salient volunteerism and lack of fundamental investment, further bolstered the image of ongoing dilettantism and incompetence.

Third, the book analyses the development of the German communications network (Chapter 6) and of Shelter City in the Netherlands under occupation (Chapter 7). Based on archive research, I study the effect that occupation had on the Dutch air raid protection authorities and the contribution the Germans themselves made to the development of Shelter City by building shelters for their high-ranking functionaries, senior police officials and other German citizens living in the Netherlands. It seems that the top German administrator, Reichskommisar Dr. Arthur Seyss-Inquart, acted as principal and had a separate department for German civilian projects in the Netherlands, the *Abteilung Siedlung und Bauten* (Department of Housing and Public Works). Between 1942 and 1945, this department played a leading role in planning and building air raid shelters, of which Seyss-Inquart's nerve centre at Clingendaal, near The Hague, was the most important (Chapter 7). *Siedlung und Bauten* also played an active part in the design of the bunkers needed for international communication, as well as for purely military projects. The architecture that *Siedlung und Bauten* built on the orders of Seyss-Inquart was an essential contribution to the expansion of Shelter City. Its most enduring remains – bunkers with walls up to three metres thick – were adapted during the Cold War to meet the defence requirements of the nuclear age (Chapter 8). In the matter of conservation, the Netherlands lags well behind the UK where the material vestiges of the Cold War and everything connected with civil defence have received considerable archaeological attention, with many defensive structures listed as historical buildings or sites. This has one great advantage, however. The remains of Shelter City have enjoyed a peaceful old age in the Netherlands, undisturbed in their urban or rural surroundings (Chapter 9).

The Dutch edition of this book (2006) includes three appendices which have been omitted from the present English-language edition:

- a survey of *Siedlung und Bauten* projects in Scheveningen, The Hague and Wassenaar;
- a survey of the building activities of the *Siedlung und Bauten* outside The Hague;
- a discussion of the bunker in the Servaas Bastion in Utrecht.

The original version of Chapter 6 is moreover divided into two parts, and the concluding chapter has been partially rewritten, in order to give the heritage aspects the prominent place they deserve.

Of course, a book like this could not have been written without the aid and encouragement of a great many people. The publications in various fields of research that I have drawn on for facts, arguments and quotations are mentioned in the notes. The illustrations in this book have been carefully selected for the extent to which they depict the many physical and emotional dimensions of Shelter City. What is it that makes the visual and verbal vocabulary of Shelter City so unmistakable? Why do the images of Shelter City continue to move, astonish and overwhelm us, despite the many intervening years in which we have been increasingly saturated by and thus inured to scenes of disaster and human misery? Due to our historical distance and the lack of modern documentary techniques in those times, we are fascinated by the mysteries of an unfinished story, with all its imperfections and improbabilities and the sense of raw survival the images exude. These pictures often have something of a still life, of a reduction to the barest margins of existence, of Shelter City doomed to become a *memento mori*.

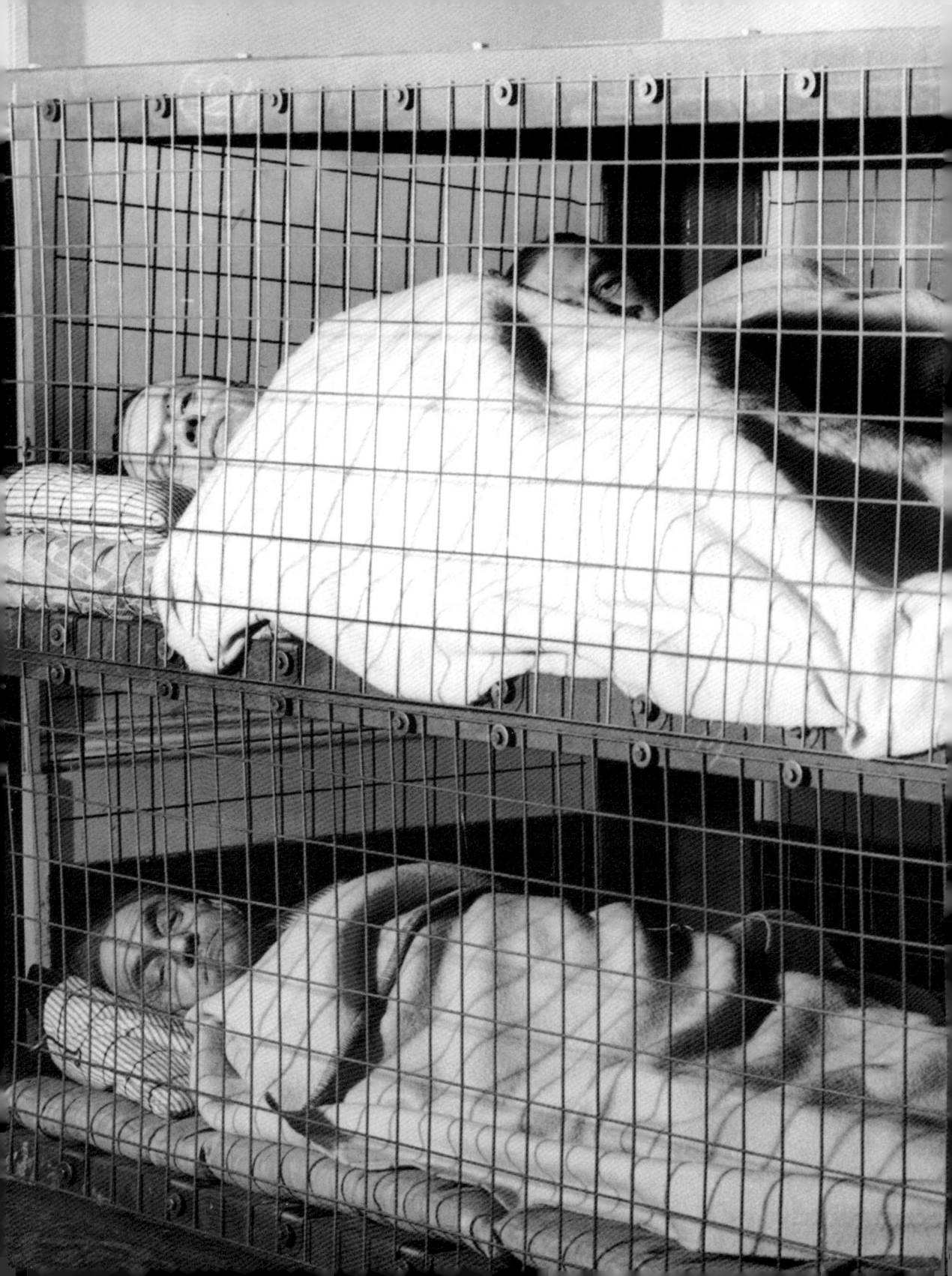

North Sea

Enschede

Zeist
Delft   Deelen
     Driebergen   Arnhem

Zierikzee

Venlo

0   30 km

Maastricht

< *Page 18 and 19*
3. Indoor steel cage, Morrison Shelter, London 1941

CHAPTER 1

"Gunpowder is heaping up in Europe and sparks could fly!"

Contours of a Shelter City

AIRSPACE AND AVIATION

The narrator in Dostoevsky's novel *Notes From Underground* (1864) explains why he lives in a cellar (his "mouse hole") and absolutely refuses to leave it. In a monologue, he contrasts his underground den with a "Palace of Crystal", a prominent building in another part of the city which is inviolable, impervious to doubt and permitting no denial; you may not even poke out your tongue at it. Dostoevsky had visited London in that period and seen the Crystal Palace with his own eyes. He sets its ostentation against the misery of his mouse hole, which nonetheless lends him ample opportunity for shady affairs, destructive behaviour and unfettered emotions. He is convinced that "man will never renounce real suffering, that is, destruction and chaos".[1] In a twist of literary irony, a novel by H.G. Wells, *The War in the Air* (1909), chooses the Crystal Palace in London as a place where plans are forged for worldwide aerial warfare.

Turning to the twentieth century, we can interpret the Crystal Palace and the mouse hole as symbols of, on the one hand, the official city with its imposing buildings whose occupants issue decrees on war and peace, and, on the other, of the parallel city that skulks in the long shadow of the official one and offers secrecy and shelter to those who seek it. The threat of war justifies the existence of Shelter City. War boosts industrial production, accelerates and standardizes technical innova-

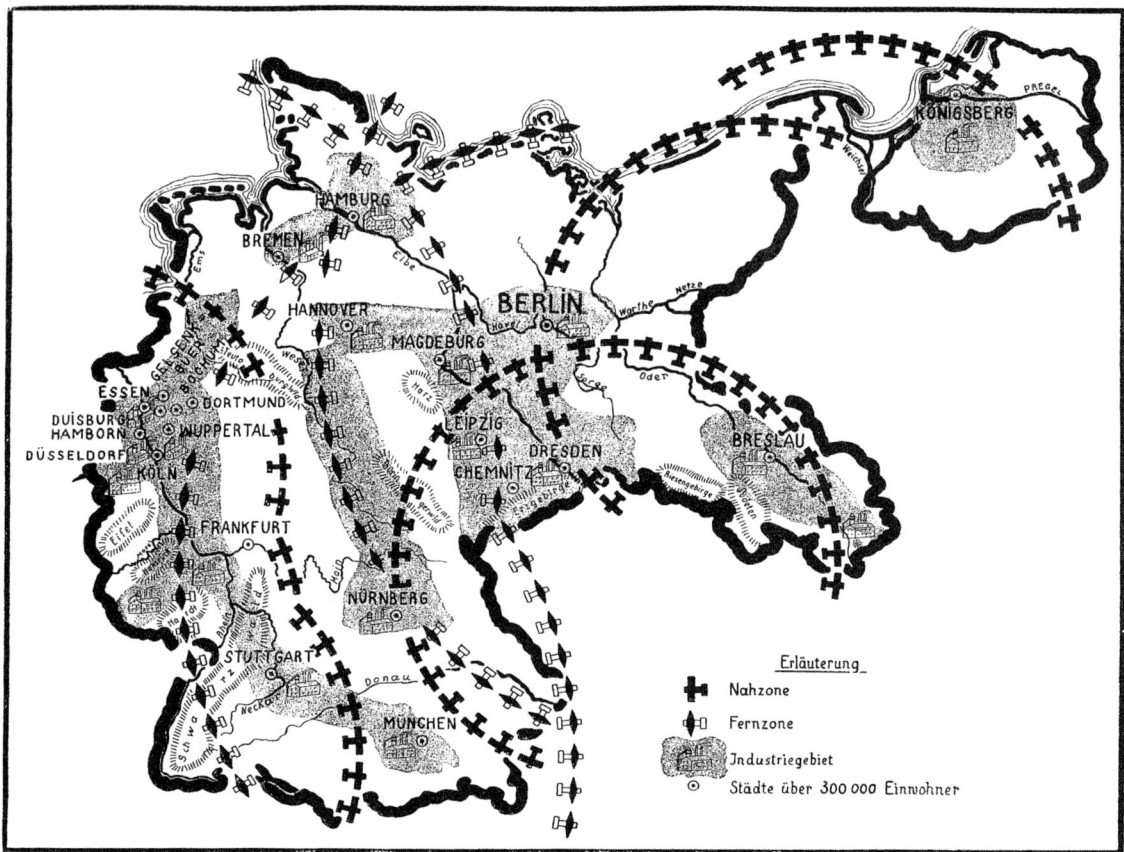

4. Threat levels in German airspace, 1934. Inscriptions from top to bottom: near zone, far zone, industrial areas, cities with a population over 300,000

tions, simplifies ideologies by cultivating an enemy concept, and legitimizes actions by claiming a monopoly on morality. The Shelter City shields its inhabitants against attack from the air. It is the dark alter ego of the existing city: unlovely and primitive, forever unfinished and always betraying a scent of fear that underlies its design.

The modernist progress towards mechanization, towards a civilization shaped by the capacities of engineers, has been interpreted as an alienation of human nature ever since the first publications of Karl Marx. Mechanization as an extension of the human body, with modern warfare as its eventual outcome, spawned a recurrent international discussion on the arduous peace negotiations, on the hazards of progress, and the psychological and political consequences of bloodthirsty militarism.[2] During the first decades of the twentieth century, the mechanization process culminated in flying machines. The appearance of these wonders of technology symbolized the dawn of a new era, breaking with every tradition. This zenith of modernity, however, exerted not only a poetic heroism but also the threat of turning the urban surroundings into a theatre of war. The Hague Convention of 1907 banned attacks on civilians from the air. But this prohibition did not apply to the colonies; there, it seems, the idea of treating the natives as civilized beings was beneath serious consideration. The symbolic and geopolitical implications of the flying machine were demonstrated by the French pilot Louis Blériot, who flew across the Channel in 1909 and so robbed Great Britain of its long cherished self-image as an inviolate island realm. The potential of flying machines (and initially airships, too) as weapons of war was recognized from the outset.[3] The Spanish air force conducted an airborne assault on Tripoli in 1911, although without fatal casualties. After Spain, Italy, France and Great Britain attacked the populations of their colonies from the air as a method of "pacification".[4] The French coined the term "colonial bombing" and developed a purpose-built aircraft, the *Type Colonial*. In the UK, the objective was described as "domination without occupation".

In the course of World War I, planes were equipped not only with machine guns but with devices for discharging bombs; warring empires were thus able to re-apply the art of colonial bombing to their civilized neighbours. The prospect of using aircraft to spread poison gas over enemy territory did not go unnoticed either. Pandora's Box was open – but so far by a mere fraction, so that theories on the potential of an air force in an escalating conflict remained somewhat speculative.

The speculation continued between the wars especially in military circles, for example at the Air Corps Tactical School of the American Army and as part of the secret German-Soviet technical collaboration in Lipetsk. Studies on related topics appeared in specialist journals such as *Revue de l'Aéronautique Militaire* (from 1921) and *Rivista Aeronautica* (from 1925).

A conspicuous feature of twentieth-century modernization was its domestication of air space into an extension of everyday life. The idea of conquering an infinite, abstract space, independent of both land and sea, reinforced the belief that man and machine would one day detach themselves altogether from the face of the earth. The reach of both military and civil action underwent a radical change. The geopolitical clout of established empires had been founded on a dominance of the high seas which served them in their conflicts with rival continental powers, but now this made way for a delocalized and spatially unconstrained style of warfare that set little store by the distinction between land and water. A criss-cross of trajectories now sullied the stainless mantle of the planet, hitherto the preserve only of clouds and birds.

Air space became increasingly cluttered by flying machines and the noise of new communication systems (radio waves, radar, flares and searchlights) as the twentieth century gained pace. This development called for conscious design, an architecture of communications, for all the airborne movements must inevitably be managed from ground stations. The worldwide proliferation of these teletechnical systems raised the spectre of remote detonation, and hence of an attack on the habitat of the city dweller. The domestication of air space sparked off the fear of attack by poison gas, bacteria and explosives.

Civilian life thus had to shield itself against attack from the air. Now that cities were potential targets for bombers, it was necessary to develop survival machines whose architectural manifestation would claim their place in the cityscape. As H.G. Wells wrote, a hallmark of the "century of science" was that progress in technology was not necessarily matched by advances in social spheres: "mechanical invention had gone faster than intellectual and social organization, and the world with its silly old flags, its silly meaningless tradition of nationality, its cheap newspapers and cheaper passions and imperialisms, its base commercial motives and habitual insincerities and vulgarities, its race lies and conflicts, was taken by surprise."[5] The difficulty people had in gauging the potential destructiveness of these technical advances is illustrated by an opinion prevalent in the 1930s that a war of aerial attacks on cities was bound to dislocate every aspect of culture and civilization and must therefore be abhorrent.

The Hungarian author Sándor Márai described the emotional difference between fighting physically and mechanically in graphic terms: "It makes a difference if we put our hands around the throat of a fellow being and break his neck, or if we wound him with a sharp object. And propelling a lead bullet into the body of a distant opponent by explosive means is something else again."[6] The next stage in the mechanization of conflict would be the large-scale, anonymous attack on the biotope of the city dweller.[7] People would turn into mere numbers and be assaulted collectively from above.

THE AIRFIELD AS A BASE OF OPERATIONS

In order to make the best possible use of aircraft, it became necessary to develop the airfield as a base of operations.[8] The first generation of airfields (1900-1919) combined military and civil functions; typically, the airfield was a meadow fringed with barracks and hangars. Little was required for a landing site: the surrounding buildings could not be too high, and the tract of land had to be flat and well-lit. In fact, the first airfields were little more than facilities for amateur stunt men in their flying machines. However, World War I soon put an end to the carefree pioneering days, when it was discovered that both dirigibles and winged aircraft could be deployed as instruments of war, for example for dropping bombs on the enemy. The number of aircraft and the number of people employed in the aviation industry consequently soared, to the extent that once the war ended the airfields continued to be used as a base of operations for freight and passenger transport. Civil aviation came into being in 1919, the year in which the first aircraft constructed entirely of metal left the factory. "The first postwar machines on the air routes were rebuilt bombers, with windows cut into the fuselages and small passenger cabins built in. An infrastructure for a future air traffic network was already in place, for many cities already possessed military and factory airfields. And there were a lot of unemployed pilots and unnecessarily large airplane industries that faced an unavoidable downsizing."[9] The growing use of aircraft drove a feverish quest for safer, more comfortable and more advanced machines, as well as an increase in their speed and range. Flying machines gained tail wheels, wheel brakes and accurate instrumentation. The military versions were now equipped with mounted machine guns and bomb racks.

The second generation of airfields (1920-1935) was marked by the separation of civil and military facilities. Aircraft were conveying passengers to increasingly far-off destinations, so a civilian airfield was typified by a passenger terminal, a car park and a control tower. Its military equivalent had no need of a terminal, although the number of barracks and hangars rose rapidly. Both military and civilian airfields required a flat, grassy field for takeoff and landing.

The third generation of civilian airfields (1935-1945), with their iconic terminal buildings, played no part in military air transport and appeared in only a few European cities (for example Tempelhof in Berlin and Gatwick near London). The larger, heavier aircraft, which had retractable landing gear, metal fuselages and pressure cabins, needed longer, hardened surfaces for takeoff and landing. Both military and civilian airfields were provided with tarmac aprons for parking the aircraft alongside the hangars and terminals, and multiple concrete runways aligned to different wind directions.

THREE-DIMENSIONAL WARFARE

Submarines operating in the deepest waters, tanks rolling in wide formations over the countryside and planes high in the sky transgressing all borders: these technologies turned warfare into a three-dimensional phenomenon. "The superior speed of the diverse means of communication and destruction is, in the hands of the armed forces, the privileged means for an insidious but creeping social transformation, a projectile for the destruction of the social continuum, a weapon, an *implosive*."[10] Airspace was formerly an abstract, measureless, emptiness; but now aircraft changed the space above land and water, and especially above towns, into an important factor in transport and communication. The reach of military might changed accordingly. The sky above the continents became a field of energy, activity and velocity.[11] As the national air fleets proliferated, aircraft speeds tripled compared to those prevailing at the end of World War I. Their bomb-carrying capacity quadrupled, and the range of action of bombers quintupled.[12] This acceleration entailed a new understanding and organization of geopolitical space.

THE THEORY OF AIR WAR

The Second World War differed markedly from the First in the capabilities of the fighting equipment and the availability of long-distance communications. Highly mobile, technically sophisticated machines such as tanks, submarines and aircraft gave warfare a mechanized character and, in principle, an almost unlimited geographical reach. These rapid developments made it easy to bypass traditional defensive structures such as the Maginot Line, the Siegfried Line and the Atlantic Wall, and to engage the hinterland of the front in the action. Those who stayed behind in the cities were now regarded simply as enemies. The traditional tactics for overpowering cities, such as siege, blockade and artillery bombardment, were now augmented by a vertical dimension of aggression.

The experience gained in aerial bombing during World War I was already looking outdated by the 1930s. The bomb strike locations recorded on the maps of Paris and Venice in those days reveal a completely arbitrary pattern. The bomb craters in London formed more of a regular line, perhaps indicating that the bombs were dropped at fixed intervals. On the night of 31 May 1915, the City of London was attacked by Zeppelins, claiming seven fatalities. Nineteen aerial assaults on the English coast had taken place in the preceding five months, resulting in 58 military and

498 civilian deaths. From 1916 to 1918, London became the target of two-engine planes which claimed 836 dead and 1,994 wounded. Most of the bombs landed on roads and open spaces, and most of the casualties occurred in low-income neighbourhoods.[13] Half of the enemy planes did not even reach London, and one-fifth of those that did were shot down. Yet the psychological effect of the bombing campaign now seems incredible: "For several weeks afterwards, London's Underground stations were packed nightly 'to suffocation' by an estimated 300,000 people, while half a million others went into cellars."[14]

The British revenge on Germany in 1918 achieved 746 fatal victims and 1,843 wounded. The French had already taken revenge for the German assault on the small, undefended town of Bar-le-Duc in 1916, when 85 civilians were killed. In a French bombardment of Karlsruhe, each two-engine plane dropped eight bombs on the city. The first five bombs landed on a circus marquee where an audience of 2,000 people were enjoying a performance; 120 were killed, including 85 children.[15] Even the Netherlands, neutral in World War I, suffered an aerial bombardment. In fact, it was a targeting error by British bombers. In February 1917, British planes started bombing the Belgian ports of Oostende and Zeebrugge, where German submarines were moored, taking a route over the region of Zeeuws-Vlaanderen in the southwest of the Netherlands. On the night of 30 April, a bomber strayed off course and discharged eight bombs on the Dutch town of Zierikzee. A fireman described the effect of a direct hit on the house of a couple with a foster child: "They were thrown out of the house, beds and all. The man was slung across the street, over a three-metre high wall and into the garden of Mr. Korsten. Later, we could still see blood on the wall. And who knows what trajectory the woman must have followed; she landed several houses away on the other side of the street, on a manhole cover. Her head was gone and her bosom squeezed out, so to speak. Skin hung in shreds from the neck." The child was found buried under rubble.[16]

Bombings by airships and two-engine aircraft during World War I prompted the South African general Jan Smuts to comment in 1917 that "the day is not far off when airborne operations, with their devastating effect on the enemy's territory and their large-scale destruction of centres of industry and population, will have become the primary acts of warfare."[17] Churchill shared his view. As the Minister of Defence, he had conceived a plan to attack Berlin with thousands of bombers. "The campaign of 1919 was never fought; but its ideas go marching on."[18] Churchill argued that national leaders had the means to render their opponents helpless, for the first time in the history of Western civilization. "The air opened paths along which death and terror could be carried out far behind the lines of the actual armies, to women, children, the aged, the sick, who in earlier struggles would perforce have been left untouched."[19]

Post-World War I discussions on the use of airborne action generally considered three alternatives. "There has been the tactical versus strategic argument, which is about whether air power is best used in conjunction with other arms on the battlefield or as an alternative, independent, offensive operation. Second, there has been the choice of objectives of attack – between the traditional, Clauzewitzian goal of the destruction of the enemy's armed forces, or (more fundamentally but less directly) the destruction of the national will to continue to resist. This argument becomes entangled with the debate about the selection of precise or more diffuse targets: precision as against area bombing, with the latter being used as something of a euphemism for city bombing."[20] The reality of that precision was wryly characterized by World War I flying ace Major Oliver Stewart in 1925: a bomber "can hit a town from ten thousand feet – if the town is big enough."[21] The English-language literature tended to focus on the permissibility of air aggression under international law and on its potential as a way of breaking the morale of the population. "Future war will see aircraft used in great units, employed in much the same manner as regiments and brigades in an army."[22] The books on air war published between the wars by Britain's leading theoretical authority, James Molony Spaight, survey the available knowledge and speculations, although his work does not offer any general strategic theory on the use of air power.[23]

A theory of air warfare was formulated in 1921 by the Italian pilot and officer Giulio Douhet in his book *Il dominio dell'aria* (The Command of the Air), which Hitler and Goering read in the German translation.[24] Douhet was not so much an original thinker as a compiler of existing theories, some of which had already been published before the start of World War I – for example, the tactic of the knockout blow (a ominous combination of the psychological effects of air raids, such as: mental collapse, profound rage, panic and riots), and descriptions of the material effects of mass bombings of large cities such as Paris and London. The hallmark of Douhet's writing was the frank way he pursued the strategic potential of air power to its logical conclusions, unfettered by moral qualms.

In Douhet's view, the flying machine's independence from the ground and its superior speed made it an ideal weapon of aggression. It would render conventional military strategies obsolete and put an end to the static trench warfare of World War I. The air force should exist alongside the army and navy as an equal partner, he argued. Its primary tactic should be to pound an area of a city with explosives of different calibre, and then to deposit a blanket of poison gas to impede the extinguishing of the resulting fires. "One must imagine what it will be like in a great city when a twenty-ton load of air ordnance lays waste to a central zone of some 250 metres radius. Strike after strike! Fires, explosions, collapsing houses. And the poison gas rolling over the whole scene. The searing flames consume everything around them, no longer constrained to the original seat of conflagration, ever fiercer and brighter, while the gas continues on its frightful path."[25]

Douhet predicted not only that future wars would take on a three-dimensional character due to the military use of aircraft, but that they would be total wars with the front line extending all the way to the home front. Every member of society would become a combatant. In total war, it was essential to strike the first blow, to destroy the enemy's air forces and supporting infrastructure, and to pursue the merciless destruction of social, governmental and economic bases.[26] Douhet saw bombing the material structure of an enemy city, with the inevitable disabling of the urban population, as a necessary psychological tactic. An air war aided by explosives and chemical and bacteriological poisons could be fought out in any desired zone of the enemy territory. Thanks to the first, devastating blow, the future war would result in less bloodshed; all the more since the bombing and gassing would so undermine the morale of the enemy that the civilian population would soon press for capitulation.

Douhet did not look at other technical advances such as searchlights and electronic communications, which were to become key elements in World War II, while despite his great expectations of clouds of poison gas, they scarcely figured as weapons then. Yet the fear of a coming war being fought mainly with chemical ordnance was far from ungrounded. In the course of World War I, the air had become a manipulable commodity; breathing was a privilege that could be withheld. The first major gas attack had taken place in the trenches near Ypres on 22 April 1915. Engineers clad in gas masks opened the taps of 5,730 cylinders of liquid chlorine. Ten minutes later, the easterly breeze drove the yellowish cloud of chlorine, one and a half metres thick, six kilometres wide and six to nine hundred metres deep, across the front line. The chlorine created a breach in the French ground formation.[27] Most men of the Algerian division, who were crouching in the trenches in its path, were asphyxiated where they lay; those who managed to flee were blinded, blood trickling from their noses and mouths.

A few years after the gas attack at Ypres in 1919, the artist Marcel Duchamp acutely symbolized the new existential condition by packaging samples of air in vials and sending them round the world as "ready made" gifts. By the 1920s, gastight chambers were in use for fumigating sofas and other household goods to remove insect pests, and some American states adopted the gas chamber as a "humane" option for executing condemned prisoners. The use of poison gas in warfare was restricted to ground attacks in the 1930s, apart from the war in the Rif mountains in Spanish Morocco, in which the Spanish conducted the first gas attacks from the air using various poison gases they had obtained from German laboratories. The Italians also deployed poison gas as an aerial weapon in their colonial war in Abyssinia in 1936. Opinions were divided about whether gas bombs were likely to be used in a future non-colonial war; some people saw the use of gas on civilized towns as inconceivable, while others were seriously worried about the "friendly gift from the enemy, intended to sow panic in the city".[28]

Elias Canetti eloquently described the fear of gas warfare that beset people in the 1930s: "It is the defencelessness of our breath of which I finally wish to speak. It is a threat that is hard to exaggerate. Man is exposed to the air as to nothing else. In it, he still moves as Adam did in paradise. (...) Air is the last straw at which man clutches. It comes to us all alike. It is not divided, and even the poorest may partake of it. (...) And it is precisely this last thing that we still had in common, that will poison us all in common."[29]

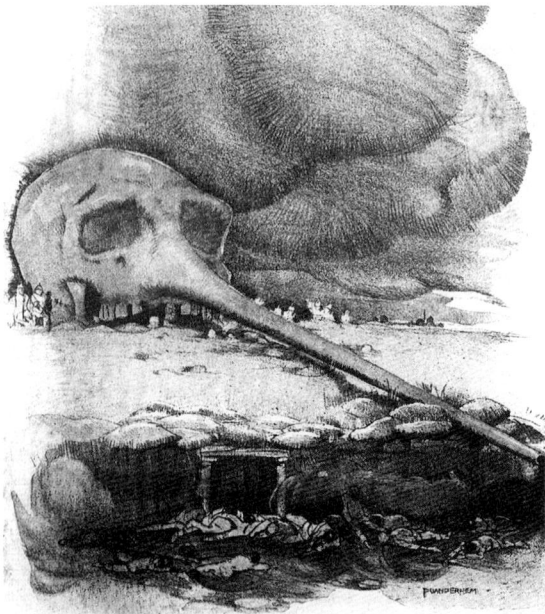

5. Piet van der Hem, poison gas as "The New Death", undated

6. The French engineer Le Witte devised a stretcher with a gasproof aluminium cover. When in use the compartment is automatically ventilated with filtered air. The invention was exhibited in Paris in the 1930s

SUDDEN DEATH: THE ASSAULT ON GUERNICA

Summoned to the aid of Franco in the Civil War, the Nazis saw Spain as an experimental laboratory for their military ambitions. Here they could hone their skills in burning down selected villages and towns, which they did without even waiting for explicit orders from General Franco. The German Condor Legion consisted of several air squadrons, a tank corps and a corps specialized in communications and radio technology. With this force they were in a position to put their Blitzkrieg tactics to the test – the combination of rapid ground and air forces, able to communicate with one another using the latest technology. As part of their Spanish experiment, the German army tried out 27 different types of aircraft for their suitability for different tactics such dive-bombing and area bombing. They also practised night flying guided by advanced navigation techniques.

In their attacks on Spanish villages in 1936, they developed a crucial assault tactic: area bombing in three waves. The first wave consisted of bombs of roughly 800 kilograms intended to destroy concrete buildings. These were followed by bombs of approximately 100 kilograms to shatter the main blocks of rubble. Finally, there was a wave of firebombs, combined with fragmentation bombs to kill the firemen who rushed to quench the flames.[30]

Not only had aircraft design meanwhile advanced by leaps and bounds, but the ordnance had undergone considerable refinement. The various categories of bombs and their effects on civilian targets were well known to professionals.[31] The heavy, general-purpose, high-explosive bombs had a delay fuse and were designed to penetrate the target building, undermining and destroying it by the powerful shock wave of the blast. The lighter-weight fragmentation bombs also contained high explosives, but their purpose was to propel deadly shards of metal in all directions. The shards consisted of splinters of the bomb casing and additional shrapnel which was packed around the explosive charge.

Incendiary bombs, which usually contained a charge of thermite or phosphorus, were light in weight since they only had to penetrate the roof of a building and start a high-temperature blaze. They could be dropped individually or in carpet formation. Incendiary bombs were more likely to damage the attics and upper storeys of buildings. Another category of bomb was the gas bomb, although poison gas could also be deployed as an aerial weapon by spraying it directly from tanks carried by the attacking planes. Gas weapons were feared most of all because of the invisibility of the poison and its insidious ability to permeate the narrowest of cracks and open-

7. Madrid civilians, some raising a clenched fist in the Communist salute, sheltering in the Sevilla Metro Station, 30 November 1936

ings in buildings. The military gases included choking agents which cause flooding of a victim's lungs and airways, vesicants or blistering agents which could penetrate the skin and poison the bloodstream, and lachrymatory agents which could disable victims by extreme irritation of the eyes, nose and throat.[32]

The attacker chose the type of bomb according to the target. As the war progressed, increasingly lightweight incendiary bombs and increasingly heavy high-explosive bombs were dropped to destroy the urban fabric, after which chemical warfare agents could be applied to kill or disable the surviving citizens. In daylight raids, which generally took advantage of cloud cover, the bombers were equipped with bomb racks under the fuselage; they would fly in a straight formation towards their target.[33] The hours of darkness were the true preserve of the heavy bombers, however. These less manoeuvrable planes did not fly in formation, but followed one another at regular intervals, swooping low over the target zone to discharge their payload as accurately as possible. Compared to lighter planes, the bombers not only carried a heavier load but were equipped to aim the weapons with greater accuracy using bombsights and trajectory tables. The electrically driven bomb-release devices allowed the airmen to discharge bombs in a single batch or one after another, according to the size of the target and the likelihood of destroying it with a single bomb. Bombs could of course miss the target due to errors of aim or calculation. The closer the plane approached its target, the larger the probability of hitting it. The planes would therefore often skim just above the target, discharge their payloads and climb rapidly out of danger.

General Wolfram von Richthofen launched the Luftwaffe attack on the small Basque town of Guernica (population: seven thousand, plus three thousand refugees) on Monday, 26 April 1937, which was a market day. Using the three-wave system, the bombardment lasted four hours. The number of fatalities has been estimated at figures between 250 and 1,600.[34] The saturation bombing was supplemented by machine gun attacks from diving fighters. Since Spanish architecture differed substantially from that of Central and Western Europe, the attackers decided not to use the heaviest high explosive bombs but lighter ones weighing from 100 to 250 kilos. The aim was to score as many direct hits as possible on the densely built town with its low-rise houses.[35] The first wave consisted mainly of incendiary bombs intended to set the roof frames of the houses alight. These were followed by high-explosive bombs intended to demolish the buildings and join up the individual conflagrations into a firestorm. Some seventy percent of the buildings were destroyed, and the effect on morale in the small town, without any air raid protection or shelter facilities, was devastating. The bombs actually missed their purported targets – a strategically sited bridge and a factory – but the Luftwaffe command nonetheless considered the attack a great success.[36] This strategic bombing offensive may therefore be regarded as the prototype of air raids on cities during World War II.

A VIRTUAL SHIELD

The military concept of the "front" took on a dual meaning in the twentieth century, with the old fortification concept no longer applying.[37] The front line formed by soldiers and their supporting materials, engaged in defending their national territory

or winning new ground, was now accompanied by a second, vastly more pliant, kind of front. It was the front of warplane fleets that could penetrate the air space of other nations and assail the civilian population of large cities with all the brutality of modern warfare. Germany's Minister of Aviation, Hermann Goering, described the new duality as follows: "Horizontal warfare has gained a vertical dimension, which reaches deep into the hinterland of the enemy and brings the battle of fronts to the *Heimat*."[38] It is no coincidence that it was Goering who wrote the preface including these incendiary words in what was otherwise a dry and technical handbook of civil air raid defence.

World War I had been dominated by a land war with a static front and with national frontiers at stake, but a more dynamic situation was in prospect in the run-up to World War II. Aviation was clearly going to play a more important role, but no one could foresee its full implications. In this connection, it is interesting to compare a French defence line with a German one. The French Minister of Defence, André Maginot, initiated the construction of a defence line along the French-German border in 1929. Its main constituents were bunkers, barbed wire and tank obstacles. Along the line of barriers, observation posts and medium-sized bunkers, 49 large *ouvrages* formed the nerve centres. These almost totally self-reliant subterranean forts were spaced 30 kilometres apart and could each house some 1,200 troops.[39] The underground buildings were generally eight storeys deep, and each had its own

9. Soundproof chamber for acoustic testing of
Dutch air raid sirens, Delft, late 1930s

electricity supply provided by diesel generators and hot and cold piped water. They
had corridors with narrow gauge railways for the horizontal transport of wagons
loaded with armaments, and hoists for vertical transport. There were ventilation
systems with filtered air inlets for extracting smoke from the interior. Large stocks
of food and ammunition were held to keep the fort in action for a lengthy period.
Light therapy with sunray lamps and cinema films were available to relieve depres-
sion and other stress symptoms suffered by the troops such as ringing in the ears.
Although the Maginot line did not hold out long against the eventual German attack, it would be going too far to say it was useless, for it apparently exerted sufficient threat in 1940 to persuade Hitler to invade France via the Netherlands and
Belgium.

This experiment in underground living, the most advanced of the twentieth
century, contrasts with German efforts from 1940 onwards to defend the airspace
above *Festung Europa* (Fortress Europe), as Nazi propaganda termed the occupied
territory of the continent. The threat of falling projectiles made it imperative to find
an effective armour for the home front. Protecting the airspace and the cities of the
Reich meant designing a shield to ward off attacks from the sky. The mobile, virtual
shields needed to intercept and disable enemy aircraft were to be found in the ar-
moury of the modern radiant technologies: light, radar and radio.

At the start of the occupation, the Germans used Holland – especially its airfields – as a testing ground for their night fighter system. It was one component in the Kammhuber Line, a virtual shield to defend the frontier of Fortress Europe. The line consisted of a chain of radar stations equipped with the most sensitive antennas available for detecting enemy planes. Each station covered its own rectangle of approximately thirty by thirty kilometers.[40] The line stretched from the coast of Denmark to the Schelde Estuary. At night, the ground station would detect an approaching enemy aircraft using a combination of techniques: radio, radar, listening and imaging devices and searchlights, together with anti-aircraft batteries and patrolling night fighters. General Josef Kammhuber, who set up the night fighter defence system of the Third Reich, the 'Kammhuber Line', initially operated from the country house, Slot Zeist, in the middle of the Netherlands. A safer command post, a large bunker with the codename Caesar, was later built specially for his use in Driebergen near Utrecht. In late 1942, moreover, the command bunker dubbed Diogenes went into action at Schaarsbergen near Arnhem, guiding the First and Third Air Divisions operating from the airfield at Deelen. This formed the centre from which the Germans conducted their air defence of large areas of Europe. After the Luftwaffe was forced onto the defensive in 1941, Kammhuber created his *Himmelbett* system of high-power radar stations for locating and following enemy aircraft, which covered the whole of the Dutch territory in a grid of circular zones. The purpose of the *Himmelbett* was to transmit information to Diogenes and thus alert fighters in the defence line of Maastricht-Venlo-Arnhem-Enschede (the buffer zone for the Ruhr).

Along with this attempt at military immunity, the defensive measures adopted in the largest Dutch cities formed a second virtual shield. As well as anti-aircraft guns and fighter aircraft, bombing tactics such as those described above were fended off by nets held aloft by barrage balloons, intended to impede the planes as they descended to seek their targets. At night, the cities were blacked out, while searchlights scanned the skies for approaching bombers. Spotters on the ground were equipped with night binoculars and listening devices to provide early warnings of attacks.[41] The immune system of searchlights, anti-aircraft artillery and fighters was far from foolproof, however. There were inevitably planes that found the gaps in the urban roof and managed to discharge their explosive payload. During an air raid, the sky would be full of movement, sound and colour. Once an imminent air raid was detected, the sirens began their undulating wail, warning the civilian population to seek a safe shelter. The growl of the approaching bomber squadrons swelled, and the bombs started falling, smashing into the urban body. All around was the massive, metallic drone of engines, the whistle of plummeting bombs, the smell of explosives, the smoke, rubble, soot, burning wood, clouds of explosive fumes and whirling dust. The air was filled with groans and screams, the city shook to its foundations, and buildings burst into flames. The billowing smoke and plumes of dust darkened the city skyline. High overhead, the air vibrated with beams of light, radio waves and radar. Above the blacked-out streets, the swirling anti-aircraft searchlights wove criss-cross patterns with the descending parachute flares which the attackers dropped to illuminate the target zone. War in the air seemed like a battle between light and darkness.

CIVILIAN PROTECTION ON THE HOME FRONT

During the 1930s, most of the countries of Europe were already concerned about the danger of an air war. There was a general anxiety that active air defence would be inadequate and that city dwellers would bear the brunt of the action. "Gunpowder is heaping up in Europe and sparks could fly," an adjutant inspector of the Air Watch opined in 1937 when international tension was palpably rising. Terms like "aerial threat" and "air protection" started appearing in official language, revealing a growing awareness of the need to prepare citizens to take measures in the event of air raids and to ready them mentally for the horrors to come.

The measures against air raids consisted of a shield (intercepting the enemy), individual and collective bomb shelters and the evacuation of town dwellers. Evacuation of civilians was already being prepared in Britain and France, but this was not considered a serious option in a small country like the Netherlands, which therefore lacked a scenario defining what categories of people must be evacuated or how and where they would be sent.

Most European cities started building fragmentary Shelter Cities in the period from 1935 to 1945. The main physical component of a Shelter City, the bunker, was a dark, windowless, inward-looking monolith with an artificial indoor climate. The exterior of a bunker was disguised either with a layer of earth or with an architectural costume, camouflaging the caged existence within from the eyes of the outside world. The duplication of the city consisted largely of trenches (covered or open) and bunkers – technical facilities without any kind of representational exterior, decoration or style. All that mattered was the protective effectiveness, size and capacity of the structures. Gasmasks were required to assure a supply of breathable air. Existence for city dwellers in these Spartan interiors was simply a matter of survival; for some they would be salvation and for others, a sarcophagus.

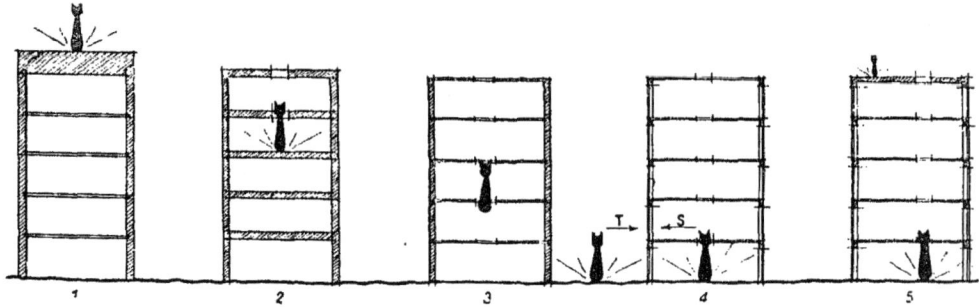

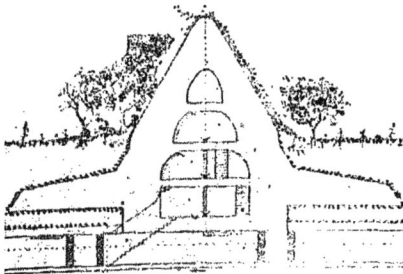

Top

10. Hans Schossberger, diagram of five
architectural methods for calculating bomb
impacts on apartment buildings: 1. barrier;
2. retardation; 3. protective walls; 4. safety valve;
5. combination of 1 and 4

Bottom left

11. Alessandro Romani, partially above-ground
bunker as the primary component of Shelter City,
1927

Bottom right

12. Prof. Mariani, elaboration of the Romani
concept into a ground-level bunker city

IDEALIZED SHELTER CITIES

Realistic assessments of the possibility of air raids existed well before the outbreak of World War II.[42] What was known in the Netherlands about air raids and the requisite structural defences for the home front came from German and English books. It was clear that city dwellers would have to seek their safety in reinforced cellars in old and new buildings, in a shelter on the ground floor or under the stairs, in free-standing towers and underground passages built of steel, concrete and hard brick, in a buried hut in the garden or in tunnels, shafts and bunkers.

A city of mouse holes could stand up to vertical attacks better than one of crystal palaces, and those mouse holes could take many forms. For convenience, we will consider them here under the collective term bunker, primarily in the sense of a more or less bombproof survival machine, and secondarily as a cultural, technical and architectonic phenomenon whose conspicuous presence had an important impact on the cityscape. The bunker, with its airlock and gas filter, was a protective container, an empty shell where the city dweller, torn out of his familiar habitat, could survive.

ABOVE GROUND

The ideal supply of mouse holes for the urban population took shape on the drawing board in three extreme models. One was the above-ground bunker city, another the underground city, and the third was the linear city. A colonel of the Italian military engineers, Alessandro Romani, took Douhet's theory to its logical conclusions in 1927 by designing a city consisting only of bunkers.[43] No more is known of this early Shelter City than a general view and a cross-section of an individual bunker. In Germany, two types of above-ground bunker were built and provoked widespread interest in the North German ports before the outbreak of World War II. Hamburg, for example, established a new municipal department to supervise the construction of the ever more standardized bunkers. The well-oiled machine, headed by engineers and architects, prepared separate series of bunker designs for filling gaps in the city

13. Karl Friedrich, linear Shelter City, circa 1932

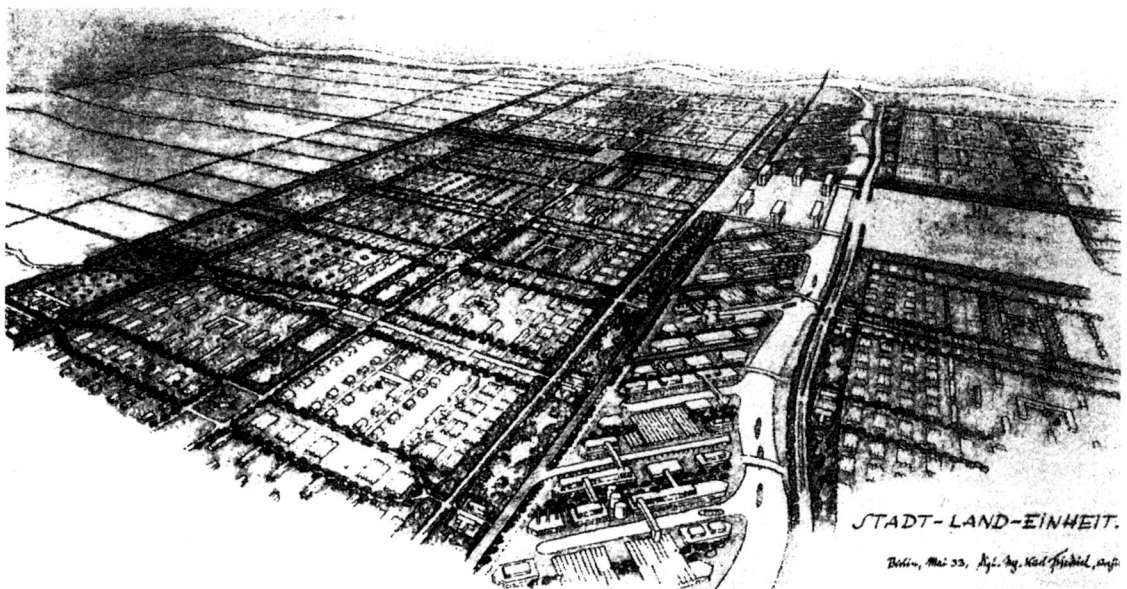

STADT-LAND-EINHEIT.

Berlin, Mai 33, Dipl. Ing. Karl Friedrich, arft.

fabric or for building in the city outskirts.[44] During the heaviest air raids on Hamburg, the citizens could take shelter in any of 124 public bunkers (some of which had five above-ground storeys) with room for over 92,000 people. The city also had shrapnel-proof tubular collective shelters with a total capacity of nearly 63,000 people and 89 shrapnel-proofed trench shelters with room for 6,000. Many lives were saved by Hamburg's Shelter City.

UNDERGROUND

A striking example of the underground model is provided by the study for air raid shelters in London published by the structural engineer Ove N. Arup in 1939.[45] Arup was a member of the architecture firm Tecton, headed by the flamboyant Russian emigré Berthold Lubetkin. The socialist local council of the London Borough of Finsbury commissioned the firm to conduct a series of studies into more effective protection against air raids.[46] Arup studied the design principles, construction and strength of air raid shelters, and devised an ingenious method for comparing the protective strength of different shelter designs in relation to the size of the bomb hitting it, and hence deciding on their cost-effectiveness. He compared seven covered trench shelter designs with earthen protection (capacity varying from 50 to 450 people), five rectangular basement shelters with concrete walls (capacity 350 to 500 people) which could be built under existing buildings, and eight designs for bunkers capable of withstanding direct bomb hits. The last category, with capacities ranging from 50 to 12,300 people, comprised bunkers equipped with toilets, mechanical ventilation, gasproof airlocks, lighting, generator rooms, decontamination rooms and food stores. The largest of these bunkers were to be run by a professional staff including doctors and nurses.[47] The most economical bunker shape was in Arup's view a round one. Given the huge thickness of the covering layer (about three metres of concrete), it was logical that a bunker of this type should have multiple levels, thereby reducing the building cost per user; but five levels was considered the maximum. The entrances and stairways of such a large bunker required special consideration because of the risk of panicking crowds; Arup resolved this by replacing the floors and stairs by spiral ramps – two contra-directional spirals in the case of the largest type. In peacetime these bunkers could serve as underground car parks. The image that emerges from Arup's study is of an underground Shelter City, a duplicate of the existing city that would form the backbone of a civilian defence system for all the city's inhabitants – not just Finsbury, but the whole of London.

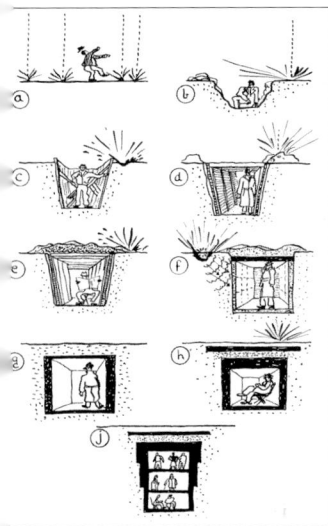

14. Ove Arup, scale of individual protection

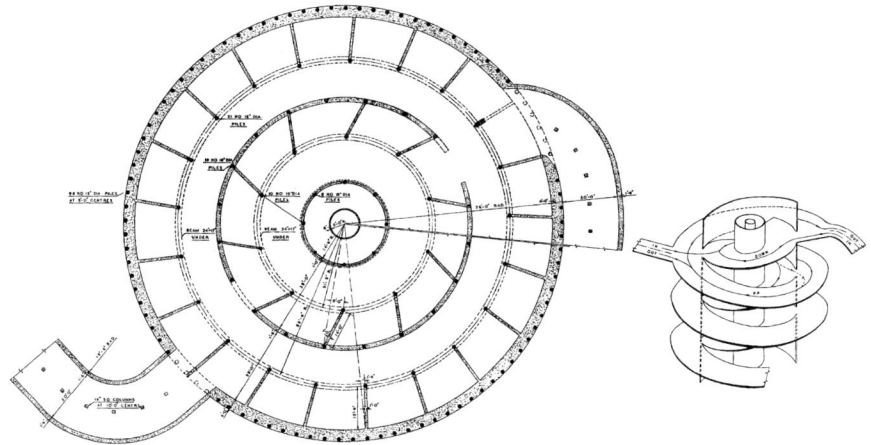

15. Ove Arup, underground shelter for 12,300 people, 1939

LINEAR CITIES

Arup devised a system of detached survival machines, but another plausible approach was to design cities that would be much less vulnerable to attacks from the air. An ideal city in this respect was outlined in 1934 by the German architect Hans Schoszberger.[48] His model was intended as an ideal to be aspired to, although it could never be realized in its totality. His underlying assumption was that a future air war would mean the death knell for large cities in their present form, and he therefore sought ways of decentralizing them. Numerous plans for breaking up existing cities and returning their population to the countryside had been devised in the first quarter of the twentieth century. The long-term aim was to eliminate the distinction between town and country without dispensing with the cultural advantages of the city. Out of the range of existing models for the modern city, Schoszberger selected a combination of the garden city with Le Corbusier's skyscraper vision, *Plan Voisin*. The latter did not incorporate any architectural air raid protection measures, although they did appear in Le Corbusier's later plans for Algiers.[49] Schoszberger regarded Le Corbusier's designs as at most a halfway house, since the skyscrapers would present an attractive target for aerial attackers. The decentralized city designed by the German architect Paul Wolf, which was a synthesis of several other German urban growth models, was similarly vulnerable.[50] Wolf's model admittedly had wedges of greenery penetrating deep into the urban body, while the low density residential areas were attached to the mother city as satellite suburbs; but the city centre remained as a potential target. In 1933 Wolf radically updated his concept: now the main railway station occupied the city centre, and this was surrounded by a green belt; the commercial and residential districts were also separated by 700-metre-wide building-free green strips. Much as Schoszberger appreciated this proposal, the star shape of the model struck him as vulnerable. His preferred long-term solution was the linear city, which he saw as meeting all the defence requirements: with a transport corridor forming the backbone of the conglomeration, there was no core "city" to be attacked.[51] He cited Russian linear cities and Frank Lloyd Wright's concept of Broadacre City, which was essentially also a linear city. The best design for a linear city, in his view, was *Stadt-Land-Einheit* by Karl Friedrich (1929).[52]

Idealizations like those of Arup and Schoszberger were attractive as individual designs. Neither of them was feasible, however, as a strategy for long-term air raid resistance, with their soaring ambition either to duplicate the entire city structure underground, or to decentralize it and spread it so thin on the above-ground surface area that it would be a different kind of city altogether. Yet even as designers theorized feverishly about the ideal Shelter City, the ultimate Shelter City was actually being built, a mere stone's throw from Berlin.

ZOSSEN, THE ULTIMATE SHELTER CITY

In deepest secrecy, the Germans built an underground settlement beneath the village of Zossen, near Berlin, in 1936. It was to be the nerve centre of the accelerated warfare in which the latest communication technologies would be combined to enable a surprise attack and a decisive first blow on the enemy.[53] Communications between the central command and the occupied territories were perfected late in 1940 when the army leadership settled permanently into the Headquarters of the Reich at Zossen. The upper command of the army occupied the bunker group Maybach I (1938; blown up after the war), and all the communications lines converged on bunker group Maybach II (1939-1940; still existing).

Cables led from Zossen to all the theatres of war in Europe. Besides providing direct lines to the army commands on the various fronts, the headquarters compiled all incoming intelligence traffic for the information of the staff of Goebbels and Goering. The nerve centre of the Zeppelin underground communications facility provided space for incoming and outgoing telegrams, facsimile (160 lines for

16. Schematic map of underground buildings in Zossen (Berlin); the Zeppelin Communication Centre is near the centre

17. Map of upper and lower floor beneath Zeppelin communication centre, Zossen (Berlin), 1938

the transportation and army networks), telex, television, telephone (1,500 lines) and radio. Beneath these spaces was a level for machinery and all the supporting technical apparatus, and the bottom level consisted of tunnels for cables and pipes. This huge command centre consisted of 23 gas-tight bunkers, camouflaged as ordinary houses, each with two underground levels. These bunkers were linked by a 600 metre long ring tunnel at a depth of 10 to 12 metres. The dense cable network of the political and military command structures provided the flexible telecommunication links considered necessary for rapid troop manoeuvres. It made it possible for the order to attack Poland on 31 August 1939 to be sent simultaneously from Zossen to all the military units involved. For the invasion of the Netherlands on 10 May 1940, the army signals corps were able to benefit from the knowledge gained in Sudetenland and Poland.[54]

Hitler's star architect, Albert Speer, observed that the power of the Zossen facility was something of a mixed blessing: "The communications apparatus at head-

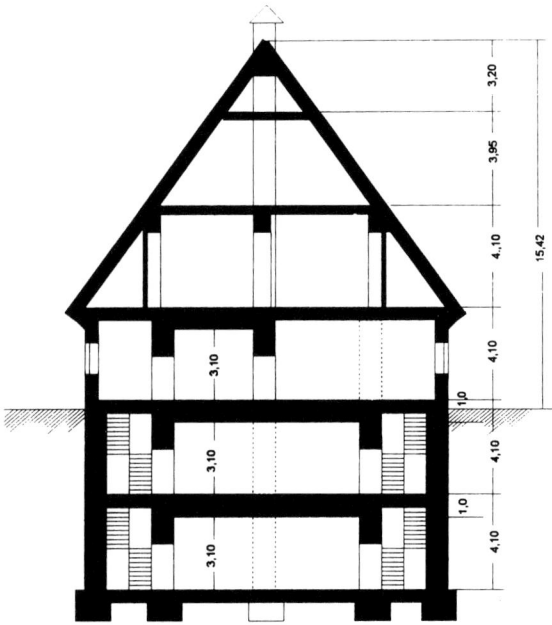

Top left
18. Cross section of exemplary bunker house, Zossen (Berlin), 1938

Top right
19. Bunker camouflaged as semi-detached house, Zossen (Berlin), 1938

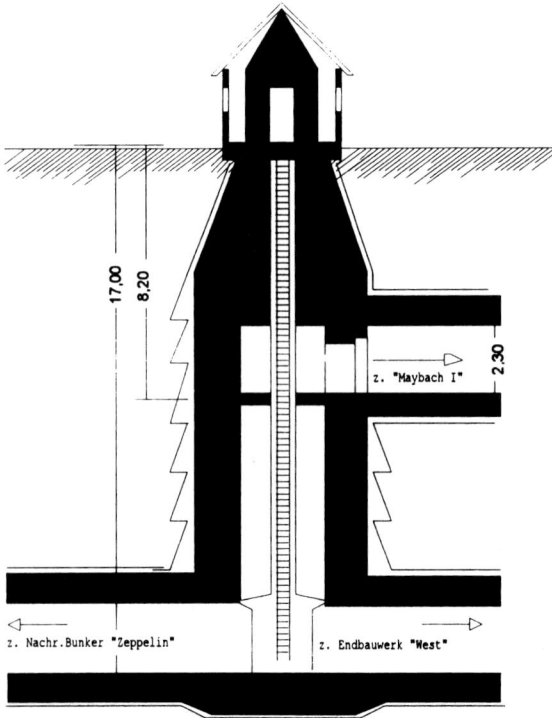

20. Cross section of bunker with camouflage and staircase to the underground "ring road" of Zossen, 1938

quarters was remarkable for that period. It was possible to communicate directly with all the important theatres of war. But Hitler overestimated the merits of the telephone, radio and teletype. For thanks to this apparatus the responsible army commanders were robbed of every chance for independent action, in contrast to earlier wars. Hitler was constantly intervening on their sectors of the front. Because of this communications apparatus individual divisions in all the theatres of war could be directed from Hitler's table in the situation room. The more fearful the situation, the greater was the gulf modern technology created between reality and the fantasies with which the man at this table operated."[55]

World War II was conducted from the underground bunkers of Zossen and from Hitler's own hardened headquarters.[56] In the endgame of the war, Hitler pulled back into the well-known *Führerbunker* in Berlin, a mouse hole in the garden of the Nazi counterpart to the Crystal Palace, the *Reichskanzlei* that Speer designed.

North Sea

Amsterdam
Haarlem
Hilversum Amersfoort
Kijkduin The Hague Zeist
Utrecht
Rotterdam Arnhem
Nijmegen
Middelburg
Eindhoven

0   30 km

< *Page 46 and 47*
21. Balloon barrage in the UK, 1939–1940

CHAPTER 2

Gimme Shelter!

Air Defence in Great Britain, Germany and the Netherlands, 1930-1940

The advances in aviation not only offered the wealthy traveller almost unlimited opportunities to fly to places all over the world, it also presented an intangible threat to his hometown. The opinion that cities would become significant targets in an air war was widely held by specialists. Bombing raids targeted at military objects and places of production, and direct attacks on the city dwellers with the aim of "exerting so much pressure through terror and intimidation that the population of the enemy nation would beg for peace to be made",[1] became core tenets of modern warfare strategy. The international tensions rose to such a pitch from 1938 onwards that national governments began considering concrete measures to protect the cities against enemy air raids with bombs and poison gas. It is useful to compare the situation in some of the main countries in Europe.

GREAT BRITAIN

British government officials were already pondering the possibility of a future *Blitzkrieg* in the latter half of the 1920s. Their sketchy scenario was based on World War I experience and on grossly exaggerated extrapolations from the effects of German bombardment of cities in Spain. The report predicted a wave of bombing lasting sixty days, beginning with a massive first attack delivered by the entire German air

Left
22. Poster by Nazi Propaganda Department: "when there's ack-ack fire, seek cover"

Right
23. Training course for instructors at "The Civilian Anti Gas School" in Falfield, Gloucestershire, February 1937

force, which would result in 600,000 deaths and twice that number of wounded. The aggregate bombing load was taken to be 600 tons daily, and each ton of bombs falling on a densely populated location was expected to claim on average 17 fatalities and 33 wounded. This meant one Briton in 25 would be a bombing victim, with a relatively heavy toll in the prime target area, London, which had eight million inhabitants.[2] The scenario had all "the features of the knock-out blow, of centres of government and industrial production, communications and power stations as the most likely civil targets, and of bomb-aiming of high precision (...)."[3] Something clearly had to be done, but the official position was that the cost of air raid protection would have to be shared between the local authorities and the public.

BLACKOUT

Stanley Baldwin's National Government sent its first circular on anti-air raid measures to the local councils in 1935. The councils were free to implement the advice as they saw fit, and they started doing so in ways that ranged from inaction to the planning of completely new fortifications. Then, in 1937, the Air Raid Precautions Act made it mandatory for local authorities to prepare plans for civilian defence and to set up air raid protection services. The main steps towards building a Shelter City would be to recruit new personnel and to train them – for example in how to use the specially designed equipment they would need. The hundreds of thousands of volunteers in the Air Raid Precautions (A.R.P.) service would need protection against falling masonry and poison gas by means of helmets, gas masks, lightweight and heavyweight gas suits, gloves, rubber boots and goggles. The local police force and fire brigade required special training in responding to gas attacks.

Handbooks circulated by the Home Office had already acquainted the general public with the official fears about the effects of bombs and gas attacks. "When the intelligent citizen thought about war, he saw in his mind's eye, not the noble if heart-rending scenes of 1915, not the flower of the nation marching away to fight in a foreign land, but his own living-room smashed, his mother crushed, his children maimed, corpses in familiar streets, a sky black with bombers, the air itself poisoned with gas."[4] During the first eight months of 1938, the British Shelter City began making deeper inroads into everyday city life, as the plans and warning systems became more concrete. The first experiments took place with blackout curtains, masked vehicle headlights, reflectors, white-painted kerbstones, dimly lit traffic signs and pedestrian crossings, and fluorescent markings on the uniforms of the wardens.[5] At ground level, the blackout often resulted in people completely losing all orientation in space and time. Familiar streets turned into hazardous environments, with risk of violent collisions against kerbstones, walls and trees which could result in serious injuries or even death. Reconciling the demands of air raid defence with the

24. Air Raid Protection member demonstrates blackout curtains with ventilation grilles, 1940

25. Car with masked headlights, Westminster

26. Marking roads for the blackout in the UK. Accompanying propaganda text: "Wartime England gives not the slightest clue for the positioning of enemy aircraft. From coast to coast blackness prevails: there is literally no light by which an enemy navigator may correct his dead reckoning."

27. Special lighting at intersections during the blackout, London, 24 August 1939

28. Firefighting exercise with stirrup pump, Newbury, Berkshire, January 1931

inconvenience and perils imposed on the public proved immensely problematic; vehicles would have to drive at night with heavily dimmed headlights, factories and railway yards had to take precautions to prevent stray light escaping, and street illumination had to be cut to a minimum. The Civil Defence Bill of March-July 1939 directed industry to take its own blackout measures.[6] The electricity companies found it took them some six hours of preparation to dim the street lights in time. London's blackout was first tested on the night of 9-10 August 1939.[7]

The government then launched an astonishing plan to provide every inhabitant of the designated danger zones with a gas mask. Circulating these respirators to the public at large had a dual purpose: to win public confidence in the government's war preparations, and at the same time to remind people that air raids were more than a distant possibility. As well as the gas masks, a newly designed hand pump – the stirrup pump – would help boost public self-confidence. The idea was that anyone could extinguish the fire of an incendiary bomb with this new pump.[8]

Left
29. Young people wearing bathing attire and gasmask backpacks help with sandbagging on South Coast, England, 10 September 1939

Right
30. Two children with a stack of sandbags, Rosebury Avenue, London, circa 1938

THE MUNICH CRISIS

After annexing Austria into the Third Reich with the acquiescence of the British and the French, Germany declared its intention of invading Sudetenland in September 1938. The negotiations between Hitler and Chamberlain ground to halt, and the resulting impasse has gone down in history as the Munich Crisis. Hitler threatened Britain with air raids if they did not quickly accede to his demands. A week-long collective frenzy with all the hallmarks of mass hysteria ensued in Britain. Practically the entire population believed that the island realm was about to be annihilated. People prepared for their descent into Shelter City. Anti-aircraft batteries and searchlights appeared on the roofs of tall buildings. Walls were reinforced with heaps of sandbags. The government decided to start building public shelters so that, in an air raid, the occupants of insufficiently protected homes and passers-by in the street could find protection from bomb blasts and shrapnel.

On 25 September 1938, the A.R.P. was placed on the alert, and its ranks were swelled by many new volunteers. Cellars and ground floor rooms were converted into refuge rooms. An epidemic of digging broke out. Day and night, people dug shelter trenches in the normally sacrosanct city parks, and government announce-

ments encouraged householders to start excavating shelters in their back gardens. The police took the lead in conducting warning drills with electric sirens and factory hooters and whistles. Barrage balloons, intended to make life more difficult for low-skimming bombers, festooned the skies of London. On 29 September, the government announced plans for the evacuation of two million Londoners to the countryside. Instructions on air raid precautions were issued to local councils, and a condensed version of the manual, *The Protection of Your Home Against Air raids* (1938), was distributed to every household.[9] Thirty-eight million respirators were issued to men, women and children. Despite all these precautions the public showed symptoms of mass panic, as indicated by a deluge of rush weddings, the drawing up of wills and the hoarding of sugar and petrol.[10] By 30 September, when Chamberlain had abandoned Czechoslovakia to its fate, the crisis subsided.

EVACUATION PLANS

While the Munich Crisis was still in progress, the government decided to evacuate all city dwellers who were not vital to the military and civil defence effort and who were not engaged in essential employment (cynically referred to in some documents as "useless mouths to feed"). Evacuation plans had already been brewing in government circles for some time. The first such plans dated from 1925, and six years later a committee pondered the logistics of evacuating 3.5 million Londoners.[11] The government evacuation plans were initially motivated by purely military considerations, as a countermeasure to the enemy strategy of attacking and demoralizing the general population. The new plan of 1938 concerned the voluntary evacuation of about four million city dwellers. Candidates for evacuation fell into four groups: children, mothers, the elderly and invalids in London and other government-designated cities; other private individuals who wished to move to the countryside and were capable of organizing the departure for themselves; industries, schools and other private institutions; and members of the government, top officials and sections of the civil service.

Although the official evacuation plans were still rudimentary at the start of 1938, they were put into practice during the Munich Crisis and once again the fol-

< *Page 54*
31. Sandbag reinforcement on roof of Unilever
Building, London, September 1939

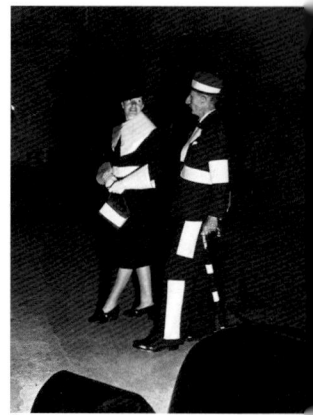

32. Evacuation

33. Blackout precautions in Waterloo Station, London, 3 November 1941

34. Reflective attire for night life during the blackout

lowing year when Hitler invaded Poland.[12] Two million people were evacuated from London, among them 500,000 children unaccompanied by their parents. Great Britain was divided up into evacuation areas, neutral areas and reception areas. The evacuation process took place in three stages. Firstly, the selected category of evacuees (e.g. the elderly, invalids or children) had to be persuaded to leave the city, followed by their transportation and finally their accommodation at designated evacuation addresses. Local authorities in the destination zones began a hectic search for suitable accommodation, starting in 1938. Tentative efforts were also made to relocate parts of the machinery of government.[13] The evacuation plans were supported by measures for the stockpiling and storage of all kinds of supplies. Hospitals, lodging houses and similar institutions in the destination areas were issued with handbooks detailing the actions to be taken in the event of an air attack.[14]

Fear of a major air attack subsided around Christmas 1938, and over half of the 1.5 million evacuee mothers and children headed back home. But the evacuation tide rose again in June 1939. It was the start of a mass migration that was to shake British society to its roots. Once Britain declared war on Germany in September 1939, somewhere between 3.5 million and 3.75 million members of the British public sought refuge in the countryside. The treasures of the National Gallery moved to a cave in North Wales, and the Bank of England set up shop in a village in rural Hampshire.

Two million city dwellers made their own way to Wales, Devon, Scotland and other destinations that were presumed safe. One man recalled "a constant stream of private cars and London taxis driving up to his mother's front door in the Thames Valley in the September of '39, filled with men and women of all ages and in various stages of hunger, exhaustion and fear, offering absurd sums for accommodation in her already overcrowded house, and even for food. This horde of satin-clad, pin-striped refugees poured through for two or three days, eating everything that was for sale, downing all the spirits in the pubs, and then vanished."[15] The exodus of 1 September 1939 seems to have been orderly enough: "The parties, clutching gas masks and emergency rations, shepherded by their teachers, were guided and controlled by an elaborate system of banners, armlets and labels. In three days, nearly one and a half million people were decanted into the countryside. (...) The children had, in most cases, assembled in a state of high excitement at seven or eight in the morning. They arrived dirty, tearful and exhausted."[16] Reception of the children at their host addresses proved to be a social experiment of an unprecedented scale and complexity. It was a confrontation between social classes, with differences in domestic simplicity or comfort, in customs and habits, in hygiene, table manners and etiquette; a confrontation between rich and poor, sick and healthy, Catholic and Protestant, and town and country.[17] For some of the arriving children, it was the first time they had seen a live cow or discovered that apples grow on trees. The young Bernard Kops, evacuated from the impoverished district of Stepney in the East End of London, recalled how his little sister reacted to their new home: "Rose whispered. She whispered for days. Everything was so clean in the room. We were even given flannels and tooth brushes. We'd never cleaned our teeth up till then. And hot water came from the tap. And there was a lavatory upstairs. And carpets. And something called an eiderdown. And clean sheets. This was all very odd. And rather scaring."[18] For him too, a new world opened: "For now I realised that the world was an open place of light, air and clouds. A tree was a miracle. How strange! I poked through the earth and stood there waving. Here I could see the sky but London was a maze of stones."[19] The evacuation campaign ended in huge disarray, especially when it involved children, due to tardy payments to the hosts, clashes of culture, the failure of the anticipated air raids to materialize and plain homesickness. Four out of ten children, and about nine out of ten mothers with children under 5, were back at home within three months. New plans to evacuate 670,000 children, which the government announced in February 1940, proved unsuccessful.

BRITISH BOMB SHELTERS

Once the Munich Crisis subsided, Sir John Anderson (then the Lord Privy Seal, soon to become Home Secretary) was put in charge of Civil Defence. Anderson threw himself into the task and, in late 1938, announced a programme of bomb shelters.

35. Promotional photo for Anderson Shelters, February 1939

36. Anderson Shelter factory, February 1939

Two and a quarter million shelters were to be provided free of charge to low-income households who lacked room to build a refuge room in the home. The Civil Defence Act, which aimed to formalize and implement the policy for air raid shelters, was passed in 1939. It authorized local authorities to erect buildings or requisition parts of existing buildings as public bomb shelters, as first-aid posts and as ambulance stations. That same year, a handbook of technical information for building shelters appeared, after long preparation, under the title of *Structural Defence*.[20] The official policy was that a shelter must be capable of defending its occupants against falling debris and bomb splinters, but could not be expected to survive a direct hit. Neither were the shelters intended for lengthy stays.

As well as being able to buy the corrugated steel shelters known as Anderson Shelters (named after the engineer responsible for their design, David Anderson, although it was widely assumed that they were named after the Home Secretary), members of the public could obtain free materials to reinforce their homes. The local authorities remained responsible for carrying out the reinforcement work. The Civil Defence Act authorized the minister to specify standards for incorporating structural air raid defences into all new buildings. Businesses with over 50 employees were now required to provide shelters for their personnel, and some of their employees would have to be trained in firefighting, first aid and gas precautions.[21]

37. Anderson Shelter deliveries, London, February 1939

38. Lord Beaverbrook consented to removal of steel railings around his London home, November 1941

Throughout Great Britain, these measures concerned some 12,000 factories with a total of 2.5 million employees, as well as coal mines with a further 1.5 million employees.[22] A special committee was charged with studying camouflage techniques for factories.

Apart from the new obligations for industry, the Civil Defence Act was largely a confirmation of existing plans, which aimed to establish an organization "to capitalize on the great volume of good will and readiness to collaborate which exists in all sections of the community".[23] These government exertions intentionally rammed in the message that the coming war was going to make World War I look like a mere picnic.

The poor results of the evacuation efforts made it clear that the cities themselves would need stronger defences. Shelter City began to spread like a stain. As innumerable citizens took steps to reinforce their homes, sandbags became a familiar sight in the streets. The Home Office ordered 42 million sacks for use as sandbags in 1938 plus another 275 million as a stock for the following three years.[24] Sandpits and the jute industry worked at full swing. Stacks of sandbags were used to protect the entrances and ground floor windows of important buildings. The cityscape also underwent another important change, the disappearance of railings. Since there was, or at least was believed to be, a shortage of iron and steel for the war industry, local councils uprooted the railings around public parks and gardens and appealed to the patriotism of private landowners to do the same. Public discussion of this action concentrated on its ideological rather than its utilitarian motives, throwing an interesting light on the political climate of the time.[25] On the one hand, it was an aesthetic matter: the railings were considered old-fashioned. On the other, it was a social one, for many saw the elimination of railings as symbolizing the birth of a more egalitarian society with less distinction between public and private property. To the adherents of this view, a railing-free London held out the promise of happier times to come.

A similar polarization was evident in arguments on the approach to be taken towards providing bomb shelters, now that evacuation appeared to be of limited avail. Leftist circles, concentrated notably in Finsbury, favoured the use of well-buried refuges, following the example of the use of the London Underground for shelter during World War I. The architectural firm of Tecton, led by Lubetkin and Arup, played a leading role in this camp.[26] In the 1930s, Tecton had been active in the wider socialist movement, which stood for the social relevance of scientific research and aimed to change the world through the planned application of science. Among architects, this cause gave rise to the Architects and Technicians Organization, in which Tecton cooperated with like-minded scientists.[27] Other groups concentrated on building research, for example the Association of Scientific Workers and the Association of Architects, Surveyors and Technical Assistants. Their research gave rise to a range of alternative bomb shelter designs which included detailed cost estimates in relation to the degree of protection offered. In August 1938, the Air Raid Protection Coordinating Committee, an informal collaboration of architects, scientists and engineers, presented a detailed scheme for a system of bombproof tunnels known as the St. Pancras Shelter. The Finsbury Borough Council backed the idea of building underground shelters to the design of Tecton and Arup (see Chapter 1). These were part of a larger study towards the location of fifteen underground shelters, each with room for 7,600 occupants. The Tecton/Arup designs took into account the varying populations by day and night, the physical conditions prevailing at ground level and underground, the effect of bomb strikes and the formal design of the shelter. A novel concept in the designs was the danger volume, which expressed the relation between the vicinity and size of a bomb explosion, and the dimensions and type of protection capable of resisting it. The general plan required the entire population of Finsbury to be able to reach shelter within seven minutes. To prevent congestion at the entrance to the shelter, Arup designed the floor as a helical ramp spiralling around a central column. The shelter as a whole was equipped with au-

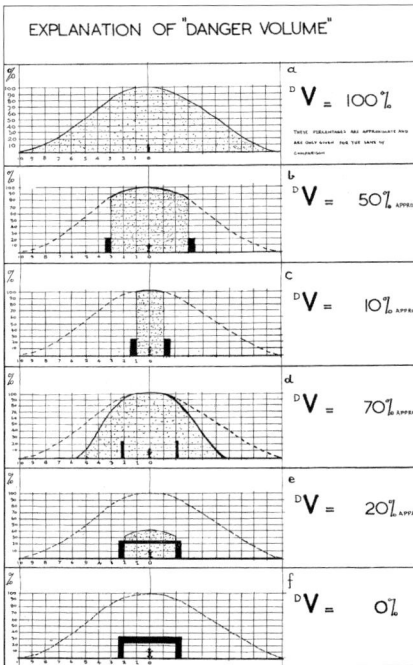

EXPLANATION OF "DANGER VOLUME"

$_D V$ = 100%

$_D V$ = 50% APPROX

$_D V$ = 10% APPROX

$_D V$ = 70% APPROX

$_D V$ = 20% APPROX

$_D V$ = 0%

39. Tecton-Arup, diagram for calculating danger volume of bomb explosions, February 1939

tonomous water supplies and electricity generators, decontamination zones and an air conditioning system; the bunkers of the Maginot line had clearly been studied carefully.[28]

The depth of the tunnels to be dug, the problems of creating suitable entrances, the lengthy construction time and fears that a disabling "deep shelter mentality" would take grip of the public dominated discussions about the underground Shelter City.[29] While the Tecton designers had hitherto drawn little public attention with their regular architectural projects (for example the Penguin Pool at London Zoo, and a health centre and a housing estate for the Borough of Finsbury), the shelter designs were widely reported in the national press and sparked off a vehement political debate.

The pragmatic policies of the government, which was fuelled by fear of an immediate invasion, contrasted with the engineering concerns of architects like Tecton. The experiences of World War I led the government to believe that members of the public who took cover in deep tunnels "would grow hysterical with fear and would never surface to perform their duties".[30] A less explicit factor in the government's reasoning was a fear that the mass panic would degenerate into violent rioting and conspiracies among the troglodytes, and that these processes would be

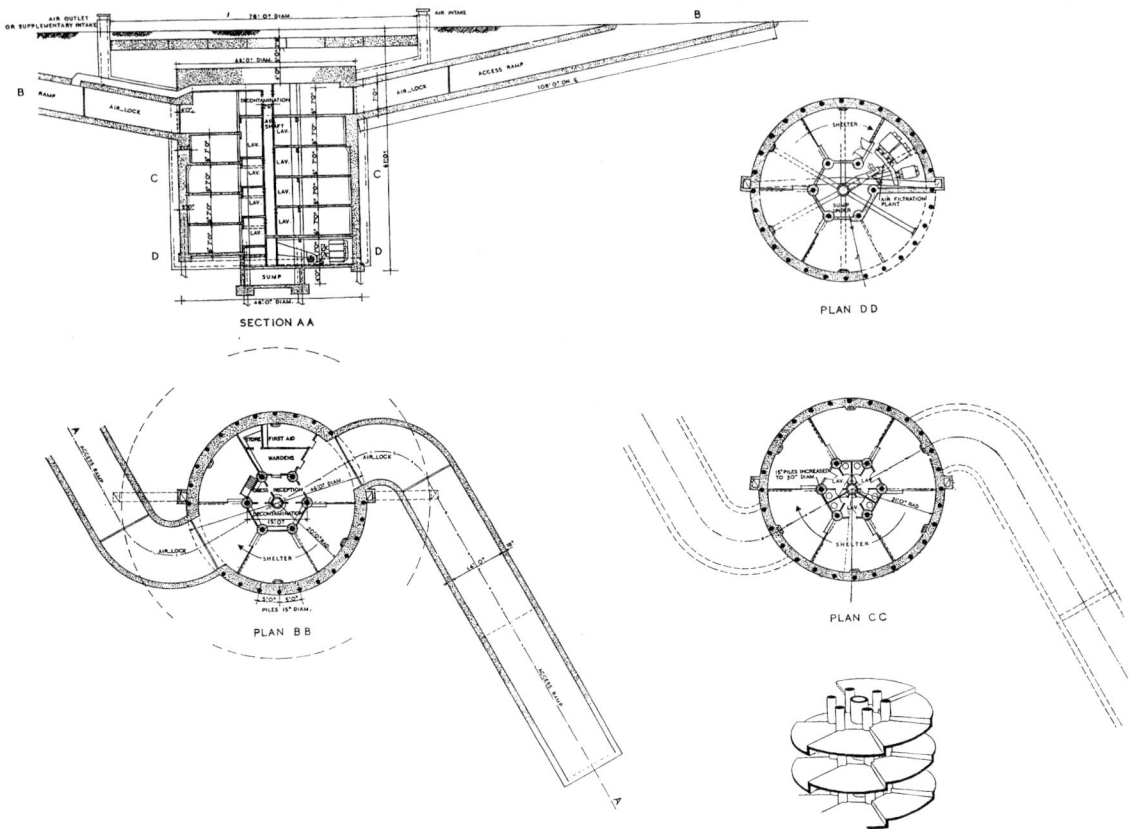

40. Ove Arup, design for underground bunker for 830 people

exploited for political ends by the communists, who were the main proponents of the use of tunnels. But the time factor was an even greater issue. The government thought that making completely bombproof shelters, whether underground or above ground, would take too long and cost too much in terms of labour and materials. Digging deep tunnels would take at least two years, but action was needed immediately. The shelters distributed by the government may have looked like a solution of desperation compared to the sophisticated and aesthetically pleasing designs of the Tecton group, but at least they could be mass-produced very quickly. What is more, the costs were so low that in principle it would be possible to offer protection to the whole population, regardless of income category, in areas where air raids were likely.

The Home Office decided to provide underground tunnel shelters in twelve large cities. These took the form of buried tubes measuring 2.15 metres high and 1.4 metres wide, and each had room for up to 50 people. The trenches for these tubes

41. An unused Underground tunnel in Borough High Street, Southwark, London, was readied as a bomb shelter with room for 14,000 people, 22 June 1940

42. Borough High Street, Underground entrance

were to be dug in public areas (mainly parks and shopping centres). The shelters would not be gas-proof, but gas masks would be distributed to everyone. Furthermore, a number of important public buildings and government offices were to be fortified. The Home Office would have a shelter for two thousand people on the ground floor of its Whitehall building.[31] In offices, factories and other large buildings with concrete or steel skeletons, the ground floors or basements were reinforced and designated as potential shelters.

TRENCH SHELTERS

The mania for digging trenches on a massive scale began with the Munich Crisis, and the results were visible in busy shopping streets and parks. But well before the start of the Blitz, the fashion for digging trenches to shelter from bombs was on the wane again. The trenches were exposed to wind and rain, and their side walls of soil soon crumbled. They were supposed to be lined with wood and brick and be roofed over with steel or reinforced concrete. The government had a standard design prepared for these trenches, and issued general guidelines for giving them some permanence. They were to have a minimum depth of 1.20 m, and be equipped with duckboards, bench seats and toilets. In the end, only the reinforced and covered trench shelters (which developed practically into bunkers) attracted any users. By the beginning of 1940, the trench shelters offered protection to a total of some 1.5 million people.

43. Digging trenches in Hyde Park, London, 1939

ANDERSON SHELTERS

The Anderson Shelters scheme, which was scheduled for completion by the end of 1939, aimed to produce 2.5 million garden shelters for the protection of 10 million individuals. The shelters were intended for the occupants of houses not exceeding two stories in height and with gardens. The factory output reached 50 thousand shelters per week, and by early 1940 the 2.3 million Anderson Shelters were delivered free of charge to those who could afford the modest price of the assembly kit.[32] Assembling and installing the shelter required little more equipment than a screwdriver and a shovel. The Anderson Shelters were in fact little more than superior dog-kennels: they were prone to flooding, too small to sleep in, and did little to exclude the noise of an air raid.[33] Their greatest disadvantage was that they were designed only for a brief stay. During the Blitz, however, people had little choice but to spend the night in the shelter, since the air raids proved to last much longer than the designers anticipated. In those circumstances, condensation proved to be an exceptional nuisance: the moisture of the occupants' breath condensed on the ceiling and dripped down onto the sleepers inside.

Although designed primarily for burying in the yard or garden, it was initially thought to have an alternative application in the interior of a small house. The latter was not recommended, however, because of the probability in the event of a bomb impact "that the occupants would be trapped by the fall of their house and killed by fire or escaping coal gas. During Munich householders had been advised to dig trenches in their yards or garden, and now, by an extension of this plan, the 'Anderson' was designed as an outdoor or surface shelter. (...). It would not, as the authorities made plain from the outset, be 'bomb-proof', i.e. protect its occupants against a direct hit. But it would offer a good measure of protection against bomb-splinters, blast and falling debris."[34]

SURFACE SHELTERS

In May 1939, the government issued instructions to the local authorities for a third type of shelter. These were surface structures built of brick and poured concrete, or of concrete blocks, with a roof and floor of reinforced concrete.[35] The first such design was for a small shelter with the same floor area as an Anderson Shelter for six people. It was intended for use in homes such as flats where it would be impossible to dig a pit for an Anderson shelter. A larger, communal version with room for about fifty occupants was conceived for other situations where small domestic shelters were unsuitable.[36] The "communal domestic surface shelter" design initially had various roof shapes, one of which was eventually chosen.[37] They started making their appearance in the streets of low-income housing districts from about March 1940, where they were placed in the middle of the street or to one side, leaving room for vehicles to pass. The roofs of the communal shelters were in many cases painted yellow with a "gas detector liquid" which was supposed to change colour when the air contained poison gas.[38] By November 1940, public air raid shelter facilities were available for only two million of the 27 million inhabitants of the urban danger zones. The communal shelters that were produced suffered from various defects, and their production rate was low. There was a shortage of cement, and in London alone some 5000 communal shelters were built with a weak concrete mix. They were poorly ventilated and were stuffy, cold, damp, dark and malodorous – even when they had a built-in toilet. Their worst shortcoming, however, was that they tended to collapse when a bomb exploded nearby.

44. Street scene with public shelters, London, July 1940

Page 67 >
45. Communal shelter, London, 1939

GAS MASKS

The British government initially aimed to produce 40 million gas masks in 3 sizes, but raised this total to 45 million (for a total British population of 44 million) by the end of 1938.[39] Later, a multicoloured version for small children (known informally as the Mickey Mouse gas mask) was added to the range, as well as a gas helmet for babies which was equipped with a hand-operated bellows by which the mother could refresh the filtered air supply. The distribution of gas masks took place amid a storm of publicity. Londoners were harangued by posters, loudspeaker vans and announcements at football matches, from pulpits and on cinema screens, pressing them to go to the town hall or a nearby school to pick up their respirators. By mid-September 1939, every British town dweller had one. An additional two million children's gas masks and 1.4 million gas helmets for babies were dispatched to the local authorities in January 1940. The government made it a condition of the free issue of gas masks that they must be carried with the user at all times.

Household pets were initially unwelcome in Shelter City, particularly in the public shelters. About half of London's 400,000 cats and dogs were put down and incinerated; the furnaces operated in daylight hours only due to the blackout. The remains of nearly 80,000 dead pets were consigned to a secret mass grave somewhere in East London. A consequence of this mass liquidation was a plague of rats and mice, after which the authorities relented and began to encourage the keeping of household pets once more.[40] The air raid precautions applied to animals, too. Animals had to be evacuated from danger zones. Stables and stalls had to be made gasproof. Domestic pets required gasproof pens and kennels, and the paws of con-

Left
47. Street scene with communal shelters, South London, 1940

Right
48. Air Raid Precautions at Monmouthshire Institute of Agriculture: gasmask practice for milkmaids, April 1938

taminated animals had to be treated with anti-gas ointment. The People's Dispensary for Sick Animals, a charity manned by volunteers, championed the cause of four-footers exposed to the risk of poison gas and developed a gasproof kennel with a bellows which could be operated by the paws of its occupant.[41]

Having sealed off his home against poison gas with adhesive tape and possibly installed an Anderson shelter in the garden, the city dweller had to rush to the shops to buy blackout fabric, curtains, black paint, cardboard and brown paper. Those who could afford it bought transparent foil to stick onto the inside of the window panes, to prevent shards of glass flying around the room when a bomb exploded nearby. The less well-off used brown gummed paper tape for the same purpose. The blackout had a huge impact on nightlife in the city. As a popular song of the time complained, "There's no place like home, but we see too much of it now."[42] In the blacked-out nights of September 1939, the number of traffic accident injuries doubled. Pedestrians tumbled into canals and down staircases, people fell through skylights and railway passengers stepped off platforms. People could incur a fine for as little as striking a match in a public place. A month later, the authorities relented a little and allowed people to carry an electric torch with the beam dimmed by a layer of paper, as

49. Training camp for dogs to work as couriers in trenches, October 1939

50. Testing new gasmasks for dogs, kennels in Surrey

51. Gas shelter for sick animals, January 1939

long as they switched it off immediately the alarm sounded. Vehicle headlight beams had to be masked off to minimize light spillage. Neon advertising signs and brightly lit shop windows were banned, and cinemas and theatres closed. The measures were gradually eased off, however, and social life recovered accordingly.

The nightly blackout was not the only visible hallmark of Shelter City. The large-scale evacuations emptied the streets. Gardens, parks and public squares were dug up to install bomb shelters. All in all, the ghostly parallel city was a very different place from its peacetime counterpart.

GERMANY

In Germany, too, considerable energy went into air raid protection in the run-up to the war, but it was concentrated in the area of knowledge-gathering. Public confidence in the Luftwaffe was so high that the most conspicuous successes of the period were those of the propaganda machine. While the British public were practising with gas masks and bomb shelters, the Germans set their store by discipline and resilience rather than extensive material preparations.

Typifying the German encyclopaedic mentality, the knowledge collected came from a wide international field in the pursuit of exhaustive completeness. The publications show examples of air raid shelters from Great Britain, France, Italy, Spain and Switzerland. The solutions clearly varied considerably from country to country, reflecting national engineering traditions, building technologies and building

Page 71 >

Top
52. French underground reinforced concrete public shelter (designed to resist direct bomb hits up to 300 kilograms)
Arrivée d'air = ventilation air intake
Sas = airlock
Abri = shelter
Chef d'abri = shelter warden
Sortie de secours = emergency exit
Protection contre les éclats = shrapnel protection

Bottom left
Shelter type: towers, passages, tunnels, bunkers, shafts, 1939

Middle right
British proposal for gradual roofing-over of trench shelters, 1939

Bottom right
"Abri Marcille", freestanding French shelter hut in concrete, 1939
Height 2.40 metres, diameter 1.80 metres, concrete thickness 0.17 metres

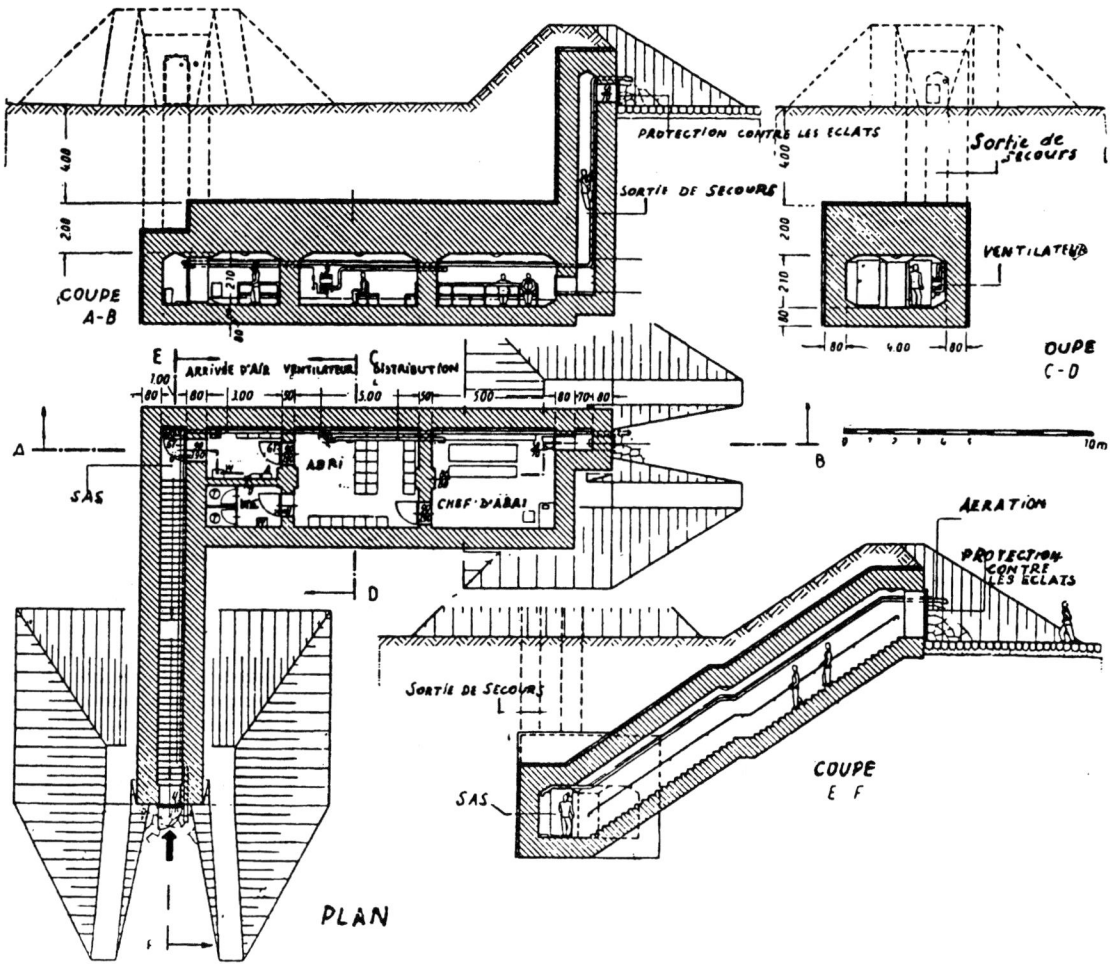

COUPE
A-B

400

200

PROTECTION CONTRE LES ECLATS

SORTIE DE SECOURS

Sortie de secours

200

210

40 210

VENTILATEUR

80 4.00 80

COUPE
C-D

E
ARRIVÉE D'AIR VENTILATEUR DISTRIBUTION C

1.00 80 80 1.00 50 3.00 150 5.00 80 70 80

ABRI

CHEF D'ABRI

A

SAS

D

B

0   10m

SORTIE DE SECOURS

AERATION

PROTECTION
CONTRE
LES ECLATS

SAS

COUPE
E F

PLAN

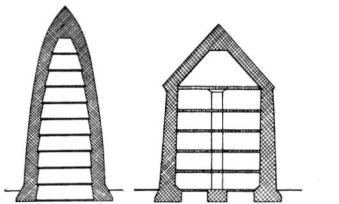

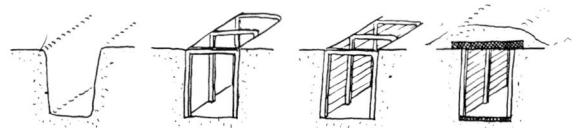

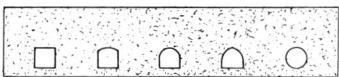

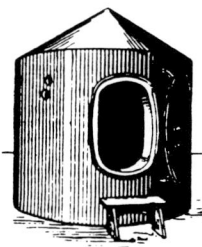

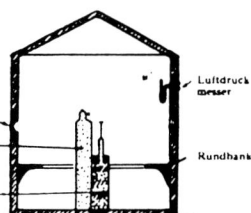

Luftdruck
messer

Guckloch

Sauerstoff

Rundbank

Kalipatronen

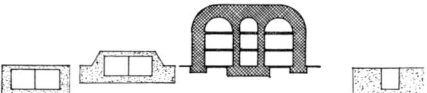

Élévation

Coupe AB

Coupe CD

Plan

Coupe EF

53.

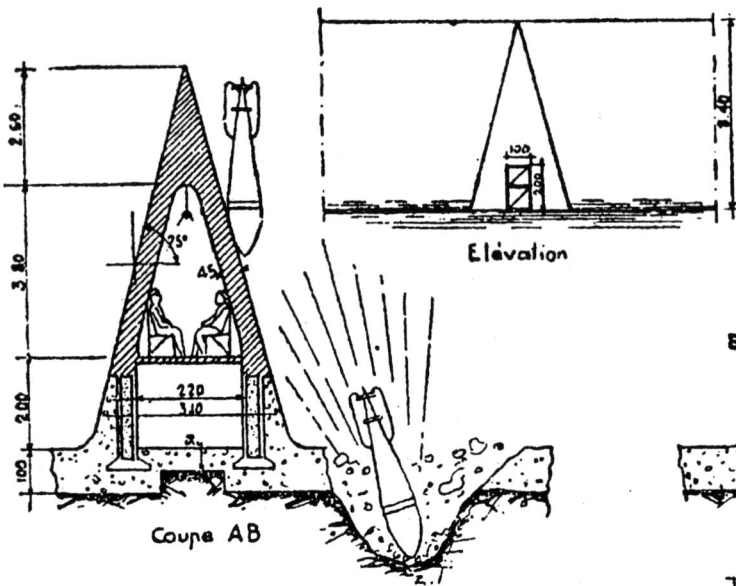

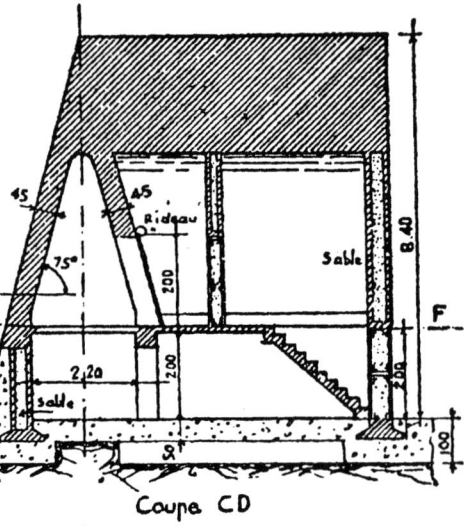

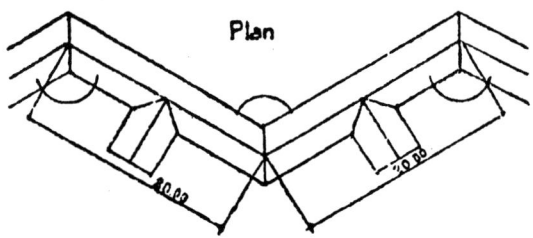

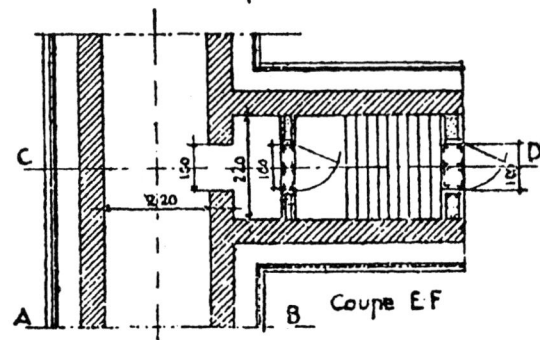

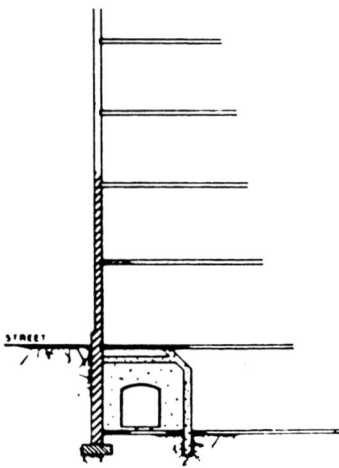

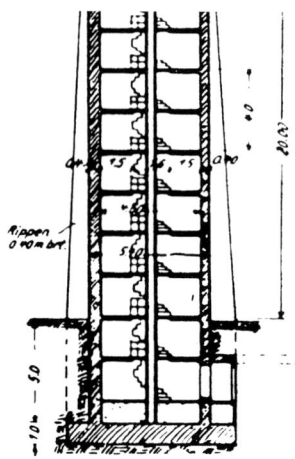

Top
"Abri Goilot", French above-ground shelter
for 80 people

Bottom
Italian above-ground tower shelter

industry capacities.[43] The technical treatises were invariably accompanied by militant prefaces: "The shelters must protect the heads and fists of the million-strong army of workers needed for the gigantic task of upholding the progress of production, health care and transport. (...) These auxiliaries are a significant element of modern warfare, dominated as it is by the motorization and mechanization of the armed forces, the use of automatic weaponry, the mounting requirement for munitions and the deployment of chemistry and technology, all of which can be crucial to the outcome of a military conflict."[44]

LEGISLATION AND ORGANIZATION

The Treaty of Versailles (1918) had forbidden Germany to build up national air defences, giving rise to numerous voluntary aerial protection groups; these merged in 1932 to form the *Deutsche Luftschutz-Verband* (German Air Defence Association). This association issued various periodicals, the most important of which was *Gasschutz und Luftschutz* (Gas and Air Attack Protection) which appeared until 1944. An intensive campaign of air raid precautions began immediately after Hitler's seizure of power. The responsibility for aerial defence fell primarily under Hermann

54. Cover of German periodical for air-raid defense, 1933

55. Exemplary attic, tidied up and equipped with sandbox, water tank and pump, Hamburg, 1934

56. Wiessendamm Tower Shelter, Hamburg, 1939

Goering, Reich Minister of Aviation and Commander of the *Luftwaffe*. Goering's ministry was backed by an organization of individual German citizens, the *Reichsluftschutzbund* (National Air Defence League) which already had 12 million members by 1937 and reached a membership of 20 million during the 1940s.[45] The league published a magazine called *Sirene* with a circulation of over 1 million.

A law of 26 June 1935, passed after Hitler repudiated the Treaty of Versailles, provided for the creation of a national air raid protection organization. The law prescribed measures such as blackout preparations and air raid defence exercises, in which every citizen could be called on to participate.[46] Absence from these exercises was to be punishable by a fine or having the electricity disconnected. The first implementation order of May 1937 defined three aerial defence sectors: production (large companies in industry and trade), private (domestic cellars and attics) and services (government buildings, large stores, banks, hotels, lodging houses, hospitals, universities and schools). Every new building had to be provided with one or more bomb shelters, complete with an airlock and a gas filter, with room for up to 50 people.

CONCRETE MEASURES

As early as 1934, Germany drew up a secret hierarchy of cities at risk of airborne attack, based on proximity to potential enemy airfields and on concentrations of military production and metropolitan functions. Only category I (originally comprising 94 cities, later reduced to 61) was eligible for state-funded bomb shelters. These cities also gained a *Sicherheits- und Hilfsdienst* (SHD or Safety and Emergency Department, renamed *Luftschutzpolizei,* Air Raid Protection Police in 1943). Category II consisted of 201 cities which were expected to take extensive air defence measures on their own initiative, and Category III covered all other municipalities. People living in Category III towns were expected to take their own defensive precautions, such as providing domestic cellars with reinforced ceilings and gasproof doors.

The implementation of air raid precautions was treated as a police matter, with the local air defence leader taking a key role. The air raid warning organization was part of the police force, although it cooperated closely with the military *Flugwachkommando* and *Luftgaukommando*. Exhibitions of air raid shelter designs were held. An exemplary bombproof dwelling, the *Luftschutzhaus*, was built in the centre of Bremen.[47] In Hamburg, a demonstration cellar was built as an example of a domestic air raid shelter, with a ceiling reinforced by wooden beams, sandbags, a water jet pump, a radio, gas masks, etc. The exhibition hoped to persuade householders to join forces to build communal shelters.[48] Although air raid protection was taken seriously, there was little to show for it by the beginning of the war. Throughout Germany, the total capacity of public air raid shelters was no more than 10,000 people. The main campaign to make up for lost time took place in 1940.

COMPARISON

If we recapitulate the main civilian measures for protecting city dwellers against air attacks – evacuation, respirators and bomb shelters – it is clear that Great Britain conducted pioneering work in all these areas, and proved capable of implementing far-reaching measures. The British version of Shelter City successfully recruited an army of well-equipped and well-trained auxiliaries. Britain also implemented evacuation on a large scale. France perceived the threat of German air raids and developed an evacuation plan, at least for Paris, but left it too late to put into practice.[49] In Germany evacuation was not even considered. Few shelter trenches were dug in Paris, but a detailed plan to create shelters in open spaces in the city was ready for use in an emergency. Members of the French public were also encouraged to rein-force the cellars of their homes as refuge rooms. Germany, too, rammed home the message of personal responsibility, but very few public bomb shelters were built. The distribution of gas masks to practically the entire population was a uniquely British step; carrying a gas mask was obligatory at all times, and people faced a fine for not doing so. In both France and Germany, obtaining a gas mask was a private matter. As regards building public air raid shelters, Britain once again took the lead. An impressive number of trench shelters were completed. Anderson and other do-mestic shelters offered most inhabitants of the danger zones at least an illusion of safety. Although none of these shelters could stand up to a direct hit, and gas masks were still necessary in the event of a gas attack, the British Shelter City was by far the best prepared for an air war.

THE NETHERLANDS

The Dutch public gradually became aware of the threat of air raids over the course of the 1930s. By the end of the decade, the rise of the dictatorship in Germany, the escalating output of weaponry and the new military strategies that were being aired prompted a national review of measures to protect the urban population against air raids. Discussions of the threat from the air in Dutch books and other publica-tions focussed almost solely on Germany. The urbanist J.M. de Casseres published articles exhaustively explaining the relation between modern airborne warfare (as a component of a total war aimed at paralysing the home front) and its prevention by urban planning. The aim of planning was in his view to scatter the population and functions more widely over the country. Town planners and the military con-curred, according to De Casseres, that the effectiveness of an air attack on a civilian target could be diminished by building tall buildings in green surroundings (the Le Corbusier approach) or by building at low densities on the garden city principle.[50] De Casseres himself favoured dispersed, open building patterns in garden cities and argued for the evacuation of children from the main towns.[51] Although this stand-point enjoyed approval in air defence circles, the compact centres of existing cities were an acute problem. "Stipulating requirements for new buildings only means that it will take years before a degree of safety prevails against dangers from the air. So the big question is what must happen with the existing buildings?"[52]

Protecting the entire population of the Netherlands was a laudable goal, but it was hard to picture how this would be realized in the light of the overwhelming practical difficulties. If citizens were to be sheltered in bombproof cellars, which needed walls three to four metres thick, a city the size of Amsterdam would need over 7000 underground spaces of that standard. The ideal air-raid precaution would be for each house to have its own reinforced, gas-proof cellar. But only a minority of Dutch houses actually had a cellar, and those that did were of relatively flimsy construction. Both the house and the cellar beneath it would be so damaged by a bomb impact that they would no longer be gas-proof, and the occupants could be overcome by fumes and smoke. It was therefore widely argued that everyone should be issued with gas masks, although achieving that on a large scale was easier said than done. A gas mask was useless unless it fitted closely over the user's face. The British had three different sizes for different age groups, but even that was not enough to guarantee a close fit. Besides, wearing a gas mask required the wearer to be trained in the proper manner of breathing, which made it impractical for very young children or the elderly. The inexpensive "popular" gas masks available in the Netherlands were practically useless: "The cap part of this cheap gas mask fits right over the head which makes it too hot after a while, and moreover has the objection that it covers the wearer's ears. The attachment of the filter container to the facepiece is too flexible, so that filter swings back and forth excessively."[53] Since a city could be contaminated by all kinds of poison gas for days on end after a major attack, it was also necessary to keep a supply of foodstuffs and other essentials in a bombproof underground shelter. "In short, if we take this type of protection (which is the only possible one) seriously, then it means building a miniature city under every city. This implies that providing anything like the necessary number of suitable shelters presents insuperable economic difficulties. Perhaps, in the course of some years and with the utmost exertion, we could fund the construction of some dozens of such cellars in each of the largest cities. This would mean providing protection to roughly one percent of the city's population. Which one percent is going to enjoy safety while the rest of the population is exposed to an air attack?"[54] This grim assessment of the feasibility of protecting civilians against air raids ran wholly counter to the slightly optimistic outlook expressed in the *Luchtbeschermingswet* (Air Raid Protection Act) of 15 August 1936. The Act separated active (military) air defence from passive defence; beforehand the War Department had offered advice on private and municipal air raid protection measures,[55] but the Air Raid Protection Act transferred respon-

57. Poster with instructions for self-protection, issued by Dutch Association for Air Raid Protection, late 1930s

sibility for the safety of the civilian population to the Ministry of Home Affairs (the State Inspectorate for Civil Air Raid Protection). The main duties of the Inspectorate were to achieve a systematic organization of the emergency services and to provide public information.

The primary purpose of the Air Raid Protection Act, which showed parallels with the German legislation of the previous year, was to delegate the implementation of concrete measures to the 1,158 Dutch municipalities. The aim of this decentralization was to bring air raid protection up to a suitable level in cooperation with members of the public. The state would itself take certain additional measures, such as building shelters in municipalities in the top two danger categories (class A and B), and would be partly responsible for organizing the warning and alarm services. The means were ill matched to the ends, however. To purchase enough gas masks for the population of the class A and B cities, for example, would take 17 years given the annual budget reserved for that purpose by the government.

DOMESTIC PRECAUTIONS

The *Nederlandsche Vereeniging voor Luchtbescherming* (or NVL, the Netherlands Association for Air Raid Defence) was founded in 1934. The association was run by professionals from the military and civil service and was open to the general public. The organizers endeavoured to gather up-to-date knowledge from air defence books and journals published in the neighbouring countries, and saw the association's task as "educating and informing the Dutch people about air raid protection".[56] They published a periodical (*Luchtgevaar*, or Aerial Danger)[57], gave radio talks, held local exercises, issued pamphlets and put on exhibitions aimed at stimulating general interest in air raid precautions and at promoting an efficient division of effort among local forces and municipal departments. The membership of the NVL reached 140,000 by the summer of 1939 and rose to 230,000 after national mobilization in September.

The NVL was particularly active in promoting air raid precautions in the home. They instructed the man of the house to clear out the attic, to give all the woodwork and glazing a fire-resistant treatment, and to keep buckets of sand, broomsticks with floor-cloths and long-handled shovels at the ready. Architects were exhorted to concern themselves with the fortification of domestic cellars. The association's first guideline on "self-protective measures for the public" advised anyone planning alterations to their own home to consult the municipal air raid defence department, the municipal architect, and the medical and chemical services.[58] Private air raid precautions were promulgated by means of professionally written instruction booklets which, very occasionally, contained some bizarre-sounding advice: "to protect one's head and hair from flying sparks, one should cover the head with some non-inflammable object or other, e.g. an inverted saucepan."[59]

In 1939, the NVL published an "instructional wall poster" with hints on the action to be taken by anyone momentarily in doubt about "What should I do now?"[60] The cardboard-backed poster was very inexpensive and had two small holes at the top for hanging it in a strategic location in the home. The Netherlands was not unique in having a poster of this kind; other countries had already made them available in their main cities.[61]

FIG III   OVERDEKTE SCHUILLOOPGRAAF

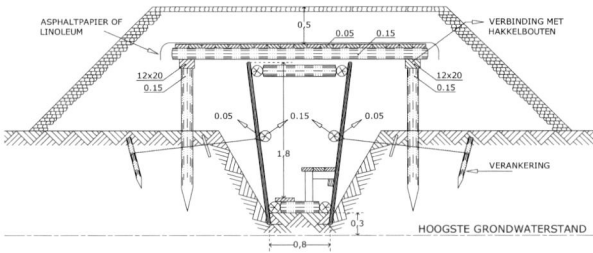

58. System trench shelters for multi-storey housing in The Hague, September 1938

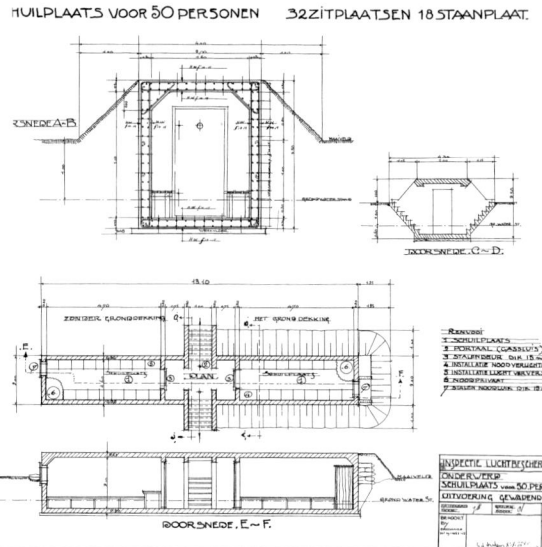

59. State Inspectorate for Civil Air Raid Protection, design for reinforced concrete shelters for 50 people, Type I, 1938

PUBLIC BOMB SHELTERS

While the citizen was out of the house, he was under protection of the government. An explanatory memorandum attached to the Air Raid Protection Act pointed out that the municipalities were expected to prepare public shelters in busy locations where "persons who are on a public road at the time of an air raid and who cannot reach home may be accommodated". The Act, in other words, was concerned solely with the safety of citizens in the urban public domain – in the street, near home or wherever they happened to be. The city councils had to distribute the shelters around the city in a systematic pattern. Building plans could be submitted to the Ministry of Home Affairs and, if approved, receive state-financed shelter accommodation.[62] The act was non-committal on the subject of private properties, and thus left it entirely up to the municipal councils to take measures in this domain.

Government officials realized all the same that something was amiss: "Protection against the risk of air raids is a matter of self-defence. Just as every citizen is obliged to protect himself and his family against fire and similar hazards, he must also take safety measures against threats from the air. Meanwhile, one cannot rely solely on the activity of the public (...)".[63] Self-protection naturally had its financial implications, but there were also practical objections. Most Dutch city dwellers lived in rented dwellings and were not at liberty to make alterations to them. The majority of the population would thus be unable to find safety in their own homes, which

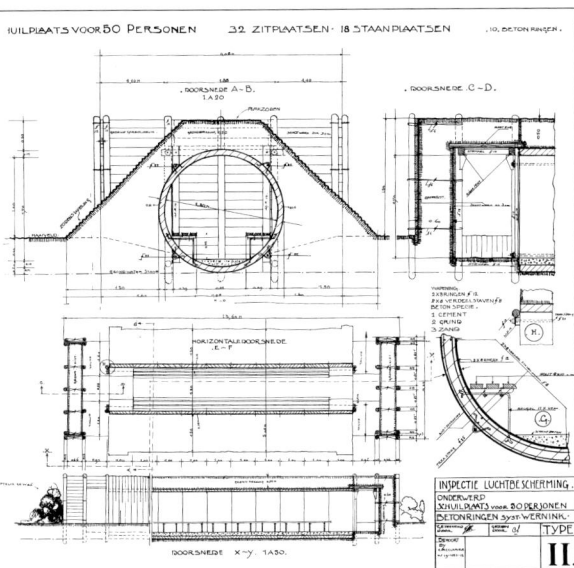

60. State Inspectorate for Civil Air Raid Protection, design for reinforced concrete shelter for 50 people, type II ("Wernink Shelter"), 1938

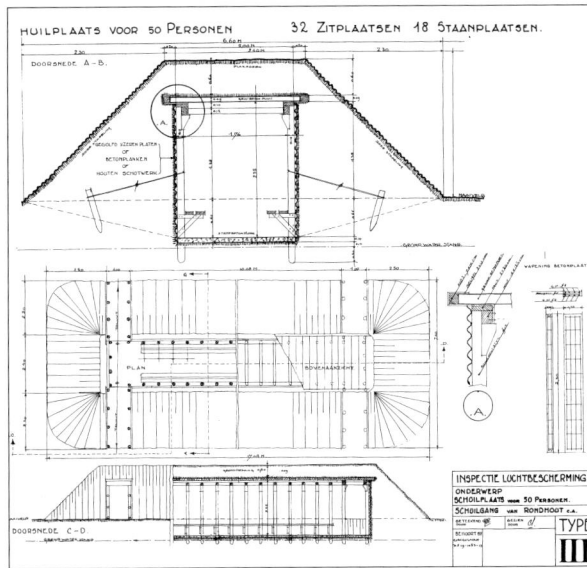

61. State Inspectorate for Civil Air Raid Protection, design for shelter in round timber for 50 people, type III, 1938

in any case generally lacked cellars and were built with single-brick walls. It was arguable that only a house capable of protecting its occupants against air raids satisfied the requirements of modern housing. But adapting the existing housing stock and all new buildings to meet this standard would place such a gigantic burden on the public housing sector that it would amount to a fortification of the entire urban fabric; or to be precise, building an underground plinth for Shelter City.

Enthusiastic advocates of air raid protection believed that the government and the public had to make a joint effort to allay the perils of air raids. Just as important as physical protection was the psychological side of aerial defence, namely the need to instill the urban population with a mental resistance to panic and demoralization.[64] The proponents lobbied municipal councils to fulfill the new Air Raid Protection Act to the letter. Local government had to implement warning systems and sirens, and delegate duties to the police, fire brigade, health service[65], public works and other municipal departments. The municipal responsibilities included organizing emergency services, providing them with protective clothing and decontamination facilities, supervising lighting and blackout[66], staff training, public information activities such as giving advice on what to do in the event of an air raid, informing business, public services and independent organizations of their duties[67] and taking measures to protect the cultural heritage of history, arts and science.[68]

The competence of the civic air raid protection agencies ranged from highly professional to quite amateurish. For example, the regular police force of Rotterdam received better uniforms, boots and food than air raid wardens despite doing the same work.[69] It was hard to find suitable non-military staff to coordinate working relationships between technical specialists and non-technical military officers, or between paid employees and volunteers – something that was all the more important in wartime since technical expertise would be thin on the ground with so many specialists engaged in the combat zone.

By the late 1930s, most large Dutch cities had a local Air Defence Department as stipulated by the Air Raid Protection Act. Amersfoort, for instance, produced a 37-page air raid protection plan which delegated duties to various municipal departments and which received the approval of the Ministry of Home Affairs.[70] The plan assigned the city's Building and Housing Department the task of drafting concepts for the layout of public bomb shelters, especially in busy city streets. In 1937, the City Architect wrote a report castigating the prevailing views on air raid protection, both regarding their degree of realism and their financial consequences. The norms issued by the Ministry required Amersfoort to build about 1000 shelter places for people at their place of work. Air raid shelter facilities in the city were practically non-existent, since far fewer houses had cellars than assumed by the government in The Hague, and many houses had only single-brick walls which could not possibly have stood up to a direct hit by a bomb. The City Architect noted ironically that the Ministry would probably refuse to pay for the fourteen new public bomb shelters proposed by the municipal council, which were supposed to be state-financed since Amersfoort was one of the cities most imperilled by air attacks, Risk Category A. His conclusion was that building public shelters was a hopeless enterprise.[71]

THE NETHERLANDS GO UNDERGROUND

Most of the shelters designed and built in Dutch cities in the period to 1940 were trench shelters. Cities in Risk Category A received a state subsidy to finance the required digging and construction. One of the first studies of trench shelters was published in 1934.[72] By civilian standards, the trench shelter was just a version of the military trenches of World War I, and people dismissed them as dank, claustrophobic burrows which offered little protection except from flying shrapnel. Nor did they protect against poison gas, so the city dweller rushing to seek shelter had to remember to bring his gas mask. The trenches were in general located next to con-

62. Meulenkamp Shelter, Rotterdam, 1939-1940

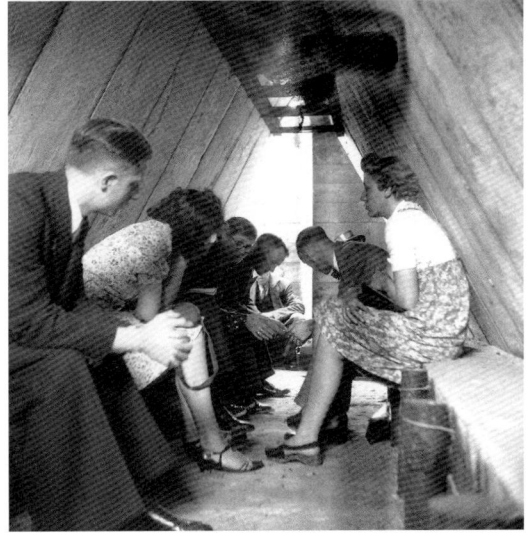

63. Interior of Meulenkamp Shelter, Rotterdam, 1940

centrations of buildings. They were dug in a line interrupted by transverse sections or zigzags, to prevent the shock wave of a direct hit travelling the full length of the trench. A covered trench obviously offered better protection against bombs than one which was open. Ideally, the trench had to be dug 1.35 metres into the ground, and where this was impossible, the above-ground defences had to be widened and strengthened. The cross-section of the trench depended on the groundwater level, and its width varied from 0.6 to 1.2 metres. Wooden bench seats could be installed where the trench was wide enough. Scanty instructions were issued for how citizens were to behave when sheltering in a trench.[73]

Relatively precise standards for the construction of trench shelters came into force in 1938.[74] The State Inspectorate for the Civil Air Raid Protection published a brochure that testifies to an understanding of the material consequences of a bombing attack. Normal shelters (for up to 150 people), according to the inspector, had to protect their users against high-explosive bombs ("except direct hits"), fire bombs (including ground vibrations and air pressure variations) and military gases. The bombproof shelters (for over 150 people) were required to withstand a direct impact. The guidelines were limited to normal shelters, which were intended for city dwellers who happened to be in a public place when the air raid alarm sounded.[75] Anyone else, it was assumed, would find shelter at home or in offices, factories, workshops, warehouses and schools.[76]

The occupants of a normal shelter had to be protected against shrapnel, falling debris and blast. The general requirements for a normal public shelter were that

it had to be within easy reach, have shrapnel-proof and fireproof side walls, a fire-proof covering, be resistant to the forces of collapsing buildings, sealed against gas, and have a ground area of 0.6 square metres per person. Without fresh air ventilation, these specifications allowed for a stay of 3 to 4 hours. For a longer period underground, the specifications recommended a special gas filter (a pipe through which purified fresh air could be drawn).[77] Some experts, however, considered the threat of a poison gas attack to be heavily exaggerated; "the spectre of an imperceptible death was continually being dangled before the public".[78] Assuring protection against a direct hit meant the shelter had to be buried entirely underground. Shelters of this kind were structurally possible but would be much too expensive because of the long entrance stairways required, among other things. The underground gas-proof shelter would have to have at least one airlock and one emergency exit, wiring, pipes and appliances, a sufficient number of toilets, emergency lighting and a supply of drinking water. Shrapnel-proof walls could be made from one of three materials: tamped concrete with gravel or clinker aggregate, reinforced concrete or clinker bricks.

The guidelines devoted a separate section to trench shelters (temporary, non-gas-proof and not necessarily covered); these had to follow a "broken" line. The walls of the trench could be made of reinforced concrete or steel sheet-piling. The main central government contribution to air raid protection took the form of job creation. Unemployed residents of the larger cities in Risk Category A were put to work digging trench shelters. To minimize the damage of a bomb impact, the cross-section of these trenches had to be as nearly V-shaped as possible.

RESULTS IN THE MAIN CITIES

What came of Shelter City in concrete terms? As far as we can tell now, shelters were indeed built in the main cities in Risk Categories A and B under job creation schemes. Owing to government austerity measures, the trenches were generally unroofed, despite the warnings of experts. "1. Is it really a good idea to drag the public out of doors at any time of day or night and force them into cold, windy shelter trenches? 2. Is it really a good idea to crowd people together, considering that a direct hit could result in mass deaths, or that panic could ensue? 3. After living through a few air raids, will people really take the trouble to go into the shelters? 4. Doesn't the home offer sufficient safety, for example in the corridor or hallway?"[79] Although the requirement was broadly similar in every city, scores of different shelter designs, both open and closed, were built in wood, concrete and steel. The Hague had 150 covered wooden trench shelters (each for 50 people), four reinforced concrete underground shelters (two for 50 and two for 100 people) and 24 cellar shelters in existing buildings.[80] Rotterdam built 300 covered trenches of the Meulenkamp model (named after the designer), each for 50 or 100 people. Amsterdam had 141 wooden and 25 concrete-lined trench shelters (13 uncompleted), 13 shelters under bridges, eight in machine rooms under movable bridges, and 30 privately owned cellars requisitioned by the city council.[81] A total of 41,500 Amsterdam citizens could find a seat in one of these shelters; and over 10,000 more if everyone remained standing.[82] The city of Utrecht dug 2,300 metres of shelter trenches (for approximately 7,000 people) and created 16 underground shelters (for approximately 2,700 people) in the arched cellars that lined the canals; the latter were below street level and could be reached via the basements of nearby buildings. The cellar arches were shored up, the interiors provided with seats and toilets, and the doors and windows protected by sandbags. Middelburg built at most 19 public shelters with a total capacity of 650 people.[83] Arnhem reported having eleven open trench shelters with a total length of 750 metres (for 2,200 people).[84] Nijmegen had 86 public shelters in the form of ten-metre long trenches, constructed in poured concrete and covered with corrugated steel sheeting; each had room for 50 people.[85]

AIR RAID PRECAUTIONS IN INDUSTRY

Industry played an incidental part in the provision of shelters. Among them were Zuidergasfabriek (South Gasworks) in Amsterdam and the shipping company Rotterdamsche Lloyd in Rotterdam.[86] Philips built a new office building in Eindhoven (1939) complete with cellars which contained advanced archiving facilities and which could quickly be converted into shelters by installing airlocks in the event of war.[87] The PTT adopted a policy of building sturdy shelters under or alongside its own buildings in 1939.[88] As a state-owned enterprise, it already had its own air raid protection department.[89] Some post offices in Rotterdam and The Hague were surrounded by Meulenkamp-type trench shelters. The PTT continued building shelters after the occupation, for example in the main post office of Hilversum which had an emergency cellar with an airlock[90] and in Rotterdam's main post office which had an exceptionally heavily reinforced bunker.[91] The Rijksgebouw voor Geld- en Telefoonbedrijf, another PTT building in Amsterdam, built eleven shelters with a capacity for 580 people.

AIR RAID PRECAUTIONS IN THE HAGUE

Although the Netherlands officially adopted a policy of neutrality, there was reason enough to re-evaluate the safety of the organs of state and of the public in the seat of government. Air raid precautions went considerably further in The Hague than in other Dutch cities. Beside the municipal authorities, the NVL was highly active there. The association's Hague section had 851 members in 1938 but 12,016 by 1939. The city had established a reputation as long ago as 1934 by building the country's first concrete public bomb shelter, with a capacity of 120 people.[92]

The municipal council embarked on building a fully fledged Shelter City in 1938, e.g. by issuing an air raid protection plan.[93] The first substantive air raid precautions were taken in December that year when the attics of municipal buildings

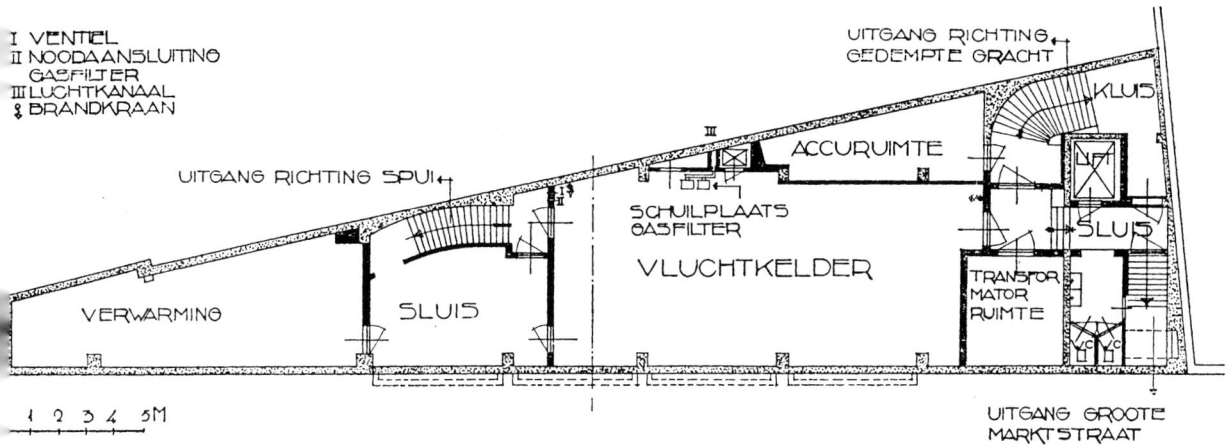

I VENTIEL
II NOODAANSLUITING
   GASFILTER
III LUCHTKANAAL
§ BRANDKRAAN

UITGANG RICHTING
GEDEMPTE GRACHT

UITGANG RICHTING SPUI←

KLUIS

ACCURUIMTE

SCHUILPLAATS
GASFILTER

VLUCHTKELDER

SLUIS

TRANSFOR
MATOR
RUIMTE

VERWARMING

SLUIS

1 2 3 4 5M

UITGANG GROOTE
MARKTSTRAAT

67. A.H. van Leeuwen, ground plan of first public emergency shelter in
the Netherlands (120 people), The Hague, 1934

68. Oval shelter with benches in Eindhoven, undated

were cleared out and their floors covered with a layer of felt paper and sand. The city also purchased gas masks, torches, first aid materials, saws, and shovels for use in municipal offices and other public buildings. They began training their staff in the use of gas masks, provided schools with alarm bells, drew up a list of cellars in the municipality and initiated an emergency telephone network. Construction began on 14 underground bomb shelters in or near police stations and on shelter facilities for the repair teams of the municipal electricity, gas and drinking water corporations. The Air Raid Protection Department was provided with a telephone exchange built strongly enough to withstand shrapnel and collapsing masonry, and facilities for the municipal health authority were improved. The city also purchased 15 short-wave transmitters.[94] A study was undertaken of how to protect members of the public who were outdoors when an air raid warning sounded; the city's technical staff calculated that the 400,000 residents of The Hague would need roughly 100 kilometres of trenches for this purpose. The report pointed out that the city centre had insufficient room to dig these trenches. Moreover, the high groundwater level of the soils meant that trench shelters must inevitably protrude largely above ground level; not only parks and gardens, but the entire look of the city would be impaired.[95]

The survey of available cellars in The Hague revealed that only ten percent of houses had them. It was decided to install public shelters under steel-framed buildings, but only if they already had an underground basement with room for at least 30 people and the possibility of making at least two entrances.[96] Where possible,

< *Page 88*
69. Public shelter in
Amsterdam, undated

70. Anderson Shelter in the
garden of the Municipal
Housing Department, The
Hague, 1939

the city encouraged the reinforcement of domestic cellars, and municipal staff eval-uated well over 600 plans for private cellar reinforcement. Later, The Hague drew lessons from the bombardment of Rotterdam in 1940: all addresses with private cel-lar shelters were registered with the city's emergency services.[97]

The decision process towards constructing 269 trench shelters for schools (with a total of 90,000 pupils) began in 1938. The original plan was to find a uni-form solution, but this turned out to be impractical. Schools with sufficiently large playgrounds could be provided with trench shelters which were resistant to shrap-nel and falling debris.[98] Where space was lacking, it was necessary to decide which schools could be given reinforced shelter spaces in units for 50 persons. A compli-cation that arose in this respect was that numerous schools were listed for requi-sitioning during mobilization. In the end, a considerable number of schools were equipped with shelters built either in reinforced bicycle sheds or in cellars under the school buildings. Most of the rest were provided with a trench shelter, in a few cases concrete-lined, alongside the school.[99]

This series of trench shelters was supplemented by 130 plans for public trench shelters, designed by the Municipal Works Department, to be fabricated in prepa-ration for imminent war. The wood required for their construction had to be pur-chased in advance. Forty of these units (each for 50 people) were to be sited at busy traffic points and built immediately – in concrete.[100] In total, 156 wooden and six concrete shelters, with room for 8000 people, were actually built.[101]

Private homes without cellars were not forgotten. The Hague pulled off a difficult feat in this area. The city council initially wanted to provide all residents who could not afford a domestic shelter a free steel shelter hut, following the British example. But this would have meant purchasing 50,000 units, which would have been hard to organize and encountered financial objections.[102] The municipality therefore bought materials for building 1000 shrapnel-proof, steel, family-sized, hut shelters of the Anderson type (each for six to eight people). Residents of The Hague could buy the materials and erect the shelter themselves in a garden or backyard.[103] The shelters apparently sold out quite quickly.[104]

THE SHAPE OF SHELTER CITY

A painful political vacuum developed in the Netherlands in 1939. On 31 May the previous year, the Minister of Home Affairs had instructed the municipalities to simplify their precautionary measures because of the tight national financial situation. Within just over a year, World War II had broken out, and the Netherlands, while claiming neutrality, mobilized its troops. There were widely varying interpretations of the responsibilities for air raid defence that were delegated to the lower echelons of government; Haarlem, for instance, did nothing, while Zaandam decided to make every home owner responsible for building and furnishing a shelter.[105]

The Public Works Departments of most cities, guided in many cases by the City Architect, designed primitive civilian shelters of a kind that was still familiar from World War I: trenches, covered or uncovered. This was the cheapest solution and thus accorded with the tight-fisted national policies of the 1930s. The Dutch government's aversion to paying for concrete measures to protect civilians against air raids contrasted sharply with Britain, which was willing to risk a considerable social upheaval, but it was not all that different from the approaches in Germany and France. Providing shelter was regarded there primarily as a private affair.

In 1940, the Air Raid Protection Inspectorate calculated the percentage of the population in the four largest Dutch cities who had a chance of finding shelter in an air raid, either in trench or cellar shelters. In Amsterdam the figure was 7.5 percent, in Rotterdam 13.2 percent,[106] in Utrecht 6 percent and in The Hague 3 percent.[107] Even the most crucial questions raised by the limited supply of shelter places, such as who would be admitted in the event of a mass rush for shelter and who would implement that selection, were left unresolved.[108]

Nonetheless, Shelter City burrowed its way under the public space of the main cities. School and city playgrounds, public gardens, parks and squares were dug over and soon bulged with giant molehills. Civilian preparations for air raids seemed if anything like preparations for trench warfare.

Politicians and government officials seemed either unwilling or unable to face the consequences of extensive air attacks, let alone back the state-funded construction of shelters for whole city populations. Imitating the examples of Germany and Britain, the Dutch launched public information campaigns with folders, exhibitions and radio announcements, all with the aim of persuading citizens to construct shelters in their own homes. The open market offered products ranging from gas- and/or shrapnel-resistant huts to bombproof bunkers. There were countless different models, and nowadays it is far from easy to reconstruct a picture of them. They included shelters made of bales of straw, a "refuge or hiding cupboard", six types of steel hut, three shelters made of reinforced concrete and segments for creating trench shelters.[109] In May 1940, the Air Raid Protection Inspectorate assessed 16 shelter systems for durability using explosives. Seen in retrospect, these experiments may be regarded as a dress rehearsal for the actual Dutch air raid precautions: German planes began their ultimate test of the Dutch aerial defences on the last day of the explosive trials.[110]

The character of air raid protection policies in the Netherlands resembled above all preparations for a rerun of the previous war. As it turned out, these measures had little bearing on the war that was about to commence. Air raids were few and far between in World War I, while in World War II they played a key role. The techniques of attack and defence had meanwhile been vastly refined. But nowhere in Europe were steel or concrete bunkers, capable of withstanding direct bomb strikes, built for civilian purposes on any significant scale.

71. "The Dove of Peace Speaks", Dutch magazine for air raid defence, 1939

< *Page 92 and 93*
72. Trenches below Eiffel Tower, Paris, 1939

CHAPTER 3

The Contest of Projectile versus Armour

Air Raid Defences in Germany, 1940-1945

THE EXAMPLE OF CARTHAGE

In the 1930s, people were widely aware of the risk of cities being bombed. It remained unclear, however, whether nation-states were really likely to employ this tactic in the event of war. The fear of air raids grew in direct relation to the growing threat of war. Efforts in the defence of the civilian home and hearth were paralleled by the growing production of military aircraft and mounting inventories of armaments on the eve of World War II. From a strategic standpoint, there was some justification for bombing raids targeting enemy manufacturing centres which supported the war effort in some way or another. There was also a current of argument that legitimized the bombing of civilian targets and even whole cities, on the grounds of weakening the enemy and breaking his morale. When the first British air raids on German ports took place in 1939, the shock and dismay were widespread. Municipal authorities in large German cities began building bombproof shelters for their inhabitants.

Prior to the air war with England, nobody had a realistic conception of the true nature of air raids, which was developing into an instrument consistent with the tactic of charred cities, in other words with prolonged, repetitive area bombing. The strategic and moral dimensions had become hard to distinguish right from the first British and German bombing campaigns. It was difficult to determine where the military or strategic targets (industrial centres engaging in the manufacture of

Flieger=Bomben

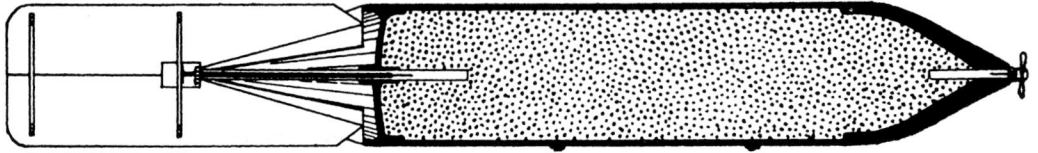

1800 Kg

Amerik. Sprengbombe   Versuchsform

900 Kg

Amerik. Sprengbombe   Versuchsform

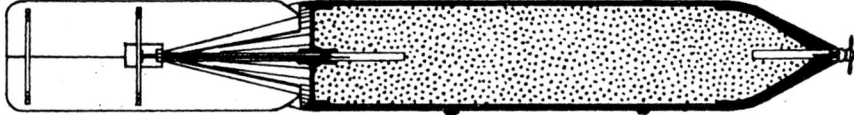

495 Kg

Amerik. Panzer-Sprengbombe   Versuchsform

495 Kg

Amerik. Sprengbombe   gewöhnl. Art

Russ. Sprengbombe
gewöhnl. Art

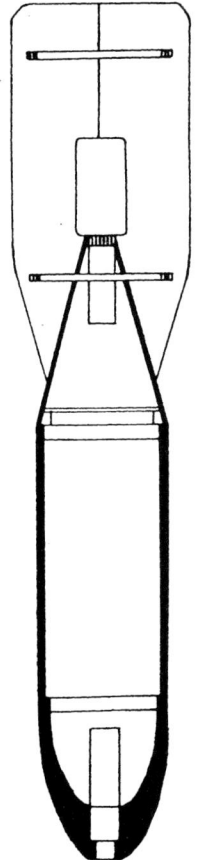

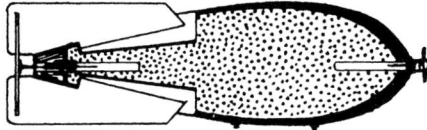

270 Kg

Amerik. Sprengbombe   gewöhnl. Art

Russ. Splitterbombe
dünnwandig

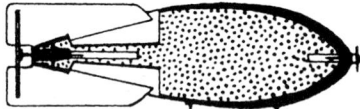

270 Kg

Amerik. Sprengbombe   dickwandig

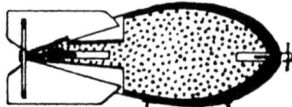

135 Kg

Amerik. Sprengbombe   gewöhnl. Art

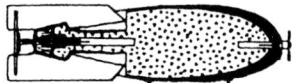

135 Kg

Amerik. Sprengbombe   dickwandig

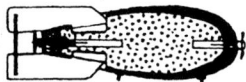

war materials) ended and the moral targets dominated (the bombing of civilian targets gauged to demoralize the enemy population). Be that as it may, civilian life was thrown into total disarray wherever the bombs fell. The air war proved to be one of the crudest possible technical incursions on civilization. This was partly because the accuracy of bomb aiming was rather poor, making it hard to tell where the strategic significance of attacking a city stopped and the moral boundary was crossed. In the summer of 1940, the British decided that the bombardment of cities, or to be more precise of the homes of the labour force needed to maintain production, was a valid way of striving for victory. They had learned their lesson from the German bombing of Coventry, where the localized fires started by incendiary bombs proved capable of merging to form large area conflagrations or even a complete firestorm in which no one could survive.

After the Germans tested this procedure on English cities in the autumn of 1940 (since when Coventry has entered history as the consummate example), the idea of retaliation started gaining support in the UK. People pointed out analogies with Carthage, which the Roman senator Cato had ordered to be wholly annihilated, never to be rebuilt. German cities became the scene of moralistic, vindictive bombing raids intended to make them share a Carthaginian fate and to degrade their citizens to cave dwellers. In the planning of Allied bombing campaigns, the concept of the city narrowed into an abstract spatial entity with primarily quantitative properties, an abstraction which had to be expunged by incineration reaching deep under the ground.

Air raids were a new adjunct to the business of war, in which the cities became laboratories for the testing of new techniques. The strategic component of this enterprise, zeroing in on the opponent's manufacturing centres, was largely a failure, after which the civilian environs of these centres and the suburbs where the workforce lived were designated as targets. Eventually, whole cities and the entire biotope of the city-dweller became fair game. The lack of precision was compensated by the deployment of huge numbers of heavily laden bombers, and the cities became the recipients of an orgy of bombing aimed at inducing fiery devastation.

The method the Allies used to attack German cities throughout a four-year period was the carpet bombing of zones marked out in advance by scout planes. The Germans dropped three times the quantity of bombs on Warsaw as the Allies did on Dresden in 1945, but the effect was more limited since the Germans aimed primarily

< *Page 96*
73. Bomb types

at military targets. In Dresden, the object of attack was the civilian population as a whole, and they were meant to vanish from the face of the earth in a firestorm.

TACTICS AND TECHNIQUES OF THE AIR RAID

To conduct an air raid, airfields were of course necessary. In the years leading up to the war, these had already been transformed from meadows with a few huts and hangars into substantial villages of some two thousand inhabitants. These villages were self-supporting, and the accommodation and welfare of their isolated rural communities were of national importance. A typical British military air base, for example, had numerous if austere communal amenities. "Living quarters were complete and self-contained, with dormitories, baths, showers, wash-hand basins, lavatories, galleys, dining halls, rest rooms, recreation rooms, a canteen, sick bays, cinemas, chapels, barber's, shoemaker's and tailor's shops and, for exercise and recreation, football, hockey and cricket pitches."[1] There were also spaces for the training of aviation personnel and for preparing aircraft for flight. Apart from the hangars, there were some 170 separate buildings designated as workshops, storage rooms, offices, training facilities and lecture classrooms. The base was also equipped with radio and radar systems, electric pumps for groundwater and electricity generators. Great Britain built 27 airfields like this at previously undeveloped or partly developed locations, while 11 existing airfields were expanded into fully fledged air bases. That work entailed the construction of concrete runways and of aprons for taxiing and maintenance. Fleetlands (Portsmouth) gained a large repair yard for aircraft. Construction of the runways alone consumed 200,000 tons of materials, roughly equivalent to 45 kilometres of modern motorway.

The airfields were busy with heavy bombers with large fuel tanks taking off in waves.[2] Besides armour plating, the bombers were equipped with mounted guns to defend themselves against enemy fighters and ground-based anti-aircraft fire. The sheer weight of these planes made them poorly manoeuvrable, slow and unable to gain much height. But they succeeded in reaching the enemy targets. Stanley Baldwin's confident 1931 prediction that "the bomber will always get through" was not yet disproved, although the question was at what price. The probability of being shot down was considerable, certainly until 1943, while the air crew were generally incapable of finding the designated targets and of discharging their bombs at the right moment. To guarantee that a target would be bombed necessitated an expensive solution: the bomber formation had to be sufficiently large to ensure that least some of the planes would reach their destination intact and discharge their munitions.

A special technical measure was required to conduct the heavy bomber formations to their destination: the pathfinder force of agile, lightweight bombers. The pathfinders had on-board radar and were guided on their course by beams from radar stations.[3] They flew ahead of the heavy bombers and dropped smoke markers and flares to identify the approach route and the target zone. In 1943-44, by which time the German air defences were seriously crippled, the Allies developed marker pots capable of illuminating the target with coloured light for a period of seven to twelve minutes. They drew, as it were, the contours of the zone of destruction in glowing lines, so that the bombers, instructed through the on-board radio, would be able to discharge their explosive cargo in the designated area. A carpet of bombs was an extremely effective way of destroying medieval inner cities. Accuracy was a different matter, however. Essen, which housed the Krupp works, was understandably an obsessive goal during the Ruhr bombing campaign, but the factories themselves were never disabled.

The Americans strove to achieve precision attacks and therefore preferred daytime raids. Yet these were notorious for their inaccuracy. One failed attack on an industrial complex in Rennes, for example, claimed three hundred fatalities. A similar course of events in Mortsel (Antwerp) resulted in three thousand deaths. The Flemish poet Gaston Burssens described the attack, which took place on 5 April 1943, as follows: "Suddenly I saw many people out on the street look up in alarm, and several of them flattened themselves on the ground. Then I heard a sudden wail of sirens, rising to a massive shriek, followed by a Paternoster of deafening explosions. Every window shattered. All the doors flew open. Boy [Burssens's dog; KB] dashed howling for the cellar shelter, while I myself scrabbled on all fours in his wake. It seemed that the air raid would never end, and I had the impression that my supposedly bombproof cellar was being shaken to its roots. Then everything was momentarily dead silent. Boy stood panting and I beside him trembling. By then I pictured my house lying in ruins above my head. I cautiously started up the stairs but no sooner had I reached the third step than the whole show started again. I tumbled over Boy back into the cellar and the steel door slammed shut like a cannon blast. Boy, I thought, we are not going to get out of this alive! Time stood still for me, and I still cannot say how I next found myself standing dazed in the street or how long had passed in the meanwhile. Not far off lay the ruins of Pompei under what seemed like a dusting of snow beneath a grey sky – while I myself stood in bright sunlight. I rambled for hours through the rubble of Mortsel; saw whole, half and

74. American high-explosive bombs of 1,800, 900, 500, 270, 135 and 45 kilograms, plus an 11 kilogram bomb, 1930s

fragmented corpses, heard the groans of the dying, children sobbing, women hysterical and men swearing as they grubbed through the debris with their bare hands in search of a wife, a mother or perhaps a child. If ever I wished to see the statesmen responsible for this skinned alive, then that was the moment!"[4]

BOMBS AND FIRESTORMS

Viewed from the bombers as they swooped in majestic formation to their destination, a city would have seemed no more than a silhouette trembling in the moonlight. It was on that abstraction that the bombs rained down. A falling bomb took thirty to forty seconds to descend, while the wind, the course of the plane and the moment of discharge caused changes in its trajectory. The calibre of British and American munitions advanced considerably in the course of the war. Besides growing heavier, they were made in ever more varieties, so that a bomb could be tailor-made for a specific target. Two million incendiary bombs were dropped on Berlin and Munich, and one million each on Frankfurt and Nuremberg in the final phase of the war.[5] Initially, high-explosive bombs weighed from 55 to 110 kilos, but by 1942 their weight rose to typically 1,800 and a maximum of 2,600 kilos. The Blitz was primarily conducted with lightweight bombs, but incidental German parachute mines with delay fuses drew the special attention of British experts. By the end of the war, a weight of 10,000 kilos was reached. During the Little Blitz of 1944, Hitler's final attempt to subdue the cities of Britain with flying bombs, V1 and V2 rockets weighing 1,400 kilos ("Fritz"), 1,800 kilos ("Satan") and 2,500 kilos ("Max") were fired across the Channel at England.[6] That same year the Americans made their own contribution with bombs of 5,400 kilos ("Tallboy") and 10,000 kilos ("Grand Slam"). The U-Boat pens along the Baltic coast were initially roofed by slabs of concrete 3.5 to 4 metres thick, but this later increased to 6-8 metres. Special bombs were developed for attacking these bunkers, such as the "Disney" (1,800 kilos) of late 1944, a rocket-propelled projectile designed to penetrate some way into the concrete before exploding.[7] The total of 2.7 million tons of bombs dropped by the Allies (of which 1,356,828 tons were on Germany) depended on a huge alliance of science, technology and logistics, backed by a feverish engineering design campaign.[8] On the home front, workers on the streamlined production lines (1.8 million people in Great Britain alone) knew only of their own task and were at most dimly aware of the dire effects of their labours.

Since the precision bombing of point targets (war production sites) with explosives was a failure, despite the use of radio and radar to guide the planes, the combatants adopted the destruction of large areas with incendiary munitions. Britain took a decision on New Year's Eve 1942 to conduct further research into the destructive effect of a firestorm on a city. The success of an air raid would henceforth be measured by the extent of the resulting conflagration, which was documented in aerial photographs after the attack. It was therefore not the tonnage of bombs that determined the urban firestorm but their incendiary qualities.

Starting in 1941, the Allies conducted intensive laboratory research into suitable chemical compositions for incendiary bombs. "A day-long bombardment with various fiery cocktails, consisting of paraffin, rubber, synthetic resin, mineral oil, liquid asphalt, gelatine, small quantities of metal oxides, fatty acids and some phosphorus, developed a level of destruction that was exceeded only by nuclear weapons."[9] A careful mix of high-explosive bombs, fragmentation bombs with delay fuses and incendiaries, taking into account the inflammability of the buildings at the location, ensured that the firefighters would have to hold back for a long while until they could set to work. The attack had to be tightly orchestrated to make this firework show possible (the responsible strategists spoke about the bombardments in such terms).

In 1942 the Allies began discharging carpets of bombs on the German cities. The attack on Cologne by thousands of bombers in a tight formation (the "Bomberkette") in May 1942 was the first experiment in the erasure of an area. One of the basic insights was that a city with houses lacking fire walls made excellent fuel. The inflammability of cities in combination with the prevailing temperature, humidity and wind determined the intensity and duration of the fire. The separate foci of fire were fed by the building materials of the houses and their domestic contents, and the localized blazes soon united to form a continuous conflagration, which was capable of developing into a firestorm. In a firestorm, a burning block or a row of houses could reach a temperature above eight hundred degrees, a wind speed of at least fifteen metres per second in a circumference of four kilometres was reached around the hot air column, and oxygen was sucked out. The firestorm worked like a furnace.

TERRITORIAL AIR DEFENCE

At first it did not look as though the Allies would be capable of breaking the German air defence lines. The first line was territorial, a virtual glass cover in the airspace meant to protect the country against intruders. The Netherlands was the testbed for the German night fighter system. The Germans planned to use Dutch airfields for launching attacks on England. Immediately after the invasion of the Netherlands, they were adapted in great haste, while new bases for night fighters were constructed in Leeuwarden and Venlo as early as 1940. The airfields of Leeuwarden, Twente, Schiphol and Gilze-Rijen[10] were considerably expanded and served as operating bases for fighters. Those at Deelen,[11] Soesterberg and Welschap and the new airfield of Venlo[12] were dedicated to bombers. Havelte, Volkel and Woensdrecht had a less prominent role.[13] The construction of these new bases probably took place in accordance with blueprints that had been prepared well in advance of the invasion, as is evident from their standardized typological concept. Besides the offensive and defensive airfields, sub-airfields and mock airfields (both intended to deceive the enemy), private airfields and airfields for the Lufthansa passenger airline were constructed at various places in the German Reich. Camouflage was the goal of the airfield architecture. Leeuwarden Airfield, for example, was made up of four locomotive sheds (low buildings with ridge roofs), a white-stuccoed chapel and, just outside the airfield proper, the Burmania complex (seven barracks for military personnel which were built in brick). They had a wall thickness of 55 centimetres and a parapet height of over one metre. The attic floor was made of concrete. The gently sloping roofs, the eaves, the tall fenestration and the windows with six or twelve panes were a recurrent feature in German military architecture.[14] Twente Airfield, which in the 1920s was no more than a large meadow with a terminal and a hangar, had the most refined camouflage of all German-built airfields in the Netherlands. The most important principle was to make the airfield blend with its surrounding so that it would be invisible from the air. The runways were therefore extensions of existing roads; the rural-looking brick-clad buildings were scattered around the landscape. The buildings in the Zuidkamp residential complex "breathe at first sight a centuries-old tradition. The interior is characterized by an almost rustic atmosphere. The communal rooms have open hearths and parquet floors. The radiators are encased in oak panelling, and Seluhofer tiles have been laid in the halls. But the extremely thick walls and the extensive use of concrete indicate an unmistakable military function. The red and green painted shutters prove, on closer examination, to be made not of wood but of steel."[15]

The defence against British air raids in the period from the autumn of 1940 to the summer of 1943 was aided by a string of radar posts with sensitive antennas reaching from the coast of Denmark to the Schelde estuary, and later extending along the French coast. They were equipped with listening devices, searchlights, anti-aircraft batteries and patrolling fighter planes. The night fighters communicated with the ground stations, which were linked in turn to the detector towers (with monitoring, measuring and transmission equipment), the centres of the air surveillance service, the anti-aircraft artillery and of course the air bases. It has been estimated that about sixty such posts existed in the Netherlands.[16] The line

75. Mobile searchlight manufactured by Siemens-Schuckert

76. Observation and listening equipment for localizing approaching aircraft

77. German radio tower at Oostvoorne (Southwest Netherlands)

was named after the night watchman of the Reich, General Josef Kammhuber, who was dedicated to creating a centrally managed night fighter organization. Consisting of a grid of rectangles each measuring approximately 30 kilometres square and with its own surveillance and warning apparatus, the line was intended to provide the air space above the German Reich with an invulnerable roof. The first Freya radar systems with parasitic searchlights were already functional by September 1940. Kammhuber created a defence line of night fighters parallel to the German-Dutch border, coupled with a series of radar surveillance stations on the Dutch side of the border.[17] The Freya detectors could sense approaching planes at a distance of 120 to 150 kilometres. The detection range of the system was such that it could even signal allied bombers taking off from airfields in the south of England. The radar gave a picture of anything approaching within a height of eight kilometres, although without indicating exact heights. This was followed in 1941 by the Telefunken-developed Würzburg system, an antenna dish with a cross-section of three metres which was capable of detecting every type of aircraft movement. An improved 1942 version, the Würzburg-Riese ("Giant" Würzburg), had a 7.5 metre cross-section and a depth of 2 metres, and was coupled to searchlights. By 1942, when nightly attacks by forces of over 1,000 bombers began, the line was reinforced with German anti-aircraft batteries and searchlights around the airfields in the east of the Netherlands. "Air Defence Zone West" on the east bank of the Rhine, which had been operational since 1940, was also activated. The next radar monitoring stations to be built were equipped with large Würzburgs.[18] Simpler types of monitoring stations (wooden towers) also appeared in 1942.[19] The dish-shaped Würzburg apparatus could trace enemy aircraft with precision and could guide the night fighters. The radio operators of the night fighters were guided to their target by means of a shortwave radio transmitter. In late 1942, the Diogenes command bunker on Koningsweg, Schaarsbergen (in the vicinity of Arnhem), went into operation to improve the guidance of the First and Third Air Squadrons (*Fliegerdivision*) based at the airfield of Deelen.[20] Data from the radar posts were used to select targets. The leaders of the night fighter squadron projected the available data onto the *Seeburgtisch* (Seeburg Table), a matt glass slab measuring 2.5 metres square. The fighters were indicated by green dots and their prey, the bombers, by red dots on the glass. Aerial combat could be followed in detail in this glass arena. The Seeburgtisch operators had radio contact with any location where a bomber could been caught in the searchlights. This gave the fighter planes three minutes to reach their targets and engage in an air duel, which the fighters usually won.[21]

Following the end of the Blitzkrieg in England, most of the German squadrons were summoned to action in the Eastern theatre. From the summer of 1941 onwards, the remaining planes were deployed to resist the British air sorties. The Kammhuber system was unable to withstand the armadas of Allied planes, however. From 1942 onwards, part of the system was further dismantled on Hitler's orders. The six searchlight regiments that made up the second defensive belt were brought back to Germany to defend threatened cities. The Dutch skies were still monitored but were far less frequently attacked. Additions to the detector equipment continued, however; by 1943, for example, Würzburg-Riese systems were in use at 25 locations, together with eight improved versions of the Freya.[22]

CIVIL AIR DEFENCE

To protect the urban population adequately against the effects of air raids would have required an armoured city, an emergency measure that in its most extreme form would have entailed a complete duplication of existing cities. The rigour with which that duplication was pursued depended on the status of the cities and the level of risk to which they were exposed. In cities such as Berlin, Hamburg and The

Hague, above-ground or underground parallel worlds were created, with survival machines that supported a surrogate life form. These places of fear and hope appropriated a place in the cityscape, and their claim on space only grew as the war proceeded.

The two most important German cities in Air Defence Category 1, Berlin and Hamburg, prepared to defend themselves against air raids in very different ways. After annexing areas of the surrounding country in 1937 and 1938, Hamburg had become the second largest city of the Reich after Berlin. As the main location for submarine building and oil refining, Hamburg was at the forefront in taking air raid precautions. It was followed by other large German cities and towns in the Ruhr, the region which was the weapons factory of the Third Reich. Hamburg got down to business in September 1939 when the police command announced a range of stringent air raid precautions. All residents of the city were obliged by law to fully black out the windows of their homes from dusk to dawn. Suitable cellars were to be cleared out immediately to facilitate their conversion into domestic shelters. Architects were involved in producing conversion designs. In the neighbourhoods, the conversions, involving the reinforcement of ceilings and walls, sealing against gas and protection from shrapnel, were carried out street by street. The high groundwater level meant that most cellars were above ground level, so the outer walls had to be reinforced. Adjoining cellars were connected by break-through walls in order to provide an escape route in case the house caught fire or collapsed above the heads of the occupants sheltering in the cellar.[23] Over 50,000 cellars were eventually converted as part of the cellar programme from 1939 to 1942, providing shelter for over 350,000 people. Domestic attics were also subjected to a systematic clearance. All woodwork was removed, fire walls and bombproof ceilings were built, and the floors were covered with a layer of sand to help extinguish fires.[24] This gigantic operation was financed by the state. In 1939, Goering proclaimed that Hamburg was protected from all possible enemy air actions, and that the active and passive air defences would guarantee the continued normal functioning of the port city. The local authorities knew better, however. They were well aware that there was insufficient bombproof shelter space for the whole population of the city. Not a single dwelling could stand up to a direct hit, a carpet bombing attack or a widespread conflagration.

SHELTER TYPOLOGY

In the autumn of 1940, the RAF intensified its air attacks on Berlin and on the maritime cities of the Baltic coast which had shipyards crucial to the sea war. The German military commanders and municipal authorities soon realized that active air defence by their own air fleet and anti-aircraft artillery was deficient, and that the protection of the civilian population had been neglected. The character of the destruction achieved by the first British bombardments showed that simple trench shelters and reinforced domestic cellars could offer at most protection against shrapnel, and were inadequate from the viewpoint of bomb resistance. An estimate indicated that, in the whole of Germany in 1940, there was room for 40,000 people in bombproof public shelters and 150,000 in shrapnel-proof public shelters. State buildings such as civil service offices, schools and museums had to be provided with air raid shelter spaces. Bunkers had been built only for the Nazi elite and others held to be essential for the functioning of the Reich.

The quality of the air raid defences differed from one city to another. It depended first of all on their ranking on the list of cities under threat of aerial attack, which determined whether or not the city was eligible for a Reich subsidy. Other important factors were the city's geographical situation, the geological composition of the ground on which it was built and municipal politics.[25] Neither Augsburg nor Heilbronn had a single air raid bunker. Nuremberg had shelter space at the start of

79. Children's home in Stuttgart, undated

1942 for only 12,500 people out of a total population of 400,000.[26] Mannheim had 51 bunkers in autumn 1943 with a design capacity for 120,000 (or room for 284,000 at a maximum squeeze). Leipzig, Dresden and Berlin had the worst standard of air raid protection of all Germany. That was because of the low probability of the bombers arriving; the quantity of fuel a bomber could carry in its tanks placed these cities practically out of range. This situation changed drastically in the final two years of the war, when it became possible to launch raids from countries closer to Germany.

The best protection for the city dweller was to be found in the lee of hills and mountains, in abandoned mines and in natural caves. In cities with a mining tradition, there was a burst of excavating new mine galleries. The underground networks of passages allowed the provision of multiple entrances, so that thousands of city-dwellers could stream in at the same time without congestion. Duisburg had 39 bunkers and 53 mine gallery systems. In Dortmund, in late 1943, a *Tiefstollensystem* (deep tunnel system) was excavated with 19 entrances strung out between the main railway station and Westpark, offering shelter to 80,000 people. Nuremburg expanded its catacombs in 1943 by excavating cross connections. After insulation against humidity and cladding with clinker brick, it had room for 15,000 people. Throughout

Germany, practically every underground space was adapted for sheltering from air raids, including corridors that communicated with buildings, crawl spaces, storerooms and beer cellars.

From a quantitative viewpoint, cellars were the most significant stock of shelters. In Frankfurt and Kassel, chains of adjacent cellars were formed by partitioning them with thin membrane walls which could easily be broken out in an emergency. Frankfurt had one such chain measuring 1,200 metres in length. The safety offered by the cellars was illusory, however.

Shrapnel-proof trench shelters (*Deckungsgräben* or *Splittergräben*) lacked any autonomous civil engineering development. The makeshift covered slit trenches that were dug in great haste in German cities following the invasion of Poland had been transplanted unchanged from the military to the civilian domain. They were generally dug in a zigzag pattern to give better protection against near miss bomb strikes. From the very first air raids, however, it was apparent that the protective potential of trenches, whether open or closed, was limited. Besides, they degraded rather quickly.

From the autumn of 1940 onwards, Germany therefore switched to building bunkers. The tubular type of public shelter (the *Röhrenbunker*) was unrelated to existing military prototypes. However, like sections of sewer, it was quick and fairly easy to assemble in urban surroundings (at road intersections and at tram or bus stops, where the entrances to the shelters were located). This variant with a vaulted roof had been in use since 1939. In some cases it was buried entirely underground and in others, partly above ground. The individual tube units varied in width and height to up to 2 metres. The side wall thickness could be as much as 1.1 metres, and the ceiling ranged from 60 cm to 1.1 metres in thickness. They varied in length from 18 to 80 metres. The tubes could also be joined in a parallel configuration, communicating through openings in the side walls. In all cases, they were unsuited to anything more than a short stay, because they were furnished only with wooden benches, simple ventilation fans and dry toilets. They generally lacked sleeping facilities or heating. As shelters, they could not protect the occupants from direct hits or explosions in the close vicinity. The underground passages had to have a minimum width of 1.65 metres or, if they were to accommodate two rows of benches, 2.3 metres. Problems with the supply of ventilation fans often made it necessary to provide the shelters with separate ventilation shafts. The tubular passage had at least two entrances, and was built with one to a maximum of three sharp, horizontal bends to impede shrapnel penetration. It also had a vestibule, a sitting area, a toilet space, a machine space and gasproof doors. By the time it became clear in 1943 that it would be impossible to provide bombproof protection to the whole urban population, it was decided to lower expectations and provide shrapnel-proof trenches or deep underground passages (*Stollenbau*). Albert Speer, Hitler's chief architect and since 1942 the Reich Minister for Armaments, ordered the design of various types which could be constructed from wood, brick or concrete. Roughly a third of the trench had to be below ground level, and raised sides were revetted with packed earth. The covering consisted of 50 cm of concrete. Each space could hold 25 to 30 people. The trench shelters were lighter in construction than the tubular ones, were more poorly equipped and had a flat roof.

An alternative that began to attract interest in that period was a collective shelter built of prefabricated concrete elements, with room for about 200 people. From 1944 onwards, the guidelines dictated highly simplified *Stollen* for a maximum of 100 people. Each entrance had to have a single angular bend, and the heating, ventilation and water supply often failed.

HITLER'S BUNKER PROGRAMME

The Nazi plans with regard to air raid protection showed bombastic and extravagant tendencies. Nonetheless, the large-scale construction of bunkers during the Third Reich was arguably the largest utilitarian building project in history. These wrinkles in the face of Mother Earth had two components. The military component, consisting of the Westwall (or Siegfried Line, 1936-1940) and the Atlantic Wall (1942-1945), was not a contribution to modern air warfare. The other component had a civilian purpose, in accordance with the notion of total war: the protection of the civilian population, important leaders, workers in wartime industries and civil servants against air raids. The bunker building campaign delivered the main building blocks of Shelter City.

Following the first air raid on Berlin on 25 August 1940, Hitler decided on a systematic approach to protecting the inhabitants of the main German cities, the military bases, the weapons manufacturing centres and traffic nodes. This was to be achieved by building bunkers capable of withstanding direct hits by bombs of up to 1,000 kilos.[27] Taking the 50 million Germans in need of concrete shelters and a space requirement of four cubic metres per person, the whole of Germany's industry would have needed roughly twenty years to realize this project.[28] Although this all-embracing survival plan (the *Hitler Sofortprogramm*) foundered on technical and financial limitations, the proportion of the intended construction that was achieved was impressive. Over 3,000 bunkers were built for city dwellers, plus roughly 3,000 more for employees in road building, industry, hospitals and the army.[29] The interpretation of Hitler's programme in the form of instructions issued by the Reich Minister for Armaments, Fritz Todt (17 and 18 October 1940), called for the construction of large numbers of reinforced concrete shelters in parks, gardens, public squares and other gaps in the urban fabric.[30] Shelter City grew quickly. German engineers were well aware that a trial of strength was imminent between ever heavier Allied bombs and ever thicker German concrete. This is why the latest knowledge had to be incorporated into the design for each new bunker. The heartfelt cry of Albert Speer, the architect charged with turning Berlin into the capital of the Third Reich, in a letter to the Reich Minister for Armaments Todt in September 1941 is thus understandable: if this development were not carefully managed, the class A bomb-proof bunkers of the Westwall (3-metre-thick walls) would be surpassed in strength by the latest bunkers in the cities.[31] This prediction was later to be fulfilled, in the Netherlands as well as in Germany. But by then not even the thickest concrete walls of civilian bunkers could stand up to the tonnage and the technical refinements of the contemporary generation of bombs. The fact that the Nazi top echelons felt forced to conduct large-scale bunker-building programmes to protect German citizens contradicted their message of invincibility. The bunkers were in this respect not so much symbols of superiority as symptoms of waning self-confidence, a herald of approaching defeat and inglorious death.[32]

Hitler's bunker-building programme took place in three stages. The first phase (from November 1940 to late 1941) was the construction of bunkers in 61 Category I cities, the highest risk class, with a total population of 20 million people. Here 839 bunkers were completed with shelter space for 400,000 individuals.[33] The second phase (from summer 1941 to January 1943) involved 31 cities with a total population of about 15 million and provided shelter for 500,000 civilians. The design of these bunkers allowed for the increasing penetrating power of the bombs as they had considerably thicker roofs and exterior walls. By January 1942, the structural work was complete on 1,215 bunkers, and a further 513 were under construction. By May 1943, the total rose to 3,000. The Allied attacks were increasing in intensity, however, and necessitated a supplementary building programme in May 1943 consisting mainly of underground passages. This was a stopgap measure, for the bulk of the building industry (materials, labour and transport) had already been shipped off to work on the Atlantic Wall and to protect the armaments factories. By July 1943, the shelter builders were again opting for tunnel shelters, especially where the groundwater level allowed for their excavation.

The bunker-building programme was not standardized, either organizationally or technically; or at least not at a municipal level. The pattern of competences was apparently more complicated in the civil sector than in the military one, where standardization was held to be the highest ideal. The delimitation of responsibilities made the coordinating hierarchy of the bunker programmes opaque, and they were marred by competition between those involved – the Air Force, police, Nazi Party members, administrators and local technical specialists. The strategic planning, the siting and the order of construction were the province of the Reich Minister of Airways, the commander of the Air Force and Herman Goering, the Representative for the Four-Year Plan. The allocation of quotas, the logistics and the material execution fell to Organisation Todt, which was organized along military lines. Fritz Todt held the post of *Generalbevollmächtigte für die Regelung der Bauwirtschaft* (GB-Bau, the Plenipotentiary for Organization of the Building Industry) and was the Reich Minister for Armaments from 1940 to 1942. His successor in this post was Albert Speer. Organisation Todt had proved itself capable when implementing the national road-building plan and construction of the Westwall from 1938 onwards. The organization had its own propaganda resources, including a fortnightly magazine, as well as 500,000 workers.

The shelters developed in Germany during the 1930s were normally single-storey underground buildings with a maximum design capacity of 250 people. The guidelines assumed that these shelters would offer protection against bomb shrapnel and falling masonry, although they were not designed to cope with direct hits or area bombing. In other words, there was no attempt to anticipate exigencies of the coming war. Some structural engineers such as Leo Winkel or Paul Zombeck had already designed round, above-ground tower shelters that could stand up to the explosive force of modern bombs. These precursors of the above-ground bunker city disproved the widespread assumption that only underground shelters could offer adequate protection.[34] From 1941 onwards, a transition was made to above-ground bunkers. These had the advantage that only the outer shell and the walls of the ground floor needed to be reinforced; underground bunkers, by comparison, required extreme reinforcement of the foundations and walls.

Three models prevailed in the range of bunker types: above-ground bunkers (the narrow air raid shelter towers of Winkel and Zombeck, and square or rectangular multi-storey blocks), partly submerged trenches and underground tunnels. It was soon established that the above-ground bunkers required less building material to withstand a given blast pressure than underground ones, and could therefore be built with thinner walls. The great majority of bunkers in northern Germany (except

Berlin) were therefore built above ground. The officially prescribed wall thicknesses for bombproof tower shelters trailed behind developments in the destructive power of the bombs, however. In May 1939, for example, Goering mandated a wall thickness of 1.4 metres for above-ground bunkers for 200–500 people. The above-ground wall thickness rose to 2 metres in 1941, and by 1943 the bunkers for leading officials had to have walls as thick as 3 metres.

The shortages that developed in steel, cement and wood as the war proceeded forced the bunker designers to develop new bunker types. As a way of saving time and construction costs, they concentrated mainly on building a small number of large, centralized bunkers instead of many smaller, neighbourhood bunkers.

LIFE IN THE BUNKERS

The weakest points in a bunker were its entrances, of which there had to be at least two. The doors consisted of armoured steel for withstanding bomb blasts and had rubber strips around the edges to provide a gasproof seal. Each entrance had an airlock equipped with decontamination requisites for mustard gas and mist sprays for other poison gases. The quality of the ventilation systems determined the temperature, particularly in the absence of heaters, which could range from 16°C in winter to 24°C in summer. The humidity might range from 25-75 percent. The bunker ventilation could be powered in three ways: electricity, diesel or manually. An electricity supply, generally through an independent circuit, was indispensable for lighting landings, staircases, toilets, circulation spaces and airlocks. The bunker occupants needed washing water and, if possible, a hand shower for rinsing off contaminants. The shower walls were covered with a washable layer. One washroom was available for each 25 seats/sleeping places. The flushing toilets were soon replaced by dry closets, since the water mains were often damaged in air raids.

The staff of the large public shelters consisted of a bunker manager, a bunker warden with assistants, heating technicians, cleaners, doctors and dentists, Red Cross nurses and midwives. Some bunkers also had security personnel and fire officers. Members of existing organizations such as the fire brigade wore their normal uniforms, while special shelter staff had a specially designed uniform and armband. As an ironic note, the cost of basic equipment for the air raid brigades in Munich was met from confiscated Jewish possessions.[35]

In 1941, the Reichs Ministry Inspectorate of Air raid Protection issued guidelines on "special objectives for the construction of air raid protection bunkers". They

80. Air filter pump for gasproof shelters, manufactured by Auer

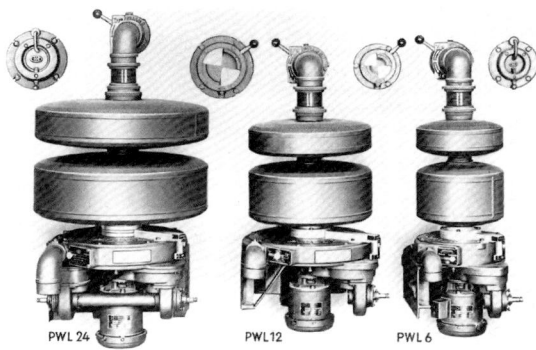

81. Air filters for shelters in a range of sizes, manufactured by Anton Piller

82. Steel cupboard with gasmasks, first aid materials and medicines, 1939

included instructions on the general design, ground plan, air supply, heating and cooling, water supply and drainage, signage in the bunkers, furnishing, bunkers in hospitals and bunkers underground.[36] The range of eligible bunker types could be classified in terms of siting (above ground, underground or partially submerged), grade of protection (bombproof, shrapnel-proof, gas-proof or masonry-proof) and the architectural type (house-like, i.e. square or rectangular with multiple storeys, round, tower-like or tubular). Within this broad classification there was much variation in size, local features and naming. Not even the standards for protection against bombs and gas were satisfied by all bunkers. Despite attempts at standardizing types and series, the municipal departments developed their own variant series. There was only one constant: the larger the bunker, the less material was required per occupant.

Practically every German construction company was involved in the first phase of the bunker programme. Technical equipment was provided by the firms Siemens & Halske, Auer, Piller and Rheinwerk. Diesel generators and electric motors were supplied by Deutz, Siemens and AEG.[37] The army initially provided soldiers to help in the construction project. Following the attack on Russia in June 1941, however, the labour forces were increasingly drawn from foreign workers, slave labourers, prisoners and concentration camp inmates. Work on the bunkers ground practical-

83. Chemical toilet for bomb shelters

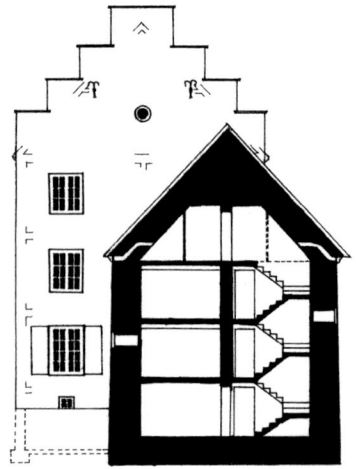

84. Carl Winand, competition design for hardened dwelling, Hamburg, October 1940

ly to a standstill in the autumn of 1944 because all available labour forces had been sent to the front.

ARCHITECTURE OF THE BUNKER

In the spring of 1941, the monumental refurbishment plans for the left bank of the Elbe in the prestige *Führerstadt* Hamburg were put on ice, and attention turned to the *Sofortprogramm* (Urgency Programme).[38] It was not immediately clear that this represented a radical change of direction, but the new bunker programme entailed a reduction of the shelter accommodation to bare essentials. A special unit was established to manage the increasingly standardized bunker-building campaign, and initially there was some concern about the architectural qualities of Shelter City. The municipal committee, which was led by engineers and architects, prepared a series of bunker designs intended to fit into gaps in the city fabric or into suburban contexts.[39]

It was thus only in the first phase of the programme that much importance was ascribed to the architectural appearance and urban harmonization of the bunkers. An exemplary publication was the book *Bombensichere Luftschutzbauten. Erste städtebaulich-architektonische Ausrichtung* ("Bombproof Air raid Shelters. First Urban Design/Architectural Orientation", February 1941). In Hamburg, the design principle of the air raid shelters, in the form of eleven round towers sited at traffic

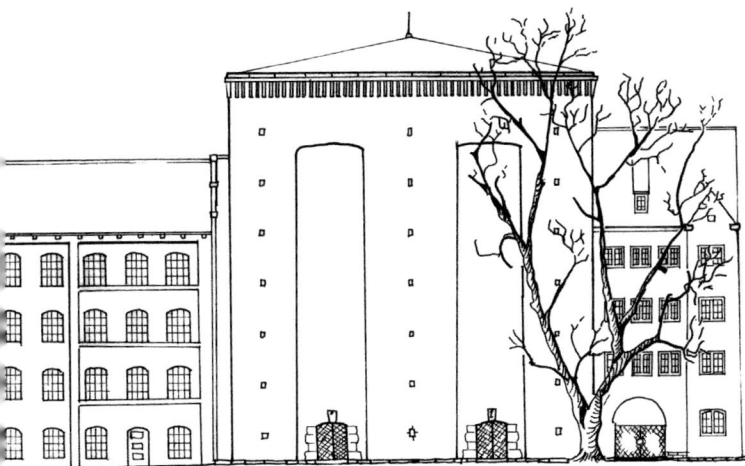

85. City of Hamburg, design for public shelter; front, 1941

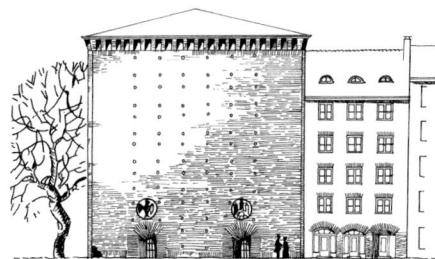

86. City of Hamburg, design for public shelter; rear, 1941

intersections which were completed in 1940, was visible to everyone: simple building volumes, each cast as a unit (*"aus einem Guss"*). The concrete shell was clad with brick and supported a gently sloping roof with Dutch roof tiles, a typical Hamburg feature. Other aesthetic choices were evident in the placing of the air holes and in the perfectly straight bands of brickwork in a contrasting colour, which could be stretched like a net over the entire brickwork surface. Another distinctive feature was the squat, arched entrance closed off by a lattice work. Rather than being naked concrete boxes, the bunkers were thus visually designed to hint at German vernacular styles and so project a sense of homely security.[40]

The need for air raid shelter also figured in the new Hamburg housing typology.[41] Each new house had to be built with a reinforced shelter in the foundations which had at least two exits; new blocks of flats were required to have a collective shelter. The architects paid some initial thought to future peacetime uses of the bunkers, but this soon became a dispensable luxury. An exception in this respect was a huge bunker for 6,000 people, measuring 200 metres in length and over 21 metres wide, on the Reeperbahn in Hamburg, which was designed with a view to potential peacetime use as a covered car park for 2,400 cars.[42]

The camouflage was initially so exuberant that bunkers were provided with medieval references such as corner turrets and city gate-like entrances. This was not seen as pseudo-architecture but as expressing the indomitability of the German people inherent to Nazi ideology. The bunkers in Emden, for instance, bore typological similarities to warehouses and grain silos, and those in Hannover, to water towers. Even in the first euphoria of bunker building, however, architectural cladding and ornament could be used only sparingly. All that really mattered was its quality as camouflage. After 1941, the bunkers were disguised with no more than a coat of paint to impede recognition from above. Organisation Todt took no interest in aesthetics. The shortage of building materials and manpower was so acute by 1942 that the brick cladding and tiled saddle roofs were abandoned. There was thus no question of a mature bunker architecture, at most of rudimentary forms. As the war progressed, the interior comfort of the bunkers similarly declined. The modernism of the bunkers, cast as they were as a single piece, declares their function: *schützenden Verbergen*, hiding from danger.

BERLIN

The ground under Berlin was churned up extensively under the National Socialist regime.[43] The start of an "intensified underground shelter" campaign was ordered for Berlin in 1939, under the management of Albert Speer. The first goal was to provide shelters in all government buildings, such as the extension to the Reichsbank and the new Tempelhof airport.[44] These received ample shelter facilities and in

87. Construction of underground bunker in Reeperbahn, Hamburg, designed for peacetime reuse as garage, 1941

88. Bunker styled to match its surroundings in Lübeck.

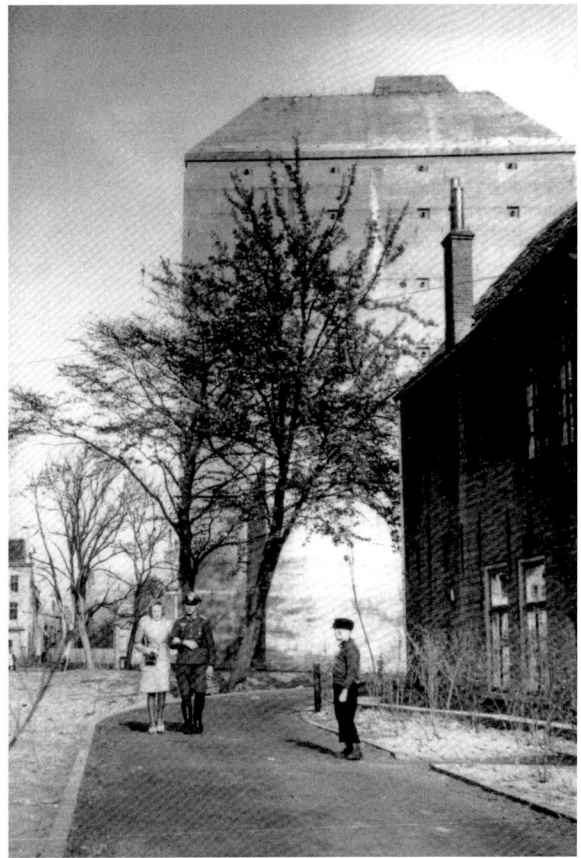

89. Bunker in Emden

some cases multi-storey bunkers. Bunkers were also built for the command centres of the military and civilian top echelons. The 16 Reichs ministers each received a bunker near their residence.[45] Underground passages were dug for the weapons industry, as well as escape and connecting tunnels, and air raid shelters in the form of cellars and trenches.

By the start of the war, less than 3 percent of Berlin's population had any prospect of safe accommodation. The available shelters were moreover unable to stand up to bombing. This was not only because of the initially boundless public confidence in the Luftwaffe but also because construction of the Westwall and later the Atlantic Wall claimed considerably more materials and money than the air raid protection of Berlin and other German cities on the A list. The Nazis apparently reckoned on heavy casualties among the general population, for the quantities of building materials, equipment and personnel available for civilian bunkers was

90. Albert Speer, Reichs Chancellery, Berlin 1935-1936

limited to whatever the military construction programme permitted. This is why Berlin resorted to digging trenches in its parks and sports fields; although covered, the trench shelters offered no protection against well-targeted bombs.[46] The first bombs falling on Berlin in the late summer of 1940 (resulting in 200 fatalities and over 1,600 homes destroyed) prompted the start of a more systematic campaign to provide shelter for a larger proportion of the population and to hide the weapons industry better underground. The measures, designated as *Bunkerbauprogramm für die Reichshauptstadt* (26 September 1940), ordered the provision of breakthrough sections in the party walls between houses in large perimeter blocks to create potential escape routes.

New bunker complexes were built, such as the two-storey bunker on Alexanderplatz. The Alexanderplatz shelter had room for 3,000 people and an escape route through a connecting staircase to the underground railway. Including the shelter capacity of the metro tunnel, the Alexanderplatz facility could protect some 10,000 Berliners. Albert Speer drew up a balance of the bunker-building programme in

1942: Berlin had 237 bunkers with approximately 60,000 berths; 53 bunkers were under construction with room for approximately 21,000; and 100 bunkers were planned for a total of about 94,000 people. Despite all these efforts, not even 6 percent of the four million population of Berlin had any prospect of a bomb-resistant shelter place.[47] By 1943, the demand for personnel and materials at the war fronts thwarted further ambitions to build bombproof accommodation for city dwellers. Berlin resorted to assembling inferior shrapnel-proof tubular collective shelters and covered trenches in the face of increasingly frequent attacks by low flying fighter bombers.

BUNKER COMPLEXES FOR THE REGIME

A total of 16 *Führerhauptquartiere* (Führer Headquarters) were built in the course of the war in Germany and in the occupied territories. Some of them were extensive bunker settlements, and Hitler actually used six of them. Wolfschanze in East Prussia and the uncompleted Riese in Silesia still give some impression of what they were like. No coherent organizational concept can be detected in these headquarter complexes; rather, there is evidence of a continual adaptation to local circumstances. They consisted of an ever increasing number of bunkers for varied users and applications. The wall thickness rose from two to five metres in some cases. The buildings for working activities, leisure and sleeping in the centre of each headquarters had simple square or rectangular ground plans. Despite a persisting myth, the "Führerbunker" in Berlin was not at all an exceptional object in a governmental district.[48] The first round of bunker construction in that zone took place back in 1935. The reception hall built as an extension to the Old Reich Chancellery had a bunker for 150 people extending into the back garden instead of a normal basement space. Its ceiling and outer walls were 60 cm thick. A larger air raid shelter was built that same year under the plaza at the intersection of Wilhemstrasse and Leipzigerstrasse. Half of this facility was intended for the staff of the nearby ministries who could flee from their offices into the bunker via two underground passages. The other half was meant as a public shelter and could be reached from the plaza via an airlock. The relatively thin reinforced concrete proved incapable of withstanding the bombs that were dropped in the area in 1944-45. It was not until 1938 that two bunker complexes were built explicitly in connection with the imminent German offensive. One of them was under the middle of Vossstrasse, and the other, smaller one under the Presidential Chancellery near Wilhelmstrasse. The roofs and walls of

91. Banqueting Hall of Reichs Chancellery, 1935-1936. Hitlers *Vorbunker* was located beneath it.

these shelters were 1.7 metres thick, and they were equipped with up-to-the minute technical features – heating and air conditioning systems, and a heavy duty vehicle lift in which a lorry could deliver coal at a depth of 4.5 metres.[49]

HITLER'S BUNKER

The New Reich Chancellery designed by Albert Speer did not have a proper basement space. The lack of deep foundations had made it possible to erect the building with exceptional speed, only two years after Hitler took office.[50] This imposing new crystal palace could not exist without its accompanying mousehole counterpart in the immediate vicinity, the icon of Shelter City, so a specially hardened underground bunker was built as an extension to the Chancellery.

By 1943, Allied bombs had made it painfully clear that the existing bunkers were inadequate both in construction and in capacity. New bunkers were therefore built in the summer of that year under Pariser Platz and Wilhelmsplatz, connected by underground passages to the adjacent hotels and ministries. One bunker under the courtyard of the Ministry of Transport had a link to the metro network which could provide an escape route in the event of a firestorm.

The Führerbunker was built in two stages: first the basement under the side wing of the New Reich Chancellery (1935), followed by the bunker 8.5 metres underground in the garden (1943). The latter was connected to the *Vorbunker* ("fore-bunker") by an underground passage. "Hitler's bunker, while not yet reaching the mausoleum-like dimensions it would have by July 1944, had the thick walls and roof of a prison. Steel doors and steel shutters sealed off the few openings, and the rare walks he took within the barbed wire gave him no more daylight or contact with nature than a prisoner in a prison yard."[51] Including the entrance in the garden, the bunker measured roughly 28 by 26.5 metres and had a usable floor size of 19.5 by 18.8 metres, while the roof and walls were about 3.5 metres thick.[52] It was connected to the 1935 bunker by a staircase. A bunker for Hitler's bodyguards and drivers was built in the underground garage on Herman Göringstrasse in the period September

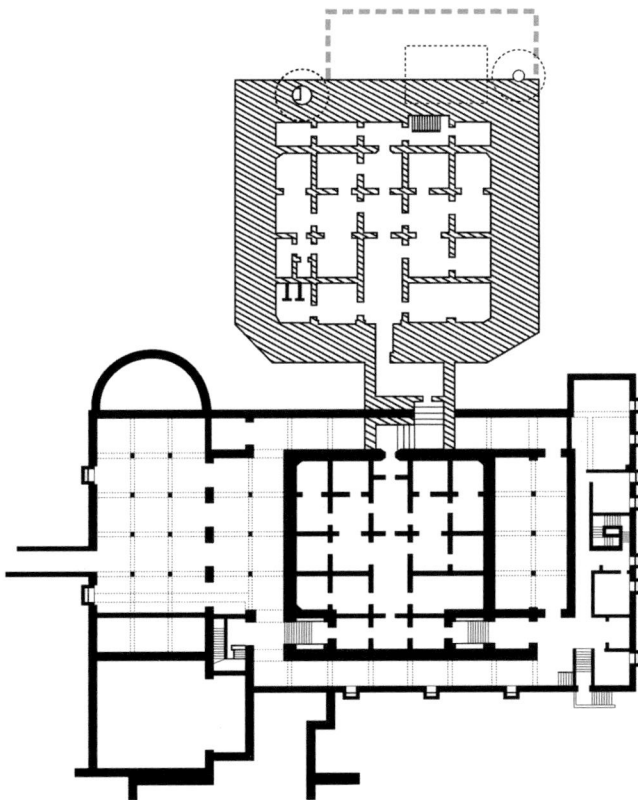

92. The *Vorbunker* (1935-1936) under the Banqueting Hall of the Reichs Chancellery, Berlin. *Above* (hatched), the deeper-lying *Hauptbunker* (1943-1944)

1943 to March 1944. Work continued on Hitler's bunker until the end of the war. One of the two cylindrical ventilation towers, which doubled as guardrooms, remained uncompleted. In 1944, Martin Bormann portrayed the atmosphere in the claustrophobic, grey painted bunker with its tiny rooms as follows: "I am now at least in a big room, roughly seven by seven metres; I have four big windows and plenty of light, and I can sleep with the windows open at night. The Führer, on the other hand, is living underground in his bunker and only has electric light and stale air, and the air pressure is constantly too high because the fresh air has to be pumped in. It is as though he had to live in an unlit cellar. Living cooped up in a cellar is bad for health and in the long run is practically unbearable for any living being. An ordinary plant would die from lack of light and fresh air. (...) He grumbles, too, about our brick-walled huts which, he claims, would be blown down in the first heavy air raid, and then everyone would have to make do with much less space!"[53] The Fürherbunker was in the first place inadequate as an air raid shelter and the very opposite of a fully equipped headquarters. This bunker was living proof that, in the race between projectiles and armour, the bombs remained one step ahead.

Der Führerbunker

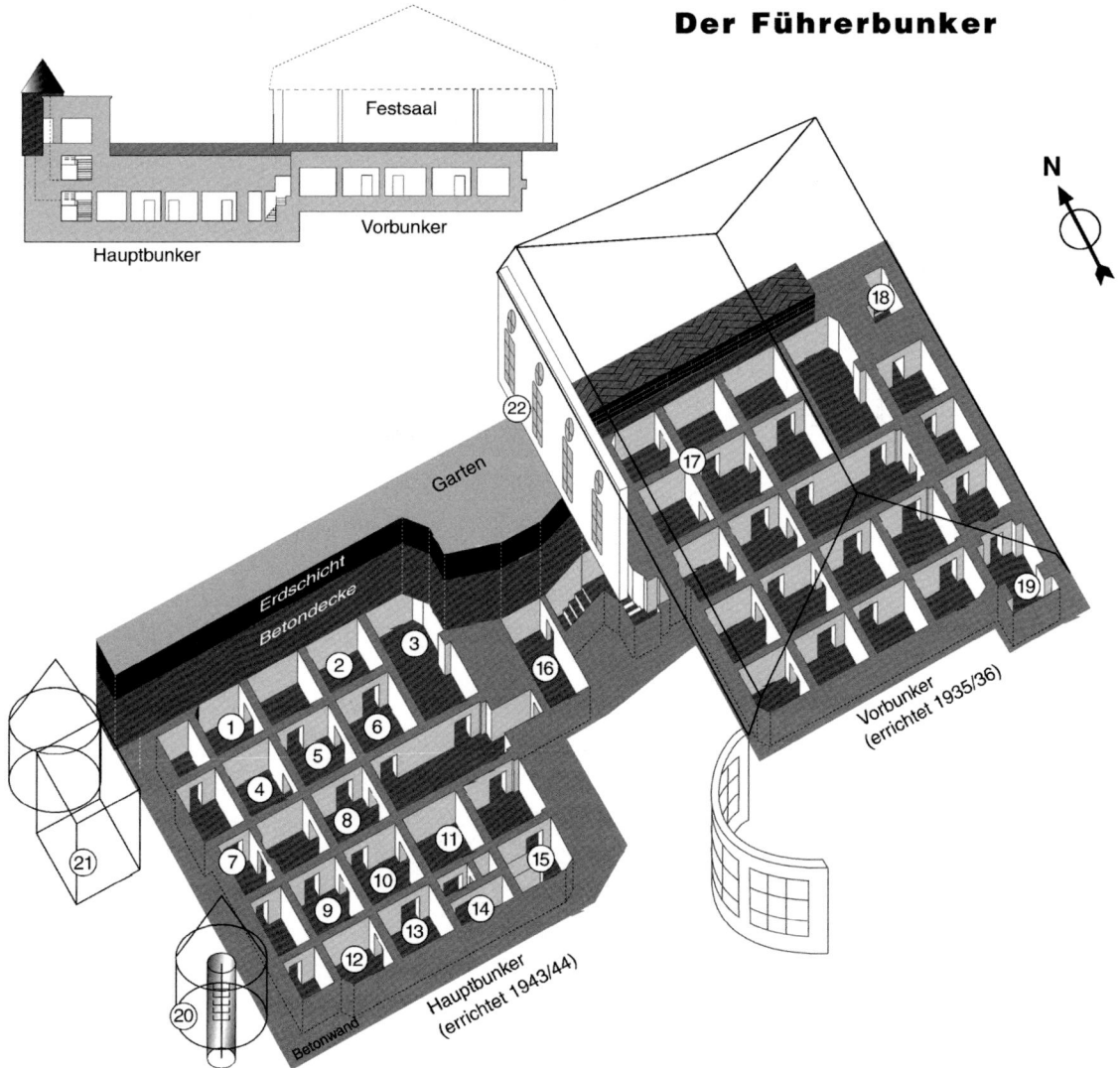

Festsaal

Vorbunker

Hauptbunker

N

Garten

Erdschicht

Betondecke

Vorbunker (errichtet 1935/36)

Hauptbunker (errichtet 1943/44)

Betonwand

93. Cutaway view and cross section of *Führerbunker*, Berlin

1. Surgery of personal physician
2. Guardroom
3. Machine room
4. Goebbels' bedroom
5. Goebbels' office
6. Telephone exchange
7. Airlock guardrooms
8. Corridor and waiting room
9. Hitler's conference room
10. Vestibule
11. Eva Braun's bedroom
12. Hitler's bedroom
13. Hitler's living room/office
14. Hitler's bathroom and toilet
15. Toilets and washrooms for general use
16. Passages and stairs
17. Rooms of the Goebbels family
18. Emergency exit
19. Main exit
20. Ventilation tower
21. Exit to Reich Chancellery garden
22. Outer wall of banqueting hall

< *Page 126 and 127*
94. Henry Moore, sketch for *Pink and Green Sleepers*,
drawn in London Underground, 1941

CHAPTER 4

Life and Death in Shelter City

The Air Duel between Germany and Britain

WARMING UP

In 1937, the United Kingdom was the scene of an ambitious experiment in anthropological fieldwork.[1] Thousands of observers fanned out over the country armed with questionnaires. Among other things they had ministerial permission to interview two thousand conscript soldiers about their state of mind and their outlook on defence and imminent war. The data was collected by a variety of methods including asking members of the public to keep diaries of their experiences. It proved of inestimable value, not only to science but also to the intelligence services. For example, the continuing Mass Observation project enabled them to monitor the state of mind of the public during air raids on London and the cities of the south coast. Countless diaries, generally illustrated with photographs and mostly kept by women, have been preserved. They provided uncensored reports on the German air raids on British cities, their life in the shelters, their feelings before and after air raids, and their day-to-day life.[2] Besides benefiting from the Mass Observation surveys, the War Cabinet took advantage of eavesdropping techniques and infiltrators to keep abreast of public morale during the Blitz.[3]

The Battle of Britain (August 1940 to March 1941) finally put modern air warfare to the test. In the period of the German invasion of Denmark and Norway (9 April 1940), the bombing of Rotterdam (14 May 1940) and the subsequent invasion

95. Air raid practice; office workers conducted to specially designed shelters, 1939

96. German press photograph of the first large-scale air raid response exercise in London. Over 5,000 children, labelled and laden with satchels, on their way to their evacuation departure point.

of France, Britain had enjoyed relative peace and quiet. Once the Germans had conquered the innumerable airfields along the North Sea Coast, however, British fears began to mount. They took the likelihood of a German invasion by sea seriously. After Churchill's appointment as Prime Minister on 10 May 1940, over 100 meetings of the War Cabinet took place in the reinforced basement under the Treasury building in Whitehall.

From May to August 1940, towns in southwest England and the Midlands were bombed by German planes based at airfields along the French North Sea coast.[4] These attacks provided the German pilots with valuable training and were also a warm-up exercise for the British aerial defence forces. The British airspace, like that of Germany, was sealed under an invisible dome. Radar posts ranged along the East Anglian coast signalled approaching German planes, after which fighter aircraft would take off to challenge the invaders.[5] Inland, some 30,000 volunteers from the Royal Observer Corps were equipped with special sound and visual equipment to help the RAF pilots navigate in their hunt for enemy aircraft intruding on

Mass-Observer, Sept.1939
Housewife
Age 37
London SE3

(1289)

Three days after two
landmines - small debris
not yet cleared from lawn
Oct. 1940

Digging Trench Shelter
1938

Pond Shelter   Jan.1941
Self in raid kit

Trench Shelter
abandonned and this one
built in 1939

97. Snapshots of shelters in London between 1938 and 1941, preserved
by a volunteer diarist

the airspace. There was little that could be done about whole formations of enemy bombers, however. On 24 August 1940, several German pilots whose designated targets were oil refineries and aircraft factories lost their way in broad daylight
and unintentionally dropped their bombs on an area of central London. Their action resulted in some substantial fires in the City, the docklands, the East End and
several suburban areas.[6] The following night Churchill sent eighty RAF bombers to
Berlin where they attacked military and civilian targets. Further expeditions of this
kind followed, but they did not rise above the status of pinprick actions. At first the
same seemed to apply to the German air raids. The British diplomat Harold Nicolson described an attack on 26 August 1940 in terms of a multicoloured light show:
"It seems so incredible as I sit here at my window in Sissinghurst, looking out on the
fuchsias and zinneas with yellow butterflies playing round each other, that in a few
seconds above the trees I may see other butterflies circling in the air intent on mur-
dering each other. (...). London is as dark as the stage at Vicenza after all the lights
have been put out. Vague gleamings of architecture. It is warm and the stars strad-
dle the sky like grains of rice. Then the searchlights come on, each terminating in
a swab of cottonwool which is its own mist area. Suburban guns thump and boom.
In the centre there are no guns, only a drone of aeroplanes, which may be enemy or

< *Page 132*

98. Press photograph of Denise Vane dressed as an ARP Warden. The caption is: "'Dazzling blonde' Denise Vane, 'England's most sensational fan-dancer' who, when she is not awaiting an air raid alarm, is beguiling the war weary at the Paradise Club, W., enhances her undoubted charms with two luxuriant fans – and little else." Westminster, 12 October 1939

99. Mother and child ready for evacuation from London, equipped with baby's gas mask. The baby is labelled "Jean Day (London NW)", November 1940

not." [7] Yet death came ever closer. Two days later, Nicolson wrote, 'Christopher Hobhouse's widow comes. She tells me that he left her on Monday evening at 4.30 in their little bungalow at Hayling Island. He went down to the Fort at Portsmouth and half-an-hour later there was a bombing attack and Christopher and three fellow-officers were blown into pieces. They would not let her even attend the funeral since there was so little left. Poor girl. She is to have a baby in March and wants me to be godfather." [8]

BOMBS RAIN DOWN ON LONDON

Starting on 28 August 1940, Goering commanded his air force to conduct night raids on British cities. It was London's turn on Saturday, 7 September. The first bombing which lasted from 5 pm to 4.30 the following morning was an unforgettable shock to the affected Londoners: "That day stands out like a flaming wound in my memory." [9] The first wave was conducted by a force of 320 bombers escorted by fighters. "They flew up the Thames and proceeded to bomb Woolwich Arsenal, Beckton Gas Works, a large number of docks, West Ham power station, and then the City, Westminster

100. Orphans hiding for air raid. The press caption: "Four attentive girls in the National Childern's Home and Orphanage in Hertforshire who crawled under a table inside the shelter, while listening to the rumours of air raids outside", 13 October 1940"

Page 135 >
101. Firefighting, London, 1941

and Kensington. They succeeded in causing a serious fire situation in the docks. An area of about 1.5 miles between North Woolwich Road and the Thames was almost destroyed, and the population of Silvertown was surrounded by fire and had to be evacuated by water. At 8.10 pm some 250 bombers resumed the attack, which was maintained until 4.30 on Sunday morning. They caused 9 conflagrations, 59 large fires and nearly 1,000 lesser fires. Three main-line railway termini were put out of action, and 430 persons killed and some 1,600 seriously injured. After the fire brigades had spent all day in an effort to deprive the enemy of illumination, some 200 bombers returned at 7.30 in the evening to carry on the assault. During this second night a further 412 persons were killed and 747 seriously injured, and damage included the temporary stoppage of every railway line to the south."[10]

The daily air raids reached their greatest intensity between 7 September and 3 November. Each night, an average of 160 enemy planes discharged a total of some 200 tons of bombs and 182 canisters of inflammable material. The peaks were on nights of the full moon. On 15 October, for example, 410 bombers droned over the city and dropped 583 tons of bombs, claiming 400 fatalities and 900 wounded victims and starting 900 fires. Almost the entire railway system came to a standstill.[11] One of the heaviest raids was on the night of 8-9 December conducted by 400 bomb-

REGISTERING NEW ARRIVALS-NIGHT

REST CENTRE 'A'

WASHING FACILITIES ARE PROVIDED, ALSO FRESH CLOTHES WHERE NEEDED

THE REST ROOM

A HOT DRINK & COMFORTABLE CHAIRS ARE PROVIDED FOR NEWCOMERS

CLUBLAND REST CENTRE

BEDS & BLANKETS ARE PROVIDED IN THE REST SHELTERS

CLOTHES & S... S DEPT "A QUES... N OF FIT"

ROOM FOR MOTHERS, DRESSINGS & SMALL AILMENTS

REST CENTRE 'B'

CENTRAL ENQUIRY BUREAU SOUTHWARK

BILLETING OFFICERS

CHILDREN'S ROOM

SUPPER TIME

THE FIRST HOME GONE

YOUNGEST OF FIVE

ONE FAMILY AT TEA

THE GIRL HAS A "WASHING" THE BOY PREFERS TO RIDE

THE CARD PLAYERS

D. MACHESON 1941

ers and continuing from the early evening to 7 am the following morning. Some 250 people were killed and 630 injured. Over 1,700 fires were started, and the buildings hit included Westminster Abbey, the Royal Mint, the Royal Naval College, Broadcasting House and several hospitals.[12] The Anglo-Irish author Elisabeth Bowen noted that Londoners experienced the daylight hours as "a curious holiday from fear".[13]

In November, it was the turn of Plymouth,[14] Portsmouth and Bristol. Like Southampton and Liverpool, these ports were hit harder than London in terms of the density of bombing and the percentage of destroyed buildings. Coventry (population 213,000), with its concentration of engineering equipment, car and radio manufacturing, formed the first target for a new German attack method. First, the compact historic centre was set alight with thousands of incendiary bombs; then 500 bombers dropped 600 tons of high-explosive bombs in a period of ten hours. The firestorm notion took shape here. There were 568 people killed and 856 severely injured.[15] Supplies of gas and electricity broke down, all telephone connections were cut, and drinking water was almost unobtainable. Two hospitals suffered direct hits and the injured had to be transported to other cities. "There were more open signs of hysteria, terror, neurosis, observed in one evening than during the whole of the past two months together in all areas. Women were seen to cry, scream, to tremble all over, to faint in the street, to attack a fireman, and so on... There were

< *Page 136*
102. D. Macpherson, tips for bombed-out residents – steps to take when seeking emergency accommodation, 24 March 1941

103. Promotional heroics: a family emerges unscathed from their Anderson Shelter after a direct hit

several signs of suppressed panic as darkness approached. In two cases people were seen fighting to get on to cars, which they thought would take them out into the country, though in fact, as the drivers insisted, the cars were going just up the road to the garage."[16]

PHYSICAL SENSATIONS OF AN AIR RAID

A regular ritual developed in the eight-month duration of the Blitz. Searchlights scanned the airspace in dancing rays. The German fighters lit up the docks with parachute flares, brilliant green fireworks that descended slowly from the sky to mark the boundaries of the field of action. Then hundreds of bombers discharged their cargos, gnawing away at the silhouette of the city. Evelyn Waugh described the London sky during an air raid as "glorious, ochre and madder, as though a dozen tropic suns were simultaneously setting round the horizon."[17] The bombs, according to one Londoner, made "a tearing sound as well as a whistle; they did not fall, they rushed at enormous velocity, as though dragged down towards the earth by some supernaturally gigantic magnet."[18] The bombs plunged into a sea of fire, and the roaring flames of burning wood shot out fountains of sparks. Streets were sud-

< *Page 138*

Top
104. St. Paul's Cathedral bathed in searchlights

Bottom
105. London suburb after a heavy air raid. The public shelters in the middle of the street are still intact

106. London shelter, three-level bunk beds, collapsible for daytime storage, 16 November 1940

denly covered with incendiary bombs, hissing and dazzling the eye with a green glow. A firebomb weighed only a few kilos but if not extinguished immediately it could be the most destructive of weapons. "In December, the sport of 'I.B.' incendiary bomb hunting which was popular with London's doughtier citizens was spoilt when the Germans began to drop a proportion of incendiaries with explosive charges; thereafter, far greater caution had to be used."[19] High explosive bombs produced a simple red or yellow flash on detonation. They could cause deep craters and not infrequently damaged the city's subterranean nervous system of cables, water mains and sewers. The landmines dropped by the Germans were large cylinders measuring over two metres in length and fifty centimetres in diameter. They floated gracefully down from the sky and exploded without penetrating the ground, which made them all the more destructive. The explosion could throw someone hundreds of metres. An 18-year-old boy recalled a bombing raid on London as follows: "Then from that point I was well aware, because bombs began to fall, and shrapnel was going along King Street, dancing off the cobbles. Then the real impetus came, in so far as the suction and the compression from the high explosives blasts just pulled you and pushed you, and the whole of this atmosphere was turbulating so hard that, after an explosion of a nearby bomb, you could actually feel your eyeballs being sucked out. I was holding my eyes to try and stop them going. And the suction was so vast, it ripped my shirt away, and ripped my trousers. Then I couldn't get my breath, the smoke was like acid and everything round me was black and yellow. And

these bombers just kept on and on, the whole road was moving, rising and falling."[20] The unexploded bombs that remained after an air raid – as many as 3,000 in October 1940 – presented serious problems. Bomb disposal experts were required to disable the time fuse and if possible transport the bomb for disposal elsewhere.

The staff of Shelter City rose to the heavy test. Rescue workers dug away the soil on top of buried Anderson Shelters and pulled the survivors, dazed and half suffocated, back into the outside world. Injured people lying in bombed buildings were usually white from the plaster of collapsed ceilings, with streaks of dark red or black congealed blood. As the rescuers carried them off, some of the shocked victims might utter a cheery joke while others snivelled uncontrollably. Their injuries were also psychological. "Those people who had experienced a 'near miss', who had been buried alive or who had suffered directly from blast commonly showed marked neurotic symptoms, and many others seem to have suffered from apathy, lethargy and general despondence as a side effect of the raids and the weariness they brought with them."[21]

The smells associated with bombing were penetrating. When the Luftwaffe destroyed a main sewer in the City, the Thames stank of excrement and the powerful disinfectants that were added. People were so worried by the bittersweet fumes that hung around a bombed pharmacy that they resorted to wearing gasmasks in the vicinity. But memories of the "harsh, rank, raw smell" that rose from the interiors and rubble of bombed-out dwellings were dominant; although not stated explicitly, the odour of burnt flesh was part of the mix. "Its basis came from the torn, wounded, dismembered houses; from the gritty dust of dissolved brickwork, masonry and joinery. But there was more to it than that. For several hours there was an acrid overtone from the high explosive which the bomb itself had contained; a fiery constituent of the smell. Almost invariably, too, there was the mean little stink of domestic gas, seeping up from broken pipes and leads. But the whole of the smell was greater than the sum of its parts. It was the smell of violent death itself."[22]

THE STAFF OF SHELTER CITY

In the course of the Blitz, German bombers dropped nearly 9,000 bombs of 280 kilos or more on England every night.[23] For London alone, the total weight of bombs dropped between September 1940 and May 1941 was 19,000 tons. The city had insufficient anti-aircraft artillery, whose function was largely a ritual one, and no night fighters. Nonetheless, the personnel of Shelter City stood ready every night. "Anti-aircraft crews, studded around fields, parks, and streets, were momentarily silhouetted against the sky by the sudden flash of their guns. The Auxiliary Fire Service, spread out in a network of squads through the capital, was standing by, ready at a moment's notice to deal with the inevitable fires; air raid wardens, tireless in their care of shelters and work of rescue, patrolled areas watchfully."[24] The civilian in the front line gained currency as a political notion. The public were required to show behaviours normally ascribed to soldiers – loyalty, subordination, automatically obeying commands and withholding criticism. These exhortations were not always easy to put into practice and did little to help city dwellers stand up to the emotional and nervous strains of the Blitz.

The undermanned and politically divided local bureaucracy of London also hampered an effective response to the air offensive. Apart from the courageous actions of the fire brigade and professional rescue squads, most other forms of assistance were organized and implemented by volunteers. This cultivated a new type of democracy that was far from typically British. The assault on London landed the unarmed civilians who manned Shelter City – police, rescue workers, nurses, doctors, clergy, and telephone operators, almost all of them volunteers – in an 8-month-long battle not only with the effects of continual bombing but also with the authorities. A regular source of friction was "the contrast between laggard councillors, obsessed with their own prestige, and the self-sacrifice of the volunteers who strove indefatigably to remedy the position which bumbledom had created."[25] As J.B. Priestly put it, the new network of voluntary associations was a symptom of Britain "now being bombed und burned into democracy".[26]

During the eight-month Blitz, London experienced a period of 76 successive days (with only a single day's respite) of German air raids. The volunteers toiled day and night, and shared the fear and tragedies of their fellow citizens. Saving one's own skin was the first priority, followed by helping others, repairing homes, caring for children and cooking meals.[27] Money played a secondary role, among other reasons because the distinction between mine and thine had become irrelevant to many people. Robbers and thieves, including organized gangs, joined in a veritable epidemic of looting; after all, if household possessions were scattered all over the street by a bomb blast were they not now common property?

Bomb shelters were not immune to the air raids. They were designed to withstand a maximum bomb size of 250 kilograms. Although most of the bombs dropped during the Blitz were in the range 50 to 250 kg, some 4,000 parachute mines with charges up to 2,500 kilograms were also used. An Anderson shelter could survive a 50 kg bomb explosion no closer than two metres away, and a 250 kg bomb explosion no closer than six metres away. Brick and concrete above-ground shelters were less durable, however, since the shock waves of a bomb blast could easily shake the walls and roof apart.[28] Trench shelters were similarly vulnerable. The Underground Railway stations were relatively safe, although fatal bomb strikes were not unknown. Nine people sheltering underground were killed at Trafalgar Square station, 19 at Bounds Green and 64 at Balham. Fifteen people were wounded in Camden Town Underground station.

Public shelters that suffered direct hits claiming numerous casualties were Stoke Newington, Stepney, the Druid Street railway arches in Bermondsey and St. Peter's Crypt, Southwark.[29] An interviewer for the Mass Observation project reported the experiences of a rescue worker as follows: "There was a shelter just underground with about 18 inches of concrete roof. The whole thing was blown to bits. He was superintending the digging out of the bodies. 'I don't want to be on another job like that again. There were heads and arms and legs and feet lying about. The only way you could tell the girls from the men was because of their hair. Their faces were all blown away. There were a lot never identified.' I say it must affect the men who are digging them out badly. He says it doesn't affect you at the time but afterwards. 'It's not the sight of the bodies. I tell you what it is – it's the smell. The smell of human flesh and the blood. It gets you afterwards. Two or three days after that I felt myself heaving.'"[30]

Night after night, countless Londoners found themselves fighting for their "few feet of concrete".[31] The main problem was that most of the public shelters were designed for a short stay, but the nightly air raids during the Blitz forced people to seek extended protection. This made it necessary to convert the shelters into dormitories with sanitary facilities.[32] The shelter became a second home, and for homeless people it could be practically permanent. Measures had to be made to make social life bearable, to prevent congestion, to tackle the hygienic problems and to provide heating and lighting. Chemical toilets, camping stoves, electric heaters, ventilating fans, foldaway beds (standardized from December 1940 onwards), libraries and entertainments made their appearance. The Anderson Shelters also had standardized foldaway beds. Each public shelter was run by a warden assisted by a number of shelter marshals. The marshals were empowered to perform specific functions such as checking the entrance tickets that were introduced in October 1940. "They could direct any inmate to use a particular part of a shelter and refuse to admit or expel anyone who might be dangerous or offensive to others or whose presence might cause over-crowding. These wardens also helped to prevent property in shelters from being pilfered and shelters being misused when empty."[33] The public shelters developed distinct characters, with their own clientele; not infrequently, they were an alternative to the local pub. Between December and May 1940, bunk beds were installed in the shelters, as well as coal or electric heaters, and food supplies were stocked up. Various forms of entertainment were arranged with official support, including gramophone music, concerts, prose and poetry readings, debates on current affairs, religious services, film shows and libraries.[34]

Railway arches, although not particularly safe, provided a semblance of shelter and were widely used by those at the lower end of the social scale. It was not until after the arches were taken into use that the local authorities started introducing sanitary facilities, soup kitchens and other necessary amenities. A poll held in November 1940 indicated that most Londoners did not stay overnight in the purpose-built public shelters. Nine percent slept in the public shelters, four percent in the Tube and 27 percent in private shelters. The rest stayed in their own warm beds.[35] Although the local authorities wanted to keep the Underground free in order to assure efficient transportation, the crowds seeking an improvised shelter conquered the subterranean tunnels through the pressure of numbers. Over 150,000 people

108. Man spends the night on an Underground escalator, 10 October 1940

Page 145 >

Top
109. Bill Brandt, Liverpool Street Underground Station, London; buckets of sand and fire extinguishers on the wall, 12 November 1940

Bottom
110. Bill Brandt, Liverpool Street Underground Station, London, 12 November 1940

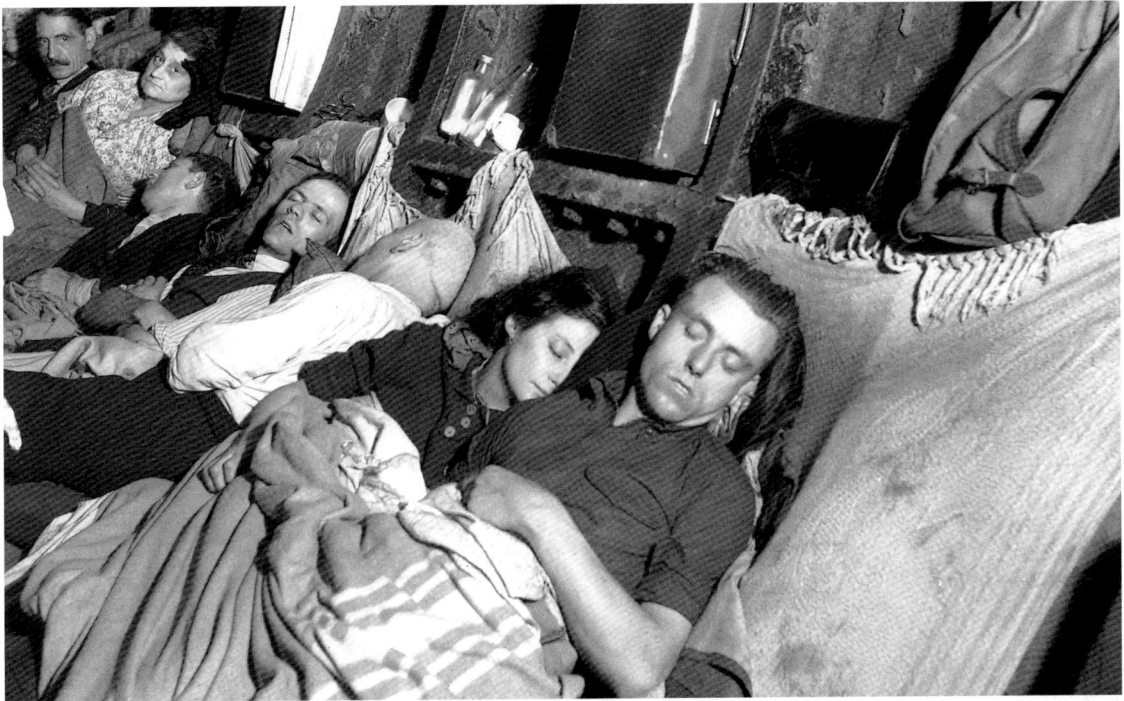

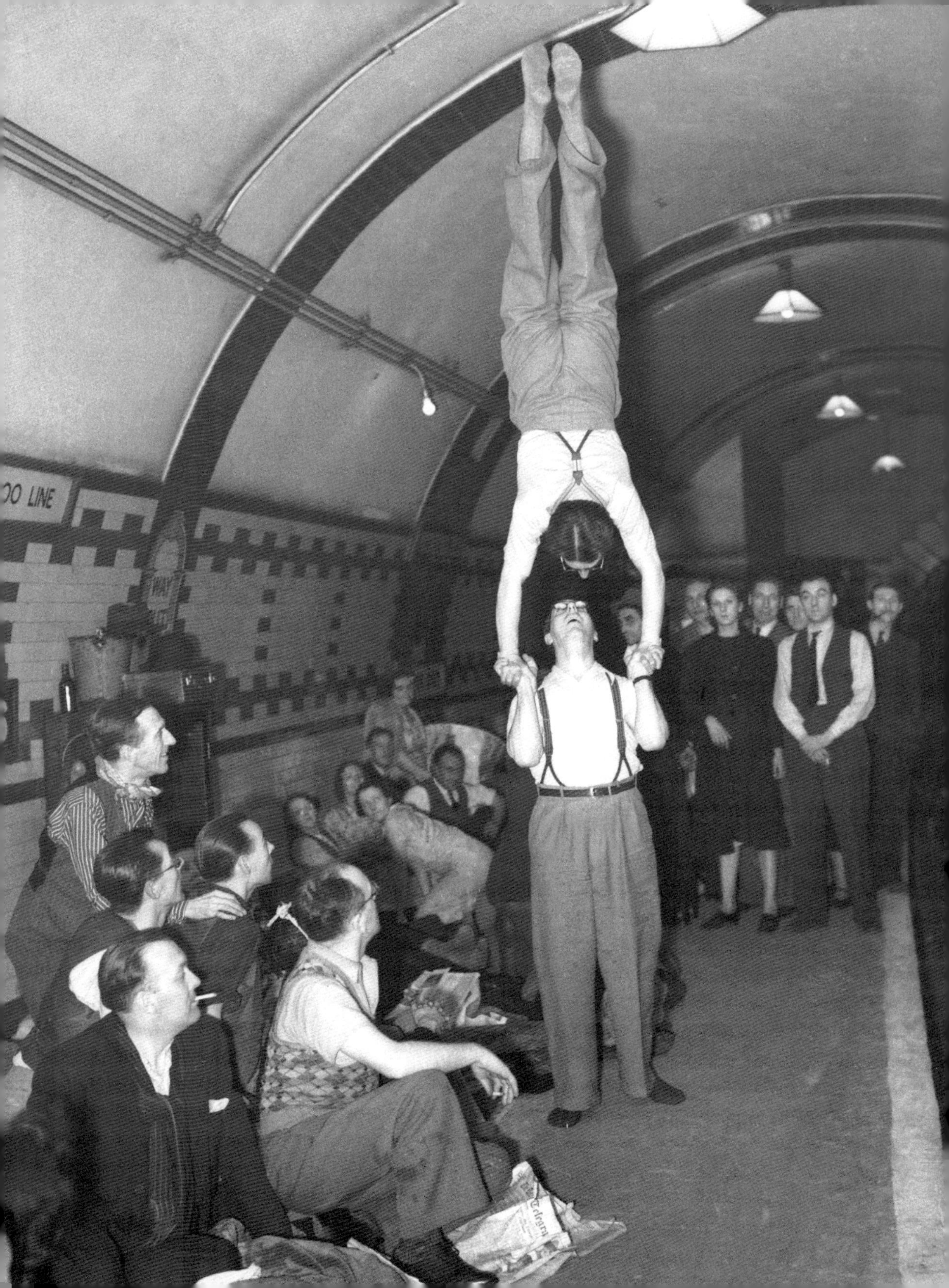
OO LINE

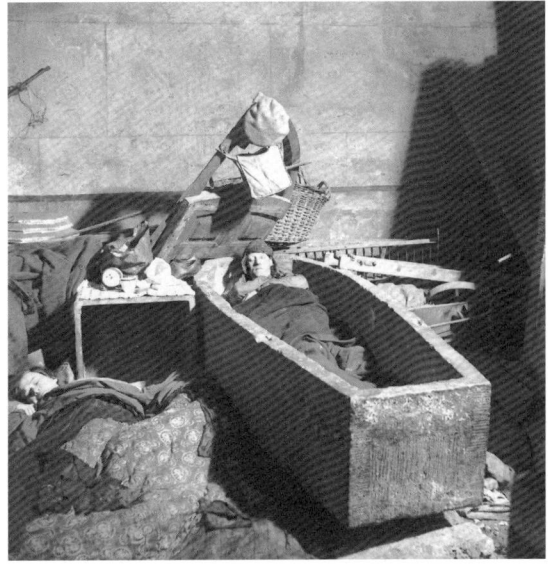

112. Bill Brandt, a Sikh family takes shelter in the crypt of Christ Church Spitalfields, London, 5-6 November 1940

113. Bill Brandt, man sleeping in a stone sarcophagus, Christ Church Spitalfield, 5-6 November 1940

< Page 146
111. Piccadilly Circus Underground Station, London, undated

took overnight refuge in 80 Underground stations. Compensating somewhat for the tightly packed conditions, spending a night in the Tube was much more comfortable than in the public shelters above ground. The Underground provided a curiously isolated, artificial environment. The tunnels were relatively safe, warm, dry and well-lit, and the droning planes and bomb explosions above were inaudible.[36] But the air was often foul, and there was little privacy: "Where the Tubes lay below the level of the sewage mains, there were no sanitation or washing facilities on the platforms. Winds, now hot, now cold, howled through the tunnels. Mosquitoes flourished in the fug; lice crawled from head to head. In the mornings, people shook the dust and germs from their blankets over the line. One witness remarks that 'The stench was frightful, urine and excrement mixed with strong carbolic sweat and dirty, unwashed humanity'".[37] It was pure *esprit de corps*, as Churchill wryly remarked.

The government attempted to wring some propaganda from the unsavoury experience by setting up a War Artists Advisory Committee. The committee commissioned artists like Paul Nash, Edward Ardizzone and John Farleigh to immortalize their view of life in the Underground. Henry Moore had already started doing so of his own accord and sold some of his work to the official patrons.[38] "Here was a new life, a whole network, a whole city under the world."[39] A small proportion of this population were in the grip of a "deep shelter mentality"; these were mostly homeless individuals who took up permanent resident in the Tube, forming a new type of community. Even in 1943, over two years after the air raid peril had ebbed, crowds of Tube dwellers including babies and children were noted living in the London Underground. They could not bear to part with their new multicultural lifestyle and were loath to resume their place in the lower strata of the class society.[40]

NEW SHELTER TYPES

The only new shelter manufactured on a large scale was the Morrison Shelter (launched in 1941 and named after the new Labour Home Secretary, Herbert Morrison). In a sense it was the indoor counterpart of an Anderson Shelter. "It had a steel plate on top which could be used as a table in the daytime, and sides of wire mesh, two feet, nine inches high. Though few were in use by the end of the blitz, over half a million had been distributed by November 1941, and they gave good service in later attacks."[41] Churchill took a great interest in the new shelter and had one installed in 10 Downing Street. The Cabinet approved the production of 400,000 of these steel cages, thereby offering protection to approximately 1,200,000 people.[42] They appeared too late to play a significant role in the Blitz. The version of *Your Home As An Air raid Shelter* issued in June 1941 under the title *Shelter At Home*, promoted three different types of shelter: the Morrison, a commercial steel shelter, and a wood-framed shelter designed by the Ministry of Home Security.

Work meanwhile continued on improving the existing public shelters for fifty occupants. Steel was used to reinforce brick and concrete walls, with the reinforcement extending from floor to roof. Under the pressure of public demand, London moreover gained eight enormous concrete shelters built 24 to 35 metres underground, each with room for 1,000 people. Construction of these shelters started in 1940 but they were not ready until the end of the Blitz and were never used. But four

Page 149 >
114. Press photo, Morrison Shelter after an air raid. According to the caption, the inhabitants "would still be alive" if they had used their indoor shelter

further reinforced concrete structures, nicknamed fortresses or citadels, were started in central London in the first half of 1941.

Finally, in late 1940, political pressure led to the construction of a deep shelter with some resemblance to the Finsbury plans designed by Tecton: "two parallel tunnels, 16 ft. 6 in. in diameter and 1,200 ft. long, underneath the platforms and tunnels at each of ten Tube stations. The tunnels, divided in two decks, would include kitchens, first aid posts and sanitation and be entered through existing station entrances. They would accommodate 9,600 shelterers at each station."[43] Setbacks delayed completion of the first tunnel until March 1942, and by May that year a second tunnel was half complete and usable as a shelter for 4,000 people. The excavation of two more tunnels was sufficiently well advanced to accommodate 3,000 people in each. Eventually eight shelter tunnels were completed, each with a capacity of 8000. Countless technical problems arose during their construction, and the costs soared. Moral prejudices also played a part in evaluation of the tunnels, as typified by descriptions of the tunnel shelter at Ramsgate as resembling a "Gypsy camp". Plans to dig further tunnels were put on ice in late 1941, but the existing ones were maintained in an operational state. One of them served as General Eisenhower's London Headquarters.

The output of new shelters declined sharply from spring 1942 onwards. A new problem had emerged in the autumn of 1941, how to protect the unused shelters from misuse and vandalism. By 1943, people were starting to use their Anderson shelters as sheds for bicycles, garden equipment or even as chicken coops. During the Little Blitz of 1944, when London was startled by assaults with V1 and then V2 rockets, 17,000 new Morrison Shelters were issued to London households. Many people took to spending the night in their shelter once more.

THE HOMELESS AND EVACUEES

Homelessness rose to unprecedented levels. No less than 1,400,000 people, or one Londoner in six, lacked a permanent place to live. The figure includes orphaned children: "Terry, aged two years. Both parents burnt to death. Terry pulled out of blazing house with sight of one eye gone."[44] The homeless were accommodated in schools and cinemas where they were also provided with meals. Others moved into encampments in Epping Forest. Many took up residence in the caves of Chislehurst; the tunnels of the ancient chalk mines were equipped with electric lighting and water, and the people sheltering there raised funds to provide cleaning, toilets, can-

115. Air raid, London, 31 December 1940

teens and a cultural programme.[45] The 5,000 troglodytes appointed "captains" to preserve order[46] and developed into a well-knit community.

London's social life was extensively disrupted by the aerial bombardment. One in five schools was severely damaged, while others provided accommodation for homeless families. Juvenile delinquency mounted. Shop windows were invariably blown to pieces by the bombs. "The impromptu shop signs became favourite blitz jokes. 'More open than usual' was a common one. (...) One pub advertised, 'our windows are gone but our spirits are excellent. Come in and try them.'"[47] By late November 1940, the city had lost about a quarter of its population (including those already evacuated).

CONFLAGRATIONS IN LONDON

On 29 December 1940, the historical and commercial centre of London suffered such heavy bombing that it resulted in the most devastating conflagration since the Great Fire of 1666. Despite the adverse weather, the bombs set off nearly 1,400 fires during an attack lasting two and a half hours. Guy's Hospital had to be evacuated, and several other hospitals suffered bomb damage. Bond Street and Burlington

Street took a heavy toll, the Guildhall was destroyed, and Buckingham Palace was hit. Seven churches designed by Christopher Wren were burned down, although the defenders succeeded in extinguishing an incendiary bomb that lodged in the roof of St. Paul's Cathedral, just in time to save the dome. That night 163 people were killed, and 509 were severely wounded.[48]

Following heavy raids in the week of 16-23 April,[49] 550 planes carried out the last major assault on London at full moon (the "Bomber's Moon") on 10 May 1941.[50] In the course of a five-hour attack, they dropped 440 tons of high-explosive bombs and firebombs as well as numerous landmines. Fires blazed from Hammersmith in west London to Romford in the east. The water pressure in the fire hoses was insufficient due to low tide in the Thames. There were 1,436 fatal casualties and 1,792 seriously injured. National treasures such as the Chambers of the House of Commons and the House of Lords, the Royal Mint and the Tower of London were hit. St. James's Palace, the War Office, the London Museum, the Public Record Office, the British Museum, Mansion House and the Guildhall Art Library were also damaged. So were many churches: St. Clement Danes, St. Stephen's Walbrook, St. Mary-le-Bow, Holy Trinity Sloane Street and St. Columba's Pont Street.[51] The East End was targeted and so later were more outlying boroughs including Croydon, Wandsworth, Plumstead and Ilford. Districts in the west of London were also hit, including Paddington and Hammersmith. The densely populated multicultural districts of Stepney, Poplar, Bermondsey, Lambeth, Deptford, Shoreditch and Bethnal Green sustained heavy damage, with Holloway hit hardest of all, leaving over 40 percent of its housing stock in ruins. Only two railway stations still functioned in these areas. "Next morning, a drifting cloud of brown smoke blotted out the sun. Charred paper danced in the woods thirty miles from the City. Churchill wept over the ruins of the House of Commons. A third of the streets of Greater London were impassable; 155,000 families were without gas, water or electricity. Every main railway station but one was blocked for weeks. Not for eleven days were the last pumps withdrawn from the fires, while exhausted civil defenders and a badly shaken population waited for the blow which must surely finish off the capital; the blow which never came."[52]

THE BALANCE OF THE BLITZ

London mourned 15,000 dead in the course of the Blitz.[53] The figure for Great Britain as a whole was twice that. By June 1941, two million houses had been damaged or destroyed, sixty percent of them in London. In some of the affected areas such as the East End, Churchill joked, it could be regarded as slum clearance by the Luft-

< *Page 152*
116. Press photo, following a German air raid on Central London, "Saving the catechism of the plutocracy. Clutching bank ledgers to their breasts like bibles, the men pick their way through the rubble in a tight-lipped procession", 11 March 1941

117. Plane shot down, undated

waffe. London seethed with vengeance. As Nicolson wrote on 2 January 1941, "I walked up to St. Paul's, where things are still smouldering and then back along Holborn and Guildford Street to the Ministry, and all along there were little groups of people talking quietly but quite determinedly about revenge. There is no doubt that the feeling is growing that similar treatment of the Germans is the only thing they will understand. I also went to a News film and saw the film of London's fire, and when the commentator spoke about doing the same to Germany, there was a decided applause."[54]

Severely frayed though the nerves of the city population were, the strategy of moral bombing, aimed at breaking the will of the public, had proved ineffective. The same would apply when German cities were later subjected to the massive Al-

< *Page 154*
118. Berlin during a nighttime air raid in January 1945; searchlight beams of the German anti aircraft batteries mix with marker flares dropped by Allied pathfinder planes for the bombers that follow them

lied bombing campaign in 1942-1945. Goering's air fleet had moreover little effect in slowing British war production during the Blitz, as would prove true conversely in the bombing of German cities. Whether or not for these reasons, after May 1941 German attention turned to the Eastern Front, and the Blitz was over. The war withdrew beyond the horizon for Britons on the home front, playing itself out on the map of continental Europe.

GERMAN CITIES IN ASHES

After the German bombers disappeared from British skies in May 1941, the counterattack started. The string of defences along the North Sea coast, the Kammhuber Line (see Chapter 3), had been designed to cope with sporadic attacks, not with formations of over 1,000 planes. The Line was ineffective in sealing off the continental airspace, although the Allied losses were substantial. By early 1942 Britain had a fleet of some 4,000 bombers and the output of new planes escalated throughout 1943 and 1944. The sixteen factories engaged in making warplanes scored well in production figures (despite their widespread distribution and complicated system of suppliers): 3,000 aircraft in 1938, 8,000 in 1939, 15,000 in 1940, 20,000 in 1941, 24,000 in 1942, 26,263 in 1943 and 26,461 in 1944.[55] Some 1.7 million people were employed in civil engineering and in the chemical and metal industries.

Although Britain had over 125,000 airmen, the Royal Air Force had to be thrifty with its pilots. In 1942 and 1943, one-on-one attacks by German fighters, who would seek blind spots on the flanks of Allied bombers, caused huge losses. Some 14,000 Allied pilots died in 1943 alone. The survival odds for a pilot in that period were about 1 in 6. In the course of the whole air war, the British lost 73,741 or about 44 percent of its flying personnel, to death, injury or capture.[56] The Germans feverishly dismantled any enemy aircraft they captured to probe for the latest Allied technical innovations.

From January 1943 onwards, attacks by the British Air Force (generally at night) and by their American allies (generally in daylight) were combined. It marked the start of an Allied campaign that took the tactic of "the scorched city" to a surrealistic extreme.[57] Over half of Britain's tonnage of bombs was dropped on German cities

in the last nine months of the war. The monthly average death toll among German civilians was 8,100 from the start of the Battle of the Ruhr until the end of 1943, and from July 1944 onwards this figure rose to 13,500. Between these episodes lay the disablement of Germany's aircraft industry and the destruction of German airfields by the American air force. The Allies were able to conduct their bombing raids almost unimpeded from January to May 1945. Flames devoured the cities of Germany. The raids targeted not only industrial facilities on the city peripheries with their firebombing tactics but also the city dwellers, their homes and the historical fabric of the cities themselves.[58] The incendiary bombs acted as firelighters, and domestic furnishings were the fuel. The shell of a building functioned like an incinerator. The firestorm dealt out from the sky was moreover portrayed by the Allies as a moral lesson. Their propaganda presented the destruction of Potsdam, for example, as a punishment for Prussian militarism.

The retaliation for the Blitz started on Saturday evening, 30 May 1942, with the first 1,000 bomber raid on Cologne. The searchlights blinked on, and the heavy anti-aircraft artillery opened fire. The 1,500 tons of ordnance dropped by the planes – 8,300 small incendiary bombs, 90 high explosive bombs, 116 phosphorus bombs, 81 firebomb canisters, four liquid bombs and three heavy mines – left a wall of flame

< *Page 156*

119. Factory site for assembly of Focke-Wulf planes in Bremen, 1944; in middle, two Winkel Tower Shelters

Top
120. Lübeck, city centre immediately after the air raid of 29 March 1942

Bottom
121. Berlin, 1 March 1943

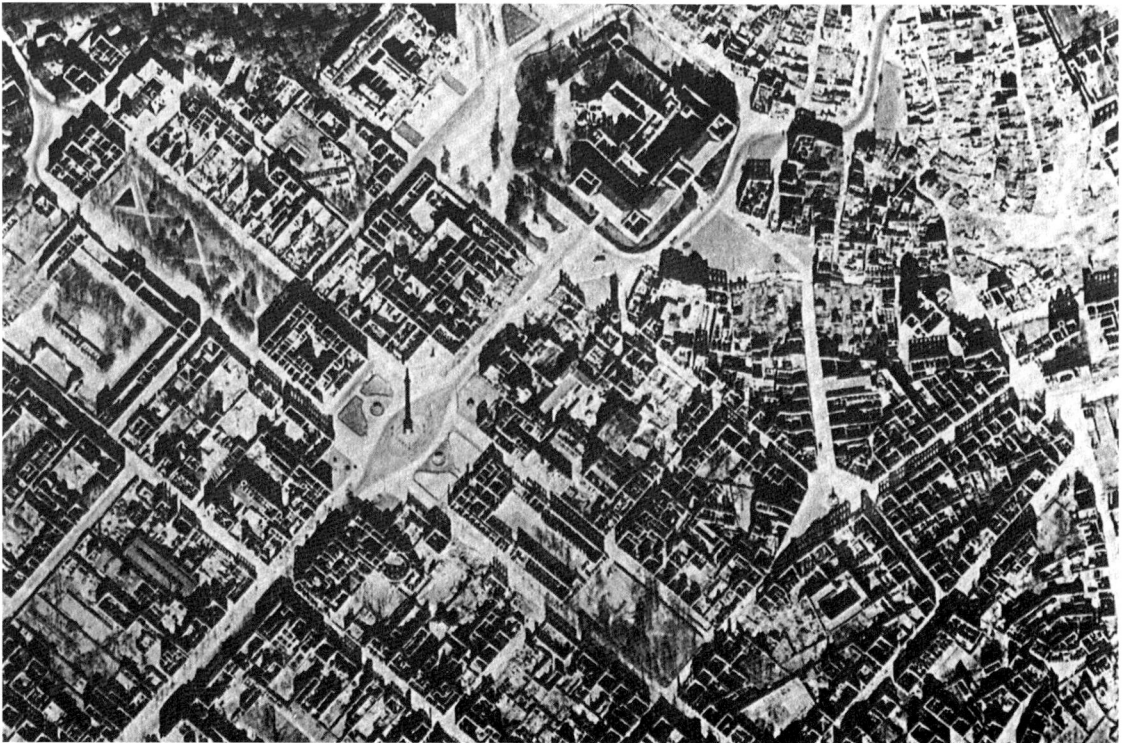

Top
122. Darmstadt after carpet bombing, 12
September 1944

Bottom
123. Steffenstadt, Bremen, 24 April 1945

124. Bremen; mid background, the
Diakonissenbunker, nicknamed Noah's Ark

behind them. The face of the city was marred for ever. Suddenly 100,000 residents
of Cologne were homeless. The number of fatal casualties was modest, at 460, in the
light of the tonnage dropped and of the doom that British area bombing scenarios
had predicted in the run-up to the war. Although the RAF planes dropped heavier
ordnance and used a much more refined mix of bomb types than the Luftwaffe, the
excellent training of the German air raid precaution services, fire brigades and rescue squads helped stem the number of casualties, as did the much greater capacity
and solidity of the air raid shelters in Cologne. Friction between the local authorities
and volunteer initiatives was moreover absent, in contrast to the British cities, and
air raid protection formed part of a disciplined state apparatus. Cologne possessed
over 500 shrapnel-proof shelters with a joint capacity of 75,000 people. Twenty-five
bomb resistant bunkers offered further protection to 7,250, and total of 42,000 shelters had been built in private homes. Fourteen emergency hospitals were available
with a total of 1,760 beds, backed up by 27 first-aid posts and 14 clinics for minor
medical assistance.[59] The German bureaucracy functioned smoothly at this stage of
the struggle. A few hours after the fires were extinguished, vans with clothing, soap,
cigarettes, etc. cruised the streets. Within a month, 140,000 damage compensation
claims from Cologne residents had been processed and paid.[60] The quality of these
public services declined sharply, however, as heavy raids continued on 32 other German cities in the remainder of 1942. Some cities were attacked four or five times. A
severe shortage of domestic necessities ensued.

Let us get away from the abstraction of mechanized mass air attacks on the cities and descend to the *locus delicti*. Let us consider the concrete sensations, and in particular the emotional impact on the city dweller, as must have been experienced at ground level.[61] Each kind of bomb made its own characteristic sound. A shell full of stick bomblets sounded like a flock of pigeons taking off. A 12-kilogram incendiary bomb, with a damage range of 80 metres, issued a short, sharp crack; its 14-kilogram equivalent, which spattered a mix of liquid rubber and petroleum a distance of 50 metres, resembled a bucket of water splashing out over the ground. An incendiary canister containing 20 litres of benzole flopped down like a sack of water. A 106-kilogram incendiary bomb struck with a creaking boom which flung the bomb's charge of wads of fabric soaked in petroleum or heavy fuel oil all around; a similar incendiary of 112 kilograms smothered the surrounding houses with thousands of sticky lumps of benzole and rubber. Then there were the high-explosive bombs and mines which blew away doors and shattered windows, feeding oxygen to the voracious flames.[62]

The smell of an air raid was even more horrible than the sight of it, as confirmed by experiences recorded by doctors and historians. Noses were assailed by the fumes of fire, gas and corruption. Skin reacted to the rise of temperature, heat and gusts of air. Veins trembled with the shock waves. A ferocious wind sucked clothing from the body. Tongue and muscles refused to function, and heart, arteries and secretions worked harder than ever. That was manifested as palpitations, sweating and goose flesh.

125. Mine tunnels with sleeping facilities in the Ruhr region

Page 161 >
126. Cellar shelter entrance, Bremen, September 1942

By the next wave of bombing, people could no longer control their emotions and started screaming. And that was often merely the beginning of the attack, for it was followed by an hours-long struggle for survival by the city dwellers, buried by rubble in their cellars and waiting for rescue. The immediate reactions of those who survived the attack was one of two extremes, either euphoria or apathy. The next task was the search for family and friends. Those who perished were found as three different varieties of sculpture. Those sheltering in a cellar could not stay long, for the conflagration soon penetrated with its heat and fumes. The cellar would quickly take on the temperature of its surrounding and act as a crematorium; or the air inside was soon saturated with suffocating smoke. The heated coal in the kitchen did not catch alight but filled the house with deadly carbon monoxide. Seventy to eighty percent of the deaths were from gas poisoning. Those who suffocated in their cellars were found in a standing, sitting or prone pose, as though instantly petrified.

Those victims who were incinerated by the firestorm would be found charred and unrecognizable, and often dwarved, shrunk to lumps of roasted flesh a mere fifty centimetres long. Of those caught in a powerful explosion or struck by the detonation of a nearby incendiary, only body fragments would be found. Who can ig-

Galerie links

128. Destruction
in Hannover,
undated

nore the images of survivors trudging to the cemetery with a sack or bucket full of
detached limbs of their relatives, seeking a decent place of burial?

LIFE IN THE MOUSEHOLES

The impacts and explosions of the bombing had a force approaching that of an
earthquake. The perceptions of the city dweller were numbed, a mental filter blur-
ring the duration and horror of the scene. The dislocation and assault on the senses
could be admitted only partially, so that the immediate experience was fenced off
and armoured by diminished awareness.

In the final year of the war, Germany's civilians were on the edge of hysteria;
that applied above all to the women, for the men had nearly all been sent to the
front or were working day and night in the war industry. They slept little, rarely
changed clothes, and were startled by the air raid sirens a dozen times a day. Asleep
or awake, a certain sound would remind them of the horror. They felt like hunted
animals. With each air raid, a stream of nervous city dwellers rushed to seek shelter in the nearest bunker. The surprise tactics used by the Allies in the latter half
of the war meant that the air raid warnings were sounded only at the last moment,
so many would rush to the bunker in their nightclothes or even naked. Those who

129. Damage at Cremon-Insel, Hamburg, July 1943

Page 165 >
130. Damage to house of G.W. Leibniz, Hannover, undated

slept at home would do so in a track suit with a bag of air raid requisites close at hand, since a moment's delay could prove fatal. At first, the bunker officials checked the papers of everyone who sought shelter, but this was abandoned in the heavy bombardments from 1943 onwards; there was simply no time for that. Reaching the safety of the bunker interior did not mean an end to the stress. Children were lost in the packed crowds, and pregnant women miscarried in the heat and stench. In the crush at the bunker entrance, people would find themselves stumbling over the prone bodies of the dead and living. Those who arrived too late and faced a closed bunker door were sometimes crushed against it by those arriving after them. After a nearby bomb explosion, a stack of corpses might be found blocking the door outside. Foreign workers and prisoners were refused admission, but Nazi party members could count on privileges. A witness of the heavy bombardment of Emden in June 194 recalled the interior of the bunker during a raid: "There was no electric

lighting, just a few candles. I found my family with great difficulty and they told me that our house had been completely destroyed by a bomb. The bunker instantly became our temporary home. But what a home! No light, no water, no drains, no ventilation! The toilets were soon blocked and in a revolting state. People brought all kinds of rescued household goods in with them, so the proper seating layout became impossible, and everyone went to the upper floors to look for a place to sleep. The bunker warden was there, but he couldn't do his job because everyone did what they liked and especially because a few big shots took command. For example, an officer from the Reichsarbeitsdienst turned up with all his workers whose barracks had burned down and decided to quarter his workforce in the bunker."[63] Nobody was keen to occupy the upper floors of a bunker since the risk of a direct bomb hit was considerably higher there. Serious problems continually arose in forcing people to take a place upstairs.

Not only were the bunker interiors claustrophobic, but they were vulnerable to the less than public-spirited behaviour of some occupants. The fittings and furnishings of the bunkers deteriorated increasingly as the war progressed, and anything that was not nailed down (such as a light bulb) was soon stolen. People brought their most treasured possessions, including pets, with them into the bunker. Many of

131. Air raid casualty, Kassel, October 1943

132. Strewing corpses with bleaching powder, Kassel, October 1943

them had believed Hitler's promise that they would be able to sleep in the bunkers during air raids, and there were indeed rooms furnished with bunk beds (although users had to bring their own bedding). The day rooms had bench seats, tables and collapsible chairs. These furnishings were all removed from the bunkers in 1943 to make room for more people.

COPING WITH THE STRAIN

Against the background of anti-aircraft fire and howling sirens, tension ran high in the shelters during an air raid. City dwellers soon developed a certain bunker routine, but it was impossible to keep it up because the bunkers were in almost continual use. Not only did thirst and fear make life in the bunker unbearable, but the equipment functioned poorly: unreliable heating, stale air, humidity, leaks, filthy and blocked toilets. Viruses and bacterial infections could spread rapidly among the people sheltering in the confined air conditions. The rising tension manifested itself as tight muscles, hawking dry throats, quaking bodies and all conversation falling still. Amid the anxious silence, the mood would swing back and forth between a sense of safety and fear. But much as people screamed, cried and jumped up in shock, others were there to help suppress a mass hysteria. Interruption of the electrical supply added to the panic, especially since everyone knew that the bunker could not withstand a direct hit. A witness to an explosion in an air raid shelter in Osnabrück in late March 1945 recalled: "The Palm Sunday raid already seemed to be over for more than a thousand people in the damp underground passages when, around 10 past 10, a heavy mine exploded with a massive thump just in front of the entrance. It demolished the two protective walls, split the door open and cast its immense explosive power unchecked into the innermost of the lair. For a distance of roughly eighty metres scarcely anyone remained alive. The first rescuers later found a ghastly scene the like of which had not been seen in the whole bombing campaign against Osnabrück. Over a hundred people were killed outright, struck by rubble or shrapnel, bleeding to death or poisoned by carbon monoxide and explosive fumes. Among the corpses lay the dying and the wounded amid fallen lumps of masonry and blocks of stone. (...) After the explosion, panic broke out in the dark passages adjacent to the place of destruction, claiming even more victims."[64]

On the whole, however, the bunkers stood up well even in a firestorm. In Braunschweig, for example, 23,000 people were shut up in two tower bunkers in the middle of a firestorm. The fire brigade used their fire hoses to create an "alley of water" where people could run under the arched jets and escape to a place of safety.[65]

AFTERMATH OF THE ORGY OF FIRE

The Allied bombers were rarely successful in starting a firestorm which would extirpate an inner city at a first attempt. The historic centre of Cologne, for example, was 95 percent destroyed only after 262 air raids. Berlin too resisted annihilation by a fire. Still, the lack of shelter capacity there had inevitable consequences when the city became the target of systematic bombardment by the Allies, and whole suburbs were reduced to ashes. From 1 February to 21 April 1945, Berlin withstood 83 further heavy air raids. The most severe was in February 1945 when, although the number of fatalities is unknown, over 18,000 dwellings were destroyed, and 120,000 Berliners found themselves roofless.[66] The surviving civilians led the life of cave dwellers in the cellars, bunkers and traffic tunnels, relying on tallow candles, open fires and hand pumps.[67] The Allied raids instigated a firestorm with a death toll of over 10,000 in more than a dozen cities: Braunschweig, Darmstadt, Dresden, Hamburg, Heilbronn, Kassel, Koblenz, Leipzig, Magdeburg, Pforzheim, Stuttgart, Swinemünde and Würzburg.[68]

133. Dresden bodies gathered on the Altmarkt on a grid of railway rails

Dresden surpassed all others in its destruction.[69] At the time of the air raid in February 1945, the city housed 640,000 residents and 300,000 refugees. The number of dead was long estimated at about 80,000, although more recent studies indicate a lower figure in the range of 18,000 to 25,000. On 27 February 1945, Erich Kästner wrote: "Yesterday evening Orthmann's courier arrived with terrible news. Dresden existed no longer. He said that the firestorm of the burning Neue Rathaus had sucked people fleeing from Waisenhausstrasse through the air and into the flames, as though they were mosquitoes or moths. Others leapt into the water, trying to save themselves; but the water was boiling hot, and they were cooked like lobsters."[70] The majority of lives were lost in the 158 repeatedly bombed and incinerated medium-sized German cities, of which little remained but skeletons. Hitler's revenge with V1 and V2 rockets, claiming 15,000 victims of whom nearly 9,000 were in Great Britain, was tiny in comparison to this orgy of fire. The causes of death in the bombing of Germany were 5-30 percent due to explosion, pressure and falling masonry; 5-15 percent due to heat and burns; and 60-70 percent due to smoke and gas inhalation.[71] The combustion gases were perhaps a surrogate for the poison gas attacks anticipated between the wars.

The death toll of the air war, 600,000, the millions of homeless people and the incredible misery into which the German people were cast (clothing, household goods, kitchen utensils and food were rationed from 1942 onwards) were formidable. Although the strategic air offensive of 1943-1944 was meant as a prelude to the later invasion, the aerial attacks on the cities and their populations failed in its explicit objective: the German weapons industry did not falter. Germany could draw on a huge labour reservoir from all over occupied Europe, and the population did not rise in revolt against the Nazi regime as some had expected.[72] There were nonetheless civic authorities that considered abandoning their bombed-out city altogether and making a new start. Hannover, for example, formulated a plan to put all traffic underground, to scatter residential areas around the countryside in green surroundings, and to build a new city centre made up of above-ground bunkers.[73]

The idea that heavy bombardment would ripen the civilian population for capitulation was not borne out; or at least, any decision to capitulate was out of their power, so there was little left to them but a passive role as victims. "That barrage from the air which mutilated, suffocated, burned, and destroyed, did not so much breed fear and a desire to bow before the storm, but rather a certain fatalistic cussedness, a dogged determination to survive and, if possible, help others to survive, whatever their politics, whatever their creed."[74] The reality of 1944 and 1945 was that families were torn apart geographically, in so far as they had not been decimated by the bombing, their members scattered over the Eastern Front, industrial zones, evacuation locations in the countryside and cellars or bunkers in the cities. The primary concerns of civilians were physical survival, the prospect of journeys to visit family and friends, and nurturing revenge. "Reprisal was the narcotic of the bombed-out community. But the German V-weapons deployed after the Allied invasion killed fewer people than the attack on Pforzheim alone. The rest of the revenge consisted of getting together to lynch parachuted bomber pilots."[75]

The German bunker programme certainly had its benefits. At the start of the project, the assumption was that eight to ten percent of the urban population could be sheltered in bomb-resistant accommodation. This percentage rose in the course of the war due to substantial evacuations and because the city dwellers who remained behind utilized the bunkers far beyond their design capacity. Back in 1940, in parallel with the bunker programme, Hitler had ordered the evacuation of all children under 14 from Berlin and Hamburg. Another component was the *Führerprogramm* "Aktion Mutter und Kind"; as a precaution, mothers with young children were to sleep in a different bunker complex every night, in such places as converted gasholders, beneath public squares and parks and in unused branches of tunnels. The spaces were divided into small cells connected by a long, narrow corridor.[76]

Starting in 1942, large contingents of the population were transported to the countryside[77] so that those who remained behind and were making an essential contribution to the economy were assured of a place in the bunkers. In November

< *Page 170*
134. Clearing debris after an Allied air raid, Dresden, 13-14 February 1945

135. Hamburg, August 1943

1942, 335,000 children aged 10-14 were sent to Hitler Youth camps, and 800,000 mothers with children were sent out of the cities. This migration required 1,684 special trains and 78 ships: "127,000 tubes of toothpaste, 7,500 first-aid kits, 9,900 musical instruments, 140,000 complete clothing outfits for boys, 130,000 for girls, and 110,000 pairs of wooden shoes had been provided for these new residents of rural Germany."[78] Munich gives a representative picture of the waves of voluntary evacuation in Germany. Immigration from the west and north of the country increased the city's population by over 30,000 between 1940 and December 1942, bringing it to 865,000. By 1943, however, Munich lay on the front line and suffered heavy bombing; the population shrank again to 680,000 and shortly before the end of the war, to 430,000.[79]

In 1943 and 1944, at least half the population of Germany could rely on a place in a bombproof shelter. The survival machines were crucial, as one example is enough to illustrate. The seven notorious Operation Gomorrah raids on Hamburg took place between 25 July and 3 August 1943,[80] preceded by 18 heavy bombings of other German cities (total 24,000 tons)[81] that turned out to be a mere prelude. The acting commander of the British air raids, "Bomber" Harris, chose Hamburg on account of its size rather than for its U-boat building facilities. "I had always wanted to have a real dead set at Hamburg. It was the second biggest city in Germany, and I wanted to make a tremendous show."[82] On 25 July 1943, 1,100 Allied bombers flew towards the port city. They completely disabled the German radar warnings by scattering small strips of aluminium foil, and were unchallenged as they cast a total of 12,000 mines, 25,000 high explosive bombs, three million firebombs and five hundred canisters of phosphorus onto the city. The wind speed measured four kilome-

136. Fatalities, probably through carbon monoxide poisoning, in a cellar shelter, Rothenburgsort district of Hamburg, undated

Page 173 >
137. Survivors amid the ruins of Altona, Hamburg, 26 July 1943

tres from the city shortly before the air raid on 28 July was six metres per second. That speed rose due to the conflagration to 15, and at the epicentre of the firestorm, wind speeds of 45 metres per second were measured. Horizontal flames shot from one burning building to another at a height of 25 metres. The cloud of smoke above Hamburg rose to eight kilometres in height.[83] Sunlight could not penetrate through this thick blanket. Only a quarter of homes were left undamaged, and 900,000 citizens of Hamburg lost all their household possessions. Trucks filled with corpses sprinkled with chlorinated lime rumbled back and forth to deposit their loads at cemeteries, where forced labourers and concentration camp inmates were set to work digging mass graves as quickly as possible.

Most of those who perished in the firestorm were victims of radiant heat rather than direct contact with the flames. Nearly 40,000 city dwellers were killed, a figure which would have been considerably higher if it were not for the 124 bunkers which offered shelter to 92,000 people. There were also shrapnel-proof tubular public shelters with a capacity of nearly 63,000 and 89 shrapnel-proof trench shelters with

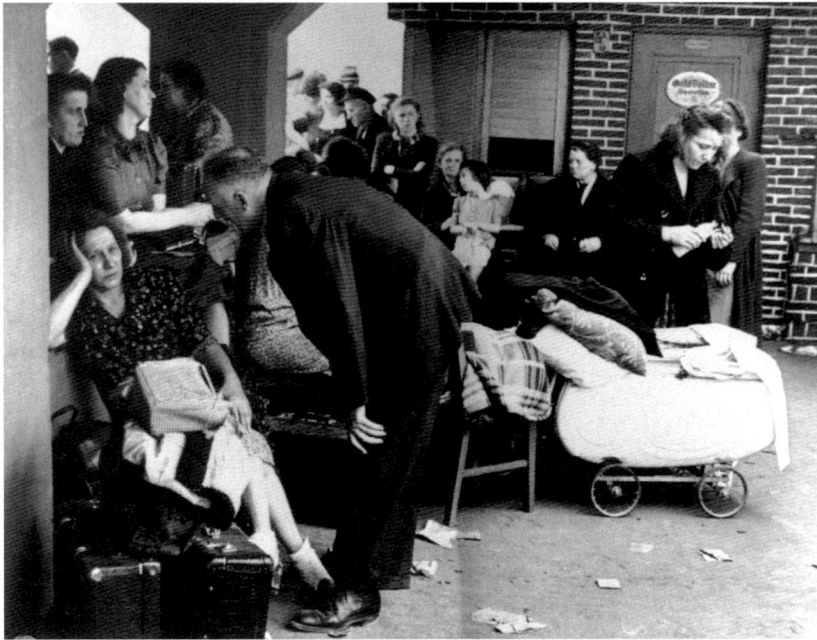

138. Shelterers in the bunker on Reeperbahn, Hamburg, July 1943

Page 175 >
139. View of River Elbe from Sankt Pauli district, Hamburg, 1945-1946

room for 6,000. None of these shelters offered a guarantee of survival. Some bunkers were completely surrounded by the firestorm which sucked away all breathable oxygen, resulting in the suffocation of thousands.[84] Eleven of the 22 bunkers still under construction were destroyed in the conflagration. In some cases later reconstruction was pointless even though the shell survived because the surrounding residential district had been wholly eradicated.[85]

American strategists concluded in 1945 that the losses among German civilians were only one-twentieth of their previous estimate.[86] The total death toll in the cities was somewhere between 420,000 and 570,000 (including 75,000 children). Whether the bombardment of Germany (in particular in 1944 and 1945) accelerated the end of the war is a question that is still debated today. Some hold that the pounding of German cities into craters was not without effect: although unable to halt the production of armaments, it dislocated the logistics and the infrastructure, so that the Germans were forced to improvise while devoting more and more money and materials to the aerial defence of cities. It would also prevent Germany from re-emerging as a super-power after the end of World War II. Others emphasize the pointless destruction of historic cities and their cultural heritage, besides the mass slaughter of civilians from the air.[87] The necropolis that many European cities had become by 1945 was full of overflowing burial grounds with disconcerting signs marking the tragic human remains – "unknown female", "unknown male" or "unknown child".

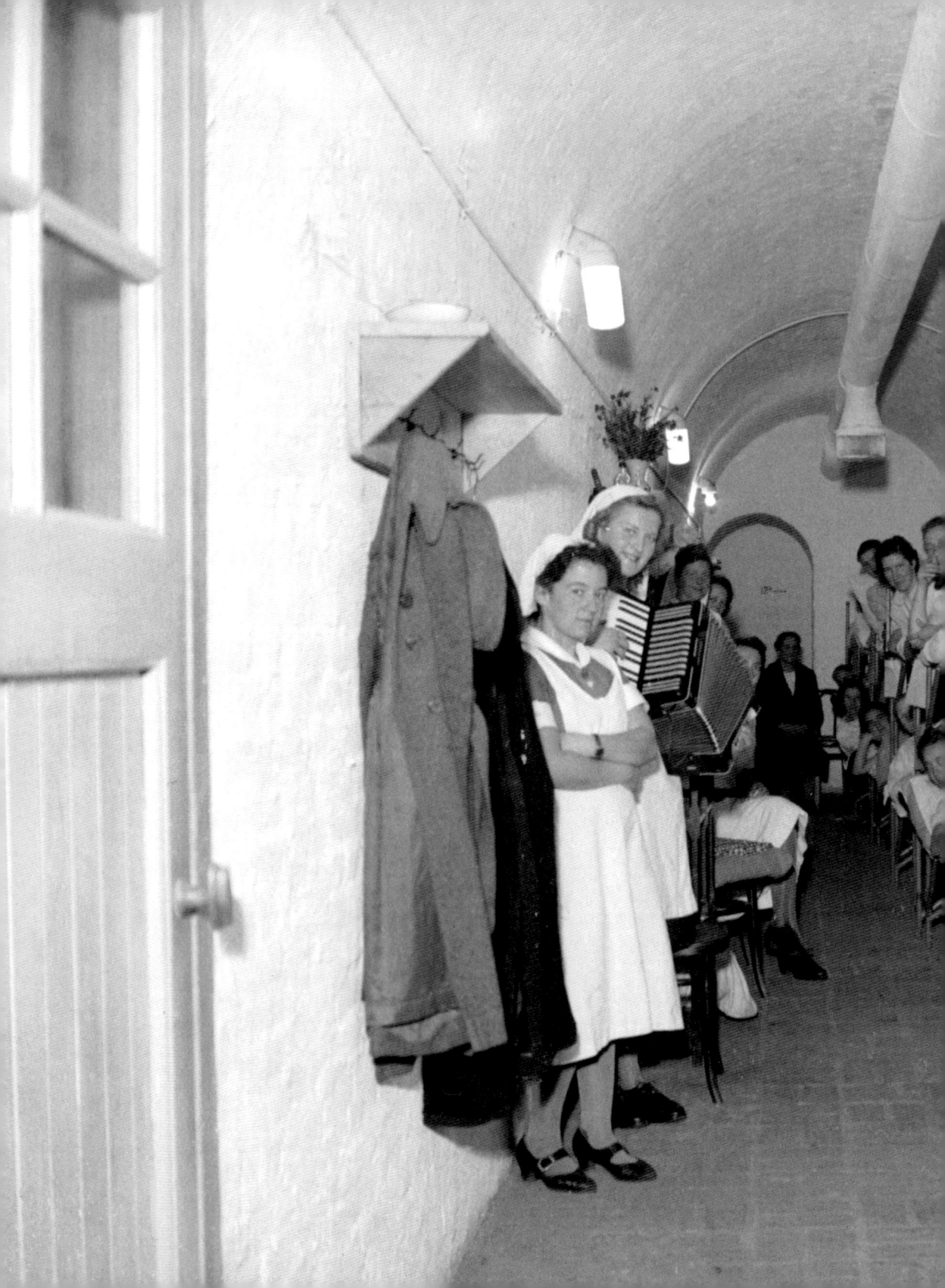

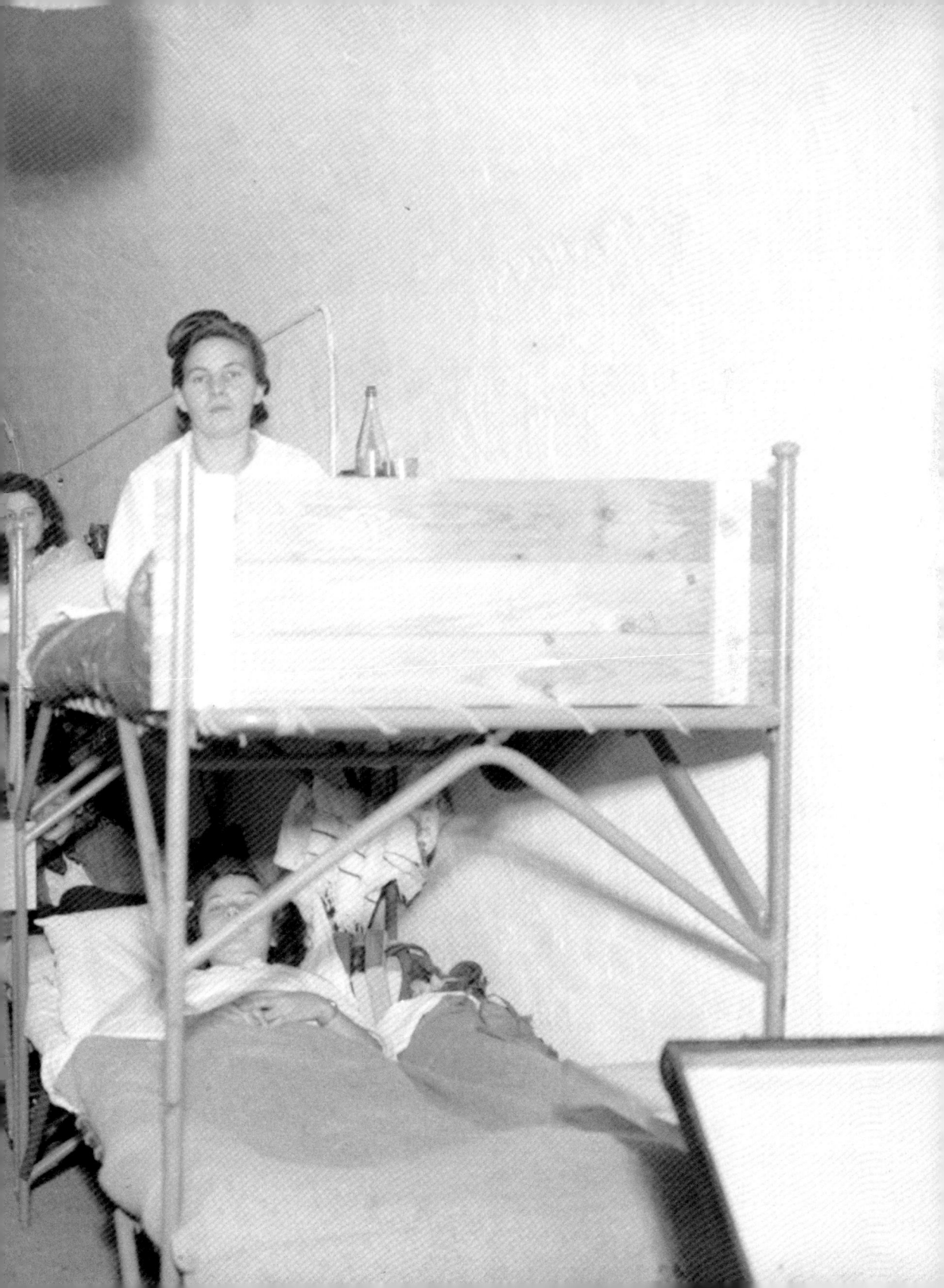

Map of the Netherlands showing: Groningen, Den Helder, Alkmaar, Amsterdam, Haarlem, Valkenburg, The Hague, Utrecht, Arnhem, Rotterdam, Nijmegen, Groesbeek, Enschede, Domburg, Middelburg, Vlissingen, Eindhoven.

North Sea

0   30 km

<   *Page 176 and 177*
140. Shelter in Oud Burgeren Hospital, Nijmegen,
1945

CHAPTER 5

"The glass falls like paper and the roof tiles like cotton wool"

Dutch Air Raid Protection During the Occupation

When they invaded Poland on 1 September 1939, the Germans could have chosen either to lay siege to Warsaw (1.3 million inhabitants) or take it by force. The former strategy would starve the enemy into submission, while the latter would result in heavy damage to the fabric of the city. In the end they deployed both methods. The Wehrmacht encircled the entire city from 1 to 20 September. The Germans would never allow an evacuation of the civilian population, because Polish forces would then be free to defend their city to the last drop of blood.[1] An air raid (code name Aktion Wasserkante) was planned as early as 10 September but postponed on account of the bad weather. On 18 September, Hitler decided it was urgent to take the capital before Russian reinforcements could come to the defence of Poland. This decision was virtually a sentence of annihilation for the city. On 22 September General Wolfram von Richthofen, a veteran of Guernica, volunteered to undertake the destruction of Warsaw. Two days later an air assault started with 487 tons of high-explosive bombs and 72 tons of incendiaries, which lasted for three days. The tactics of the attack consisted of the area bombing of industrial centres plus individual dive bombing attacks on busy city streets, in both cases supplemented by artillery barrages. "Thus the weapons had to have their say, and they spoke an unambiguous language. Anyone who witnessed the bombardment of Warsaw by artillery batteries disposed all around the city and by continual air raids of German flying machines will retain ineradicable memories of this episode. Hundreds of cannons launched their gre-

141. Air raid warning in Warsaw, 1939

nades into the city, which was soon burning on every street corner and in all directions. Meanwhile German fighter planes swooped down in rolling formations over the city unleashing their bombs, and a huge cloud of smoke and flames soon hung over the city. (...) Warsaw had become an underworld. The ethnic Germans who had remained in Warsaw recounted later what the inhabitants of the city had to endure. Food supplies were exhausted, and hunger was widespread. Hundreds of houses collapsed, crushing and killing those who crowded into their cellars in search of protection. Whole districts of the city were ablaze, and there was no prospect of extinguishing the flames for the water mains were destroyed. On top of these horrors came the whistling of the German shells and the deafening explosions of the German bombs which rained down constantly on the city."[2] The Luftwaffe began its carpet bombing attack on 24 September with 600 bombers backed by artillery in an initial offensive which reached its peak on 25 September. Water and electricity supplies were ruptured. The main attack followed two days later, but the heavy bombing failed to subdue the Polish resistance. Then the artillery and aerial bombing intensified even further on 26 and 27 September until the starving city, aware that the rest of the country already lay largely in German hands, capitulated. Over 60,000 people were killed, of whom 20,000 were civilians. Twelve percent of the city's buildings lay in ruins. Warsaw was hit by more bombs than would later be dropped on Dresden, although their total destructive effect was less, for increasing experience with this mode of warfare boosted its efficiency.

On 4 November 1939, Hitler issued a decree prohibiting the reconstruction of Warsaw. He liked watching the film clips of the bombardment of the city, and fantasized about toppling the skyscrapers of New York.[3] This fantasy was not new, however, for as long ago as 1909 H.G. Wells had pictured an attack on New York City in which German Zeppelins dropped bombs on targets in Manhattan such as Broadway and Brooklyn Bridge.[4]

"Fortress Holland", the densely populated coastal provinces once deemed inviolable behind their floodable defence lines, was no match for the modern German invading forces who saw the Netherlands as a fast route into Belgium and France. An essential ingredient of their plan was to gain mastery of Dutch air space. The German attack of 10 May to capture the airfields around The Hague, and with them the seat of government, met with failure, however. They successfully targetted the airfields, as well as the base at Waalsdorp and the Alexander Barracks, with their bombs, but the 3,500 German paratroopers who landed were so widely scattered that they were unable to capture the airfields quickly, let alone the city of The Hague. The Germans even found themselves on the defensive and had to await the arrival of reinforcements. The fresh troops were expected to enter Fortress Holland through Rotterdam, but first that city had to be taken. Their plan was to test the Blitzkrieg concept, the idea of delivering a *coup de grâce* from the air. Even before the German ultimatum expired at 1 p.m. on 14 May, the bombers were on their way.

The message of the Blitzkrieg had the required impact in Rotterdam, claiming a death toll of 650 to 900, with 26,000 civilians left homeless and the destruction of 27,000 dwellings (in 11,000 buildings), 1,200 small businesses including 500 cafés, 70 schools, 12 cinemas and two theatres.[5] In these circumstances, the commander-in-chief of the Dutch forces saw no other option but to abandon resistance and surrender. It is not the intention here to exhume the political and military debates among historians as to whether the bombing of Rotterdam could have been averted by an immediate capitulation. The basic principles of air warfare established in earlier German bombardments make this seem unlikely, however. Given the pattern of bombing in Guernica, Warsaw, Kristiansand and Elverum (Norway, April 1940), there was no reason to suppose that Rotterdam would escape the same fate. As soon

as the Germans felt threatened with a stalemate or a prolonged positional conflict, the bombs began falling on civilian targets.[6]

The Dutch army command did not capitulate immediately to the German ultimatum but insisted on procedures and hoped to gain time for negotiations. The bombardment, which Goering had prepared in advance, seemed to bear little connection to the ultimatum: the first squadron arrived at 13.10 hours and the second, ten minutes later.[7] Perhaps the bombing itself should be regarded as the real ultimatum. At 16.50 hours, General H.G. Winkelman telexed an order to his troops to lay down their arms. This induced the German commander in Rotterdam to cancel the next wave of bombers, which were by then already in the air and approaching the city.[8]

The Netherlands was thus the third country in Europe, after Poland and Norway, to buckle under the threat of continued air raids and to capitulate. In early April 1941, Belgrade suffered two days of continuous bombing with 2,200 fatalities. The last major German bombing campaign took place on 23 August 1942 with the aim of subjugating Leningrad. As the local Party Secretary, Alexei Tschujanov, observed, "Many industrial premises were severely damaged. Oil terminals, railway stations, housing areas, hospitals, palaces of culture, theatres, museums and schools – all that had been built up over many years – stood in flames. The population sought protection where possible in public shelters, trenches, house cellars and hallways. The firestorms put the city itself on the front line."[9] A complete statistical overview is still lacking, for the number of victims was initially kept secret. The death toll in Leningrad was probably about 40,000 with a further 150,000 wounded. Of the 450,000 inhabitants, 300,000 were evacuated, a process which itself claimed innumerable fatalities and injuries.[10]

The Blitz of Rotterdam was not severe in comparison to the attacks on Belgrade, Guernica, Leningrad or Warsaw, and certainly not when compared to the Allied bombardments of German cities from 1942 onwards. The reason that Rotterdam has taken such a prominent place in historical accounts was the propaganda impact of the successful air offensive which the attackers stood ready to repeat. This effect was amplified by the British press which considerably exaggerated the savagery of the Germans, reporting among other things a death toll of over 30,000.

The air raids of Tuesday, 14 May, took place in warm, calm weather, starting at 13.10 in the afternoon and lasting no more than 15 minutes. An air raid alarm had been sounded. German reports detail the quantity of munitions used as 97 tons of

143. Two Meulenkamp Shelters that survived the bombing (in the dark triangular area), Rotterdam, photo July 1940.

144. Land van Hoboken, Boymans van Beuningen Museum (right),
Rotterdam. Civilians assemble at the trench shelters, 14 May 1940

high-explosive bombs (158 pieces of 250 kilos and 1,150 of 50 kilos). Approximately 90 Heinkels conducted a short, concentrated carpet bombing of the city centre. Two squadrons approached from the east and overflew the city, one on either bank of the River Maas. It has been disputed whether or not the second squadron, which arrived over its target ten minutes later than the first, actually dropped any bombs.[11] Presumably it did, since Rotterdam civic officials precisely mapped an impact pattern of two distinct rectangular areas.

Besides the centre of Rotterdam, the districts Kralingen, Bergpolder, Provenierswijk, Liskwartier and North were hit. "Refugees streamed out of the inner city in all directions, mostly leaving all their goods and chattels behind them but in some cases encumbered with hurriedly gathered possessions. A few, generally elderly, people refused to leave their familiar surroundings and later had to be brought out by the spontaneously formed rescue squads in the ambulances which the municipal health department hastily deployed."[12] One hour after the air raid, only three buildings on Coolsingel were still ablaze.[13] The great conflagration did not break out until hours later. What made firebombs superfluous in Rotterdam was the urban design (narrow streets) and architectural structure (large windows, many single-brick walls and much woodwork) of the inner city itself. The firefighting work was hindered by strong winds and by a direct hit on the principal water mains; it was not until one and a half hours after the bombing that effective extinguishing became possible, using fireboats and water drawn from the river and canals.[14] "People in Rotterdam generally lost their heads during the air raid; the telephone exchange was deserted, for example. Members of the public were distraught."[15] A fireman described the burning of Rotterdam as follows: "The wind grew stronger all the time and fanned the conflagration. Houses and churches collapsed noisily, with thundering violence. The flames soared, and sparks leapt into the night sky and blew into other areas. The city turned into one huge, terrible funeral pyre."[16] Some foci of the fire reached temperatures of 1,800°C. The clouds of smoke resulted in an eclipse of the sun that was visible as far away as the Betuwe. Flakes of soot whirled down over a huge area around the city. In some spots the fire was still smouldering 16 weeks later.

FIFTEEN MINUTES OF SHELTER

In the panic of the air raid, the inhabitants of Rotterdam sought refuge under the stairs, in cellars, in refrigerators, in bank vaults or in one of the 300 Meulenkamp shelters that were scattered around the city. People had already left their places of shelter by the time the fires broke out. Members of the air raid protection service made themselves useful here and there, but they were insufficiently prepared to deal with a real air raid.

The main telephone exchange took a direct hit, but the cable conduits in the basement, used as a shelter, remained intact despite the huge weight of collapsed masonry above them. Only a few buildings in the main central street, Coolsingel, were on fire. Despite rumours circulating about burned and drowned shop assistants in the shelters, the 450 people in the basement of the Bijenkorf department store were all unharmed. The same applied to those in the basement shelter of the C&A-Brenninkmeier department store, although the rest of the building burned down completely. The basement shelter of the main Post Office, where 300 people sought refuge, was undamaged.[17] The shelter under the Schouwburg (municipal theatre) eventually burned out because its ceiling and walls were reinforced with wood, but the people sheltering had enough time to escape unharmed. The city hall had a basement shelter with 80-cm-thick walls, and those who sought refuge there also survived. The Coolsingel Hospital had to be abandoned and burned down, but the other three hospitals in Rotterdam were undamaged.

145. Grote Markt, statue of Erasmus unscathed in the bombing, Rotterdam, May 1940

Page 187 >

146. Grounds of Boymans Van Beuningen Museum, statue of Erasmus placed horizontal and packed in sandbags

City dwellers fled their homes in panic, except for those who had taken the initiative to convert their cellars into bomb shelters. It is quite possible that some people were left buried under the rubble in their reinforced cellars while the rescue squads were unable to help them, for the addresses of private domestic shelters were not registered. The rescuers began with nothing. As a medical orderly recalled, "I went to the old Jamin confectioner's near Kruisstraat. The first thing I saw was a pair of legs sticking out from under the rubble of a house. Naturally I started pulling at the legs and eventually I extracted a woman from the rubble. I saw that she was still alive. I found six or so others there, but they were all dead. (...) That first day I picked up maybe 20 to 25 corpses, and I helped about 20 injured people. The most difficult cases were those who lay dead under the rubble, skulls smashed or legs gone. Yes, they were the worst. Finding the legs, and putting them together with the rest."[18]

Rotterdam possessed over 300 public shelters of the Meulenkamp type for 50 to 100 people, spread around the city. A newspaper report in the NRC of 27 May 1940 described these concrete structures as follows: "things were tense now and then in many of the shelters, either because a bomb had exploded in the close vicinity or because nearby buildings collapsed. None of the shelters gave way."[19] One Meulenkamp shelter was struck by a collapsing wall, but its side walls stood up to the impact.[20] A senior official of the Air Raid Protection Inspectorate confirmed that these

shelters had withstood the air raid extremely well except for direct hits: "You can take refuge in them with the greatest confidence, for you stand a reasonable chance of surviving the attack."[21] It would be nonetheless interesting to know how many shelter places were located in the bombed areas, whether people sought refuge there, whether there was a crush of people trying to enter the shelters, and whether anyone who happened to be out in the street could obtain a place there. This information is unavailable and is hard to reconstruct from archive documents. An inspector from the Building Department stated: "As to whether many of the victims in Rotterdam were killed in or outside basement shelters, open trenches or roofed trench shelters, the Head of the Air Raid Protection Inspectorate was unable to give us an answer. He could not state any figures."[22] Considering the short duration of the bombardment and the relatively lightweight bombs used, a stay in a Meulenkamp shelter was reasonably bearable. But some of the people who entered them were already injured. Koos Postema, later well known as a television presenter, wrote: "You could hear people crying and praying, and there were others who continually shouted the names of their spouse or children. (...) Opposite me sat a man, dead silent. A little girl stood between his knees and gazed constantly into his face. She softly repeated his name over and again, but he responded only with his eyes, which he opened and closed very slowly. Suddenly a narrow stream of blood trickled from his mouth. His head sagged to one side and his eyes remained closed. The girl stopped gazing in his face. She stared straight ahead to his chest and continued whispering his name."[23]

MIDDELBURG

Following the bombing of Rotterdam, the Dutch government in exile ordered the fight to continue in Zeeland, since French and British troops were also active there. In particular, the French forces held the Sloedam, which provided access to the island of Walcheren. The German attack on this dam on 17 May 1940 encountered stiff resistance.[24] By about 13.00 hours they began firing shells onto the city of Middelburg from a vantage point in Zuid-Beveland. Word later spread that Middelburg, the capital of the Zeeland region with a population of about 18,000, had been carpet-bombed, and this was long believed to be a historical fact. It was not so, as recent research has shown.[25] The morning before the German attack, the mayor had the presence of mind to advise the civilian population, especially women and children, to leave the city. Partly due to this, the death toll was eventually limited to 22.

Middelburg's eight electric sirens began to howl at around 13.30 on 17 May 1940. The city was shelled by field artillery and was bombed once by a few German planes. The first damage was caused by shells falling on Rotterdamse Kade and on the Oost-Indisch Huis (a complex of office buildings and warehouses) which immediately burst into flame because of the munitions stored there. Impacts followed on Rouaanse Kaai and Lange Delft. Small fires broke out in the inner city, primarily on the roofs, attics and gutters of houses. The isolated point fires joined up.

Immediately after the first wave of the attack, only fifteen houses and one public building were aflame.[26] Firefighting proceeded tardily, however, due to the absence of civilians who might have helped quench small local fires had they remained in the city. Fanned by a stiff north wind, a conflagration took grip of the city centre that evening. The city hall burned like a torch. "The carillon of Lange Jan [the tower of the Abbey Church], used as a lookout tower obstinately persisted in jingling its tunes amid the sea of fire, until the end of the day when the mighty tower collapsed."[27]

Firefighting by sixteen city fire brigade units with a total manpower of 350 and equipped with seven fire engines, fourteen fireboats and five manual pumps was difficult because pressure in the water mains declined from 16.30 onwards, and the water in the city's canals was low due to drought.[28] Driven by the fierce north wind, tongues of flame shot across the wide canals and streets, igniting more and more properties. The absence of the civilian population made access to the buildings difficult so that it was impossible to tackle incipient fires. It was not until two days later that the fire was hedged in sufficiently to prevent further expansion. Fires continued to blaze up from the rubble here and there over a month after the bombing.[29]

The white flag was raised at 17:00 hours. The silhouette of Middelburg was visible from Domburg (15 km away) as "a fiery line on the horizon" in which "Lange Jan stood out sharply against the flames."[30] Once more, it was evident that the city fabric was incapable of withstanding a modern attack; 573 properties were devastated, including 253 houses, 320 industrial buildings and 18 government buildings. A resident wrote, two days after the attack, that "the destruction is so violent, so thorough, that you cannot utter a word and your eyes fill with tears. Everything you see is unrecognizably ruined. Heaps of rubble lie all around. You have to look hard for the entrances to the streets that converge on the market square; you can't find them and you can hardly tell where you are. Mounds of masonry, blackened walls, smoking, charred beams, bent and twisted rods, pipes and girders of steel – it's terrible! Only the frontage plus a few fragments of the side walls of the city hall, and the base of its tower, remain heavily damaged but still standing."[31]

Owing to the timely evacuation of the public, Middelburg's roofed trench shelters (19 in number with room for a total of 650 users) were probably barely used if at all.[32] They would have offered little defence against the fierce fires and the smoke-filled air in the city centre.

SIT VENIA VERBO

Less familiar than the bombings of Middelburg and Rotterdam, the RAF attacked the ports of Vlissingen (28 raids in 1940) and Den Helder (59 raids in 1940). The Luftwaffe bombed Den Helder for still unelucidated reasons immediately after the capitulation, and the naval base was the target of British raids in June. There were relatively few civilian victims because a more or less voluntary evacuation had taken place. The effect of an air raid on the mental state of the city dweller was observed by the physician Dr. M.G. Vroom, who personally experienced the RAF bombardment of the buildings around the old railway station of Den Helder, together with his wife and children, on the night of 24-25 June 1940. An attack by three bombers claimed a death toll of 38.[33] "Just as I arrived home and met my family, all downstairs and dressed, several bombs struck close to home, so that all the windows broke, furniture fell over, paintings shook from their hooks, and the plasterwork fell from the walls. The lights went out at the same time. We rushed to our small shelter between concrete and sandbags, primitively assembled for lack of better. I can no longer tell how long we remained there, together with several other adults and children from the neighbourhood. The bomb explosions, that followed one after another, were deafeningly loud and had an effect on us as though every aspect of our existence and life came to a stop, and everything was being destroyed. Only naked life itself remained."[34] Vroom observed his own response as "a sensation of suffocating tightness in the lungs, rising to the throat, with heavy palpitations and a moderate pulse frequency, and furthermore a dry sensation in the throat."[35] Another of the symptoms was temporary deafness, which made it seem as though "the glass falls like paper and the rooftiles like cotton wool", combined with forgetfulness (an impossibility of retaining new impressions), concentration problems and inward shuddering at the sound of aircraft engines. Vroom designated the effect of the events on the city dweller as a traumatic neurosis (sit venia verbo). "In this category we include that by which an outward mass psychological happening has such an overwhelming effect on human existence, that this existence is uncovered in all its insignificance."[36] The bombing had provoked a mental tunnel vision that was aimed exclusively at self-preservation. After the raid, Vroom noted a specific form of euphoria among his patients – a joy at having come through it alive and a disinterest in material matters – as well as insomnia, nervousness, sweating and a vegetative response (weight loss combined with a heightened appetite). Traumatized patients shut off part of their personality and the associated emotions (repression), or were instead irrepressibly conscious of what had taken place as though it were an open wound. It is striking how closely these observations correspond to the health effects reported following the disastrous crash of an Israeli freight plane into flats in the Amsterdam district of Bijlmermeer in 1992.[37]

Den Helder, and especially its naval shipyard and airfield, remained a target of bombing raids (in total 117) throughout the period of occupation. An effective civilian evacuation took place. Farms in the vicinity of the city turned into refugee camps where families spent their nights sleeping in the cowsheds. The city dwellers "found accommodation in the towns, villages and farms to the south of the city, as far as Alkmaar. The farmers were not invariably hospitable, and the refugees sometimes had to take satisfaction with a place in the barn or the hencoop. Every morning, a large procession of people travelled by train or by foot back to Den Helder in order to work, only to return to their places of refuge in the evening."[38] A small number of North Holland municipalities built village extensions to provide the refugees with overnight shelter. Out of the 37,700 residents of Den Helder, only a few hundred still lived and/or worked there by the end of the war.

SHELTER CITY IN EVERYDAY LIFE

The skies were busy with bombers for over a thousand of the 1,800 days of Dutch occupation. Some 600 air raids were directed at Dutch targets in that period.[39] From 1941 onwards, the air space of the Netherlands became one of the main routes to German territory for Allied bombers – at night for the British and in daytime for the Americans. The fact that the Allies met little difficulty in using the air space was in itself encouraging for the Dutch, but there could be no sense of security. Everyone had to stay alert and keep a grip on themselves, because some areas of Dutch cities, such as docks and factories involved in manufacturing war goods, were often targeted. What is more, the bombs and artillery shells not infrequently fell wide of their targets. The greatest danger came from navigation errors by the Allied air forces who thought they were dropping bombs on German cities when in fact they were well inside Dutch territory – for example at Arnhem, Enschede and Nijmegen on 22 February 1944. Shelter City was thus an invaluable resource.

The mysterious and partly secret Shelter City phenomenon took hold of the existing cities of the Netherlands every evening. It had something of a traumatic mirage, blacked out at night and full of perils.[40] The continual threat of air raids transformed the life of the individual city dweller. Specially shielded street lamps cast a dim light at crucial locations. The pavement kerbs were whitewashed to give a glimmer of guidance to pedestrians. Illuminated commercial signs and shop windows were prohibited. Public space was a yawning emptiness for there was no nightlife. After dusk, city dwellers shuffled through the gloom, stumbling over tiny obstacles and desperately seeking recognizable landmarks aided only by a *knijpkat* (a dynamo-powered hand torch which made a whining noise when operated). They stayed indoors at night in houses with numbers painted in phosphorescent paint and windows blacked out by extra curtains. Everyone was prepared for a possible air raid.

Extra manpower was assigned to lookout points on tall buildings. In Eindhoven, for example, the Air Raid Protection Department built a lookout tower on top of the Van Abbemuseum, and the Germans constructed a barracks on the roof of the Philips Light Tower. A system of radar warning stations and sirens gave warning of an impending attack, summoning the city dwellers to descend into their crypts.

During the attack they entrenched themselves in reinforced cellars, in shelter huts in the garden or in collective trench shelters on public squares, on grassy roadsides, in a school playground, in a public garden or in the park; or even in collective bunkers. The bunkers gave an illusion of immunity to the bombs. Air-conditioned containers of this kind sucked in city dwellers, torn from their comfortable niches while they waited fearfully for better times. The bunker visualized a breach with the normal urban living pattern and was in fact no more than an extra article of clothing – a thick, concrete cuirass.[41] This lump of concrete or other reinforced space with its artificial climate represented a microcosm that communicated a lot about the outside world. The city at ground level was not a good place to live when a rain of bombs was falling.

The transition from one "city" to the other was generally abrupt, a border situation where the mental switch was not easily thrown. As someone from Rotterdam wrote, "Dad was the 'deputy marshal' of the Air Raid Protection Department and had a heavy grey asbestos suit in the attic, alongside the box of sand for quenching fires. New buildings, each with a sign saying 'Public Shelter' above the entrance, appeared in the parks. Inside, the damp soil stank of piss, and boys in my class told me 'there are French letters lying around there'. What use were the buildings if not for that? But now it was wartime. Air raids, sandboxes and shelters changed like magic into important things. I had to move my bed to the middle floor and now we really did hide in the cellar when the sirens went off. Even my little brother, not yet three, used to babble 'toot, toot, out of bed'."[42]

147. Painting the kerbs white as a blackout precaution, Rotterdam

Page 193 >

Top
148. Building a Meulenkamp Shelter with wooden railway sleepers, Rotterdam

Bottom
149. Central canteen flanked by Meulenkamp Shelters, Rotterdam, November 1940

The Guidelines issued by the State Inspectorate of Air Raid Protection gained a supplement in June 1940, following the German assault that gave the Dutch their first experience of air raids, heavy bombardments and fires. The modified guidelines were also the result of explosive tests carried out in the week before the invasion, "in which among other things the usability and functionality of the systems of public shelters used in the three biggest cities (Amsterdam, Rotterdam and The Hague) were observed."[43] On 16 May 1940, the Ministry of Home Affairs instructed the deputy inspector to study the likely consequences of air raids in different municipalities.[44] It was already as clear as day that building open trench shelters was inadvisable, mainly because such trenches could be mistaken from the air for military targets; besides the risk of injury from shrapnel and bombs was high, and winter conditions made a stay in an open trench far from attractive. These observations put an end to uncertainty among local councils, although suitable substitute shelters were still unavailable.

The guidelines were accompanied by drawings of three types of covered (and camouflaged) trench shelters,[45] which could be constructed with steel as well as concrete reinforcement.[46] In November 1940, the deputy inspector issued the municipal governments with a drawing for a fourth type which had been designed in consultation with J.A. Ringers, the Commissioner-General for Reconstruction, and allowed for the prevailing shortages of materials.

Air raid defence activities by Dutch organizations went into a decline during the Nazi occupation at a local as well as at a national level. The air raid protection departments were subjected to tighter regulation by the occupiers,[47] and the alarm-raising system was placed entirely under German control. A side-effect of this was that the Air raid Protection Service was able to disclaim responsibility for any disruption of public life or of work in industries producing essential war goods.[48] The assignment of materials for building shelters fell under German control, and what is more, Dutch initiatives were generally rejected or adjusted to meet German requirements. The Law was admittedly upheld during the Occupation, but it was supplemented by countless orders promulgated by the highest civil authority, Reichskommissar Seyss-Inquart, which had the force of laws. A striking aspect of these orders issued in the period from 1941 to 1943 was the centralization of powers with much greater emphasis on the *Führerprinzip*, the "leader principle" embraced by the Third Reich. For example, the mayor no longer took charge of civic air raid defence, rather the local chief of police did.[49] The air raid protection departments were

150. A.F. Hens, drawing of Meulenkamp Shelter in Rochussenstraat during air raid alarm, Rotterdam, 13 October 1943

moreover obliged to make their staff more "German-friendly".[50] The total Germanization of the vocabulary is also striking.[51] The hardening of the legislation is not surprising, for the occupiers took over the entire organization of air raid protection in 1943 and quickly built a series of bunkers and other shelters to protect the families of their own civilians and officials and to enhance the security of companies working for the German war industry.

It became clear in 1943 how impotent the Dutch air raid protection organization had become when the Air Raid Protection Inspectorate once more advised the use of open trenches as an emergency measure, citing the "unfortunate neglect" that prevailed, even though these shelters failed to meet "reasonable requirements of safety".[52] It was yet another illustration of the occupying authority's indifference towards protecting Dutch civilians from airborne attacks; the return to prewar shelter types was sharply at odds with the increasingly powerful Allied bombs.

THE THIRD BOMBING OF ROTTERDAM

In the third major bombing of Rotterdam, the result of a navigation error by the American air force on 31 March 1943, 70 high-explosive bombs fell on the district of Tusschendijken and on a triangle between Marconiplein, Mathenesserlaan and Schiedamseweg. Police reports spoke of "unshowable" human remains. "The charred rump of a woman was dug up in the presence of her husband; sometimes no more than a shapeless mass was found, and pieces of limbs were retrieved in a bucket or tin. The powerful explosion had in some cases rammed the corpse three to four metres into the ground."[53] The death toll was 369 with 112 injured, and some 2,750 houses were destroyed.[54] German records report 97 tons of high explosives (158 bombs of 250 kilos and 1,150 bombs of 50 kilos) dropped on the machine hall of the Wilton Feyenoord shipyard in the failed American raid on 28 January 1942 (200 deaths and 400 wounded),[55] but by March 1943 the bombs were much heavier. This naturally had consequences for the safety of public air raid shelters. Of the seven shelters in the bombed zone in 1943, two were destroyed by direct hits, two partly collapsed and three remained standing. The whole length of tube shelter no. 132 (100 people) was devastated, and two of the five boys sheltering there were killed. Tube shelters 591 and 592 (for 60 and 120 users, respectively) both partly collapsed, but a schoolmistress with 20 pupils came out alive. A Meulenkamp shelter which had been modified to meet German standards, with two tubes at right angles, was totally destroyed, claiming 32 lives.[56]

The rescue operation following this severe air raid degenerated into total chaos. The work of the fire brigade, the medical services and the air raid wardens was impeded by ill-coordinated interference by German authorities and by German-paid Dutch auxiliaries. "The area turned into a sightseeing attraction. Cars blocked the roads, making passage of the Fire Brigade impossible. And pillaging was rife!"[57]

How well did the various troops of Rotterdam's Shelter City function during the Occupation? During the air raid of 14 May 1940, it was apparent that the Air Raid Protection Department, which had been headed by the deputy director of Muncipal Works since 1 April that year, was incapable of effective action in an emergency.[58] To start with, the organization lacked an effective command system. There was only a single reporting centre, which had just moved from the main police station to the ground floor of city hall. Then the air raid warning system, consisting of 27 small sirens on pillars erected by the police and 26 large sirens, proved inoperable when the air raid occurred.[59]

The fiasco of 14 May 1940 resulted in a non-existent Air Raid Protection De-

151. Clearing debris of bombed buildings following Allied bombing error, Rotterdam, 31 March 1943

partment for several months. There was no need for sirens immediately after the raid of May 1940 because there were no longer any private cellar shelters available in the city. Following several attacks by the RAF, the department was revived with German aid. This transitional period lasted until the summer of 1942 when the Germans were forced onto the defensive.[60] A central command post was established in October 1940 in the basement of the city hall, with fixed telephone links to the main businesses and services. One duty was immediately taken over by the Germans: pushing the button that activated the sirens. The air raid warning centre issued industrial alarms to German organizations and German-managed docks and factories, and civic alarms to all city dwellers.

The issue of sirens remained a source of conflict and confusion throughout the Occupation. The interests of employers, employees, police, industry, marshals and individual civilians conflicted, and these groups held different views on the dangers of air raids. In retrospect, it was fortunate that the Germans operated the central alarm system themselves because a continual stream of Allied formations overflew the Netherlands from 1942 onwards, and the sirens sometimes sounded for hours on end, sharply reducing productivity in businesses working for the German war industry.

After 1942, the Air Raid Protection Department was no longer as busy cop-

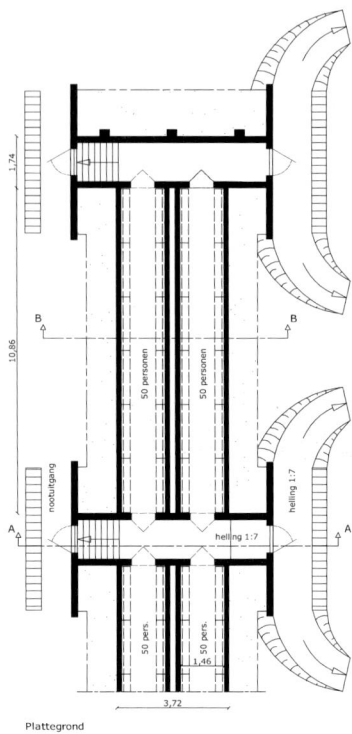

Plattegrond

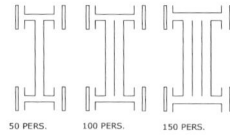

50 PERS.   100 PERS.   150 PERS.

Schema's
Schuilplaatsen

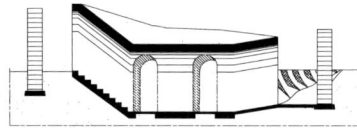

Doorsnede A-A

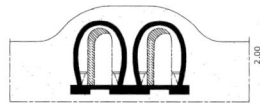

Doorsnede B-B

152. Shelters with capacity 50, 100 or 150 users, consisting of earth-covered oval tunnels assembled from tamped concrete modules, with blast walls at entrances

ing with Allied air raids as with mitigating the effects of German orders. The situation persisted until German air raid defence officials left the city in September 1944, thinking the war was lost. The Air Raid Protection Department had a permanent core of some 1,200 mobilized men, forming a Public Order Service.[61] These marshals were used to having a command hierarchy and were considered a reinforcement of the regular municipal services such as the police, the fire brigade, the ambulance service and the bomb damage clearance and reconstruction squads. The voluntary air raid warden corps that had been organized for each city block and neighbourhood before the war were retained. Considering the frequency of incidents such as air raids, plane crashes, anti-aircraft munition falling back onto the city and V1 rocket explosions, both the permanent air raid wardens and the volunteers had plenty of work on their hands.[62] The existing municipal services objected to the full-time wardens because there were so few trained professionals among them. The Public Order Service functioned largely as an ancillary arm of the police force, and was responsible for tasks such as blackout monitoring, guarding the shelters and cordoning off bomb impact sites. Friction thus arose "through the understandable preference of the official employees for their own specially trained people over the part-timers whom they saw more or less as factotums."[63] The technical arm of the Air Raid Protection Service (originally 148 men) consisted largely of building workers borrowed from a construction company. After the bombing, however, the section was filled increasingly with completely untrained individuals supplemented by staff from the municipal technical departments. This too led to resentment. From 1943, the technical service grew increasingly depleted due to the requisitioning of trained staff by the Wehrmacht.

The Air Raid Protection Service remained critical of the available shelters. The city had practically no real underground shelters, and the public shelters that existed gave little but trouble. "Nor were those few basements, most of which were voluntarily provided by the proprietors of houses and businesses, satisfactory. There was a continual hullabaloo about these basements; light fittings were stolen, then they had been used as a rendezvous, and then there would be an authoritarian squabble between zealous city block wardens and cellar owners."[64] The system of mainly above-ground shelters of the Meulenkamp type was not expanded during the Occupation; only malfunctions were repaired. The damp ground on which they were built was shielded by a floor of clinker bricks. "The concrete trench shelters built before the war should also be mentioned. (...) These shelters were subject to considerable tinkering. The water that accumulated in them was the greatest problem. A solution for this problem was not found until the trenches were roofed over and given a connection to the drains. Until then, you saw the rather sad sight of a couple of air raid wardens working day and night with a shovel, a broom and a small pump to keep the trenches in a usable condition."[65]

ARNHEM

Arnhem and Nijmegen, both close to the German frontier, were the cities where Shelter City was most heavily used. The inhabitants of Nijmegen stayed in their shelters for seven months in a row, and in Arnhem the threat of Allied air raids was so great that the entire civilian population was eventually evacuated.

The air raid defences of Arnhem were in a fairly dismal condition at the start of the war. Only a few open trenches were available.[66] Similarly, little progress had been made with the requisitioning of private shelters for public purposes. An important recommendation in the Guidelines of 1938 was for every municipality to inspect and register private basement shelters for public use, and before the war Arnhem had traced suitable cellars in five inner city streets with a total capacity for at most 575 people.[67] These still had to be officially requisitioned from their owners, and this indeed took place in July 1940. Compensation for the cellar owners was the subject of bitter dispute both during the Occupation and after the war. A fire brigade inspection in 1944 revealed that these shelters lacked illuminated signs and were hard to find at night.

The municipality of Arnhem had to house the invading Wehrmacht and was therefore obliged to provide them with barracks and military hospitals. Space was required for numerous German military staffs, administrative offices and workshops, and their personnel had to be quartered. Hundreds of buildings were confiscated for these purposes. This situation deteriorated after the bombings of the Ruhr. Goering, who was in charge of German anti-aircraft defence and air raid protection, planned to pillage the Netherlands and find homes in Dutch cities for 100,000 Germans who had been bombed out of their homes in Allied air raids. Arnhem was ordered to release houses – complete with furniture and fittings – for the homeless Germans. This process dragged on endlessly due to the delaying tactics of city officials. It took six months before a list of dwellings was ready (instead of the six weeks allotted) and even then it contained only half of the 300 homes demanded.

153. Arnhem Department of Public Works, earth-covered shelter for 50 users, modified version of Type IV with additional retaining wall

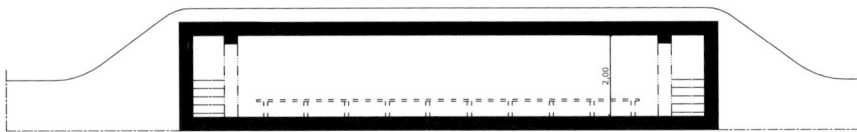

Doorsnede C-C

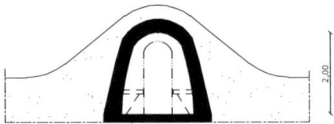

Doorsnede A-A

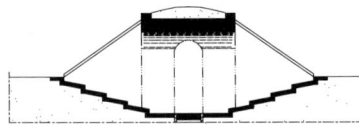

Doorsnede B-B

Aanzicht I
ingang

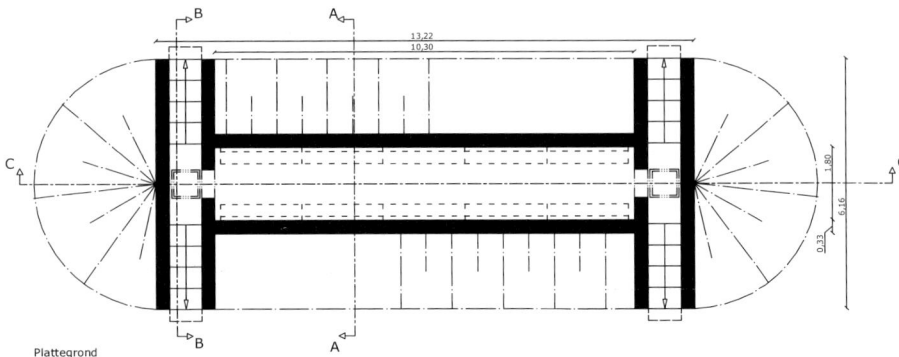

Plattegrond

The Germans meanwhile did their own requisitioning. Air raid protection of German citizens and officials, on the other hand, was treated with considerable urgency. A special situation arose in Arnhem, in the sense that the shelters conformed to Dutch models. The occupiers preferred to build shelters in schools that had been requisitioned for German pupils. However, the Arnhem Public Works Department designed variants of Dutch shelter types. Luftgaukommando Holland, the German office in command of occupied Dutch airspace, had the final say on the allocation of building materials. They insisted on changes to the Public Works designs for shelters on the Gasworks and Water Company sites, where Dutch personnel were employed.[68] These shelters were completed in June 1943.[69] It was clear by then that only shelters which the Germans considered important to their war effort would be built, and that the occupiers would have had no hesitation in requisitioning shelters built for the civilian population if it suited their purposes.

When Allied bombing of the Ruhr accelerated in 1943, the Germans took the initiative to build a series of more or less standardized shelters. Their plans to build shelters in schools were not realized until March 1944, when Seyss-Inquart intervened and put his Siedlung und Bauten Department (see Chapter 6) to work on the project. These shelters, designed at least partly by Public Works, took the form of tubular or trench shelters. One model was an improved version of the Type IV introduced in 1940, now with a German seal of approval, which was capable of rapid construction by untrained builders. It incorporated the latest instructions issued by Luftgaukommando Holland in August 1943 (see Chapter 6) which stipulated additional measures against phosphorus fumes.[70] The design was principally a long tube sealed at each end by a double wall. An entrance with steps was located between the walls at each end. There were versions with a single tube for 50 people, two parallel tubes for 100 and three parallel tubes for 150. These tubes could be linked together in many different ways. The tubes were oval in cross-section and built up from prefabricated units of tamped concrete.[71] The shape and technical detailing of these designs indicate that they benefited from experience with the fabrication and assembly of sewer pipes.

UTRECHT

The municipality of Utrecht built mainly open trenches in the period 1939-1940, until the State Inspectorate admitted in May 1940 that these shelters would be incapable of standing up to a serious air raid. The city conducted a catch-up exercise in

< *Page 202*

Bottom
155. Shelter for
Public Works
Department,
Utrecht, 1939

156. Bomb shelter,
Utrecht, 1945

1940-1943, building 20 public bomb shelters with the help of a credit of 200,000 guilders from the Inspectorate. The plan was to make it possible to accommodate four percent of the city's population in public shelters and to dispense with the prewar trenches.[72] In 1940, the city's Public Works Department designed a series of covered trench shelters of rectangular cross-section to the Type IV standard; four of them had a capacity of 150 people each, and one was a shelter for 600 users that could in future be converted into an underground car park. Designs for a further 15 locations followed in April 1941. In May 1942, the month when a building freeze was announced for the whole of the Netherlands, the Public Works Department reported to the mayor that 20 roofed, concrete-lined trench shelters were ready, and seven more were in preparation. Completion of the latter ground to a halt, but the city "massaged" the Luftgaukommando in Amsterdam to obtain exemption from the building freeze. In February 1943, no less than 11 new designs were put out to tender: half-underground types in brickwork, to be constructed with a parabolic cross-section to save material. The modification was also motivated by more stringent requirements for the entrances, which had to prevent the shock wave of an exploding bomb from propagating with full force through the shelter.[73] In other words, the same changes were implemented here as were imposed in Arnhem. By September 1943 they were largely finished. The fact that an exceptionally large number of shelters were completed after the building freeze came into force indicates that the Germans attached great importance to them. It is not improbable that, in the event of severe bombings such as those suffered by German cities from 1943 onwards, the occupiers intended to requisition them for the use of the local German civil authorities.

AMSTERDAM

The Air Raid Protection Service of Amsterdam (1938-1945) similarly had a far from easy time. As in most larger Dutch cities, the Germans allowed the service to continue its activities but as an arm of their own air defences. Anyone unwilling to cooperate faced the prospect of forced labour in Germany. Jews had already been prohibited from participation in all such "active emergency forces" as early as July 1940. The service, which was organized to draw on the personnel of the Public Works Department for clearance, demolition and repair tasks, functioned to the best of its abilities in the 25 air raids (358 dead, 714 wounded and 249 destroyed houses) and three planes crashing on the city (16 dead, 32 wounded and 25 destroyed houses).[74] On 13 August 1940, Allied firebombs fell on and around the Wilhelminagasthuis hospital, followed by nine night raids on the extensive grounds of the hospital (49 dead and 150 wounded). Probably that is why the Germans built no fewer than 22 bunkers there, with the Wilhelminagasthuis buildings serving as a military hospital.[75] Many of the attacks focussed on Amsterdam North where the Fokker aircraft works were located.[76]

157. Rooftop siren, Nieuwmarkt, Amsterdam

Page 205 >

Top
158. Nursery in an underground bomb shelter, Amsterdam

Bottom
159. State Inspectorate for Civil Air Raid Protection, design for brick-built shelter Type IV for 50 users (36 seated, 14 standing), 21 November 1940

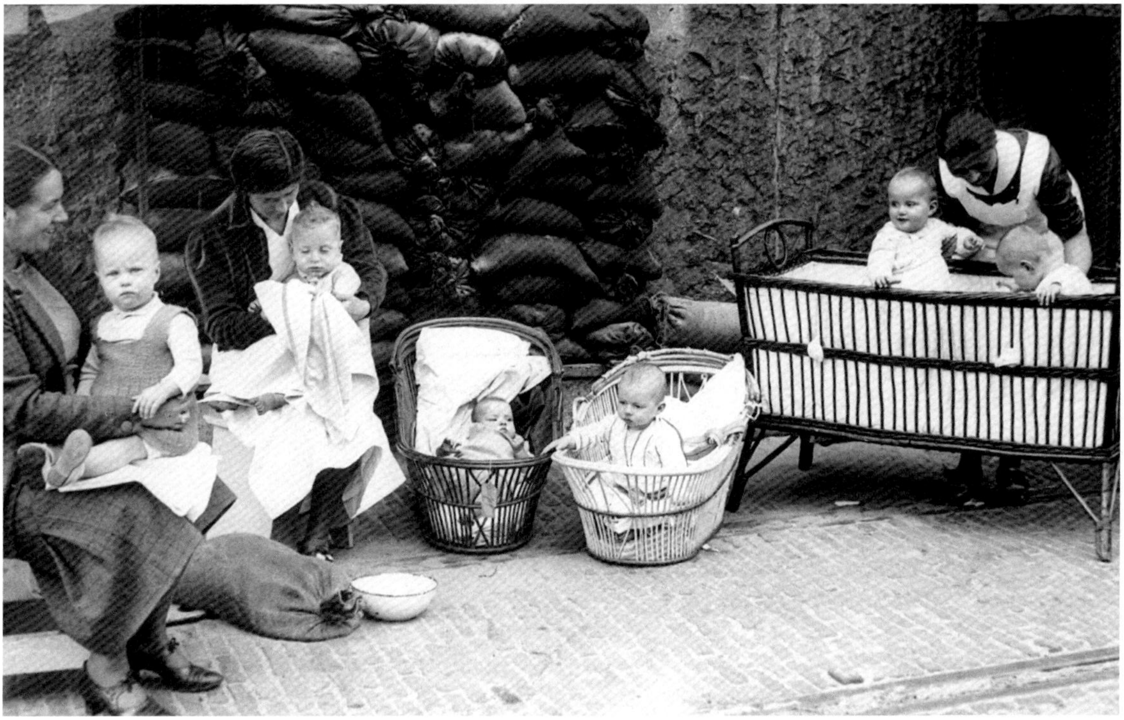

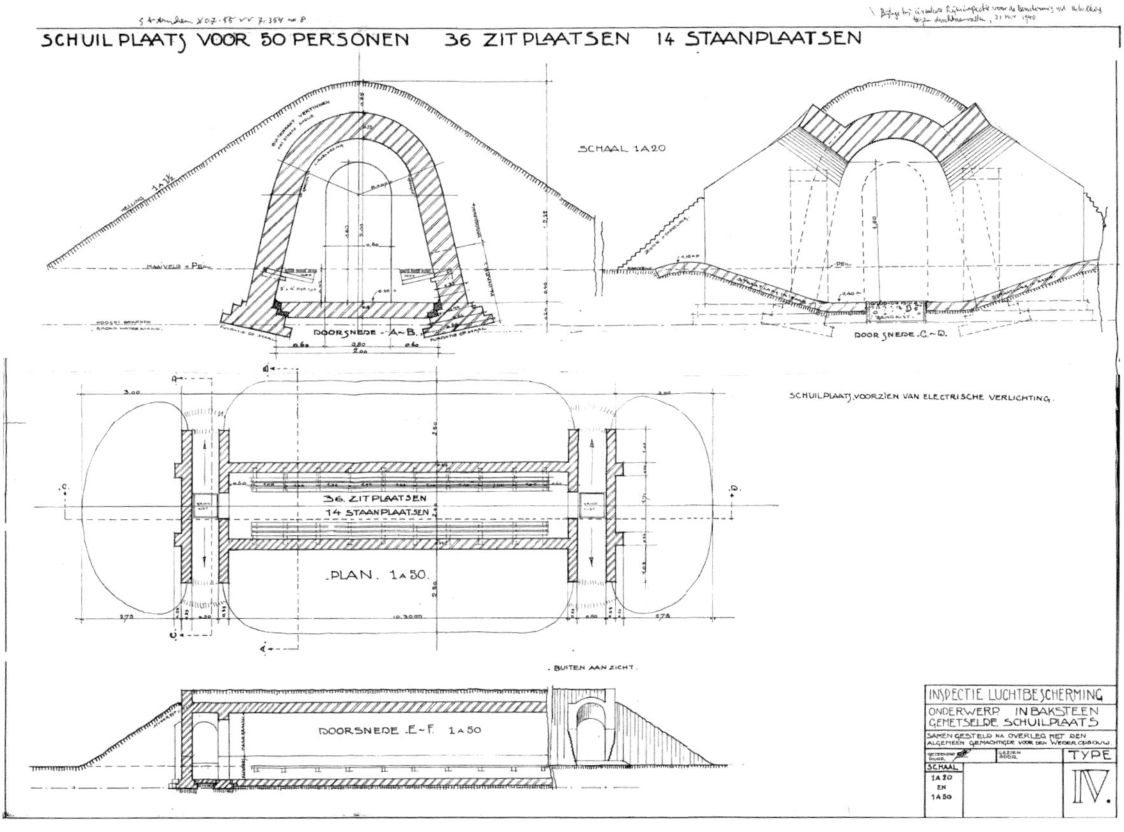

SCHUILPLAATS VOOR 50 PERSONEN   36 ZITPLAATSEN   14 STAANPLAATSEN

SCHAAL 1 A 20

DOORSNEDE · A - B ·

DOOR SNEDE · C - D ·

SCHUILPLAATS, VOORZIEN VAN ELECTRISCHE VERLICHTING.

36. ZITPLAATSEN
14 STAANPLAATSEN

· PLAN. 1 A 50 ·

· BUITEN AANZICHT ·

DOORSNEDE · E - F · 1 A 50

INSPECTIE LUCHTBESCHERMING
ONDERWERP IN BAKSTEEN
GEMETSELDE SCHUILPLAATS
SAMENGESTELD NA OVERLEG MET DEN
ALGEMEEN GEMACHTIGDE VOOR DEN WEDEROPBOUW
SCHAAL | TYPE
1 A 20
EN
1 A 50 | IV.

openbare schuilloopgraven van gewapend beton en staalplaten diverse typen

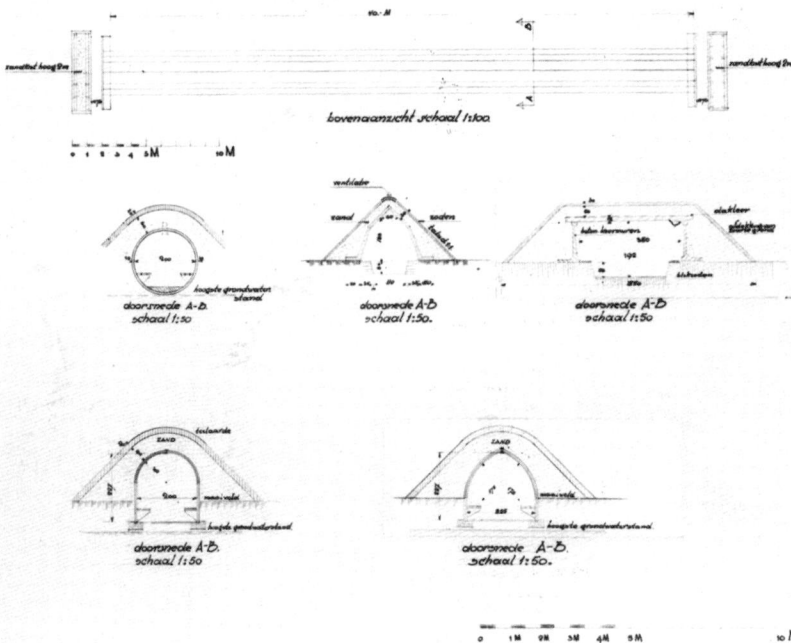

Top
160. Housing Department offices, Amsterdam, May 1940

161. Public Works Department, various shelter designs in concrete/steel, as designed and built in Amsterdam during the German Occupation

There is recurrent evidence of the unpopularity of the wardens of the Air Raid Protection Department in Amsterdam. A revealing incident occurred when an RAF plane fell on the Alphonsoschool in Westzaanstraat. "Owing to all the rushing and panic, hardly a shred of the initial rescue effort had any effect, and the block marshals and their staff found themselves in a jam. It wasn't until after a great deal of pushing and ordering people about that the air raid marshals found time to concentrate on first aid. The occupiers had given special orders about what to do about a crashed plane, and the general public weren't allowed to come near or to help. So the marshals started bashing at people, doubling the chaos. The same fate awaited the rescue squads, who only had armbands and were hard to tell from the ordinary public who rushed to help. If anything they were treated even more harshly, probably out pique at the mutual antipathy. Having got over the initial shock, hundreds of bystanders showed what they were made of and threw themselves en masse into the battle, in which quite a few telling blows fell, and the whole vocabulary of Amsterdam names were called."[77]

The activity of the Public Works Department declined sharply from 1942 onwards. Demolition of the wood-lined trench shelters, which had already been vandalized by members of the public in search of firewood, demanded attention. Civilian shelters also continued to be designed and built in the period between the

162. Public Works Department, design for shelter under canal bridge, Amsterdam

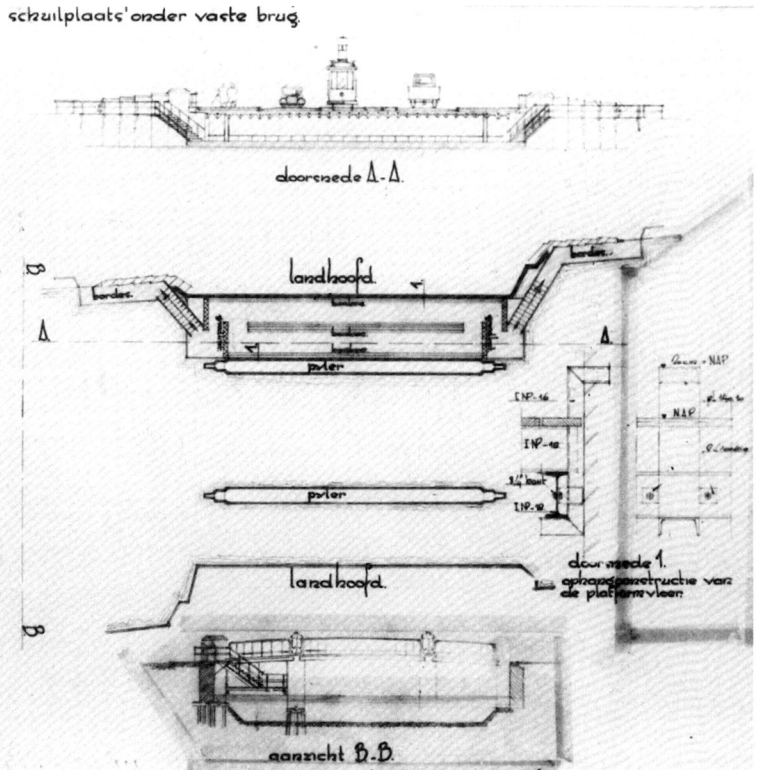

163. Public Works Department, entrance to shelter under canal bridge, Amsterdam

Page 209 >
165. Public Works Department, shelter on Waterlooplein, Amsterdam

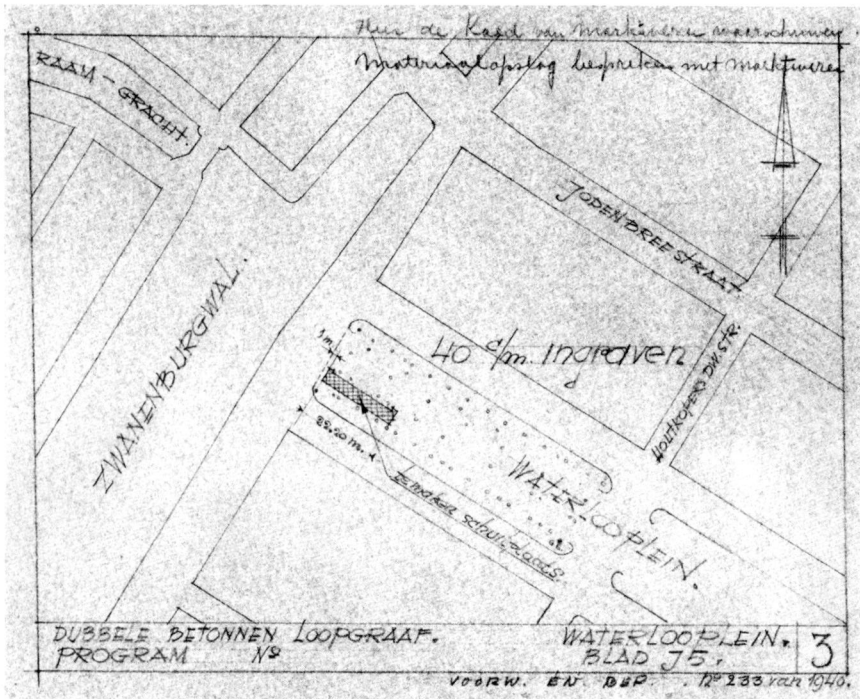

164. Public Works Department, location of double concrete trench shelter, Waterlooplein, Amsterdam

building freeze of 1942 and autumn of 1944 on orders of the occupiers, who were chiefly concerned about protecting "personnel involved in factory or other work" for their needs.[78] Most of the shelters were variations on a standard type: single or double parabolic tube shelters made of brickwork covered in tamped concrete and with entrances at the ends.[79] Requisitioning by the Wehrmacht also occurred. They commandeered eight of Amsterdam's twelve bathhouses in 1 April 1943 to adapt as decontamination facilities for use in the event of mustard gas attacks.[80]

NIJMEGEN

The Netherlands was not safe from the Allied bombing errors which occurred during their campaigns to incapacitate German aircraft manufacturing.[81] Enschede, Arnhem and Nijmegen are the best known instances. The damage caused by 80 high-explosive bombs dropped on Arnhem on 22 February 1944 could have been worse, for they landed on the suburbs of Rijnwijk and Arnhem-South and on a strip along the south bank of the Rhine (total casualties about 60).[82] The bombing of Nijmegen with 144 high-explosive, 500-pound bombs and 426 fragmentation bombs, on the other hand, was a disaster of proportions that approached the Blitz of Rotterdam.[83] The Air Raid Protection Service was on continual lookout from its post on the St. Stevenskerk, and the sirens in the warning centre in the city hall basement had already sounded that morning, but an all-clear was issued around 1 pm. Just as crowds of people emerged into the streets, a formation of Allied bombers arrived returning from Germany. Even while the sirens were sounding once more at 13:28 hrs, the first high-explosive bombs came whistling through the air. Most of the fragmentation bombs fell on the railway station forecourt. An eyewitness described their horrendous effect: "A bucket of human remains, with one arm sticking out, stood next to the station. I will never forget the sight of that immaculately manicured hand with a bracelet around the wrist."[84]

Scarcely anyone had time to reach the shelters, and most of the victims were in the open streets. Still, there were some people trapped in their cellars by the collapsing and burning houses. The Deputy Mayor, Mr. Hondius, wrote, "In the space of a few seconds, the city was transformed into pitch-black pillars of explosive fumes, smoke, dust and flying debris of wood and brick, rising to hundreds of metres in the air. All the churches I could previously see from the roof of my house had vanished from view."[85] The fire alarm centre in the police station was disabled by a bomb, and the water mains were destroyed in several places. A first aid post was quickly set up on the top floor of the Twentsche Bank, and it received a constant stream of injured victims, "often horribly mutilated, convulsing, wrestling with death. Clergymen ministered to the dying, and doctors gave injections to lessen their pain, but the number of casualties was so great that there was insufficient assistance to go round. Now and then ambulances rushed back and forth to carry victims to the hospitals."[86] Doctors and nurses worked long hours; some 87 arms and legs had to be amputated in the first few days.[87] The malfunctioning water mains hindered firefighting, and the many collapsing buildings prevented the firemen from reaching the seats of fire. The Air Raid Protection Service played a key role in clearing obstructions, repairing gas and water mains, digging out buried casualties and transporting the dead and injured. The personnel of Shelter City performed their grim duties: "Immediately after the bombing, my father, a member of the Civil Defence or an air raid warden, had to go to the city to help with the rescue and clearing up work. He dug out dozens of victims. The horrific task of juggling with all the detached heads, bodies and limbs to match them up for identification put him seriously off his balance."[88] As another survivor wrote, "Then I picked up four cast iron cooking pans from the street to put the body parts in."[89]

Some prominent buildings in the city centre were destroyed. Individual fires joined into a conflagration, making the recovery work and the rescuing of buried or

166. Grote Markt following accidental Allied bombing, Nijmegen, 1944

167. Boy in search of family following accidental Allied bombing, Nijmegen, 1944

Left
168. Shelter in front of
railway station following
bombing of Nijmegen,
1944

Page 213 >
169. Shelter in Canisius
College, Nijmegen, 1944–
1945

trapped citizens exceptionally difficult. "In Lange Burchstraat, a direct hit smashed up the lovely, big building of the Haspels fashion store. Most of the women who worked there were killed and were buried under the rubble. Diagonally behind the store, the infant school of the Sisters of St. Louis was hit, and many of the children and the sisters were killed by the explosion or by the fire that ensued. Hotel Metropole stood in flames from top to bottom. On Groote Markt, the proud department store buildings of Vroom en Dreesmann and the Hema were smashed apart by direct hits, and a hellish blaze raged there. Everything behind was a scene of destruction and devastation. The fire had free play, greedily devouring all around it, and the flames soared high out of the Augustijnenkerk and the Franciscuskerk, flapping fantastically around the church towers and leaping from one of the old commercial premises to the next."[90] The monumental tower of the St Stevenskerk was cut in half. The Augustijnenkerk had lost its spire and only one of its four corner towers was left standing.

The vicinity of Grote Markt took the heaviest punishment. The whole south side of the great market square burned. "Close to the market, V&D stood in flames. The heavy stone pilasters between the windows bulged outwards. Then the gables began to tilt, and the walls buckled with a thundering noise. The whole building collapsed. The fierce heat washed across the market square, forcing everyone back. A huge column of smoke and dust rose to the sky."[91] Eventually the firefighters succeeded in containing the conflagration in the greater part of the inner city. "In the ruddy glow of burning blocks of houses, the bitter ruin of the St. Stevens Tower,

which had once so impressively dominated the cityscape, stuck up like an unspeakably sad lamentation."[92] After two days of firefighting, it was possible to draw up the balance: 1,270 properties destroyed or damaged beyond repair, 771 fatalities and 130 people missing.[93] The dead were laid out in the buildings of the Nijmegen auction company. These halls of death also contained the unrecognizably mutilated remains of those, mostly charred in the flames, who might conceivably be identified from scraps of clothing or possessions. All these victims were buried in a mass grave at the Public Cemetery on Saturday 26 February.

The air raid alarms no longer functioned in Nijmegen after the tragedy of 22 February 1943. From the city's liberation in September 1944 until February 1945, the German artillery bombarded the Allied positions with a high frequency.[94] In December 1944, for example, the city suffered an unbroken 68 hours of artillery fire. The German shelling of the city, in addition to the bombardment, robbed countless civilians of their homes, forcing them to evacuate the city or to seek shelter in private cellars or in the basement shelters of banks, monasteries, factories, the Canisius College, the round bastion in the Kronenburgpark, Huize Bethlehem or the underground shelter of the power station on Waalkade.[95] Other locations included the Dominicus College in Neerbosch, which at one point housed hundreds of citizens, and the basement of the Robinson factory.

Whereas the local ss-Obersturmführer drove the 95,000 civilian inhabitants of Arnhem out of that city to seek places to stay in the Veluwe hills, Nijmegen, un-

170. Shelter in electricity generating plant, Nijmegen, 1944–1945

< Page 214
171. Shelter in Canisius College, Nijmegen, 1944–1945

der Allied command from September 1944 to Easter 1945, possessed over 20 underground bomb shelters, each with room for 400 to 500 users.[96] The number of refugees might change from day to day, as buildings with cellar shelters were commandeered for military purposes. The suitcases were already packed.

On 25 September 1944, a Refugee Commission went into action. Besides providing shelter accommodation to the homeless, it had the task of allocating the scarce shelter capacity over the thousands of people. The Union of Women Volunteers played an important part in this form of aid. "The historic city had many deep, solidly built cellars which were excellent for the purpose. In the suburbs, the basements of large buildings were used for that purpose, while in safer places schools and factories were chosen for accommodation. The shortage of capacity persisted, however, so that even coal cellars were adapted as shelters, and for a period several dozen people slept nightly in the hollow piers of a bridge."[97] The bunkers of the Grüne Polizei behind the Oud Burgeren Gasthuis Hospital, which the occupiers abandoned on 17 September 1944, gave shelter to some 1200 people, although they were obliged to leave two weeks later to make room for a temporary hospital due to the clearance of one floor of the Canisius Hospital for the benefit of wounded Allied troops.[98] In the Canisius College (in German hands from 5 June 1942 to 17 September 1944), the monks furnished 20 cellars to accommodate 500 refugees. The college not only had a first aid post but programmes of cultural activities.

Some people did not emerge from the shelters for months at a time.[99] Shells were the most widely feared projectiles. "The nights were very restless. The little

172. Private shelter, Nijmegen, 1944–1945

173. Shelter in wine cellar, Nijmegen, 1944–1945

ones were a continual nuisance, and the adults made all kinds of noise in their sleep, either snoring or nose blowing. The shells are the worst of all. Tonnie, who went home at 5 o'clock because she was feeling unwell, just came back and told us that the shells were whining through the air. She could hear the bangs too, but these shells were coming in our direction. Where on earth can we be safe nowadays? Oh, what a racket! You can really feel it here in the factory. How can we stand up to another day? Maybe I'll start with a morning prayer. Half an hour later: we all said our morning prayers together, because everyone is afraid. Then Cis and Hanna Holla came in with sleepy, anxious faces. They told us that fire had broken out across the street from them (Van Welderenstraat) so they decided to come back to the shelter which has so far proved safe. It was a hell again just now. We had hardly ate our breakfast, when the explosions started. I only just had time to get across. It's so full here!!! Terrible! That alone is enough to make you afraid."[100]

For months at a time, the civilians turned into cave dwellers in the evenings and at night. They were not even safe in their shelters, because German planes kept dropping high-explosive bombs. A direct hit on the kapok factory, for example, killed dozens of men, woman and children who were sheltering in the basement.[101] "People were hard at work clearing up the remains. It must have been a terrible death for those people. There were many large families. We read funeral notices in the papers for a household of twenty people, grandparents, a son and daughter in law, a married daughter and the mother with fourteen children from toddlers to grown ups."[102] Space was running out in the cemeteries.[103]

Each shelter had an appointed warden, who drew up a daily report for the Commission. It provided details, such as disinfection and insect extermination, relating to the medical, sanitary and mental welfare of the some 10,000 civilians who resided in about 80 underground shelters. The shelters that belonged to Catholic institutions gave rise to a special underground lifestyle in which the priests contributed to psychological as well as spiritual welfare. A newspaper for shelter users, the *Bunkercourant*, was even issued.[104] Entertainment was also provided. A cultural organization called *De Stuw* organized events such as choral and poetry recitals, concerts, films and lectures. The Canisius College had a weekly film show, Sinterklaas knocked on the door on 5th December in accordance with Dutch tradition, and a Christmas play was on the programme. The same happened in the Bonaventura Cloister, where over a hundred local residents sheltered for several months starting in September 1944. Evenings of varied entertainment were held, education was provided to 45 children, and a child was born on 30 December.[105]

The Dutch bomb shelters in frontline cities like Arnhem and Nijmegen, espe-

174. Shelter in tunnels of old fortification Maastricht, September 1942

cially the private shelters, also had a role to play immediately after the Liberation, and in some cases German bunkers were reused. What remained of the convents, schools, youth clubs and other Catholic institutions fell, according to the laws of war, into Allied hands. "And one will understand that soldiers do not treat furniture and school equipment with the same fearful caution that the Sisters and teaching staff are accustomed to employ."[106] Nijmegen's history of refugee problems was not yet at an end after the German capitulation. Dutch nationals returning home, famished refugees from the western part of the country, Poles, Lithuanians, Czecheslovakians, Russians and Roma all had to be scrubbed, fed and housed.

COMPARISON

The Dutch air raid defensive measures during the Occupation did not differ essentially from those taken in the UK or Germany. The circumstances which determined its functioning were wholly different, however. The occupiers of the Netherlands involved themselves in the organization, staffing and regulation of air raid protection at both national and municipal levels, and annexed significant components of it, such as operating the air raid alarm system as well as tightening up the legislation and its local implementation.

Practically no new shelters were built for Dutch civilians, apart from those locations and building complexes that were considered essential to the German war industry. Shortages of building materials from 1943 onwards moreover forced people to resort to variants of trench and tube shelters, which gave protection at most against collapsing masonry and flying shrapnel.

The character of the bombings differed as well. Whether it was the Germans or the Allies who dropped the bombs, the air raids on Dutch cities seemed to lack any logic or predictability, making it hard to use the available shelters to good advantage. Long residence in the shelters such as was common in England and Germany was not a widespread phenomenon in the Netherlands, except when Arnhem and Nijmegen were under fire in 1944.

175. Shelter in tunnels of historic fortifications, September 1942

CHAPTER 6

Seyss-Inquart as a Patron of Architecture I

The Architecture of Communications

UNDERGROUND ART

The gigantic air raid defence operation in Germany (see Chapter 3) also left its mark on the Netherlands. At first, this outcome seemed unlikely. While the urban air raid protection services were soon organized more or less along German lines, the Dutch defence agencies were left to carry out their limited duties almost undisturbed until 1942. That was consistent with the general programme of rebuilding bombed or otherwise damaged cities and villages, which was supervised by the assiduous Dutch Commissioner-General for Reconstruction, Dr. J.A. Ringers.[1]

This picture changed dramatically in the summer of 1942. Allied air raids were stepped up, forcing the occupier to take measures to protect German nationals holding civilian posts and the staff of Dutch firms considered essential to the war effort. The Germans announced a building freeze, bringing reconstruction to a halt. From then on the building industry was entirely at the disposal of the occupying civil and military authorities, who concentrated exclusively on projects related to waging war. This marked the start of not only the systematic pillaging of the Netherlands but also the destruction of many city areas and villages to make room for military reinforcements. The building of the Atlantic Wall along the North Sea coast was the largest of these operations. The area around The Hague was particularly well fortified. Besides the military base at Scheveningen, there was a base at the unlikely lo-

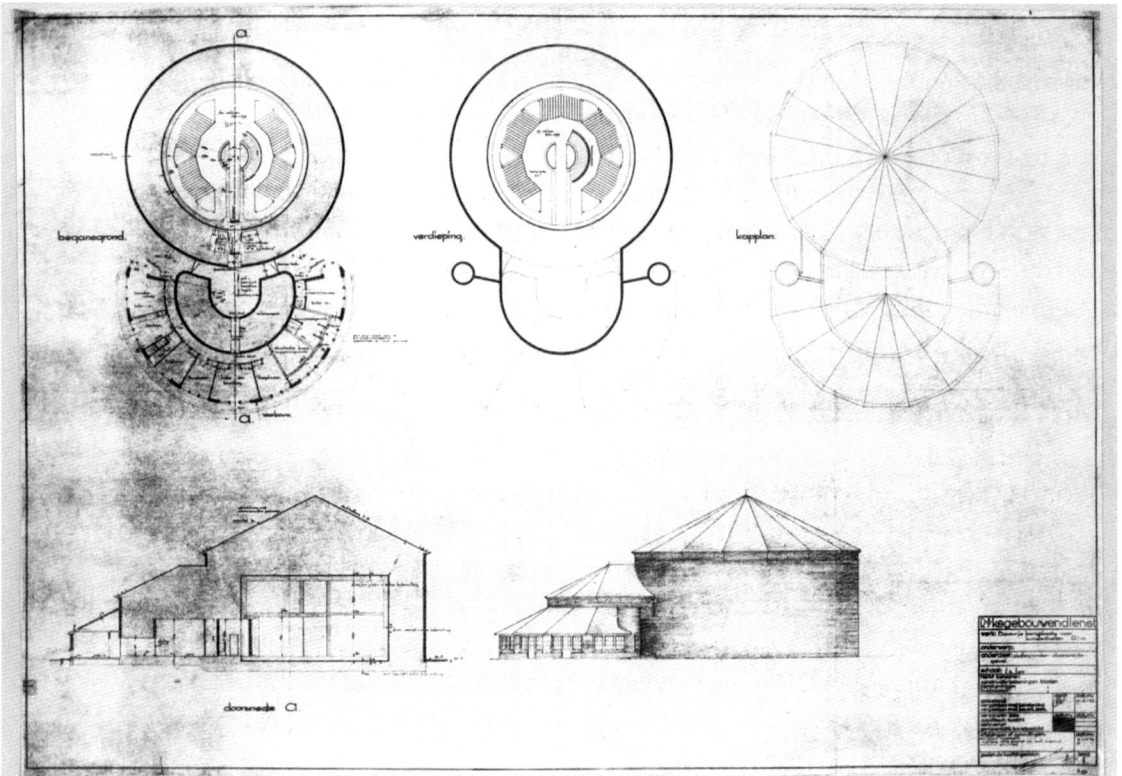

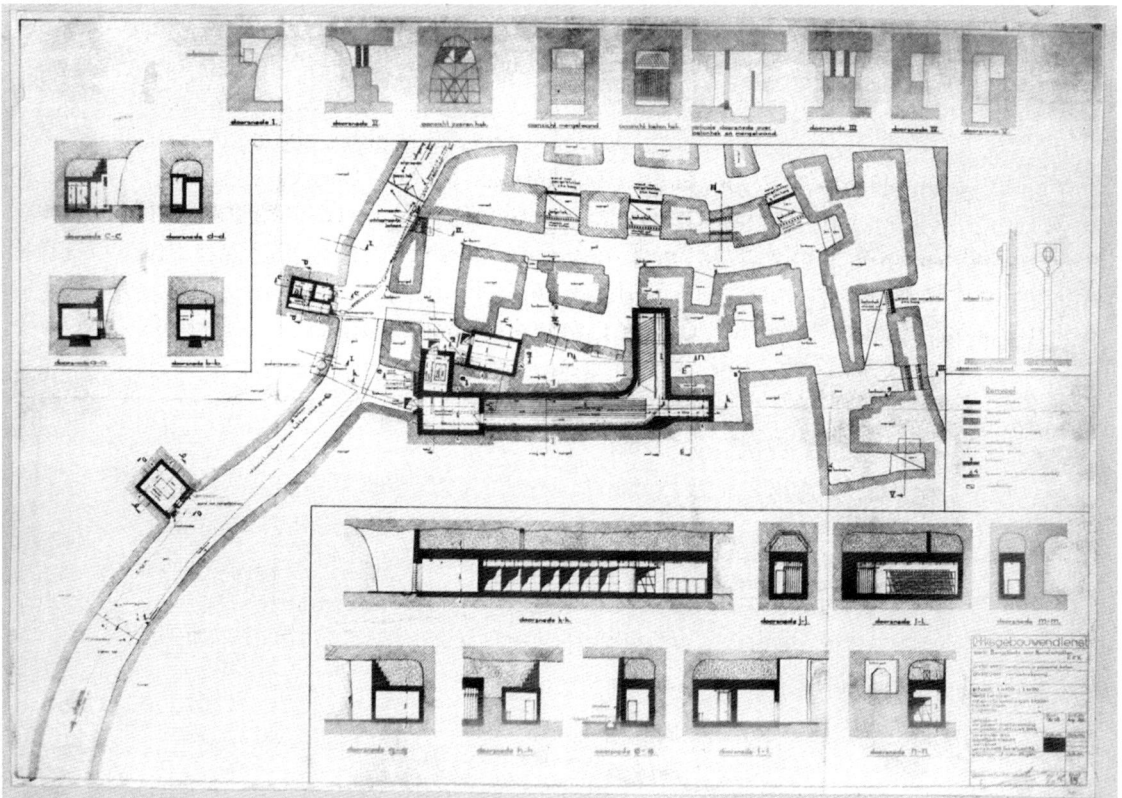

cation of Clingendaal (on the border between The Hague and Wassenaar), the home of Reichskommissar Seyss-Inquart. The resulting interventions had disastrous consequences for Scheveningen and The Hague.

The first sign of this change of direction were the steps taken to protect works of art and historic artefacts against air raids. At first sight it is hard to understand why the German authorities took so much trouble to arrange the underground storage of Dutch works of art.[2] Shortly before the German invasion in 1940, the Dutch had already built art storerooms in bombproof shelters in the coastal sand dunes[3] and in a reinforced cellar in the Mauritshuis in The Hague. An underground vault was also installed in June that year in the Kröller-Müller museum.[4] When building the Atlantic Wall two years later, the Germans requisitioned the dune depositories as ammunition dumps. Alternative storage facilities had to be found for the art.

In the spring of 1942, the Government Buildings Agency created new bombproof vaults 35 metres underground on Sint Pietersberg, a hill outside Maastricht, and built an above-ground bunker in Paaslo, in the province of Drenthe, which was completed between May and September 1942. Most of the nation's masterpieces were stored at Sint Pietersberg. The art works from the dunes and the collections of various museums and archives[5] (a total of about 3,000 art works and other items) were transferred to the Paaslo bunker.

Allowing the Dutch Government Buildings Agency to build the most impregnable bunker in the whole of the occupied Netherlands in rural Paaslo was more than just generosity on the part of the Germans, in compensation for the bunkers in the dunes. It also made up for the impact of the defences the Germans planned to build along a wide strip of coastal country, which they had known about since the end of 1941. The Paaslo Pantheon, as the new bunker became known, is cylindrical with a conical roof and is 19 metres tall. Its walls are four metres thick and the roof nine metres thick, while the interior measures fifteen metres in diameter. The entrance to the actual bunker has 17-cm-thick vault doors, is further shielded by a semicircular forecourt surrounded by four-metre-thick reinforced concrete walls. To make this monolith look reasonably presentable, it was finished with clinkers

< Page 222

Top
176. Government Buildings Agency, design for bombproof art vault, Paaslo, 17 April 1942

Bottom
177. Government Buildings Agency, design for art vault in chalk tunnels under Sint Pietersberg, Maastricht, August 1942

178. Investiture of Reichskommissar Arthur Seyss-Inquart (middle) in the Knights Hall, The Hague, 29 May 1940

and given an iconographic touch – the exterior suggested associations with an early Christian chapel. One might wonder of course whether the intended symbolism was a glorified depository – or perhaps a sarcophagus – for the spiritual peaks of Dutch art. On entering the site the first thing to strike the eye is a large majolica tableau representing the Dutch coat of arms and the national motto *Je maintiendrai*. Next to the left-hand entrance door, the following Latin text appears in alphabetic bricks: "In the Year of our Lord 1942 the Batavian people ordered this extremely strong shelter to be built, in order to protect, with the help of God, the exquisite artistic monuments of the Nation from the considerable perils of war."[6] At an extremely isolated location like this, the museum authorities could allow themselves a patriotic gesture.

The Paaslo Pantheon was the strongest shelter that the occupier would countenance in the Netherlands, surpassing anything they built themselves after 1942. The Germans who came to inspect the complex shrugged off the patriotic bravura and paid more attention to the structural qualities of the experimental bunker than to the art treasures. While the Germans had no wish to be portrayed as Philistines, one must wonder what hidden agenda the structure was meant to serve. It is obvious that a bunker with walls and roof as thick as those of the new armoured U-boat pens could not have been intended solely for sheltering Dutch art.

THE GERMAN CIVIL ADMINISTRATION

The German air raid defence projects in the Netherlands differed in character from analogous projects in Germany and were completed at a later date. The shelters that were built from 1942 onwards were meant almost exclusively for the protection of German citizens. The occupying civil authorities were highly centralized and enjoyed a measure of autonomy from the military engineering corps *Organisation Todt* in Berlin and the *Luftgaukommando* (Airspace Command) in Amsterdam. This is evident from the fact that the civilian air raid defences in the Netherlands were directed *de facto* by Seyss-Inquart and his *Abteilung Siedlung und Bauten*. Dr. Arthur Seyss-Inquart (1891-1946), an Austrian from Moravia, was appointed *Reichskommissar* (Reichs Commissioner) of the occupied Netherlands territories on 29 May 1940.[7] The civil administration was reorganized to allow him to act as the governor of a colony. He had the royally appointed Dutch governors of the provinces replaced by his own *Beauftragte* or deputies. In The Hague, the seat of government, he headed a number of *General-Kommissare* (General Commissioners) who oversaw the Dutch-run government departments. The "state secretaries" or junior ministers had stayed behind to keep an eye on things after the Dutch Queen and her ministers fled the country. While Dutch officials continued to govern at a departmental level, in the background Seyss-Inquart and his staff exerted more and more tacit leverage on their decisions. Moreover, the *Reichskommissar* pursued his own policy in response to the changing military situation and the gradual descent into total war. He and

179. Festive opening of Deutsches Theater in den Niederlanden with Mozart's Don Giovanni, in Koninklijke Schouwburg in The Hague. R. to L. in front row: Seyss-Inquart, his wife, Goebbels and General Reinhardt, 19 November 1942

180. Seyss-Inquart's political headquarters (right), Plein 23, The Hague, photo 1983

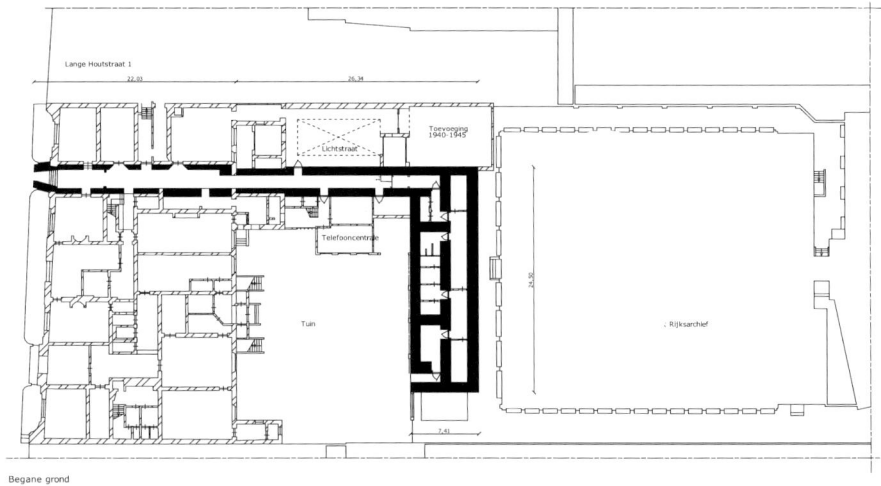

181. Bunker in Seyss-Inquart´s headquarters, 1943-1944. In black the new entrance and reinforced corridor leading to the shelter in the garden

his fellow civilian administrators were obliged to steer a course between staying on good terms with the ss leader Heinrich Himmler (and his police chief in the Netherlands H.A. Rauter),[8] and curbing the influence of the militant ss who had the potential to sideline his administrative machinery. This was no imaginary danger, for Himmler had already downgraded the "General Governor" of the conquered Polish territories to a puppet while actually holding the reins of power himself.

The appointment of Seyss-Inquart and his chief advisors, the General Commissioners Dr. Dr. F. Wimmer,[9] Dr. H. Fischböck and H.A. Rauter, to form a civilian tier over the Dutch State Secretaries was a recipe for complicated decision-making, even though Seyss-Inquart had the last word, and his decrees had the force of law.[10] The blow to the Dutch economy that ensued from May 1940 was amply compensated for by the flow of orders for goods from Germany, thereby setting in train the greater integration of the German and Dutch economies that Seyss-Inquart so enthusiastically espoused.[11] The occupier left the realization of this development largely to Dutch administrators, politicians and businessmen.

In 1942, when the building freeze was announced, two German bodies took over the reins of the construction industry: the *Abteilung Bauwirtschaft*, or Building Industry Department, under Fischböck, and the *Abteilung Siedlung und Bauten*, or Housing and Construction Department, which was Seyss-Inquart's own domain. Between them they directed the German air raid defence projects in the Netherlands.

ABTEILUNG BAUWIRTSCHAFT

In the summer of 1940, Fritz Todt, Germany's *Generalbevollmächtigter für die Regelung der Bauwirtschaft* (Plenipotentiary for the Organization of the Building Industry, succeeded on his death in 1942 by Albert Speer), appointed R. Werckshagen to represent him in the Netherlands, Belgium and Northern France. Werckshagen was empowered to "advise and monitor" the Dutch building industry and, when necessary, to employ Dutch building contractors and their equipment for the German war effort. As early as 7 August 1940, he instructed the Dutch Commissioner-General for Reconstruction, J.A. Ringers, to provide a monthly overview of construction projects, including both those planned and those in progress. The survey was to state the workforce and machinery required, the construction materials (cement, iron, wood and brick), and the total building costs and estimated construction time. This information would enable Werckshagen to apply to Berlin for building materials; the amounts always proved less than he had asked for, but he could distribute the quantities assigned as he saw fit, "so that it was possible in case of a shortage of construction materials in the Netherlands or Belgium to solve the problem with compensatory deliveries".[12] These were the first major experiments with a systematic quota system for construction materials. In June 1941 the hardly enthusiastic Werckshagen, who had his offices in The Hague, agreed with Ringers a method of prioritizing and assessing the urgency and status of requests for building permits. Werckshagen worked out the capacity of machinery and other equipment presently unutilized in the building industry and in road and waterway engineering, with a view to mobilizing it for housing projects, infrastructural works in Germany, new U-boat pens along the Atlantic coast and other *Organisation Todt* projects.

Werckshagen's activities changed in the summer of 1942, when a total building ban was imposed on the Netherlands, and the Dutch were deprived of almost all say in the construction industry.[13] In a letter from 30 October 1942, Albert Speer, who had just succeeded Todt, ordered the building industries of Belgium, France and the Netherlands to be coordinated as a single entity.[14] The deployment of Dutch materials and manpower took on a grimmer aspect. While at first these had been applied to constructive tasks such as new housing, roads and land reclamation, henceforth defence projects and war damage recovery took absolute priority. Battalions of Dutch building workers were formed, ready for immediate deployment in any bombed German city.

With total war as justification, Werckshagen effectively had free rein to plunder the Netherlands and requisition all available materials, building contractors and manpower for the war effort. His office was brought into line with the German model, with separate departments for the construction industry, the armaments industry (which in this case remained unmanned), building materials and transport. He no longer had to answer to Seyss-Inquart, and his remit now included any defensive works or other plans deemed essential for the war effort in the Netherlands. Speer later specified these projects in detail in a *Wehrkreisrangfolgeliste* (military priority list); in effect new building permits would only be granted to plans serving German interests.[15] He intervened in an increasingly proactive fashion in the distribution and transport of construction materials, and decided personally about exemptions from the construction ban and instructed his staff to verify the urgency and use of materials in construction plans.[16] Werckshagen became so absorbed in the building of the Atlantic Wall in France and Belgium in 1943 that he moved his offices to Belgium. His department in the Netherlands merged with the *Abteilung Siedlung und Bauten* in 1944 to form the *Abteilung Bauwesen* (Construction Industry Department). That was only logical since Seyss-Inquart's *Abteilung Siedlung und Bauten* had been arrogating ever more tasks to itself.

ABTEILUNG SIEDLUNG UND BAUTEN

The most important German body concerned with air raid defence in the Netherlands was the *Abteilung Siedlung und Bauten*. Walter Münster, a civil engineer from Sudetenland and director of an Austrian housing corporation, took charge of the new department on 1 January 1941. He can hardly have imagined the turn his career was now about to take. In The Hague, his post was in the tightly organized command centre of the civilian German administration with Seyss-Inquart as its chief building patron. Münster found himself directly answerable to the highest civil official in the Netherlands.

On arrival in The Hague, Münster was nearly 40 years old. He was accompanied by his 39-year-old fiancée Maria Zerbs, whom he married around Easter 1941. The letters of congratulation he received from former comrades in Austria expressed the wish that he would find a home for his family which "despite the disturbance from aeroplanes" would compensate for all the pressures of his job.[17] Initially, Münster's work mainly revolved around the prestige project of accommodating the Hague "court" of Seyss-Inquart and his three General Commissioners. But instead of enjoying a relatively unflurried career as an architect in occupied territory, Münster and his wife were soon caught up in the frenzy of protecting Seyss-Inquart and his aides from allied attacks. The change in his responsibilities and the atmosphere of his work, effectively a shift from prestige architecture to the pragmatic civil engineering demands of Shelter City, is poignantly illustrated by his first transaction after the birth of his son on 12 April 1942: an order for a child's gas mask.[18]

Siedlung und Bauten functioned entirely autonomously until halfway through 1942 and had next to nothing to do with the German military machine. The purpose of the department was to implement prestigious German civilian projects – for example providing premises for the German police officials and for the Waffen SS, which maintained a force of 20,000 men in the Netherlands until 1944. This semi-military body normally set up quarters in existing large buildings, adapting and expanding them, always taking into account special German needs with regard to domestic comfort and amusement, but new buildings were occasionally designed when something more imposing was required.[19] The estate of Clingendaal, the residence of Seyss-Inquart and his wife, underwent various alterations in 1940. For security reasons, the entire balcony on the front facade was demolished. The sanitary facilities were improved and enlarged. Seyss-Inquart's wife came up with the idea of building two film projectors into a wall of the room opening onto the conservatory. The entrance drive to the country house was widened, and a stable and a tennis court were built. The conservatory to the right of the house was converted into a hall for banquets and concerts. The house was intended to be an elegant venue for the top echelon of German cultural life. It was here that Seyss-Inquart received the leading lights of the Third Reich – men such as Himmler and Goering – and regaled them with entertainments. German, Austrian and Dutch soloists performed in the

Top
182. Entrance
to Clingendaal
country estate, with
guardroom on left,
photo 1946

183. Front entrance
facade of Clingendaal
house following
restoration in 1970s

184. Walter Münster, head of Abteilung Siedlung und Bauten, caricatured by his staff in an anniversary book, ca. 1942

conservatory, and sober banquets were served. Film footage of a tennis match between Seyss-Inquart and Himmler has been preserved. The lawns were used for croquet, dance performances, concerts and plays. In winter people skated on the frozen ponds. On taking up his post, Münster supervised the planned alterations such as building garages, dwellings for the chauffeurs and for other staff, the asphalting of the drives and erecting wooden huts for sentries.

Münster's office undertook inspection of the work, project management, assuring supplies of building materials and providing site supervision of all projects on behalf of the Reichskommissariat, such as the conversion of homes for senior officials, and building German schools and other training and educational institutions which were officially classified under public order and security. Security was the domain of Rauter, who was fanatical in his endeavours to merge SS and police functions. The schools consisted of *Adolf-Hitler-Schulen* which provided vocational training for future Party officials and *Nationalpolitische Erziehungsanstalten* (also known as NAPO-LA) which were state boarding schools charged with character building and training of the future Nazi elite. Their purpose was the political cultivation of the new man; in other words, for the Nazification of character, fighting spirit and lifestyle.[20]

185. Second premises (former Jewish Old Age Home) of Abteilung Siedlung und Bauten in The Hague

Page 233 >
186. Architect Karl Gonser designing the Police Barracks to be built on the Hague/Wassenaar border, caricatured by colleagues in an anniversary book

The conversion of housing entailed renting, purchasing or requisitioning existing buildings such as town houses, villas, country estates, nursing homes, hotels and cloister buildings together with many potential storage spaces such as garages, sheds, warehouses and stables, as well as spaces with recreational functions including summer houses, sports grounds and tennis courts. When the requirement was for a premises with a pronounced ideological or representative character, new buildings were designed. Sometimes competitions were held for these projects, for example for a projected NAPOLA in the grounds of the Royal Palace in Soestdijk,[21] and for a new police barracks in The Hague.[22] From 1942 onwards, however, *Siedlung und Bauten* were also actively involved in the transport and delivery of building materials for concentration camps such as Vught "which the *Reichskommissar* and Rauter had built on their own initiative because – according to Rauter at least – they were mildly shocked by the mortality figures in Mauthausen."[23] During the Nurem-

DIE GESCHICHTE DER POLIZEI KASERNE.

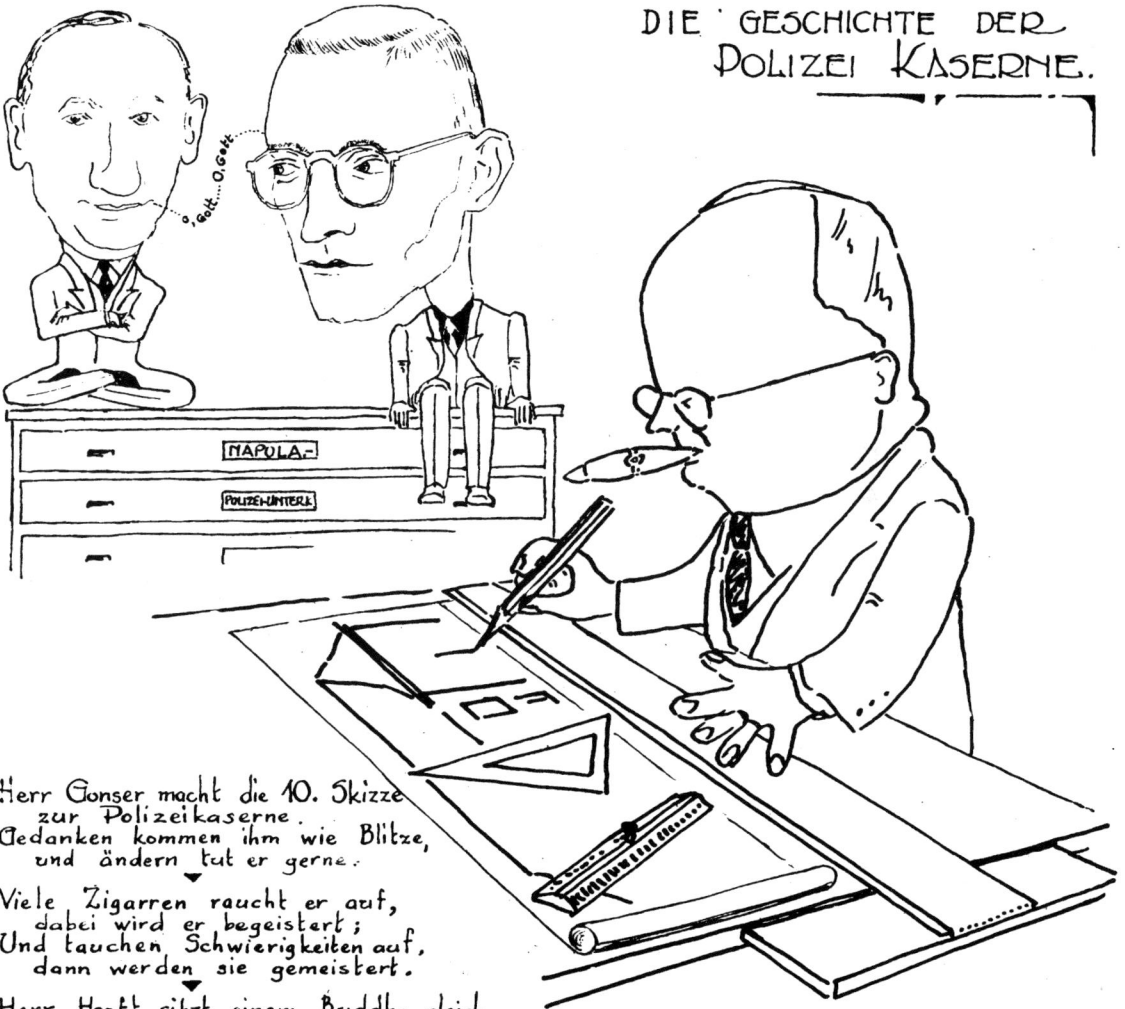

Herr Gonser macht die 10. Skizze
  zur Polizeikaserne.
Gedanken kommen ihm wie Blitze,
  und ändern tut er gerne.

Viele Zigarren raucht er auf,
  dabei wird er begeistert;
Und tauchen Schwierigkeiten auf,
  dann werden sie gemeistert.

Herr Hooft sitzt, einem Buddha gleich,
  hoch auf dem Zeichnungsschrank
Und denkt: "Die ewige Änderei
  macht mich noch völlig krank!

Wir machten alles wunderbar
  doch bleibt kein Strich bestehen.
Ich werde bald, das wird mir klar,
  zu andrer Arbeit gehen."

Bleich ist Verhoeven im Gesicht,
  ihm zuckt's in beiden Händen:
"Sollt' ich mit einem Morde nicht
  die Änderei beenden?"

Doch keine Angst - er tut es nicht.
  Hier herrscht nur Harmonie.
Sind diese zwei auch mal vergrämt,
  so raufen sie doch nie.

Drum zeichnet Gonser ungestört
  und beide helfen gern.
Sie schätzen beide, wie man hört
  den Gonser, ihren Herrn.

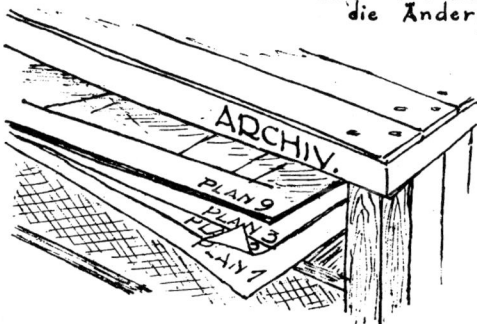

berg trials Seyss-Inquart stated that he intended to concentrate the Dutch Jewish population in Vught, Westerbork and three Amsterdam neighbourhoods.[24]

A MODEL ESTATE FOR MINERS IN HEERLEN

The available records show that out of a total of some 40-60 staff employed by *Siedlung und Bauten*, at least 12 were architects and engineers. Münster's office launched a pseudo-housing association, ostensibly in conformity with the Dutch Housing Act, with the Germanic-sounding name of Algemeene Volksvestiging NV.[25] The word "Voksvestiging" (literally Settlement of the People) betrays the National-Socialist ambitions of this organization, for despite its innocent sound, it denoted the ideology of "internal colonization", the process by which *Lebensraum* was to be won and exploited on behalf of the German people.[26] Organizationally, too, the housing association with its staff of about 20 was based on German and Austrian models.[27]

The housing association's most prominent project, executed under the direction of its own builders, was an estate for mining officials in Heerlen in the province of Limburg, designed by Karl Gonser[28] and Hans Georg Oechler (1941-1944) and completed in 1945, after the Liberation.[29] The project was largely realized during the German occupation despite the ban on construction (1942) and the quotas on construction materials. This was because building this estate was viewed as important for the war effort. Maintaining productivity in the Limburg coal mines was deemed essential to the German war economy. The state mines were requisitioned and run by German officials who were to be housed in the model estate.[30]

The planning concept of the estate is decidedly axial, with north-south rows of housing. In the original plan the main axes opened onto a parade ground with Nazi party buildings. The part that was actually completed consists of 240 large four-bedroom dwellings, thus conforming with the requirements of the German Housing Law (the *Führererlass* of 15 November 1940). Amongst other things, the act contains guidelines for *reichseinheitliche* (standardized throughout the Reich) dwelling types for large families (a hint at the blessing of having many children).[31] The *reichseinheitliche* dwellings, with their limited range of ground plans, were technically amenable to serial production. The architecture of the exterior was to conform with local vernacular building styles.

Compared with the bedrooms, the living area was small. There was a bathroom with bathtub on the first floor, and the house had a cellar which incorporated small air raid shelters. The shelter area had an armour-plated steel door with rubber seals round the edges to provide protection against gas attacks. The cellar walls were extremely thick except where the shelters adjoined those of the neighbours; in an emergency such as the house suffering a direct bomb hit, it would not be too difficult to break down the thin membrane of masonry and escape via the neighbour's shelter. At this stage of the war, the German Shelter City was still burrowing underground. That would soon change.

CONTRIBUTIONS TO DEFENCE PROJECTS

Siedlung und Bauten's tasks underwent considerable changes in the course of 1941. Seyss-Inquart cornered a share of the supplies of materials, thus making sure that his own projects were carried out. He also generated revenues for himself by setting up a legal sub-department to coordinate the bleeding dry of Jewish financial resources, an activity described as the "Aryanization" of Jewish property. Münster's offices, for their part, saw to the implementation of Ordinance 154/4, which restricted the location of Jewish residences to three neighbourhoods in Amsterdam.[32] The *Wehrmacht* expropriated the moveable property of Jewish households, while their financial assets (amounting to 300 or 400 million guilders) were written up to the firm of Lippmann, Rosenthal & Co., a Jewish bank confiscated by the Germans.[33] It goes without saying that at least part of the revenues from these transactions went into the occupiers' construction plans.[34]

To finance and implement his projects, Seyss-Inquart had his own financial resources, his own building department, a selection of contractors and a supply of building materials. A separate yard for distributing building materials was installed on the estate of Clingendaal in The Hague, which was both his home and the seat of his court.[35]

By 1941 Münster had already succeeded in cornering a sizeable personal share in the quotas of raw materials and construction materials and could thus bypass Werckshagen in executing the *Reichskommissar*'s projects. On 17 April, 1942, when German circles learned that marine defence would entail the requisitioning and demolition of properties (a coastal strip was to be evacuated to make way for the Atlantic Wall), Münster's private projects were exempted. He was even appointed *Kommissar* in charge of eviction from properties earmarked for demolition in both bases in The Hague (Scheveningen and Clingendaal) and later for the whole Dutch part of the North Sea coast.[36] His responsibilities also included the distribution and transport of construction materials for the civilian projects of the *Reichskommissar*, the

National Socialist Workers Party (NSDAP) and the SS. From August 1942 onwards, the NSDAP, the Commandant of the security police (the *Sicherheitsdienst* or SD), and those responsible for building within the Waffen SS all had to apply to Münster for their building materials. He was in charge of logistics, with the *Reichskommissar's* quota again being prioritized. The supply of materials for civilian projects was thus channelled through *Abteilung Siedlung und Bauten*, even after the armaments minister Albert Speer imposed the yoke of total war on the Dutch building industry.[37] Münster was now actively involved in the defence of the occupied Netherlands, ostensibly because of the need for air raid shelters.

Once commissions for planning and building prestigious civilian projects ground to a halt in 1942, the focus of attention turned to air raid precautions in the main Dutch cities. Bombproof shelters were built for German civilian bodies, the police, the SS, and civil servants and other employees engaged in important war projects. The small air raid shelters on the estate in Heerlen were a mere foretaste of what was to come. From 1942 onwards the building of civilian air raid defence structures proceeded apace, and in the second half of 1943 work began on defences for the Atlantic Wall (Scheveningen, Clingendaal and Wassenaar). The Germans were planning their own Shelter City.

The building freeze made it theoretically possible for a considerable part of the construction industry to be diverted to the needs of war. In 1942 Münster developed friendly relations with one of the commandants of the SS, Dr. Hans Kammler. Kammler wrote to him from Berlin on 20 May 1942: "My short stay in The Hague was worthwhile in every regard. I was particularly pleased with the brilliant cooperation between your department and ours. I also want to express our sincere gratitude on behalf of SS *Obergruppenführer* and Waffen SS General Pohl."[38] Besides strengthening ties with the directorate of the SS in The Hague, Münster developed an excellent working relationship with Seyss-Inquart. These efforts meant that he was assigned an ever-increasing number of tasks, giving him a key role in the building industry and a strong position vis-à-vis the aggressive leadership of the Waffen SS.[39] A joint coup by Seyss-Inquart and Rauter brought the construction of the Hague section of the Atlantic Wall entirely under the management of the SS. In effect, the Reichs agency responsible for building the coastal defences, *Organisation Todt*, was sidelined and replaced by *Siedlung und Bauten*.

In March 1942 a meeting of senior officials involved in air raid defence was held in Amsterdam, with figures such as Werckshagen, Münster, Gonser and delegates of the *Luftgaukommando* attending.[40] Although we have no report of this meeting, it was probably here that the air raid defence plans were hatched, and tasks assigned. The *Luftgaukommando* was responsible for defending the whole German military apparatus against aerial threats, but they also had peripheral duties such as protecting German and Dutch workers in the armaments industry in order to prevent interruptions to the flow of munitions to the forces, and to protect German civilians engaged in semi-military activities.[41]

In November 1942 the *Luftgaukommando* issued detailed guidelines for the division of tasks and for the building of air raid shelters in existing buildings.[42] The air defence ordinances were until then less than impressive by German standards.[43] *Anlage No. 3* (November 1942) was exceptionally detailed by contrast. Cellars with strong load-bearing walls capped by a massive floor or roof were recommended; in the absence of a cellar, it was permissible to use a tunnel, a mine passage or a trench instead.[44] The internal volume of the air raid shelter was set at three cubic metres of space and one bunk berth per person, for a maximum of 50 people. The shelter had to have an airlock at the entrance and at least one emergency exit. The shelters had to withstand the blast of high-explosives and the shrapnel from fragmentation bombs and were covered with earth up to a metre thick. The variant using wooden cases required a protective layer of stamped earth up to 75-cm-thick, or of gravel, crushed stone or rubble up to 50 cm thick. Brick walls had to be reinforced by a layer of earth at least 51 cm thick. Walls of compacted concrete had to be at least 40 cm thick and those of reinforced concrete, at least 25 cm. The doors of the airlocks, the emergency exit, windows and other openings had to be sealed against poison gas. The bomb shelter contained one toilet per 20 people.

The occupiers issued orders on the division of air raid protection responsibilities on 1 February, 1943. The *Luftgaukommando* was in general charge of the aerial defence of the Netherlands, while day-to-day management and supervision of civilian sector defences came under the commander of the occupier's civilian police force, the *Ordnungspolizei*.[45] The latter relied for this purpose on the liaison officers and the police units attached to the *Reichskommissar*'s deputies.[46] This accounts for the expansion of the duties of *Abteilung Siedlung und Bauten* to include "air raid protection in housing and urban planning"[47], starting in The Hague (see Chapter 7).

SIEDLUNG UND BAUTEN: BUNKER PROJECTS

Siedlung und Bauten implemented numerous air raid defence projects in The Hague and beyond. The siting and proportions of these bomb shelters suggest that they were designed for large groups of people. Sometimes the space had to allow for considerable amounts of equipment, too. They were usually built close to concentrations of confiscated buildings (cloisters, orphanages, mansions, town houses, hotels or schools) where Germans were living or working. The siting of *Siedlung und Bauten*'s bunkers was not selected primarily on military or strategic grounds, but according to the need to provide shelter for German government and police officials and other civilians where they were present in high concentrations. The shelters fall into roughly two categories: a long, narrow type designed to protect civilians at home or at work, and a more or less square or rectangular type that could also include other functions – military or semi-military ones such as facilities for domestic and foreign communications and intelligence. *Siedlung und Bauten* continued building smaller versions of the latter type until 1944, as individual bomb shelters for senior officials such as Seyss-Inquart's deputies in the provincial capitals or the top echelons of the police and the ss. Some diplomats were also provided with shelters in this style.

INTERPENETRATION OF THE DUTCH AND GERMAN TELECOMMUNICATIONS SYSTEMS

A particularly dense fog of secrecy surrounds the bunker projects that played a significant part in telecommunications. Dutch spies, members of the Albrecht group, managed to locate the premises of the various German army or civil units fairly accurately, but were less successful in ascertaining what went on in these buildings. The Germans were of course not exactly lavish with information about these projects, but comparison of various pieces of information culled from the archives has helped elucidate some details. Some riddles remain, however.

Communications were crucial to the German war effort. The latest technical novelties were put to use for scanning the airwaves, and neither expense nor effort was spared in gathering intelligence and tapping into allied diplomatic and military messages, besides broadcasting propaganda. To clarify how information was gathered and how the communication channels worked justifies a short digression on the complex relations between the Dutch and German bodies that specialized in

187. Hotel Bleumink, Apeldoorn, headquarters of Seyss-Inquart from 1943 onwards. In foreground, the oblong shelter for Seyss-Inquart and his staff, designed by *Siedlung und Bauten* (photo Anja de Jong, 2004)

188. Hotel Bleumink, Apeldoorn, headquarters of Seyss-Inquart from 1943 onwards (photo Anja de Jong, 2004)

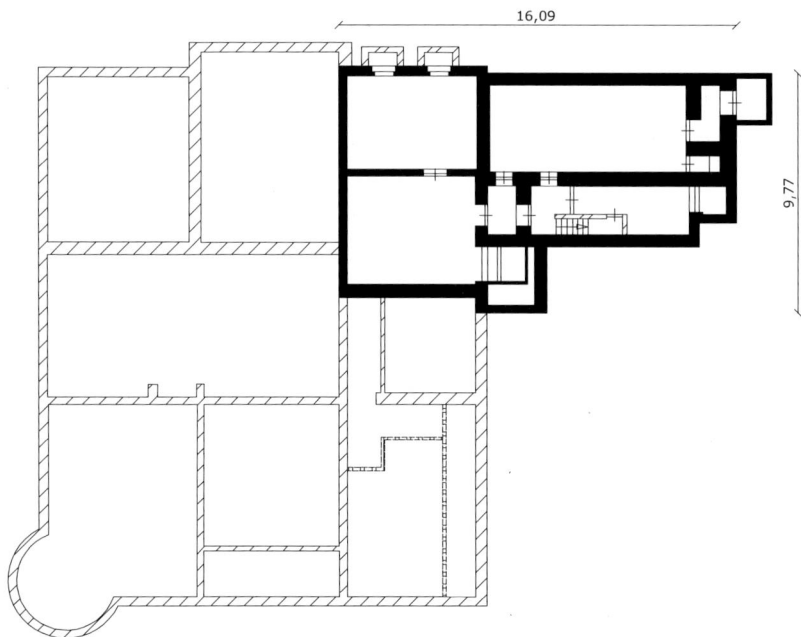

16,09

9,77

Top
189. Het Spelderholt country
estate, Apeldoorn, residence
of Seyss-Inquart from 1943
onwards, photo 1912

190. Foundations in
Het Spelderholt estate,
emergency exit and shelter
in black, designed by *Siedlung
und Bauten*

communications. The organizations involved included broadcasting corporations and channels, equipment suppliers and research centres.

The Dutch Postal, Telephone and Telegraph Company, the PTT, was invariably involved in one way or another in installing telephone lines in German bunkers and shelters. That should come as no surprise seeing that this state company was regarded from the outset as a branch of the *Deutsche Reichspost* and was therefore assigned an important role in the international communications network. Shortly after the German invasion, the director of the *Deutsche Dienstpost Niederlande* (German Postal Service in the Netherlands, DDPN), W. Linnemeyer, took over the head offices of the PTT in The Hague. The building included a radio laboratory which had satellites in Kootwijk and Noordwijk/Langeveld. One of the laboratory's most important functions was developing wireless installations for telephone, telegraph and broadcasting, a speciality in which the Netherlands excelled internationally in the 1930s. The *Deutsche Fernmeldeamt* (German Telephone Office) which coordinated instructions from Berlin set up shop in another Hague PTT office.

All the instructions from the occupying authorities were sent centrally to Linnemeyer; he then briefed the board of the PTT, and the work was then carried out in the district in question. The districts were organized around the district exchange, and from there the cables spread in a star-like formation to the sub-zone exchanges. From these exchanges, further star-shaped networks led to the terminal exchanges and then to the subscribers.[48]

In August 1940 the Germans took over the municipal phone companies in Amsterdam, The Hague and Rotterdam, incorporating them in the PTT. This step was part of the desired incorporation of the PTT in the *Deutsche Reichspost*. This had the advantage that the entire telephone network was placed under a single authority, simplifying control enormously.

As the occupation proceeded, the occupiers created their own communications hardware, both for eavesdropping and for sending messages. The repeater station in The Hague, for example, had special equipment to provide telephone connections to command posts on the Atlantic Wall.[49] The Germans consumed more and more cable lines, both for military and civilian purposes, rising from a total of 50,000 kilometres in 1940 to 260,000 kilometres by the end of 1942.

Linnemeyer strengthened his grip on the telephone network in the spring of 1943 when, for safety reasons, he, his staff, and part of the board of the PTT relocated from The Hague to Arnhem. The *Deutsche Fernmeldeamt* moved to Utrecht at the same time, and the mass of Dutch subscribers were cut off. This was not solely in order to appropriate the equipment, but also because resistance groups were suspect-

191. Radio Kootwijk, ca. 1923. In the middle: the approach drive, the cooling pond, the "Cathedral" and the main antenna mast

ed of making use of the network. From October 1944 onwards the occupiers cut off electricity supplies to a large number of telephone exchanges.[50] By the time the occupation ended, 211 exchanges had been deactivated, with 62 destroyed completely.

INTELLIGENCE GATHERING

The PTT and Philips, with their corporate expertise and high-tech equipment, were thrust into a grudging partnership with the occupying power. The laboratories of the two Dutch organizations and the whole Philips production line were placed under German management and set to work for the German war requirements. Different branches of the German war industry often depended on one another for supplies, for example for fluorescent lights. Philips was regarded as a German factory and supplied not only the *Deutsche Reichspost* but also the German army, navy and air force.[51] In 1942, for instance, a meeting with the Germans took place at Philips to discuss the radio factory's role as a supplier of technical components for essential transmitters with specialized tasks and the need to keep stocks of spare parts.[52] Neither Philips nor the PTT had any option but to collaborate in manufacturing the required products, but their efforts were hampered by acts of sabotage and go-slows.[53]

On invading the Netherlands in 1940, one of the German goals was to take over the Dutch communications facilities as intact as possible. The first stage in the German takeover of the lines of communication consisted of repairing the Dutch transmission equipment and the gradual standardization of the broadcasting networks. Once the Germans had succeeded in occupying large areas of Europe, they installed broadcast monitoring sites wherever possible to trace and listen in to the enemy. They even aimed, according to instructions of August 1940 issued to the new supervisors of the broadcasting stations of Huizen, Jaarsveld/Lopik, Kootwijk, Noordwijk and Scheveningen, to set up an "archive for international communications engineering". Despite the purported good intentions, their activity was first and foremost a contribution to the war effort.[54] The German technicians who arrived in the wake of the army were well informed and encountered plenty of equipment that was already familiar to them, since German and Dutch engineers had been cooperating since World War I.

Linnemeyer had to keep both Seyss-Inquart and Wilhelm Ohnesorge, the Reichs Minister of Posts, on his side. He disposed over a small army of German overseers who specialized in telecommunications. Following the invasion, one was assigned to each transmitting station. The main transmitters were Jaarsveld/Lopik, Noordwijk (used by Goering's air force, the DDPN and others), Kootwijk (the navy), Scheveningen (navy) and Huizen (specialized in wireless communications). Once installed, the overseers bombarded the PTT departments with demands for countless additional connections, initially for military airbases and harbours (especially for the intended invasion of England), then later for a large number of German civilian bodies. From 1942 onwards lines were also required for intelligence-gathering bunkers.[55] The German organization charts offer us not only a survey of the cities with telephone exchanges but a summary of the seven local authorities with radio services – Huizen, Jaarsveld/Lopik, Kootwijk, Langeveld/Eindhoven (also known as Valkenswaard), Noordwijkerhout, Scheveningen and Waalsdorp (Physics Laboratory of the Dutch Armed Forces).[56]

In May 1941 the Reich Minister of Posts, W. Ohnesorge, visited the Netherlands to discuss topics such as eavesdropping campaigns, improving the auditive quality of telecommunications and activating jamming transmitters. The director of *Siedlung und Bauten*, W. Münster, became involved in secret communication projects. On 11 May he attended a meeting with Linnemeyer and Ohnesorge at the Hague Zoo.[57] Under supervision of *Siedlung und Bauten* the Germans built massive bunkers on at least three of these sites. The receiver station Noordwijk Radio (NORA) scoured the airwaves for allied and underground transmissions. Both NORA and Radio Kootwijk

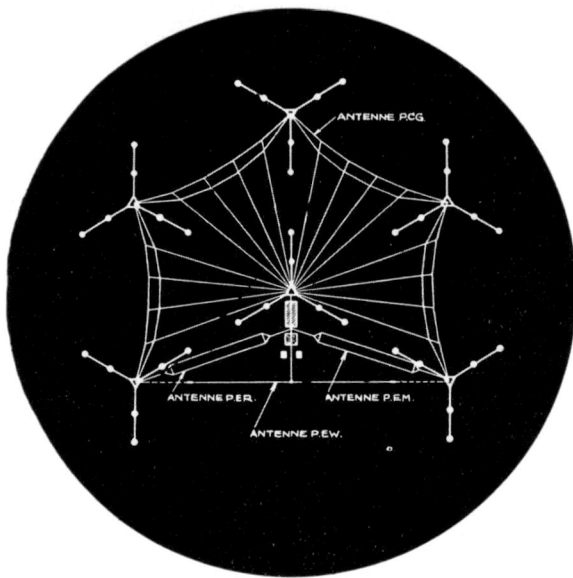

192. Kootwijk longwave Station, 1923. In the middle: the approach drive, the cooling pond, the "Cathedral" and the main antenna mast with ancillary masts

Page 245 >
193. Radio Kootwijk, interior of transmission station in the "Cathedral"

came under the authority of an intelligence department of the Ministry of Aviation. The information gathered was passed on immediately to the command headquarters in Berlin-Zossen (see Chapter 1).

The Reichspost gave orders for scientific research to be carried out into the latest techniques in the field of wireless communications, narrow-beam transmitters, high frequency technology, decryption and wire tapping. This research met with fierce competition from Goering's Luftwaffe Ministry in Berlin, which was also interested in monitoring telephone conversations and which mushroomed in size after 1940. The Germans were keen to acquire the latest equipment, especially the single sideband radiotelephony devices manufactured at the Reich laboratory in Noordwijk (Langeveld), the transmitter laboratory in Kootwijk, Philips's Nederlandse Seinfabriek in Hilversum, and the Philips Physics Laboratory in Eindhoven.[58]

RADIO KOOTWIJK

In 1920, a telegram transmitting station was built on a 450-hectare tract of land in the sandy flats of Kootwijk, in the centre of the Netherlands. The architect's design of this concrete sculpture – the truncated tower and the elongated nave both in rough-cast concrete – becomes comprehensible when we realize that the mast, over two hundred metres tall, stood exactly on the centre line of the tower and the nave.

The verticality of the tower acted as an overture to that of the transparent steel mast. The cluster of buildings included a gigantic transmitter building, a machine hall, a stockroom and a number of subsidiary buildings such as a transformer station and an overseer's building, which also included quarters for unmarried officials. The latter building was promptly dubbed 'Radio Kootwijk Hotel', and in 1928 an extra wing was added with a dining room-cum-lounge. There were also two utility buildings and four blocks with six workers' dwellings each. The operational layout conformed to Telefunken's requirements: an equipment hall (23.50 × 35 m) and a broadcasting tower executed in concrete, dispensing with nails, screws or wood. This meant the structures were less fire-prone (the intense radio waves could heat metal fixings by induction to hazardous temperatures) and had low maintenance costs. Immediately behind this complex was a tall, long-wave transmission mast.

Radio Kootwijk had telegraph cable links with stations in Europe and beyond, and a radio-telephonic link with the Dutch East Indies. Kootwijk was a transmitter station; reception occurred elsewhere, in Noordwijkerhout (NORA). The telegraph office moved to Amsterdam in 1924. Once a dedicated telegraph cable had been laid between Kootwijk and the capital, telegrams could be received and transmitted from Amsterdam.

Kootwijk "Cathedral", as the transmitting station soon became nicknamed, was a perfect example of an investment folly. On completion the building no longer complied with the requirements of long-wave technology. Sadder still, the cumbersome long-wave system had by then been overtaken by short-wave technology,

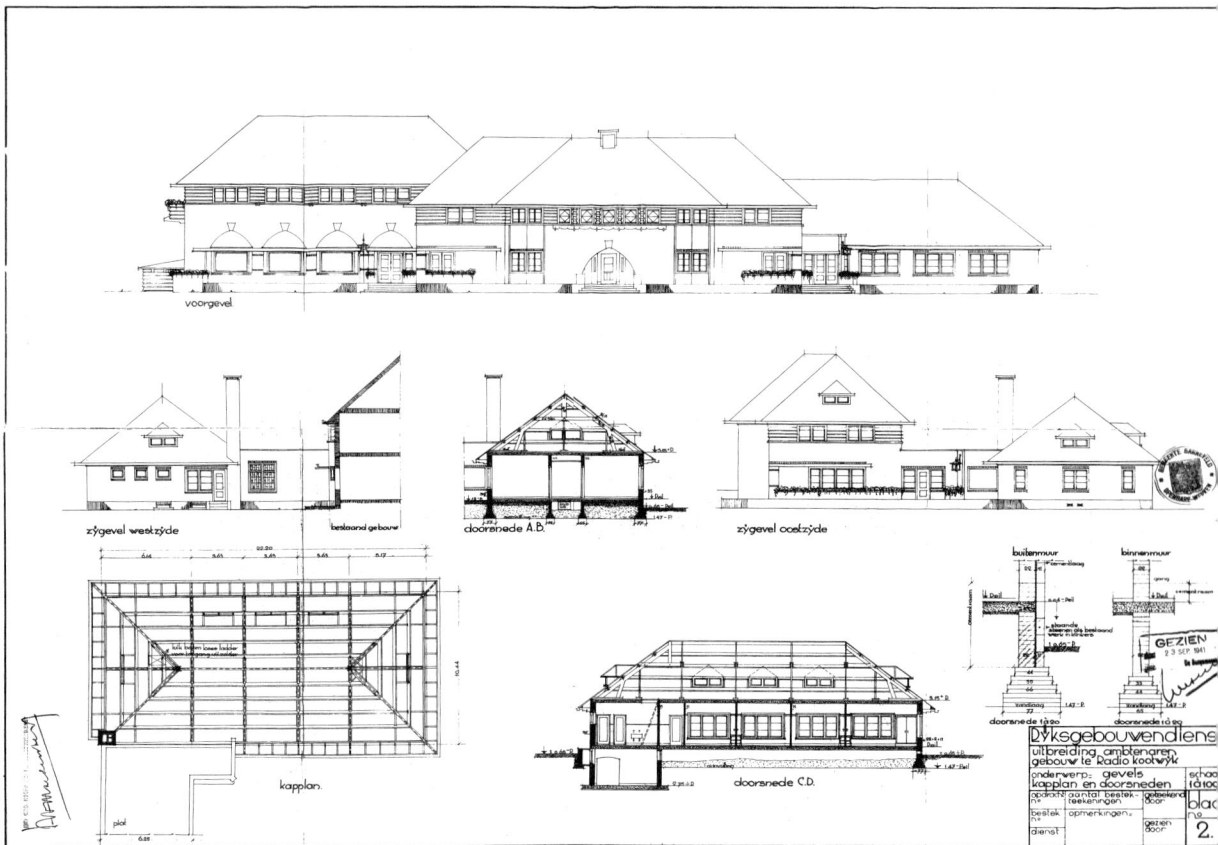

194. Government Buildings Agency, design for extension to Radio
Kootwijk (staff building), September 1941. The bomb shelter is visible
in cross section C–D

which had no need to go through life dressed as a cathedral; all it needed was a shed.
From 1925 onwards tests began in a separate wooden shed (building B). The new
transmission buildings C and D (short-wave transmitters on a PTT design, built in
brick) and E (short-wave, designed by Philips) rose at a safe distance from the cathedral. Between 1933 and 1937 a limited form of facsimile telegraphy became possible,
for instance for transmitting press photos.[59] Morse code and telex experiments also
took place there. To complete the alphabetic coding, the engineers' building (nicknamed "Pension Rustoord", or Sundown Hotel) was labelled F, while Radio Kootwijk
Hotel received an H. During the occupation Building F was given an extra wing.

"Broadcasting Group 8" came in the wake of the German troops. They soon had the transmitter working again and readied it for use by the occupiers. Reports by German officials give us precise information about the equipment they found in the various buildings of Radio Kootwijk.[60] They themselves added a G building, the "Siemens Shed", where experiments were carried out with German radio and radar systems.[61] In January 1941 the single sideband transmitters[62] were housed in C and E buildings.[63]

The huge collection of equipment gave scope for many experiments. The main activities consisted of German news broadcasts, propaganda broadcasts to the Dutch East Indies and other countries, and the jamming of allied transmissions. In August 1940 the long-wave apparatus was put to use for relaying "News for Seamen" to the western sector of the German navy in Wilhelmshafen. The equipment had to be operated by Germans, because the Dutch had qualms about working for the occupier, and they were also afraid of British air raids.[64] During the occupation Dutch-language programmes were broadcast from Radio Kootwijk and the medium-wave transmitter in Jaarsveld. From 12 March 1941, the independent Dutch broadcasting companies were abolished and replaced by the homogenized Reich Radio Broadcasting Company.[65] The Germans were extremely interested in the Dutch colonies of course and considered it vital to maintain connections with them. This state of affairs continued until 1942, when Japan overran the Dutch East Indies. Nearer home, the need to build the Atlantic Wall implied that the territories beyond the Atlantic Ocean were beyond the reach of German influence for the time being.

Kootwijk was also used for broadcasts of the Reich Ministry for Public Education and Propaganda. After 22 December 1940, this whole programme was transferred to the transmitter in Bremen and renamed "Radio Friesland".[66] The Dutch staff were also required to pass on the tapped telephone connections to the Reichs exchange in Amsterdam, where a German deciphering group processed the diplomatic and military telegrams and telex reports and sent them on to Zossen.[67] A version of the *Hellschreiber*, a device invented by Dr. Rudolf Hell in 1929 which was a forerunner of later fax machines, was used for this transfer. Texts and drawings were prepared on a special tape and transmitted electronically through the telephone lines.

The chief activity in Kootwijk consisted of relaying ciphered communications to the German navy, including submarines in the Atlantic Ocean. Only later on in the war did the British succeed in cracking the Kootwijk codes.

An unannounced German inspection of Kootwijk in June 1941 revealed a less than favourable picture of the functioning of the German staff.[68] Nowhere was a photo of the Führer to be seen, there was no duty roster, and all the activities and routines were performed in a very relaxed fashion. The German staff lacked the most elementary technical knowledge; nor did they have the proper attitude for this vital work. One of the officials even did not know the difference between long-wave and short-wave transmitters. Another was caught sleeping while the Dutch personnel were at their posts. During the weekly film show for the staff, the equipment was left unattended in all buildings except F (trials with the single sideband transmitter). There was no staff training programme. Five of the German employees wanted to be posted elsewhere because they found the work totally uninteresting. One potentially well-trained German technician was an alcoholic and ducked his responsibilities whenever he could, losing all respect. The inspector's departure was celebrated in the Radio Hotel by another alcoholic binge which the technician helped organize. The fact of the situation was that the German staff had to fall back on the technical expertise of the Dutch.

KOOTWIJK, STAGE 2

The transmission resources were allotted as follows: fifteen transmitters for the Army, one for the German intelligence office, three for the Reich Post Office ministry and one radio broadcaster ("Radio Friesland").[69] The Germans regarded Radio Kootwijk as the largest transmission facility in the European "intelligence business", so the total inadequacy of the staff[70] prompted a reorganization. With Kootwijk handling more and more of the communications work needed for the war effort, the proportion of German employees was raised and their training improved. German women were also recruited to operate the equipment.

The importance of Kootwijk for German communications is illustrated by the construction in January 1942 of a huge new rhombic antenna supported by eight 35-metre masts, although it was only completed a year later. By 1 February 1942, the frequency of one of the transmitters was set to allow troops on the East Front to listen to radio broadcasts.[71] Work on building three new barracks was due to start in July 1942, but working conditions in Kootwijk started deteriorating in the course of the year. The number of night shifts required increased sharply, and more and more often Dutch employees living outside Kootwijk failed to turn up due to problems with the buses (mechanical breakdowns and the lack of tyres or fuel) and bicycles in

195. Radio Kootwijk
following destruction long
wave antenna, 1945

a deteriorating condition. Even the supervisor lost his service car. Efforts therefore concentrated on housing as many employees as possible on the site.[72] The occupiers had already added a new wing, designed by the Government Buildings Agency, to the Radio Hotel (1941-1942). "Towards the end of the war they also planned to add a wing on the left, containing a central kitchen and with an air raid shelter under it. The kitchen was not finished by the end of the occupation. (...). One can still see remains of the shelter, for instance the vaulted ceiling reinforced with train rails."[73]

A German report from early 1943 gives an impression of the poor morale prevailing among the staff after it became necessary to boost the numbers (now reduced to 22) with female employees.[74] Boredom was endemic in the sandy wastes of Kootwijk, and an average of one-fifth of the staff was sick at any one time. Matters might have been improved by a proposed swimming pool, but it was never dug.[75] The Dutch personnel caused work stoppages whenever they could or else stayed at home, and they were encouraged in this by the supervisor who proved a master in the delaying tactics that the Germans described as 'passive resistance'.[76] Work on a new East Asia Transmitter proceeded at a snail's pace.[77] Power failures were ever more frequent, although it was unclear whether these were due to breakdowns or sabotage.[78] The PTT employees consistently absented themselves from film shows and other entertainments meant to boost staff morale. The thirty staff members, now including eight women whose sleeping quarters were assigned by the building manager and his wife, were quartered in the Hotel. The German inspector reported the situation there as follows. "Intimate transactions between the sexes, something that could never by the nature of the matter be prevented or treated as a misdemeanour, are nonetheless unsettling for the resident community, besides reflecting badly on the prestige of the occupying authorities. This is especially so when the occasional traffic between beds rises to serious proportions. The other residents in the building are not only disturbed by the nightly tiptoeing across the floors, but also by noises associated with these activities, caused by frequent visits to the toilets and the use of the water supply for washing and douching at any moment in the night."[79] The supervisor proposed packing all the PTT staff into the new but rather rickety side wing of the Hotel, and to house the women, whose responsibilities included operating the *Hellschreiber*, closer to their place of work, so that they could find their way back to bed even in the pitch dark.

At the end of March 1943, the Dutch supervisor was replaced.[80] The fear of air raids increased, and work began on two long, narrow, workplace air raid shelters. Each of them was about 18 metres in length and had room for 30 people. Built in concrete and brick and covered over with earth, they were based on a design by the Government Buildings Agency.[81] Construction continued until May 1944.

In 1943 a German plane struck one of the masts, and in May 1944 four allied bombers succeeded in inflicting serious damage.[82] There were also incidents of arson. Anti-aircraft guns were posted on and around the site, manned by old soldiers from the *Postschutz* (Postal Protection Unit).[83] They posted their guns at three points round the broadcasting station, and may have been successful in bringing down three or four allied planes.[84] Fifty soldiers guarded the grounds.[85] To safeguard their vehicles, the Government Buildings Agency built a garage with a hardened masonry roof in June 1944.[86] This was the last structure to be built at the broadcasting station. In January 1945 a direct hit on the cathedral demolished the adjacent mast, which slowly collapsed with a creak and a groan.[87]

Given the crucial role that the Kootwijk transmitter played in the German communications network, it is remarkable how few air raid precautions were taken. The staff in the cathedral could shelter in the catacombs, but the sheds housing the various short-wave transmitters were anything but bombproof. From the allies' point of view, the loose distribution of the buildings over the site, the vast expanse of the antenna fields and the height of the masts made accurate bombing difficult. On the other hand, it would have been difficult for the defenders to protect all the buildings from aerial attack, which may explain why workplace air raid protection was limited to the Hotel and the two covered shelter trenches. *Siedlung und Bauten* appears not to have been involved in the plans for Kootwijk – at least it is absent from the archives.

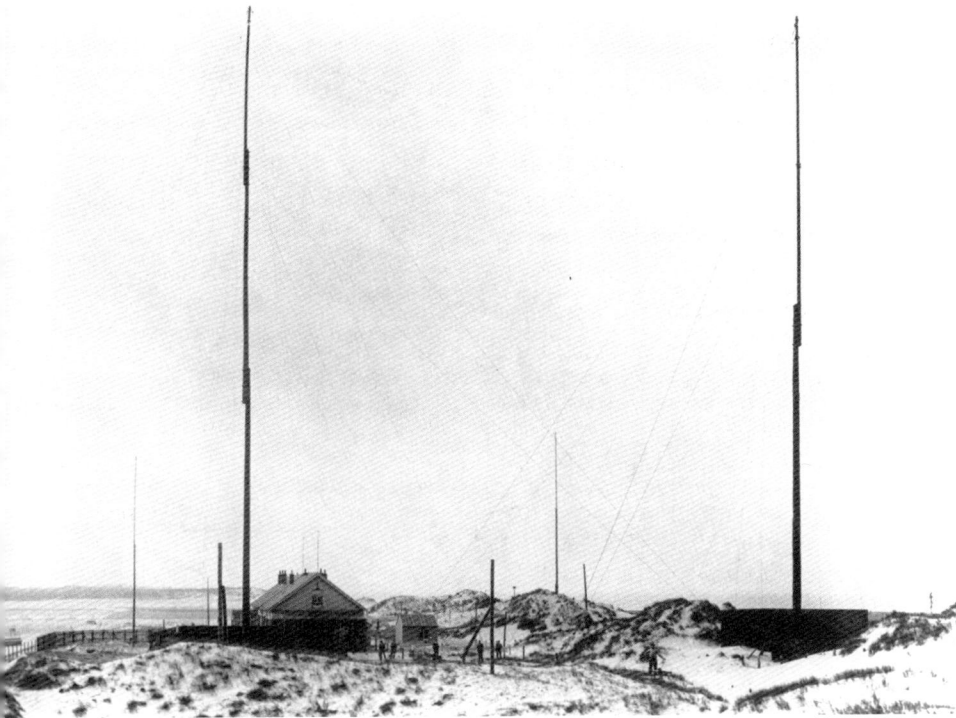

196. Radio
Scheveningen, on
seaward side of first
harbour in the sand
dunes

197. Radar installation
in the sand dunes of
Scheveningen

3,10

3,25

Onderverdieping

Bovenverdieping

32,58

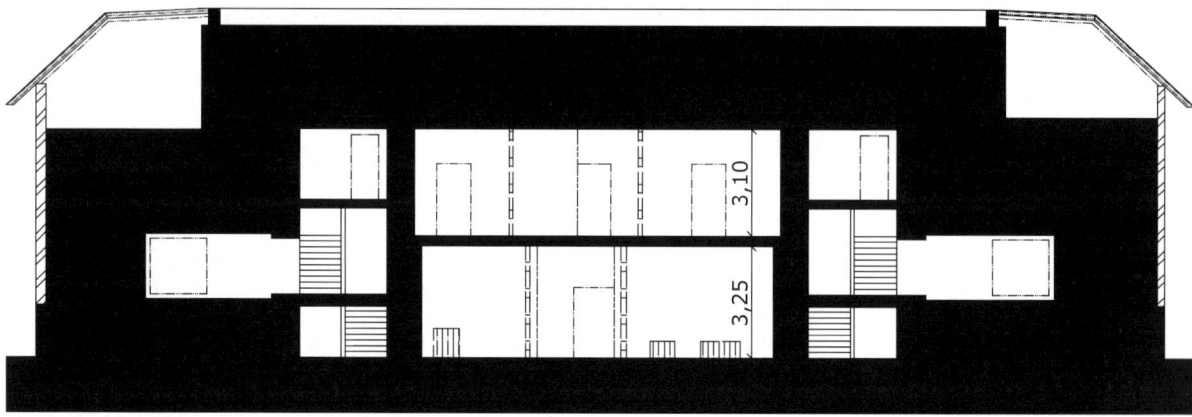

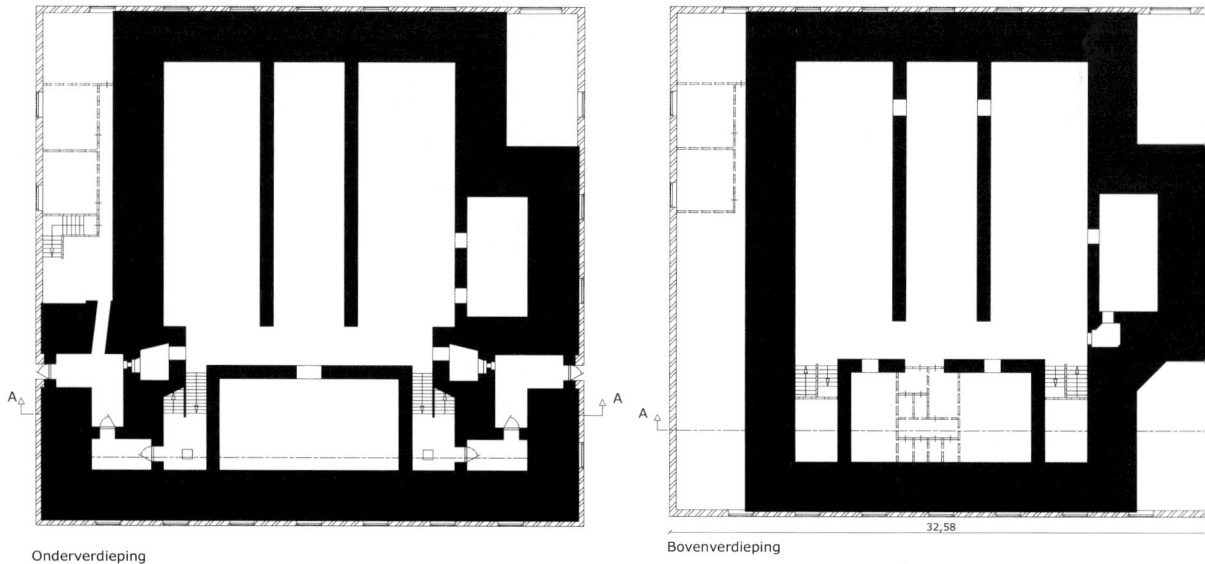

198. Section and plans of lower floor (left) and upper floor (right) of
the Servaasbolwerk bunker, Utrecht

FUNCTION OF THE BUNKER IN UTRECHT

Every broadcasting location had to be protected sooner or later (usually later, after successful air raids) with shelters or bunkers.[88] *Siedlung und Bauten* was closely
involved in the construction of some these sites (Huizen, Scheveningen, Utrecht,
Valkenswaard and Zwolle). The bunker in Utrecht is mentioned only cursorily in the
records; it was clearly a sizeable structure, but its function is hard to gauge. Follow-

199. Street facade of Servaasbolwerk bunker, Utrecht (photo Anja de Jong, 2004)

ing their departure from The Hague in 1943, a number of the bodies responsible for telecommunications ended up in Utrecht. Besides protecting their equipment, they needed staff air raid shelters, and these were supplied by *Siedlung und Bauten*. Two interpretations of this bunker's purpose have been mooted. It may have been an uncompleted first-aid bunker: for a time red crosses could be discerned on the outside walls. The other possibility is that the red crosses had a deceptive purpose and that the structure was really meant to be a bunker for radio communications centre or telephony. The latter alternative seems more likely but merits further explanation. Seyss-Inquart was constantly occupied with setting up his own telecommunications system between his headquarters in the Atlantic Wall (Clingendaal-Radio Scheveningen) and his fall-back posts in Apeldoorn (which later on communicated via Radio Kootwijk) and Arnhem. The civilian shelters, such as those for his provincial representatives and police chiefs, had to be able to maintain contact. It is plausible that the bunker in Utrecht was intended as a central relay station (*Vermittlungsschrank*) for telecommunications between the *Reichskommissar* and his countrywide civilian network. By the time execution of this plan started, however, the conditions no longer allowed the laying of new long-distance cables.

200. Servaasbolwerk Bunker, Utrecht. Camouflage facade of brickwork with windows in front of concrete wall (photo Anja de Jong, 2004)

201. Side wall of Servaasbolwerk Bunker, Utrecht (photo Anja de Jong, 2004)

202. Interior of
Servaasbolwerk
Bunker, Utrecht
(photo Anja de Jong,
2004)

203. Interior of
Servaasbolwerk
Bunker, Utrecht
(photo Anja de Jong,
2004)

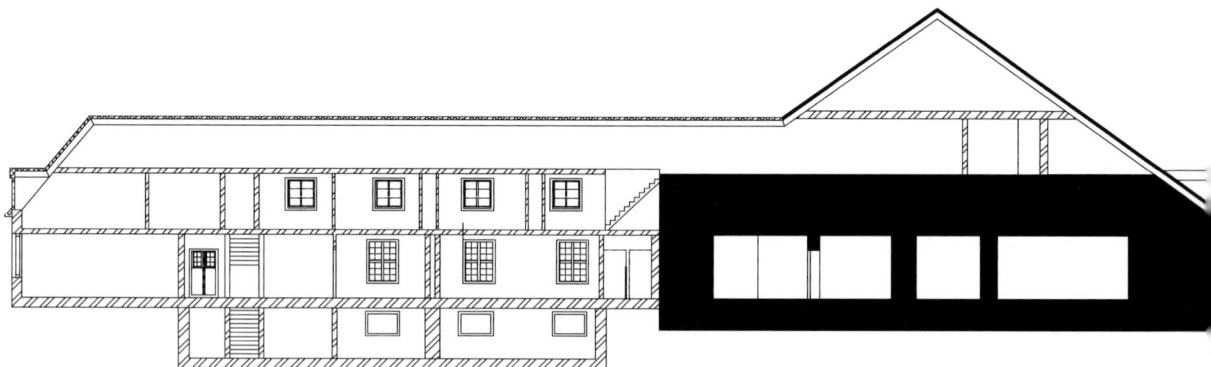

204. Cross section of communications monitoring station in Valkenswaard (bunker in black)

VALKENSWAARD: LISTENING IN TO THE ALLIES

The *Deutsche Reichspost* had its own branch in Eindhoven in order to do business directly with Philips.[89] It also requisitioned the estate of Valkenhorst outside nearby Valkenswaard. Immediately after the German invasion in 1940, the occupying postal authority moved into an office close to the Philips laboratories in Eindhoven. On 24 May that year, a number of German radio specialists moved into Valkenhorst and mounted parabolic dish antennas on the telephone exchange to establish a direct radio connection with German central communications command in Zossen near Berlin.[90] They also set up direct links with Welschap airfield on the outskirts of Eindhoven, with the new military airfield of Venlo and that of Cleves in Germany. What was the relation between the activities here and those in Noordwijk on the North Sea coast?

On the coast at Noordwijk, there was a PTT receiving station (NORA) with a rhombic antenna system. A specialized Philips support laboratory was installed in the wooden huts of a youth hostel in the nearby hamlet of Langeveld. In September 1941, aided by the expertise of the PTT and Philips, the German technicians succeeded in their mission to monitor the coded communications of the top of the allied command.[91] A telex connection was established from the Langeveld youth hostel to Zossen, and from there information was relayed to Goering's *Reichs Sicherheits Hauptamt* and thence to the Wehrmacht high command, the Ministry of Foreign Affairs and Hitler's own headquarters. Throughout the occupation, Langeveld remained the only wireless listening post in Western Europe capable of eavesdropping on wireless allied telephone exchanges.[92]

The installations in Noordwijk and Langeveld were vulnerable to air raids, certainly after the Luftwaffe's capacity to provide protection declined. On 16 April 1941, for example, the antennae on the NORA terrain were damaged by seven bombs.[93] There were two reasons why Langeveld was moved to the south of the Netherlands. The most important may have been the decision to build the Atlantic Wall, which meant transferring the civil departments to other parts of the country. Besides that, the work of the "Langeveld Research Station" had made a tremendous impression in Berlin, and the German engineer in charge (Vetterlein) was held in such high regard that he was considered worthy of luxury quarters on the estate of Valkenhorst, later with the benefit of a bombproof bunker nearby.

A specialist in advanced communications technology, Kurt E. Vetterlein had been dispatched to the Netherlands in the spring of 1941. His special assignment was to scan a wide range of wavelengths, to intercept allied radio communications,

205. Basement (left) and ground floor (right, bunker in black) of communciations monitoring station in Valkenswaard

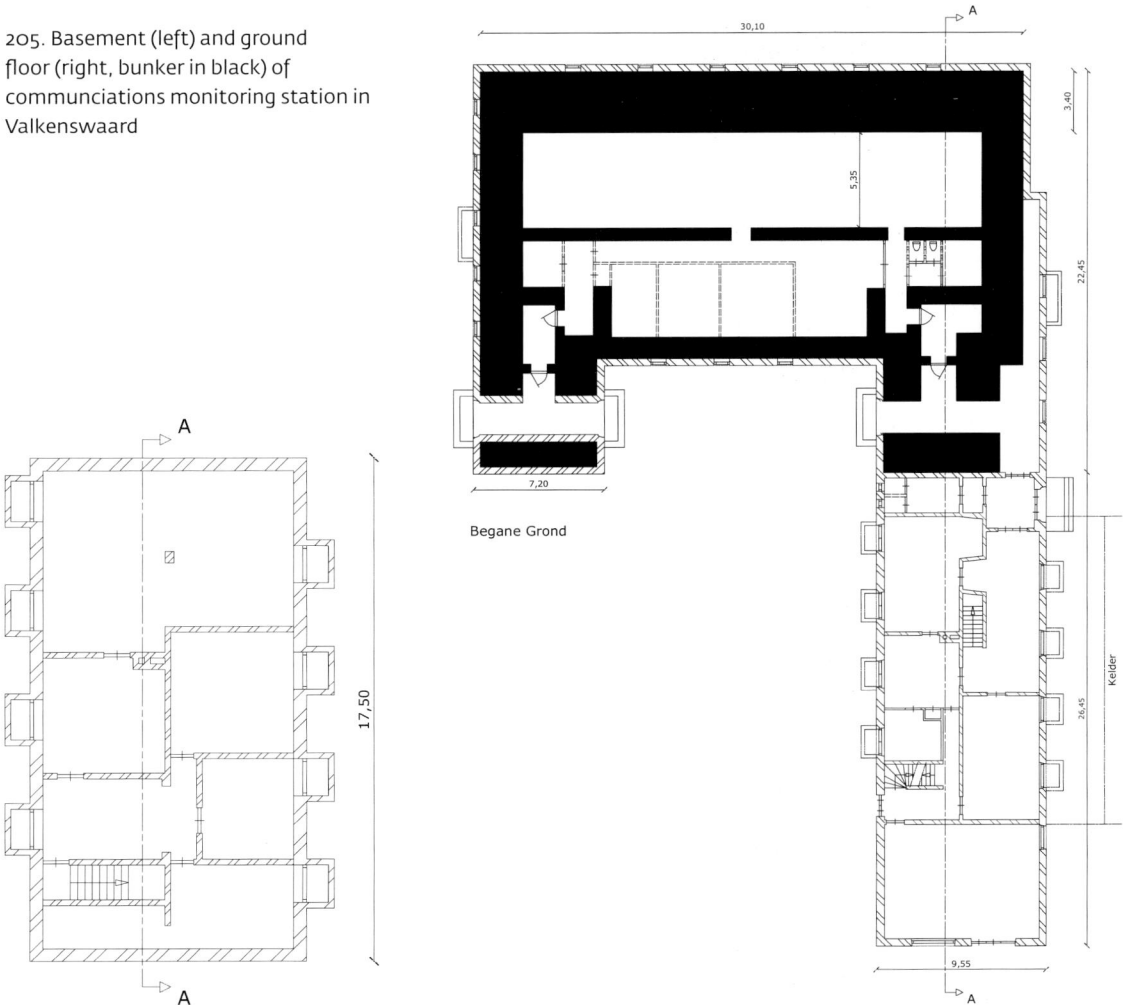

Begane Grond

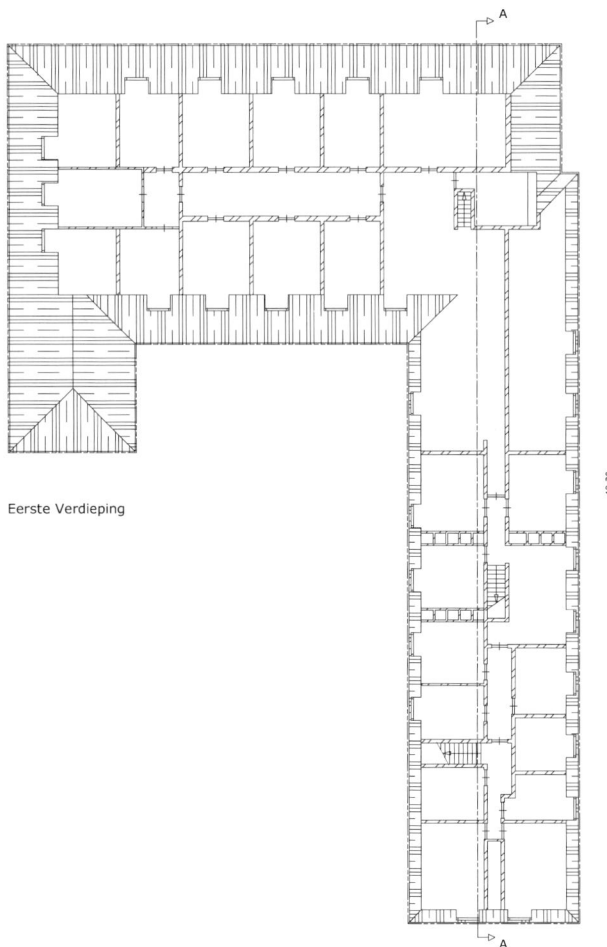

206. Attic of communications monitoring station, Valkenswaard

Page 259 >
207. Front view of communications monitoring station, Valkenswaard (photo Anja de Jong, 2005)

Eerste Verdieping

to detect and locate jamming transmitters and even to develop jamming and encryption systems himself. Vetterlein and his staff scored considerable successes.

In the late summer of 1942, the headquarters of the listening post were therefore moved for security reasons to Valkenhorst. *Siedlung und Bauten* supervised the conversion of the estate's stables into quarters for the ss.[94] Valkenhorst was in theory an easy target for air raids and moreover not immune to sabotage. The stand-by installation on the estate remained in use and was linked up to Birkenhof – the name the Germans gave to the new bunker which they built some kilometres away. Valkenswaard[95] became the home base for communications interception technology. It was here that the Germans tapped into conversations of the allies, despite their veiled speech and encryption systems, to the highest level, including the hotline between Churchill and Roosevelt.[96]

The costs of converting Valkenhorst and building the bunker in Valkenswaard were absurdly high; an investment on such as scale is only explicable if one bears in mind the exceptional importance attached to the monitoring station.[97] The shell of the bunker was completed in December, and bricks were ordered in January 1943.[98] The design of *Siedlung und Bauten* camouflaged the three-storey bunker to look like a vernacular farmhouse.[99] Construction of the bunker was carried out by the bunker-building firm of Julius Berger Tiefbau A.G. in Berlin, which had a branch in The Hague. The bunker is still there today. The walls and ceiling are two and a half metres thick and built of concrete reinforced with a standardized grid. The two entrance portals are at right angles to the doorways. The interior is divided up into two main spaces separated by a thick wall. These were subdivided into rooms by brick partition walls. The building is equipped with an airlock and a fresh air filter. The outside walls on the north and west sides have metal brackets attached to support the feeder cables to the antennae. Over the bunker is a storey with office space. The massive attic is made partly of wood and partly of reinforced concrete; it is clad with tiles and has dormer windows for the bedrooms inside. The ancillary buildings are built of brick but have ceilings of reinforced concrete.[100] The sloping roof frame is covered with a layer of engineering brick to prevent incendiary bombs from penetrating the roof. A wing with living quarters was added to the bunker.

208. Side view of communications monitoring station, Valkenswaard
(photo Anja de Jong, 2005)

This part included a shower, toilets and a kitchen for the guards, who were not sup-posed to know about the activities in the bunker.[101] The day room in particular was comfortably furnished with elegant furniture and an open fireplace. The layout of the sleeping quarters for the shift workers was later altered to create a hierarchical distinction between technicians and guards and between men and women.[102] To house the staff of the *Forschungsstelle* (research centre), various premises in Eind-hoven and Valkenswaard were commandeered.[103]

The new site was completely fenced in, and a sentry box was erected at the entrance. Inside the fencing, fourteen antennas, including four rhomboid ones,[104] were installed in the shrubbery. The bunker contained about thirty phone lines and had direct links with Zossen and the navy on the North Sea without any intermedi-ary telephone exchange being required.

The bunker went into operation in December 1943. Allied bombing raids on

209. Rear of communications monitoring station, Valkenswaard
(photo Anja de Jong, 2005)

Arnhem, Enschede and Nijmegen early in 1944 hindered the work of the monitoring posts by disabling many telephone cables. In September 1944 the installations and technical equipment of Valkenhorst and Birkenhof were dismantled and transported to Bavaria. The total operational life of the bunker had been no more than six months.[105]

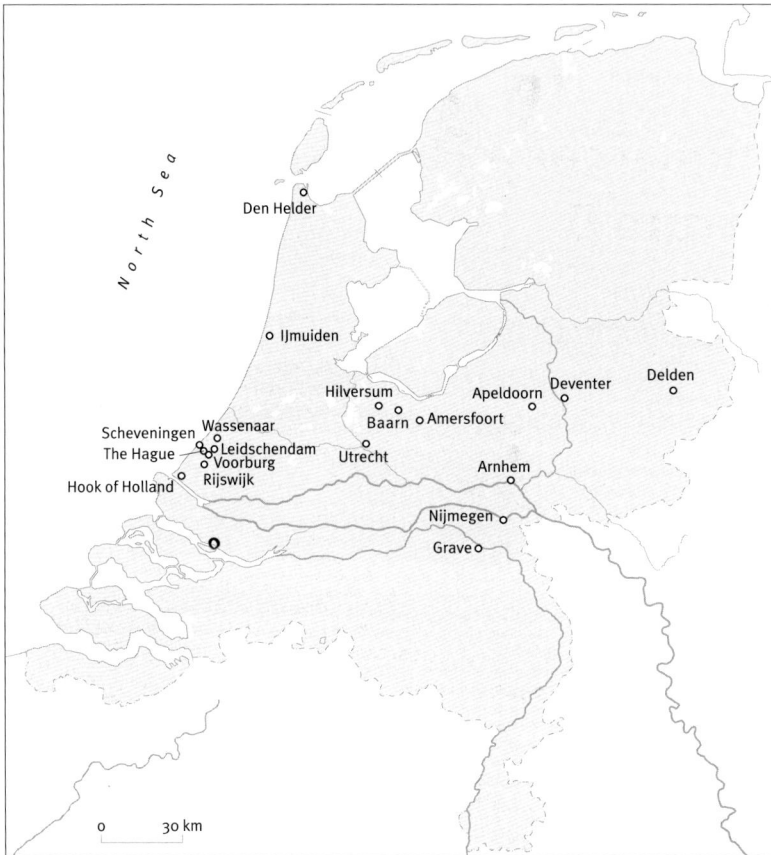

<   *Page 262 and 263*
210. Scheveningen, 1932

CHAPTER 7

Seyss-Inquart as a Patron of Architecture II

The Hague as Shelter City

As the seat of government, The Hague was unquestionably the most fully developed Shelter City in the Netherlands. More than in other cities, the local authorities there had encouraged people to build their own shelters and had supported these efforts with advice about their construction (see Chapter 2). In private cellars or gardens, in the shelters of companies, offices and factories, in government buildings and public shelters in parks, public gardens, on roadside verges and school yards, the Shelter City appropriated the city image. The longer the occupation lasted, the more wide-scale were the German authorities' air raid precautions. City dwellers had a personal experience of living in two cities at once. Right from the start the threat from the skies could be palpably felt in The Hague due to the blackout regulations. "All street lighting had to be switched off, the houses had to be totally blacked out and torches, car headlights and bicycle lamps were allowed to issue only a narrow strip of blue light. To prevent the worst accidents, the local authorities put up fences along canals and drains, and almost the entire staff of the Public Works department turned out to whitewash curbstones, street furniture and trees. The phases of the moon were the subject of unusual interest."[1] Gradually, nightlife ceased to exist. Traffic declined drastically at the very beginning of the occupation due to the lack of fuel. No new streets were built; indeed, the total area of road paving declined in the course of the war. The timetables of trams and buses were ever more limited, and traffic was dominated by bicycles. The shopping streets with their blacked-out windows looked

211. Scheveningen, 1932

dead. The more luxurious shops, such as jewellers and perfumeries, and countless restaurants closed their doors. More than anything, the exodus of the civilian population, which began in November 1942, reduced The Hague to a phantom city.

The staff of the Air Raid Protection Department in The Hague maintained its numbers during the occupation. In September 1942 the total staff in the different sectors amounted to 1,123.[2] It upheld a state of readiness on many fronts – something that proved essential in the final years of the war, from 1943 onward, when construction of the Atlantic Wall and increasingly frequent air raids put them under considerable pressure. From September 1944 onwards, the raids were partly attracted by the new V2 rocket-launching sites. Over a thousand V2s were fired from sites in The Hague (such as the Haagse Bos, a tract of open woodland on the edge of the city).[3]

The Shelter City in The Hague unexpectedly gained an extra layer, which was specifically German in origin. When Reichskommissar Seyss-Inquart's civilian regime took up quarters in The Hague, the protection of the civilian and military centre was near the bottom of his list of priorities. The top German officials claimed stately properties for themselves and took it for granted that they were in no particular danger. In 1942, however, it was decided that the bases of Scheveningen and Clingendaal, which formed the centre of Seyss-Inquart's civilian power, were to be made part of the Atlantic Wall, which included tank defences on the landward side. Ultimately, 135,000 Hague residents were evacuated between November 1942 and the beginning of 1944 – a quarter of the entire population.

THE ATLANTIC WALL

The most important project for which *Siedlung und Bauten* took responsibility was in The Hague – or rather in nearby Scheveningen, Clingendaal and Wassenaar. The development of the Atlantic Wall as a military enterprise has by now been written about in detail, but it is still worth taking a closer look at the significance of the base at Clingendaal for the civilians residing there. It was a miniature town in its own right, with shelters for the Reichskommissar and the top echelons of the ss, a communications centre and a collection of little shelters for German citizens; an ensemble which would bear comparison even with Adolf Hitler's various headquarters.

212. Four main areas neighbouring The Hague

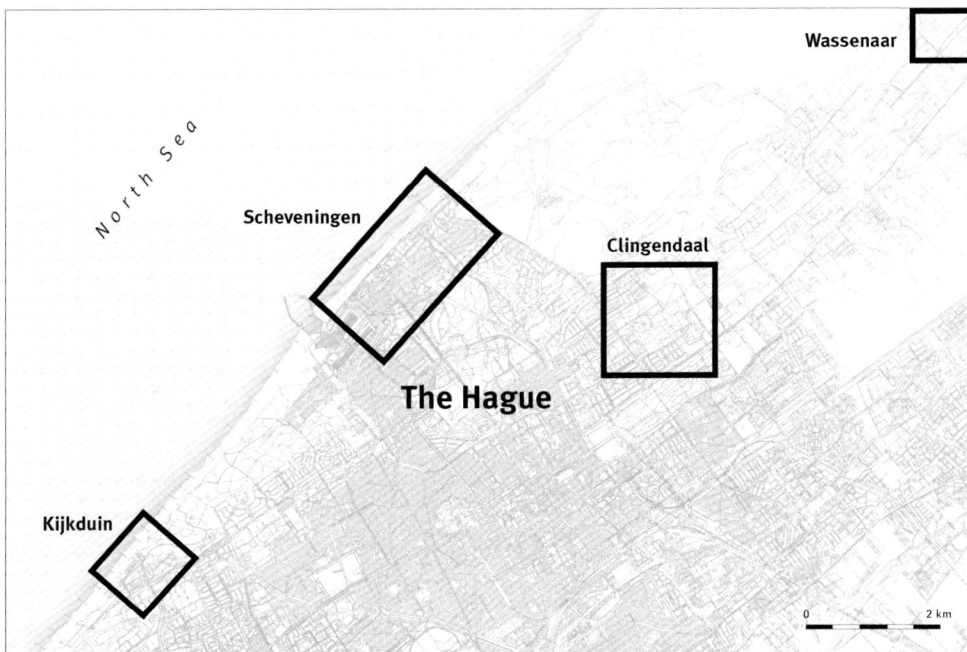

213. Public Works Department, map of The Hague showing location of all shelters with capacities indicated, 22 September 1939

GEMEENTE 'S-GRAVENHAGE
SCHAAL 1 A 10,000.

NOORD_ZEE.

GEMEENTE

WASSENAAR

GEMEENTE

VOORBURG

VOORBURG

VERKLARING.

214. Public Works Department, enlarged section of map of The Hague with location of all shelters with capacities indicated, 22 September 1939

GEMEENTE 'S_GRAVENHAGE
SCHAAL 1 A 10,000.

LEGEND

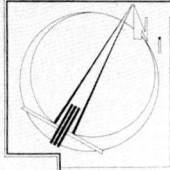

‑‑‑‑‑	tankwall
∙∙∙∙∙∙	asparagus, concrete posts and other tank traps
▫▫▫▫▫	anti-tank ditch
———	trench
✕✕✕✕	barbed wire

line of fire	line of fire
■	anti aircraft
→	entrance
①	bunker Seyss Inquart

2	command bunker
▪✈	anti aircraft with bunker
■	group of bunkers
✈	anti aircraft
■	civil shelters

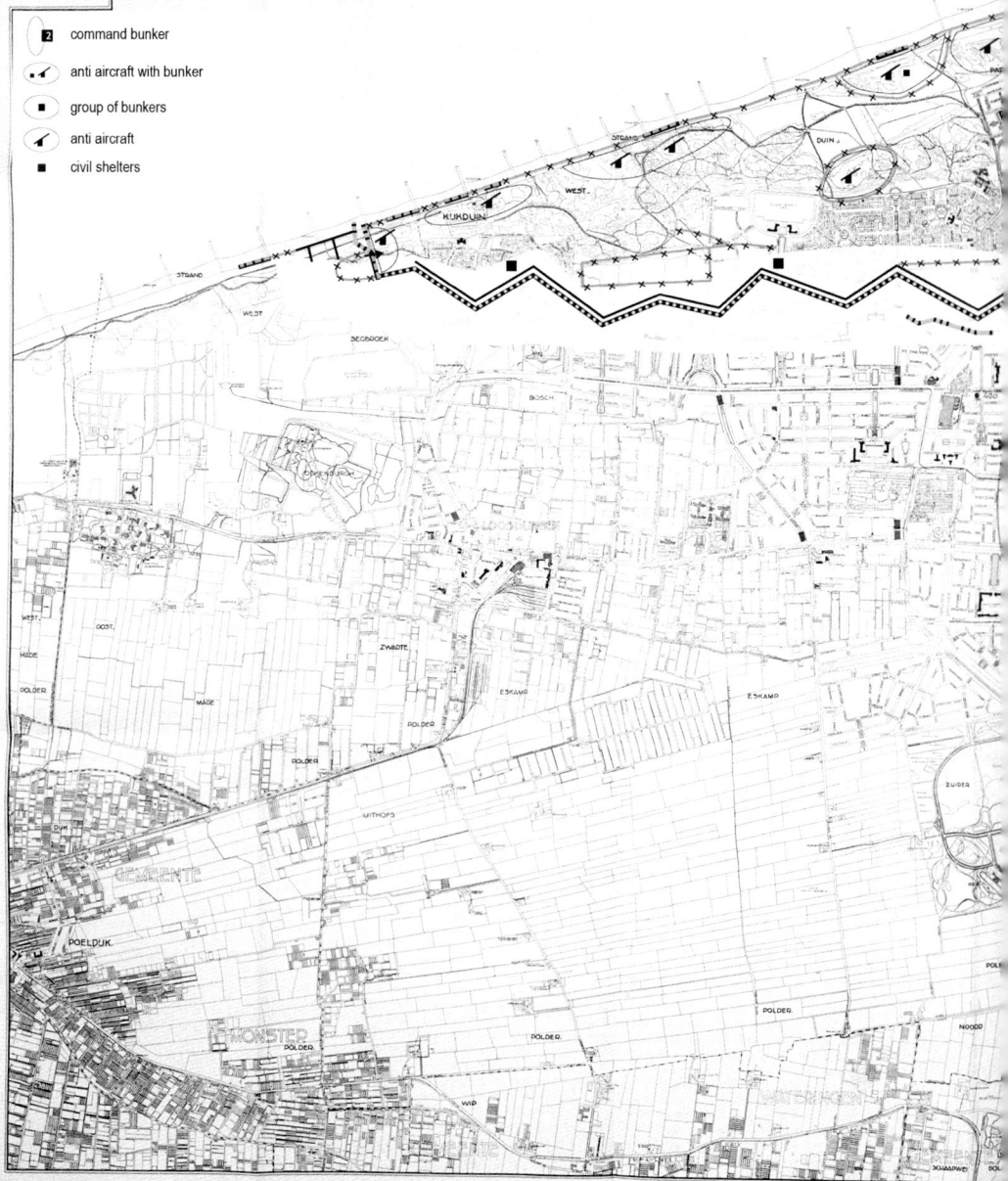

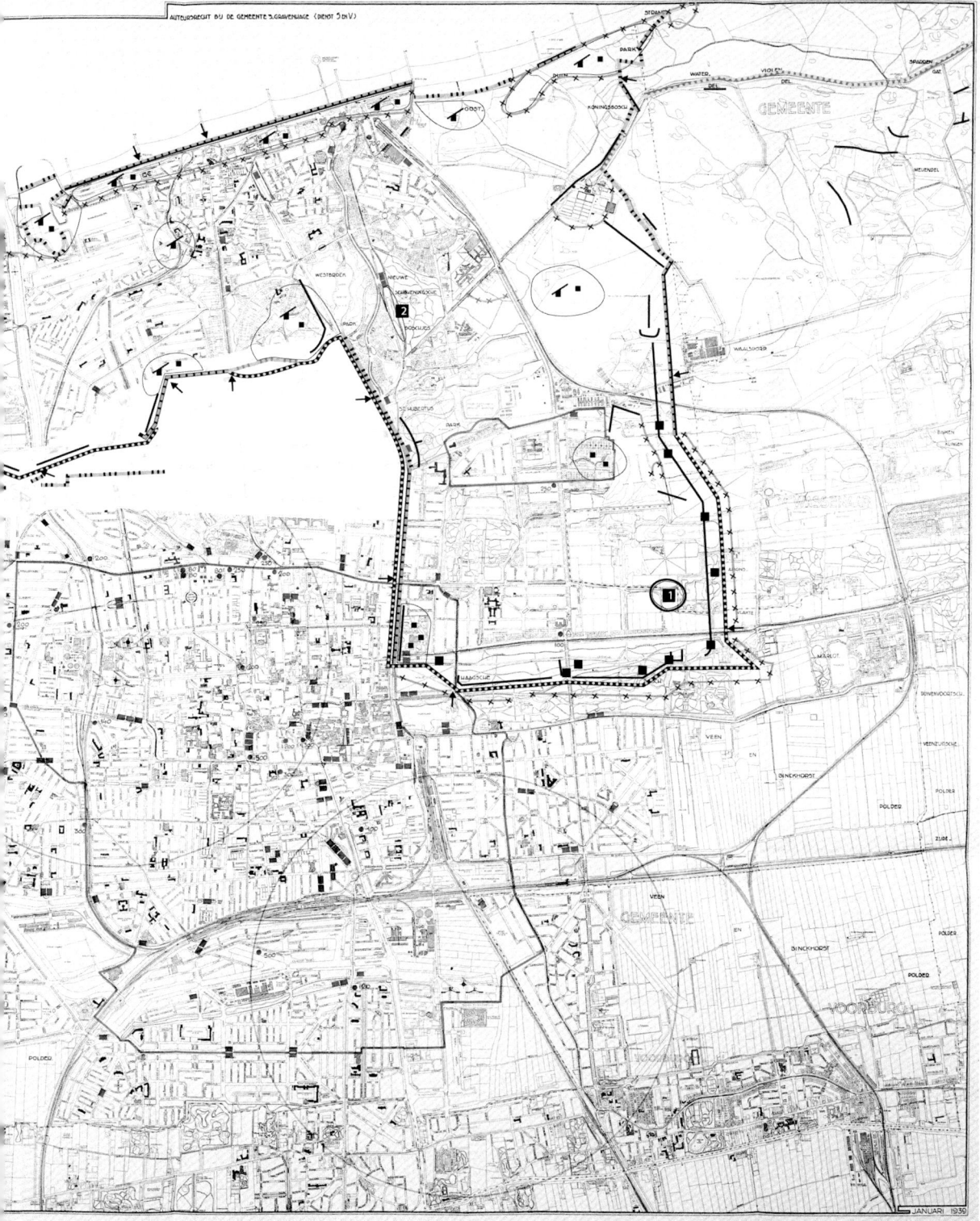

GEMEENTE

GEMEENTE

VOORBURG

JANUARI 1930

At first, the defence of the port of Scheveningen was the main priority. The need for radical measures became increasingly urgent, however, as the allies' ability to strike grew, and the Germans lost their advantage in the air. When the west coast of continental Europe was deemed a potential front for an allied attack and orders were given to build the Atlantic Wall in December 1941, the defence of The Hague as a whole came on the agenda. The plans for the defence line were only at the design stage when Hitler started putting pressure on the bunker-building programme in the autumn of 1942. Allied superiority in the skies was forcing the Germans to seek effective shelter for their armaments and materiel. The coastal defences had to be hardened with concrete. This effort to close the defensive gap – the 'Schartenbauprogramm' – was launched in January 1943. Fifteen thousand bunkers were assigned to the French, Belgian and Dutch coasts, two thousand of them to Holland. The deadline for completion of the Atlantic Wall was 1 May 1943, and *Organisation Todt* took charge of its construction.

The most important bases in the Netherlands were located in Den Helder, IJmuiden, the Hook of Holland, Scheveningen and Vlissingen. They were accorded various types of bunker based on the German manual of types for concrete fortifications (*Typenheft für die Erkündigung des verstärkt feldmässigen Ausbaues in Beton*). Crucial for The Hague was that each base enjoyed the cover and support of the one next to it. Each had to be defensible from all directions and maintain a clear field of fire around the periphery. Providing the necessary cover on the landward side meant cutting away part of the urban fabric to make room for a defensive wall and a tank ditch. Under the supervision of *Siedlung und Bauten*, a long swathe of land from Kijkduin to Clingendaal was cleared of all buildings and woodland.

SEYSS-INQUART DIGS HIMSELF IN

Now that The Hague was a possible target for invasion, both the armed forces and the German civilian administration concentrated there looked very vulnerable. In the spring of 1942, various military staff units left the city, and a year later the General Commissioners relocated to the east of the country with their subordinates. The commander-in-chief of the German army moved to Hilversum and Baarn, and the chief admiral set up headquarters in Utrecht. In 1943 construction began on a series of camouflaged bunkers.[4]

To avoid further loss of face, however, Seyss-Inquart felt obliged to remain in The Hague; in November 1942 he and Rauter obtained Hitler's leave to stay.[5] He compensated himself generously for the risk he was taking, by ordering the building of his own personal base, which strictly speaking had no military relevance to the defence of the coastline. In the end, it was decided to limit the building of fortifications to the civilian stronghold around Clingendaal, after the operation to fortify the political centre of The Hague proved too time-consuming.

In December 1942 Himmler proposed strengthening Clingendaal's defences to serve as an SS fort, while the base at Scheveningen was constructed under the command of the army and *Organisation Todt* in particular. On 8 January 1943 Seyss-Inquart wrote to Himmler, "The defence lines have been staked out, the individual defence structures have been decided on, as has an anti-tank ditch. Münster, my engineer, is taking charge of the building. He has already built the bunkers, and

216. Row of estates and royal palace in the neighbourhood of Seyss-Inquart's command centre at Clingendaal

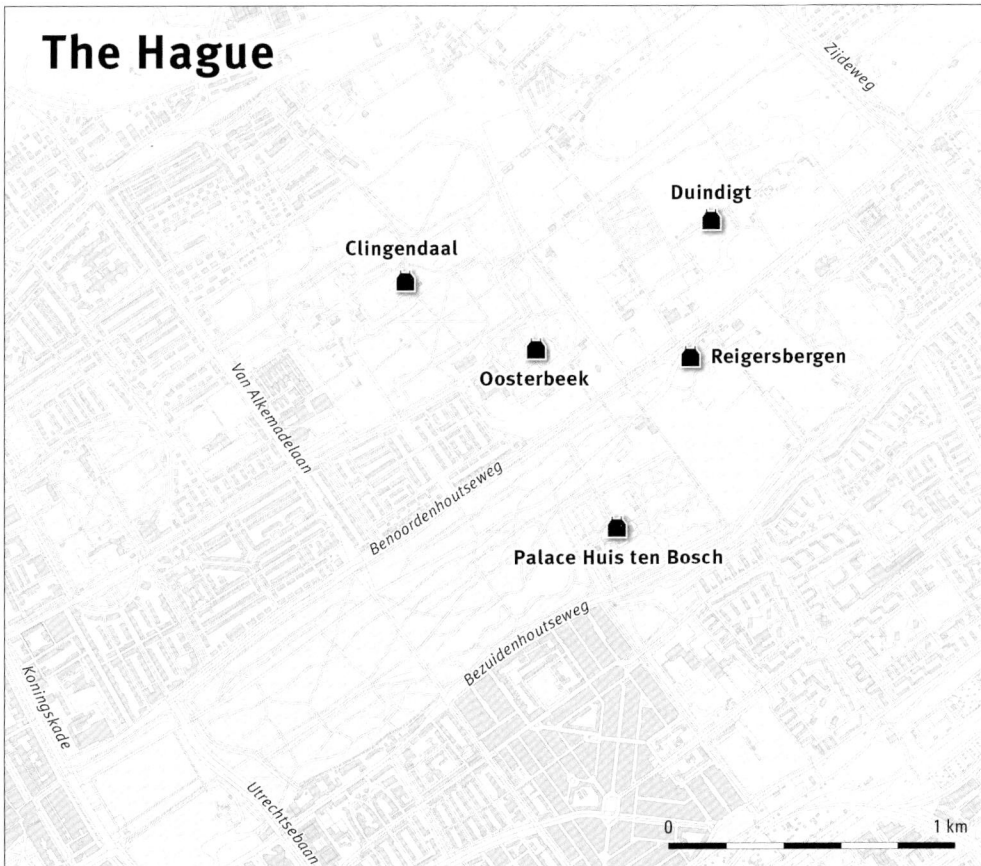

everyone concerned trusts him to carry out the work speedily and efficiently. He is definitely someone to get the job done. The situation is that Lieutenant-Colonel Pausinger also prefers certain parts of the base at Scheveningen to be supervised by Münster rather than the military construction department."[6] In February 1943 Himmler obtained permission from Hitler to put both bases under the command of the ss. This meant that the design and construction work could be delegated to *Siedlung und Bauten*, who were already engaged in clearing the Atlantic Wall zone, and Seyss-Inquart appointed the head of the organization "Commissioner of Evacuations" in an Ordinance of 20 October 1942. Münster not only supervised the building of Clingendaal but took an active part in the procedural and logistics preparation and the implementation of the entire defence line in The Hague. As it turned out, Clingendaal never became more than an imposing facade of civilian government, for soon afterwards Seyss-Inquart issued another ordinance (7 December 1942) to transfer his civilian departments to the east of the Netherlands, resulting in a drastic shrinkage in the German civilian population of Clingendaal.

Be that as it may, Münster was the one in charge of the day-to-day business of building all the defence works. In the end, the whole defensive complex of Scheveningen and Clingendaal, including civilian facilities, amounted to over a thousand structures. *Siedlung und Bauten* supervised and contracted out not just the demolition work along the Dutch coast to make way for the Atlantic Wall, but also the defensive building activities in Scheveningen, Clingendaal and Wassenaar. The organization was additionally made responsible for planning and implementing the civilian projects specifically for the base at Clingendaal.

DEMOLITION

The decision to combine Scheveningen as a military base with Clingendaal as a civilian one had far-reaching consequences for the wider urban fabric of The Hague.[7] The city consisted almost entirely of low-rise buildings interspersed with parks, woods and landed estates around country houses. Well-to-do administrators, politicians, diplomats, Dutch East Indies officials, military officers and civil servants had their residences in the exclusive neighbourhoods strung out along the coast, except in the workaday seaside suburbs of Scheveningen and nearby Duindorp. The tradesmen, shopkeepers and workers, on the other hand, lived more inland, south of a line from Loosduinseweg to Bezuidenhoutseweg which cuts across The Hague's historic centre. The "Front Line" linking the two bases had to be drawn right through the

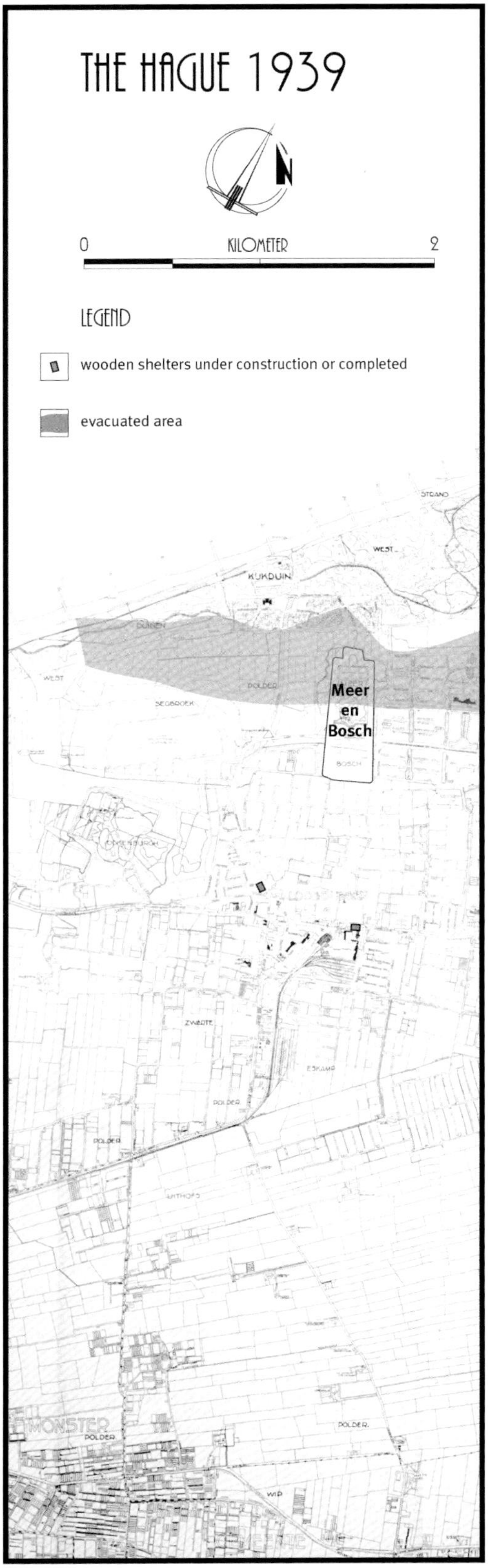

THE HAGUE 1939

0   KILOMETER   2

LEGEND

▣   wooden shelters under construction or completed

▨   evacuated area

Meer en Bosch

top left
7. Demolition in Savornin Lohmanlaan to make way for Atlantic Wall, December 1942

bottom left
8. Demolition and collection of bathtubs in Scheveningseweg, 1942

right
9. Evacuation area of Kijkduin that was demolished to pave the way for an anti-tank ditch (drawn on the 1939 map of The Hague)

220. Demolition in Stokroosstraat, November 1942

built-up area of the city. To clear an adequate firing field between them, it was inevitable that a great many buildings would be demolished and their occupiers evicted. The breach had to be at least fifty metres wide, to allow for fortifications and leave room for manoeuvring wheeled materiel.

The demolitions, mostly of housing, and then building the structures of the Atlantic Wall took three years. From Kijkduin, a 27-m-wide, 5-km-long anti-tank ditch zigzagged its way parallel to SportLaan via the woodlands of the Scheveningse Bos to Zorgvliet. At this point "crocodile's teeth" (low pyramid-shaped obstacles), iron posts and a small, dry, anti-tank ditch led to the pond. The pond was itself dug to form an anti-tank ditch, and this continued to Het Kanaal, a canal which also served as an anti-tank ditch. On the far side of the Koninginnegracht, a series of bricked-up houses and pieces of anti-tank wall led along the Raamweg to the Malieveld. Here the wall turned once more into an anti-tank ditch, which crossed the Haagse Bos just north of the royal palace Huis ten Bosch and resumed its course seawards up to the golf course.[8] Near Oude Waalsdorperweg, a checkpoint was built in the wall. From The Hague Golf Club the wall continued – interrupted by a pool – via the water tower to the coast. To provide the wide field of fire needed, long rows of houses had to be demolished on the city side of the line. Many stands of trees and shrubbery had to be cut down in the woodlands of Poot en Pex, Meer en Bos and Scheveningen. The ancient Haagse Bosch, famous for its mighty trees, lakes and winding paths, suffered heavily and lost its much-loved skating rink. "Of the whole residential quarter between Stadhouderslaan and Zorgvliet, with its priceless gardens and woods, nothing remained either; an enchanting church, the Duinoordkerk was demolished, and it proved impossible to save its fine mosaic *Last Supper* by Thorn Prikker."[9]

By April 1942 the beach and dunes were declared out of bounds to the public. The resort of Scheveningen was closed in May, and on 15 May an order came for the eviction of 309 families from homes in Duindorp and Scheveningen village. Rauter wrote to the Mayor of The Hague about the "evacuation of the Dutch civilian population from the areas along parts of the coast". On 7 November 1942 the National Socialist mayor and the director of the local public works department had to report to Walter Münster, Commissioner for Evacuations. "On his desk was a large map of The Hague with a long strip of the urban area hatched with diagonal lines, from Kijkduin south-west of Sportlaan all the way to Zorgvliet. All the houses in this area, Münster informed his visitors, had to make way for a tank barrier and an open

221. Demolition in Aronskelkweg, June 1945

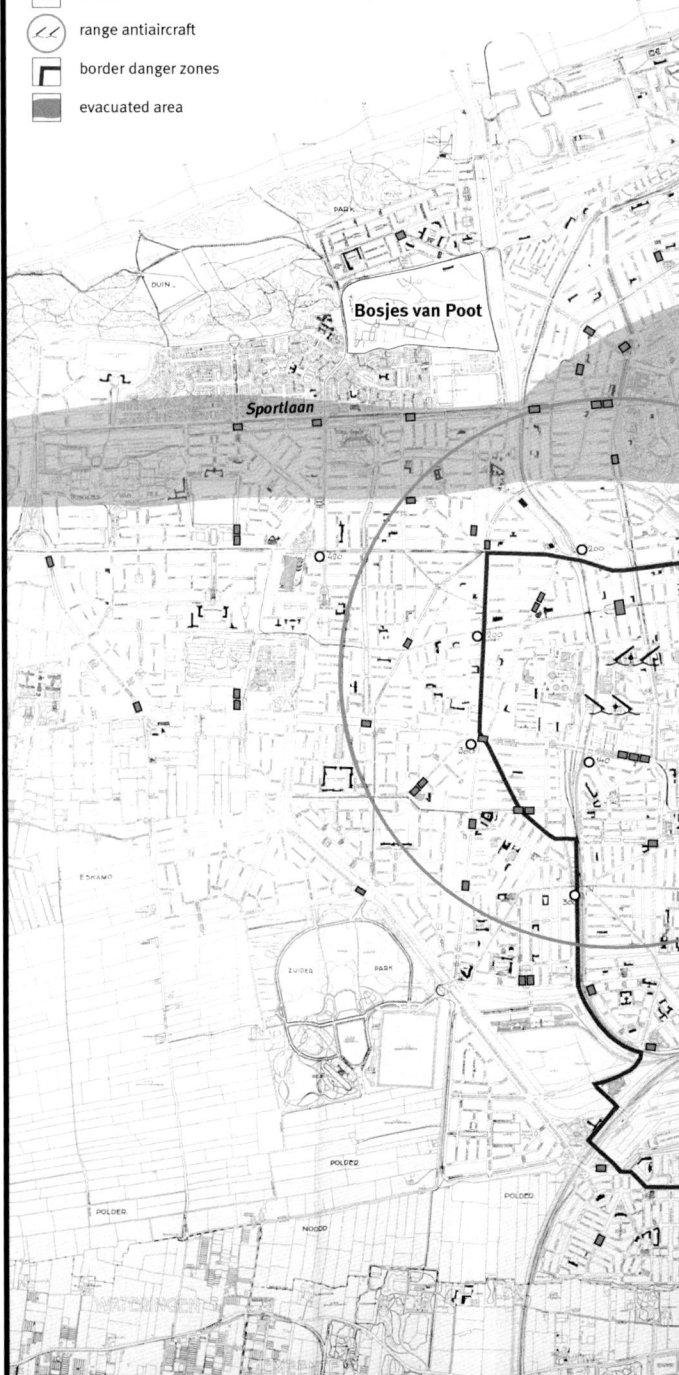

THE HAGUE 1939

LEGEND

- ▪ wooden shelters under construction or completed
- ○ private shelters under construction or completed
- ⟨∕∕⟩ range antiaircraft
- ⌐ border danger zones
- ▪ evacuated area

0   KILOMETER   1

Bosjes van Poot

Sportlaan

222. Map of the Sportlaan area showing the urban fabric making way for an anti-tank ditch (drawn on the 1939 map of The Hague)

Page 281 >
223. Aerial view of demolition in Bomenbuurt and Bloemenbuurt for construction of an anti-tank ditch. No. 1: Demolished secondary school on Stokroosplein. No. 2: Demolished Red Cross Hospital, photo 1943

field of fire. More than 2500 homes had to be levelled."[10] As the coordinator of the demolition, Münster issued instructions to the mayor for a phased evacuation of the coastal strip and a strip through the city where a line of defence would be built. In Section I of his letter of 31 October 1942 (demolition of about 220 homes), he gave instructions for the demolition operations and the disposal of materials, dealing with the labour force and the like.[11]

Given the size of the task, The Hague section of the Atlantic Wall was accomplished at astonishing speed. The municipal public works department made arrangements for demolition, the storage of household effects and evacuation in The Hague itself. The Urban Planning and Housing Department supplied the cadastral data, the electricity company removed electric meters, lamp posts and transformer kiosks, and the local water board saw to it that water supplies were cut off at the mains.[12]

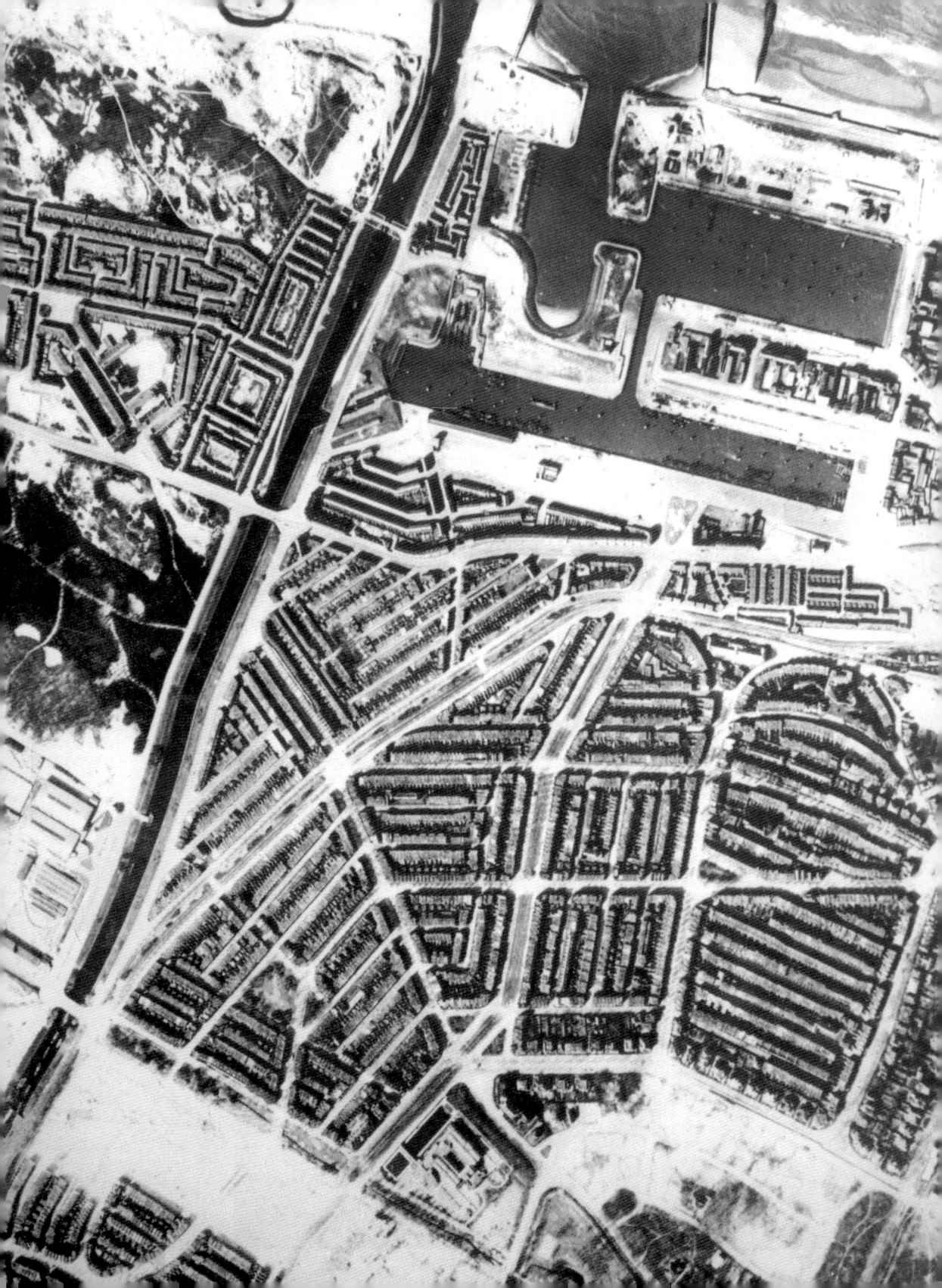

< *Page 282*
224. Aerial view of Geuzenkwartier and Statenkwartier. Diagonally, tank ditch from Houtrustweg to Oude Scheveningseweg, photo 1943

225. Aerial view of Bohemen and Meer en Bos; left, Sportlaan and Vogelwijk; middle, clearance along Daal en Bergselaan, photo 15 May 1946

In the first stage, from May 1942 to April 1943, over 1,600 homes were demolished by 65 contractors.[13] The number of houses demolished was doubled in the second phase. Between December 1942 and December 1943, 2,883 dwellings (1,692 houses) and 290 other buildings were pulled down.[14] This number was still to increase considerably. In December 1942 1,850 demolition workers were engaged in the operation, but by the end of January 1943 their number had risen to 5,800. "In as little as four months, 2,517 homes, two churches, a church tower, three hospitals, seven schools, three clubhouses, 25 company garages, 113 private garages and five bridges were demolished. This was about eighty percent of all the demolition work that would take place throughout the war."[15]

The Public Works Department made drawings of the blocks scheduled for demolition and issued the tenders for specialized contractors. A striking feature was the way *Siedlung und Bauten* organized recycling. All usable building materials were trans-

226. Aerial view of Kijkduin and Ockenburg; right, Meer en Bos (black area); above right, Savornin Lohmanplein; photo 5 August 1945

ported to the building depot in Clingendaal where they were stored. Some of the material was recycled straightway for building the Atlantic Wall and air-raid shelters.[16]

On 15 January 1944 Münster had given instructions to dismantle the interiors of those houses that were still standing, with the shells made waterproof: "The sanitary fittings were removed, the carpeting and stoves disappeared; everything was knocked down and removed, even cupboard doors, floorboards, etc.; then it was the turn of the garden fences, the tram rails were prised loose from the streets and clinkers were also removed from a number of them."[17] The rubble and any usable materials went to Malieveld, Haagse Bos and the Clingendaal building depot. A number of pre-war military trenches were also destroyed during the demolition.

EVACUATION

Münster delegated the vast operation of demolition and evacuation to the Municipal Public Works Department[18] and the Office of the Evacuation of the Civilian Population, which came under the Ministry of Home Affairs. The Evacuation Office, which was the executive body of the *Commissie Burgerbevolking* (Civilian Population Commission) instituted in 1939, had already conducted a number of evacuations in May 1940, and its activities were nationwide. At a regional level, provincial Commissioners for the Evacuation of the Civilian Population were responsible for the distribution of the evacuees around the host local authorities.

The mayor requested the Planning and Housing Department to arrange for the evacuation of 2,500 Scheveningen residents.[19] The city authorities had drawn up an evacuation plan as early as 1941, with the aim of accommodating the different groups of the population inside the city limits. The city was divided into 14 sectors, each under a 'sector head', in each of which one or more large buildings was "set aside as a temporary refuge".[20] The Hague had had a municipal Evacuation Office since October 1942. It had an initial staff of 25, but its numbers had expanded to 400 by the spring of 1944.[21] Feverishly, they endeavoured to cope with the inevitable secondary consequences of the erecting the Atlantic Wall – evacuation, requisitions, billeting and demolition.

227. Tank ditch on Sportlaan, August 1945

228. Scheveningse Bosjes, tank ditch and "asparagus" tank traps
(angled sections of rail with one end implanted in the ground), March
1946

The Proclamation of 21 October 1942, signed by Seyss-Inquart and the mayor of The Hague and intended to be put up as a poster, announced the evacuation of sections of the population to destinations outside the Randstad. By now, thousands of Hague citizens had already experienced the removal vans pulling up at the front door. To accomplish the evacuation in the final two weeks of 1942, thousands of homes were requisitioned in Leidschendam, Rijswijk, Voorburg and Wassenaar. Of the 135,000 citizens to be moved from The Hague, 15,000 went to neighbouring municipalities and 45,000 to the north or east of the country. Many of them were billeted on other Hague residents, which led to interesting but not always pleasurable social interactions. In the centre of the city, there were about a thousand empty homes that had belonged to deported Jews; these were made available for accommodation by *Siedlung und Bauten*. Any evacuees who could not find accommodation elsewhere or who were not potentially employable were housed by the local authorities in areas outside the Randstad.[22]

In September 1943 the two bases still contained a substantial Dutch population, with roughly 25,000 Dutch citizens living in Scheveningen and 17,000 in Clingendaal. The evacuation had halted the previous February, by which time 100,000 Hague residents had already left (including 15,000 displaced from their homes in the "substitute district" to make way for evacuated residents considered indispensable to local industry). The explanation for the postponement of further evacuation until September is uncertain. It may have had to do with delays in building the defences: between June and September the contractors were redeployed to the Ruhr to repair dams that had been bombed.[23] A letter from infantry General Reinhardt, dated 30 October 1943, pressed for Dutch and German functions to be moved from the two bases, leaving no more than 5,000 civilians in Clingendaal and roughly 7,000 in Scheveningen.[24] After Hitler's order of 3 November 1943 for resumption of work on the Atlantic Wall, the pace of construction of the fortifications in The Hague was significantly stepped up in any case. Evacuation also resumed full speed. A plan to evict the inhabitants of Benoordenhout (a large part of the population of the Clingendaal base, comprising 14,000 of the total 17,000 residents), leaked out in September 1943 and was partly implemented. At the end of 1943, when the German occupiers were on high alert for an allied invasion, Siedlung und Bauten sealed the Clingendaal garrison off by demolishing the temporary wooden bridges over the anti-tank ditches. In total, only seven entrances remained.[25]

SCHEVENINGEN

On the seaward side of the base in Scheveningen, a combination of artillery batteries, the dunes, a beach wall with barbed wire, the seawall and an anti-tank wall (1.5 metres thick and 2 metres high) presented an impressive defence to a potential tank-led invasion. Münster's department built standardized military bunkers at top speed, and screened designs by third parties, paying close attention to the estimated costs per item. Siedlung und Bauten supervised the construction of various defensive works,[26] as well as about 35 bunkers for artillery and munitions (including bunker types 612, 667 and 680) on the north and south beaches.[27] In 1944 Siedlung und Bauten also carried out works along the beach on the basis of an idea by Field Marshal E. Rommel: the soft yellow sands were dug up to plant buried tree trunks and posts topped with mines, converting them into a pockmarked barricade which would impede landings from the North Sea and would be impassable for tanks.

Meanwhile in The Hague and its surroundings there were 6000 Germans who

229. Cremerweg, intersection with Haringkade, demolished bridges,
August 1945

230. Turning harbour basin in lock approach, Scheveningen; left:
former slipway, August 1945

231. Keizerstraat, Scheveningen, separated from the coast by barbed wire and a concrete wall, 1945

Bottom
232. Keizerstraat, Scheveningen, from seaward side, showing concrete tank wall; left, Hotel Rauch; right, Hotel Zeerust; 1945

233. Bunkers and tank wall on present-day Eisenhowerlaan, intersection with Prins Mauritslaan, 1945

234. Bunker on present-day Eisenhowerlaan, July 1945

held civilian posts.[28] They enjoyed the cultural privileges offered by a host of elegant buildings,[29] and their children were sent to special German schools. They too needed shelter from air raids.[30]

CLINGENDAAL

On inspecting the combined stronghold of Scheveningen and Clingendaal at the end of September 1943, Seyss-Inquart and Rauter were generous in their praise.[31] The progress of the demolition campaign was already evident by April 1943, when a report from the Albrecht resistance group included a map with the course of the tank ditch and the outlines of the Clingendaal base drawn in.[32] An inspection early in January 1944 by Field Marshal Rommel, who visited the coastal defences and those of The Hague as well as other installations in the hinterland, proved equally satisfactory. A few days later Himmler arrived on the scene, and on his return he wrote to Seyss-Inquart, congratulating him "on his energetic and soldierly support"

235. SS Reichsführer A. Himmler on a visit to The Hague; front row, right to left: Himmler, Mussert and Seyss-Inquart; 17 May 1942

236. Aerial photo of the eastern part of the Atlantic Wall
(landside): Haagse Bos with tank ditch; below left to above,
Bezuidenhoutseweg; right, Benoordenhoutseweg; middle, Royal
Palace Huis ten Bosch; 5 August 1946

in the building of the Scheveningen-Clingendaal base and requesting him to inform
Walter Münster of his gratitude.[33]

This enthusiasm about progress on the base should not be taken to mean that it
was well organized or that the defence personnel had a coherent hierarchy. In April
1943, for instance, it appeared that there were no less than nine different military,
semi-military and civilian units active inside the stronghold, each of whom wore
their own uniforms and were answerable to different superiors. A commander, who
had spent a couple of winters on the Russian front, compared the situation to an international congress.[34]

The two strongholds still had a total population of 10,000 in the spring of 1944.
It was becoming increasingly difficult to arrange accommodation for them else-

where in the densely populated west of the Netherlands. The pressure was such that by 1944, three thousand Dutch nationals were given access to Clingendaal, along with a thousand German civilians. In May 1944 the evacuation of the remaining civilian population from the base was once again imminent, but the allied landing in Normandy made even that plan impossible. As a seat of government, the base of Clingendaal had become an empty sham.

SIEDLUNG UND BAUTEN: APPROACH AND PROJECTS

Seyss-Inquart's base at Clingendaal, a combination of active and passive air raid defence, was *Siedlung und Bauten*'s masterpiece. It provided a safe shelter for Seyss-Inquart and his civilian court, and it was built in next to no time.

The prime concern of *Siedlung und Bauten*'s mode of operation was efficiency, and this meant that the shelters were standardized, even though they were intended for specific sites. More importantly, the working procedures were regulated ever more precisely, with the same construction firms, draughtsmen and fitters being instructed to submit offers for carrying out the work on the bunker series.

Apart from the Atlantic Wall, most of *Siedlung und Bauten*'s designs, like the air raid defence projects in Germany, were made for a specific site, while the separate parts – doors, ventilation systems and so on – were standardised and were installed in the bunker shell by regular suppliers. For their series of bunkers and shelters *Siedlung und Bauten* employed civilian, not military standards. Despite embrasures in some of them, the prime purpose of most of them was to offer protection; armed defence was not their aim. Generally speaking, there were two types of bunker, both of which were present in Clingendaal – the long narrow ones and the rectangular or square type.

The fortress was surrounded by ditches, walls and uniform bunkers. The first phase of the construction of Clingendaal consisted of major military earthworks around the perimeter of the base: a zigzag tank ditch with some bunkers and anti-tank walls cutting across the partially felled Haagse Bos. No drawings have been preserved, and it may be that these defences were not designed by *Siedlung und Bauten*. An existing watercourse was widened to create the anti-tank ditch. The bunkers were arranged along this ditch, and some are still visible as mounds of earth. Anti-tank ditches were generally made by enlarging existing waterways or other features, but the tank ditch parallel to Benoordenhoutseweg, between Oosterbeek and the Oostersportpark in Wassenaar, was specially dug and is still visible.[35]

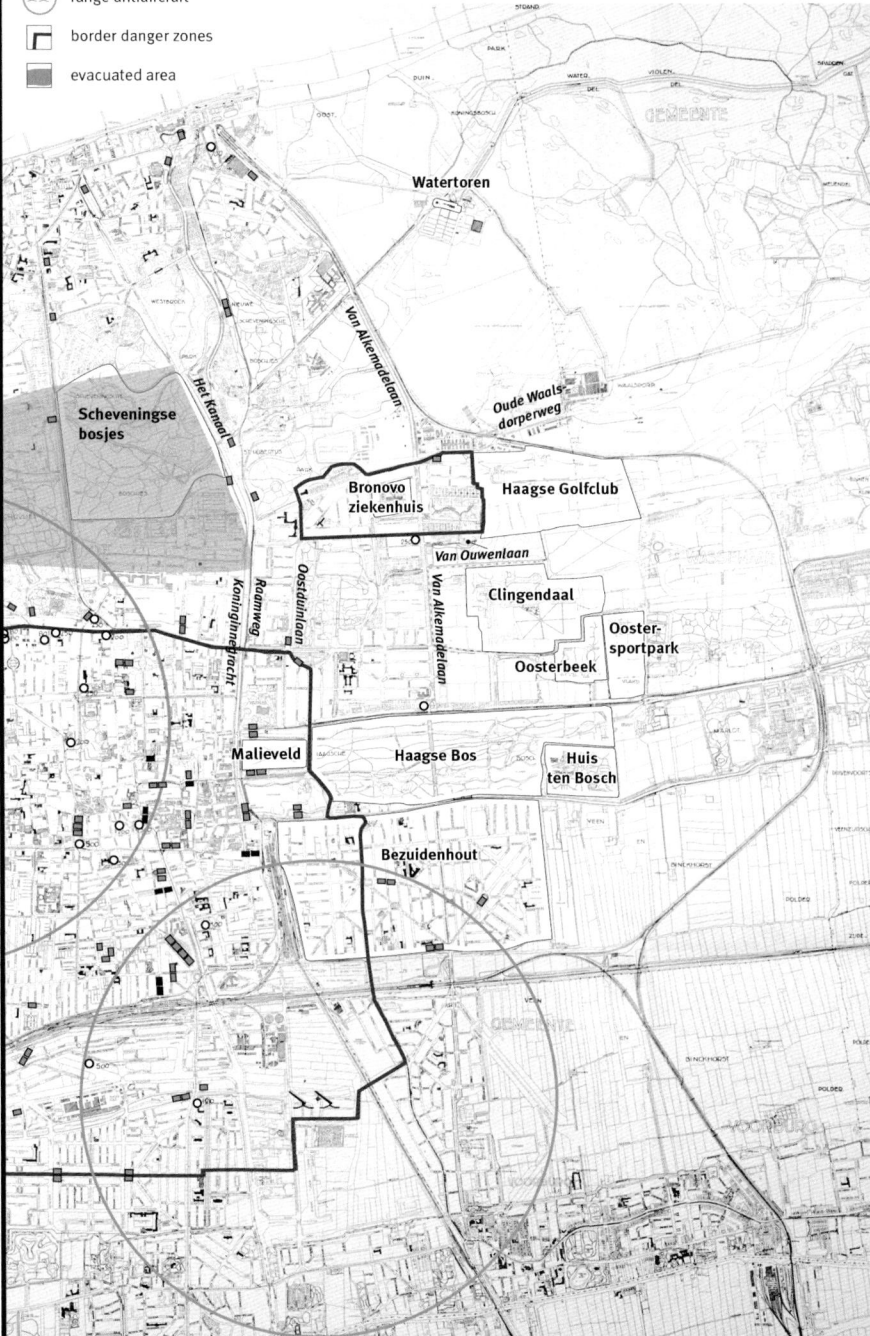

THE HAGUE 1939

LEGEND

- ▣ wooden shelters under construction or completed
- ◆ concrete shelters (planned)
- ○ private shelters under construction or completed
- ⟋⟋ range antiaircraft
- ⌐ border danger zones
- ▨ evacuated area

KILOMETER

0   2

Watertoren

Scheveningse bosjes

Het Kanaal

Van Alkemadelaan

Oude Waals-dorperweg

Bronovo ziekenhuis

Haagse Golfclub

Van Ouwenlaan

Koninginnegracht

Raamweg

Oostduinlaan

Van Alkemadelaan

Clingendaal

Ooster-sportpark

Oosterbeek

Malieveld

Haagse Bos

Huis ten Bosch

Bezuidenhout

237. Eastern part of the Atlantic Wall. The evacuation zone ended at Scheveningse Bosjes. The defence line suddenly went southward in order to include Seyss-Inquart's headquarters Clingendaal. The demarcation line went southwards along Het Kanaal, then Raamweg/Koninginnegracht, then went to the east again through the Haagse Bos and eventually northward alongside Oosterbeek, Clingendaal, Haagse Golfclub, Van Alkema-delaan (drawn on the 1939 map of The Hague)

238. Royal Palace Huis ten Bosch, 1937

239. Royal Palace Huis ten Bosch; foreground, tank ditch; left, three storey bomb shelter, 1944

240. Haagse Bos, felled trees
awaiting transportation, 1943

Bottom
241. Haagse Bos, transportation
of felled tree, 1944

242. Tank ditch from Malieveld to Haagse Bos, 1943

243. Tank ditch through Malieveld, seen from Benoorden-houtseweg, 18 March 1943

244. Bunker in Haagse Bos near Laan van Nieuw Oost-Indië,
September 1945

245. Anti-tank wall on Koningskade, seen in Javastraat direction,
July 1945

246. Anti-tank wall, bunker and dragon's teeth on Stadhouderslaan, 1945

247. Bricked-up housing in Raamweg; middle, Carel van Bylandtlaan, 1943

248. Houses on Koningskade converted to defensive wall, 1945

The base was sealed off to the south and east with an anti-tank ditch about 20 metres wide, while on the west the Koninginnegracht formed the boundary. The terrace of houses on the Raamweg and the Koningskade was requisitioned, and a wall to the height of the windows was built in front of them. In Clingendaal the line was partly determined by the features of the terrain, with the boundaries largely formed by waterways. The part of the cleared strip between Raamweg and Koningskade was 50-70 metres wide, and the Malieveld was an open meadow with the trees of the Haagse Bos forming the only remaining obstacle. The land to the northeast of the estate of Oosterbeek and The Hague Golf Club were also free of buildings, trees and bushes. On the north side there was no boundary because the barrier on the east side cut right through the dunes to the beach. On the edge of this contour were 14 uniform defensive bunkers. They projected about seven metres above ground level and were covered with sand and rubble. Sketched in on German military maps of 28 April 1943 are indications of 35 bunkers in front of Clingendaal, of which 20 were the 625 type (11 along the tank ditch).[36] In comparison with the other Dutch bases,

249. Koningskade, bunker alongside Zoo, 1945

the cordon around Clingendaal was completed exceptionally quickly, with the aid of thousands of workers, a host of machines and German specialists operating under the zealous supervision of *Siedlung und Bauten*.

The scanty records we have group the projects designed and implemented by *Siedlung und Bauten* for Seyss-Inquart's base under the heading Clingendaal I to IV. The major concentrations of buildings were on the estate of Clingendaal itself, home to Seyss-Inquart and his family (where the wine cellar was converted into a shelter), the command complex of the Reichskommissar (bunker and police barracks on the Wassenaarseweg) and three complexes with service functions in the little park on the corner of the Oostduinlaan and the Ruychrocklaan.[37] "All the other works were domestic shelters or had a service function. Most of them were situated in the gardens of the houses along the Stadhouderslaan."[38] The shelters were intended for German bodies that had requisitioned housing in the immediate surroundings. Of course the Shelter City required its own facilities: reinforced electricity substations, an emergency municipal office, emergency kitchens and two emergency hospitals,[39] a first aid post, three emergency cemeteries,[40] a morgue,[41] a water board office, a food depot, the fire brigade and the police. Huge quantities of supplies were stored, so that if besieged, the residents of the fortress could survive for several months.

AERIAL PROTECTION FOR THE REICHSKOMMISSAR

Cropping up in the records for May and June 1941 we find the term *Gesamtübersichtsplan* (master plan) for "Filmstad". The district of Benoordenhout consisted of four seventeenth-century parkland estates: Duindigt (heavily bombed), Reigersbergen (destroyed to make way for the Atlantic Wall), Clingendaal and Oosterbeek. In 1935 a Hague businessman had bought Oosterbeek with the idea of building a film studio there. He dubbed it "Filmstad" or Film City, doubtless dreaming of founding a Dutch Hollywood. In the space of a few years, his dream went up in smoke. The German film company, the UFA, confiscated Oosterbeek as Jewish property. The studio was in a good enough shape for the Germans to shoot films there. In 1944 the grounds of Oosterbeek were put to use for assembling and stockpiling V2 rockets, making it a target for an allied bombardment. After the Liberation the remains of both Filmstad and the country house were demolished.[42]

Other additions made to the Oosterbeek estate during the occupation included a police barracks, a garage and a wooden bridge, which made it necessary to shift the stables. The farm of Uilennest, on the Hague side of Oosterbeek, was demolished by the Public Works Department, and the police barracks for the Reichskommissar's headquarters was built on its site. This barracks and the accompanying bunker were designed at the same time, as the Luftgaukommando's approval of both sets of drawings in February 1942 indicates. The simultaneous construction of the two buildings – both designed by the architects Gonser (a husband and wife team) – highlights more clearly than anything else the two faces of *Siedlung und Bauten*: representative architecture and prosaic protection, building overground and underground. The style of the police barracks was that of the Stuttgart School, which meant among other things that a building must declare its position in the hierarchy. The exterior had to accord with the regional vernacular and might well make specific local references. The ground plan of the main building consists of two identical L-shaped blocks arranged to form an open rectangle. A lower garage annex, also L-shaped, closed one of the gaps to produce a rectangular courtyard reminiscent of regional farmyards. The long brick facades with their strict window arrangement

250. Fortified wall through sand dunes, Harstenhoekweg, intersection with Van Alkemadelaan, near water tower, 1946

251. Paved cycle path from the water tower to the Wassenaarseslag beach entry which crossed the anti tank wall at "Sperre 340", a 4.2 metre wide passage, March 1946

252. Clingendaal,
shelter on Van
Ouwenlaan, 1948

and the sloping roofs with dormers are severe and sober. This sobriety places all the emphasis on the restrained but representative entrance, which takes the form of a projecting portico with a windowed space above it and with the brickwork subtly set off by the stone moulding of the archways. The status of the main interior spaces is also emphasized by the tall windows, chandeliers and a stage for artistic performances.

In September 1942 work started on the barracks and the bunker. The barracks were up and running by February 1943; at the same time, right next to it, work continued on the two-storey bomb shelter, disguised as a farmhouse, for Seyss-Inquart.[43] The camouflage consisted of an outer structure clad with grey tiles, placed like a huge cheese cover over the actual bunker and separated from it by over five metres. The outer walls of the cover were painted with imitation clinkers, windows and doors. The bunker had phone and telex links and transmitting facilities, and was equipped with an emergency generator. The whole complex was surrounded by trenches, while a number of transmitting and receiving masts was installed in the garden. Excluding the kitchen bunker added in 1943-1944, the exterior measurements of the bunker were about 60 by 30 metres, with the roof reaching a height of 20 metres above ground level.

Delivered early in 1943, Seyss-Inquart's huge bunker was built a stone's throw from Clingendaal. The design work was supervised by *Siedlung und Bauten*, after which the drawings were detailed and made ready for tender by an external technician.[44] This air raid shelter was the largest and best camouflaged bunker in The Hague. The armaments minister, Albert Speer, expressed his concerns, stating that it was disproportionately large, even if Seyss-Inquart didn't intend it to be used solely by the Reichskommissariat.[45] On 14 November 1942, Seyss-Inquart rubber-stamped *Siedlung und Bauten*'s design. He regarded the police barracks as a masterpiece of quality and distinction. He spoke of it in one breath with the bunker-in-progress which, with its camouflage, would look quite charming, while offering protection against raids by fighter-bombers. Moreover, it was large enough to house the barracks' entire police force. A separate intelligence post was built into it as well. Only in extreme circumstances would it serve as a 'retreat' for the Reichskommissar himself. Seyss-Inquart, who had the backing of Himmler, acknowledged the receipt of Speer's remarks.[46] His shelter space was considerably larger than Adolf Hitler's bunker in the Reich Chancellery in Berlin.

In 1943 *Siedlung und Bauten* embarked on a new series of projects to protect Seyss-Inquart and his staff. It is clear that this was an air raid shelter system of the utmost importance from Seyss-Inquart's orders to his staff in September 1944 to

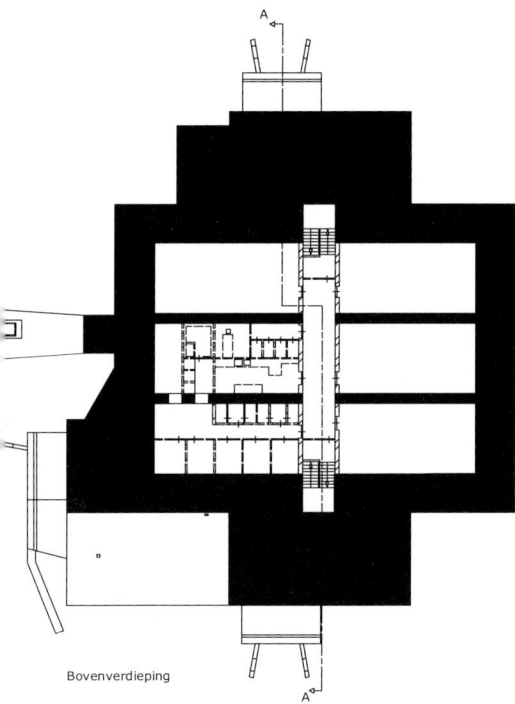

Bovenverdieping

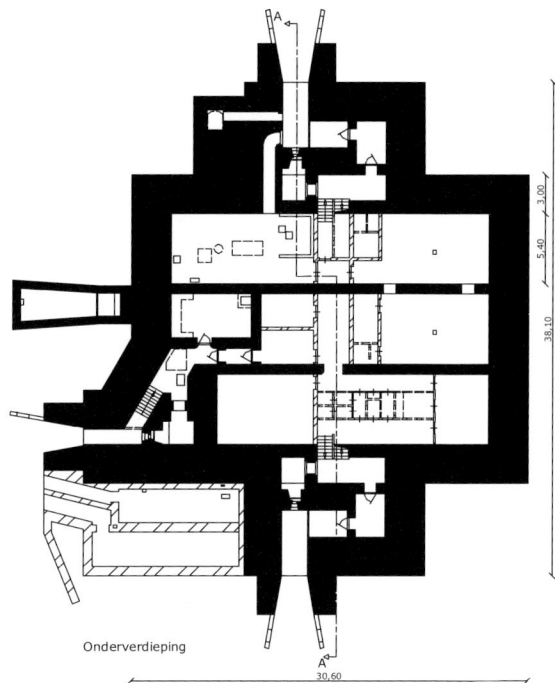

Onderverdieping

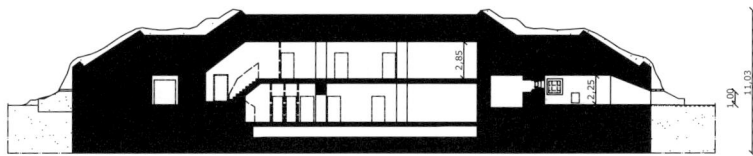

Doorsnede A-A

Top
253. Clingendaal, section, plans of ground floor and upper floor of hospital bunker on Van Ouwenlaan

Bottom
254. Clingendaal, hospital bunker on Van Ouwenlaan (photo Anja de Jong, 2004)

255. Clingendaal, entrance hospital bunker on Van Ouwenlaan (photo Anja de Jong, 2004)

256. Clingendaal, entrance to Van Soutelandenlaan shelter (photo Anja de Jong, 2004)

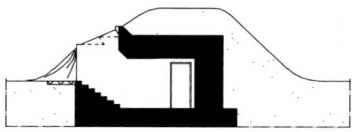

Doorsnede B-B

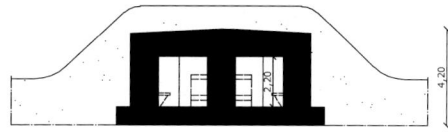

Doorsnede A-A

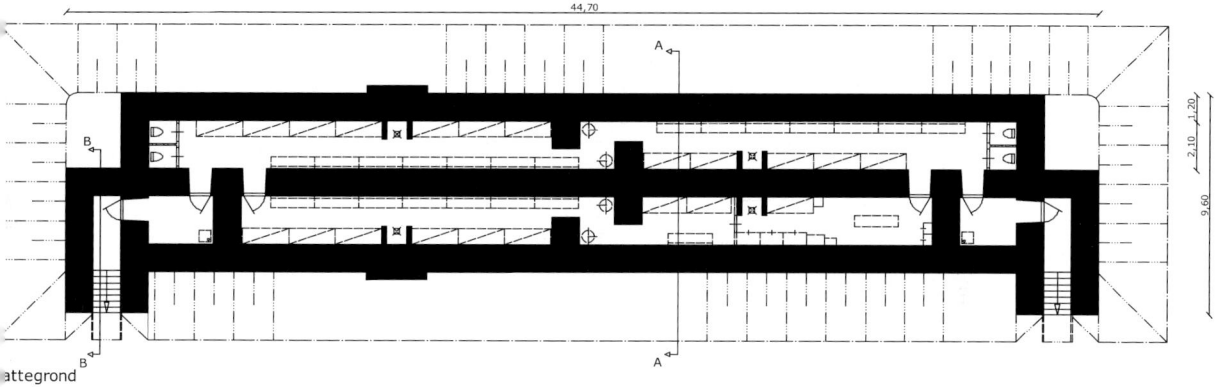

Plattegrond

257. Clingendaal, plan and sections of earth-covered shelter on Van Soutelandelaan

258. Clingendaal, shelter on Wassenaarseweg at intersection with Van Alkemadelaan, May 1946

take up quarters inside the base. Seyss-Inquart himself continued to make use of his offices on Het Plein, in the political heart of The Hague – outside the base, that is. This meant that conversions were required in the sense of improvements to buildings and air raid protection measures. A new porch on the front facade led to the corridor in the basement, which was thoroughly reinforced with 45-cm-thick brick walls and a concrete ceiling 40-60 cm thick. This bombproof corridor continued under the courtyard behind the residence and led to a concrete shelter with walls of a similar width (see Chapter 6, illustration 181).[47]

Siedlung und Bauten also designed a "first aid bunker" on Van Ouwenlaan (April 1943; completed May 1944).[48] It is a nearly square, two-storey block (roughly 30×40 metres) with bulges at both entrances and at the emergency exit. The exterior walls are three metres wide and the roof, two metres wide. The entrances include embrasures and an airlock. The interior was divided by walls into three units of 5.5 × 11 metres. The machine room was situated on the ground floor. The bunker cannot be described as a hospital, but it was a superior first-aid post with nurses, midwives, doctors and male nurses. Ordinary bunkers were not laid out in a way that allowed room for medical facilities, because the water supply, electricity supplies and corridor width were not suited to this purpose. This shelter was essential because the German army had requisitioned the Bronovo Hospital, which was situated on the estate of Clingendaal.

In 1943 and 1944 *Siedlung und Bauten* produced a series of at least 13 shelters for civilian purposes; the few remaining drawings are signed by the staff. It is necessary to look at the concept of a "shelter" for a moment. According to H.F. Ambachtsheer in his book about the Atlantic Wall in The Hague, the gamut of typologies in The Hague includes two types of building that he denotes as residential accommodation and shelters.[49] The underground city of The Hague had countless public shelters, which were partly entrenched and which could serve both military and civilian purposes. They provided storage spaces for weapons, victuals, water and the like, and contained toilets, saunas, hospitals, kitchens, canteens and bakeries. As these spaces could not strictly speaking be classified as civilian shelters, I will not describe them in detail. The second type is the long narrow shelter in brick and concrete with entrances at each end. With their steel doors and airlocks, the entrances also served as buffers to the actual shelters. Extractor fans were installed in the interior. The brick walls were 133 centimetres thick, and the concrete roof was one metre thick. Benches were placed parallel to the walls. Each 125-cm-wide bay had room for two adults. There was also a version with thin brick walls and vaults heavily reinforced with packed earth.

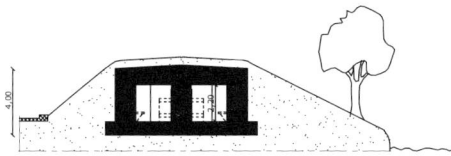

Doorsnede A-A

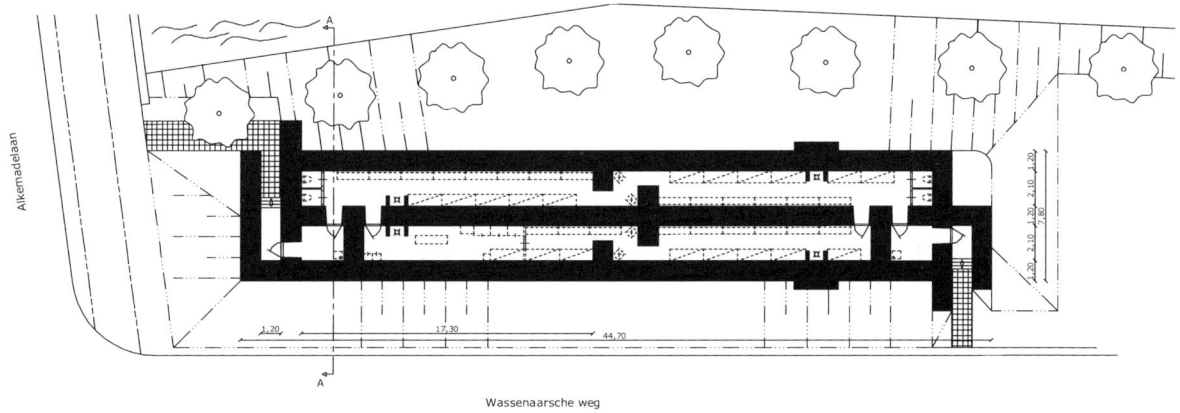

Alkemadelaan

1,20 1,20 2,10 2,10
7,80

1,20   17,30   44,70

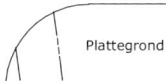

A

Wassenaarsche weg

Plattegrond

259. Clingendaal, situation, plan and section of Wassenaarseweg
shelter at intersection with Van Alkemadelaan. Standardized layout:
two entrances, airlock, toilets and bunk beds along walls

260. Clingendaal, situation, elevation, sections and plan of shelter on
Jan van Nassaustraat, next to a school

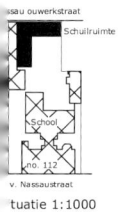

sau ouwerkstraat
Schuilruimte

School

no. 112
v. Nassaustraat
tuatie 1:1000

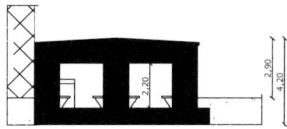

2,90
2,20
4,20

Doorsnede A-A

oorsnede B-B

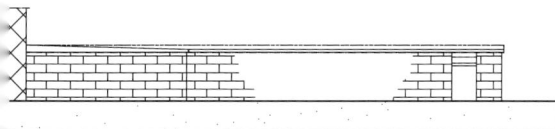

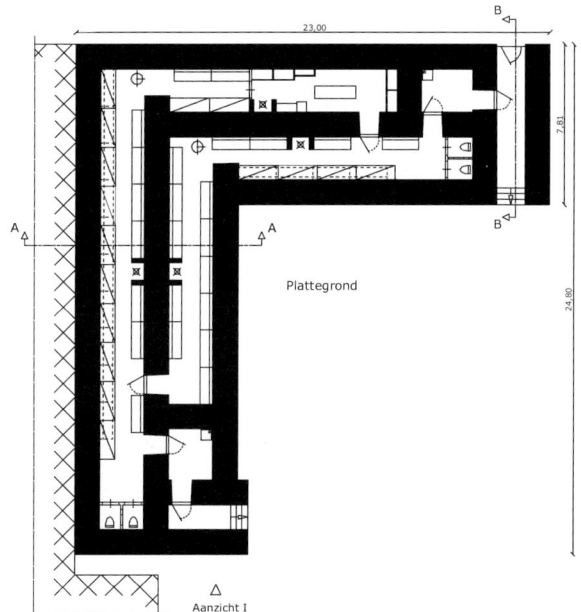

B

23,00

7,81

A A   A

B

Plattegrond

24,80

Δ
Aanzicht I

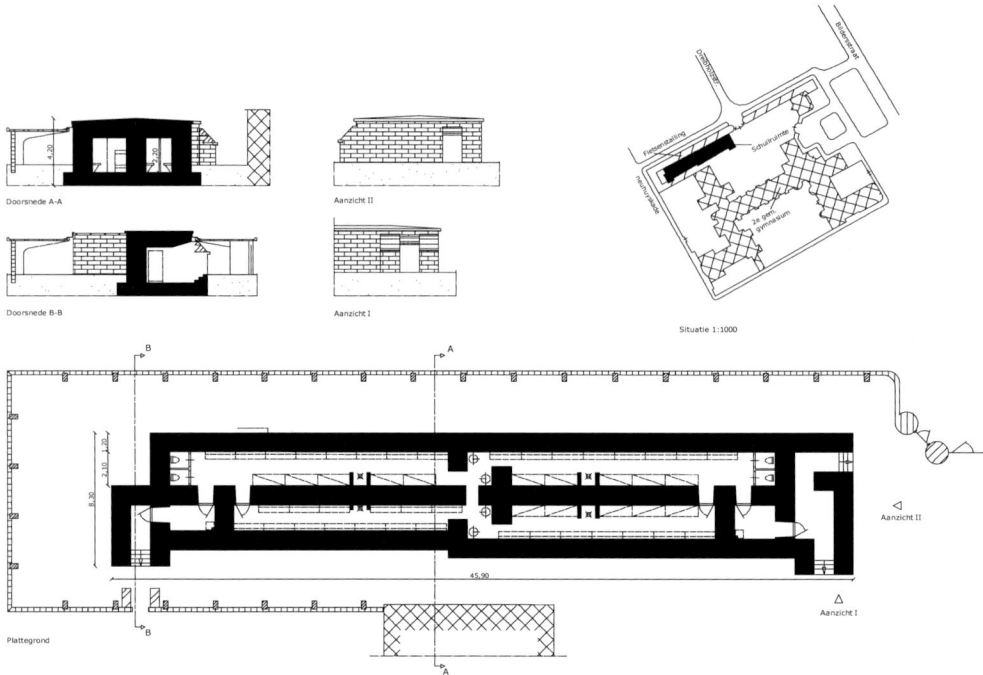

Doorsnede A-A

Aanzicht II

Doorsnede B-B

Aanzicht I

Situatie 1:1000

Plattegrond

Aanzicht II

Aanzicht I

45,90

261. Clingendaal, situation, elevation, sections and plan of shelter on
Bilderstraat, next to a school

262. Clingendaal, situation, elevation, sections and plan of shelter on
Carel van Bylandtlaan

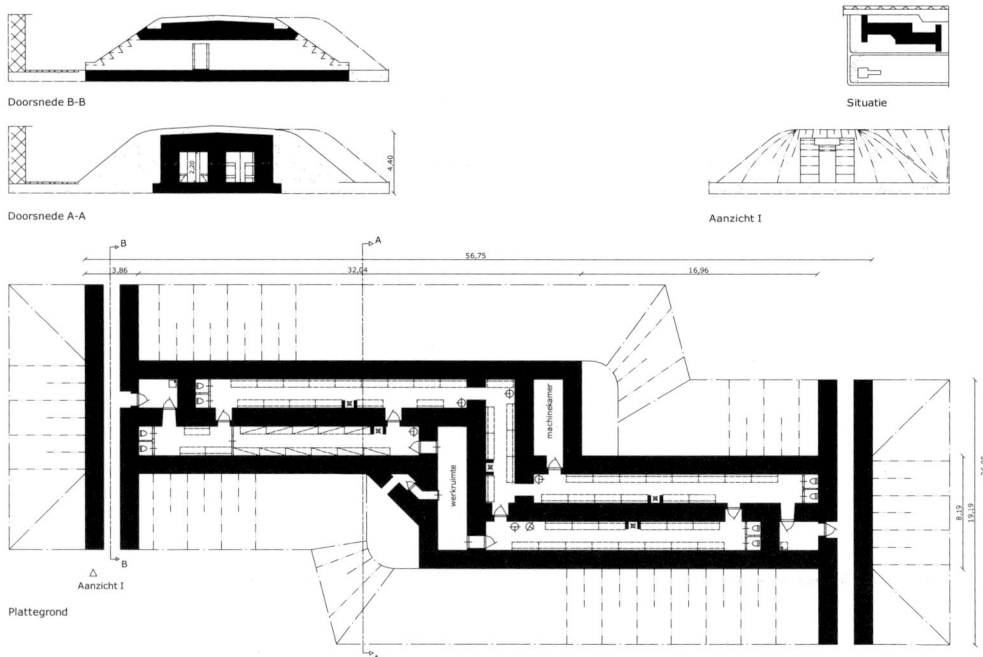

Doorsnede B-B

Situatie

Doorsnede A-A

Aanzicht I

Plattegrond

Aanzicht I

56,75

32,04

16,96

3,86

26,05

19,19

8,19

machinekamer

werkruimte

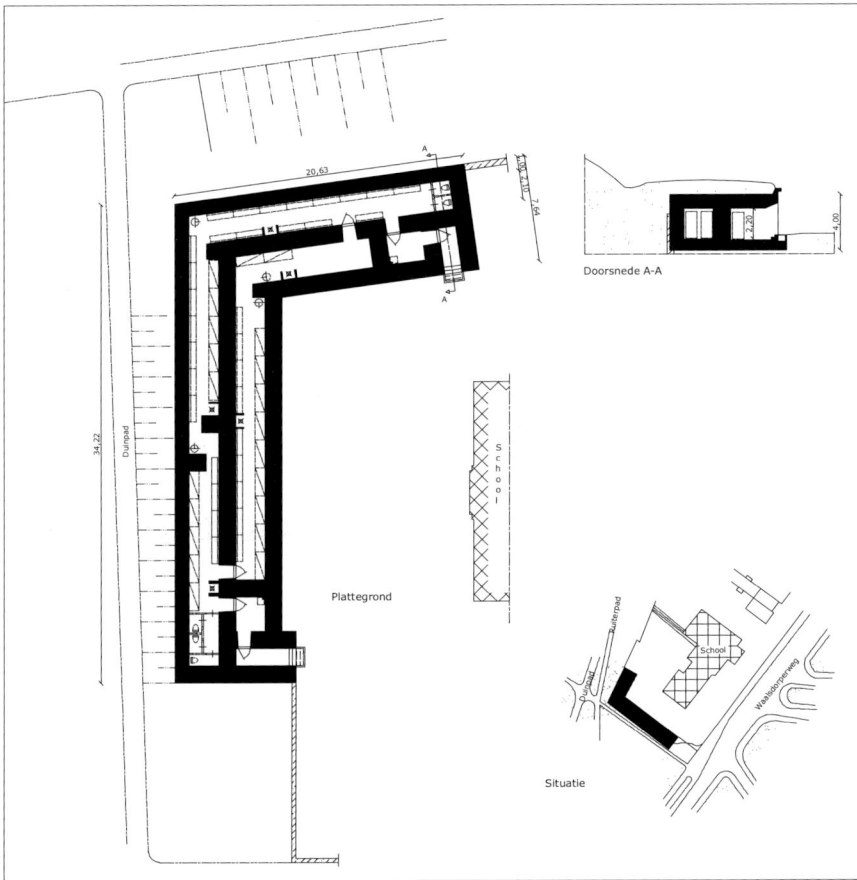

263. Clingendaal,
situation, elevation,
sections and
plan of shelter on
Waalsdorperweg

Doorsnede A-A

Plattegrond

School

Situatie

264. Clingendaal,
postwar house
built on bunker in
Ruychrocklaan (photo
Anja de Jong, 2004)

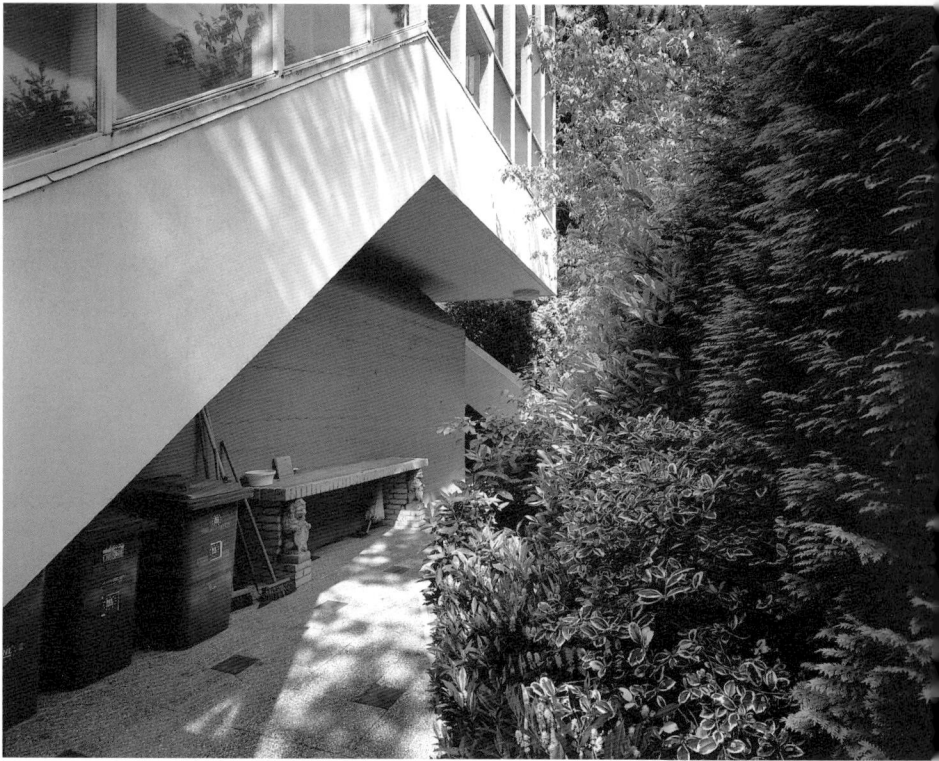

265. Clingendaal,
postwar house
built on bunker in
Ruychrocklaan (photo
Anja de Jong, 2004)

266. Clingendaal,
postwar house
built on bunker in
Ruychrocklaan (photo
Anja de Jong, 2004)

267. Clingendaal, Elisabeth and Karl Gonser, police barracks on
Wassenaarseweg (1942-1943, photo 2004). The bunker for Seyss-
Inquart and his staff, camouflaged as a farmhouse, is to the left of the
barracks, separated by a road and ditch

268. Clingendaal, main
entrance of police
barracks

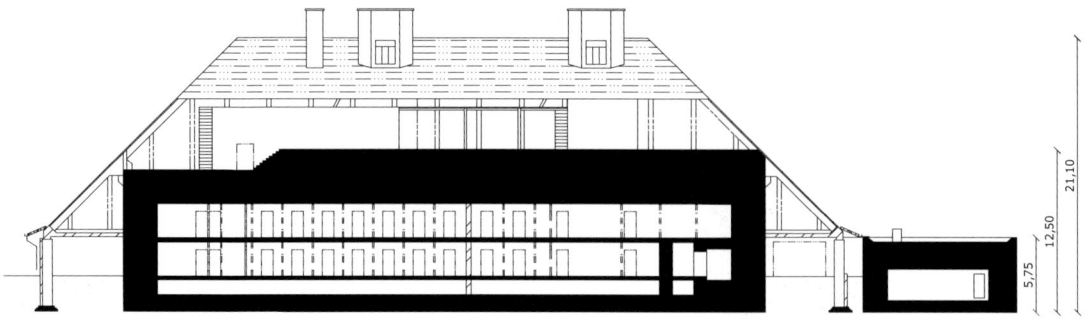

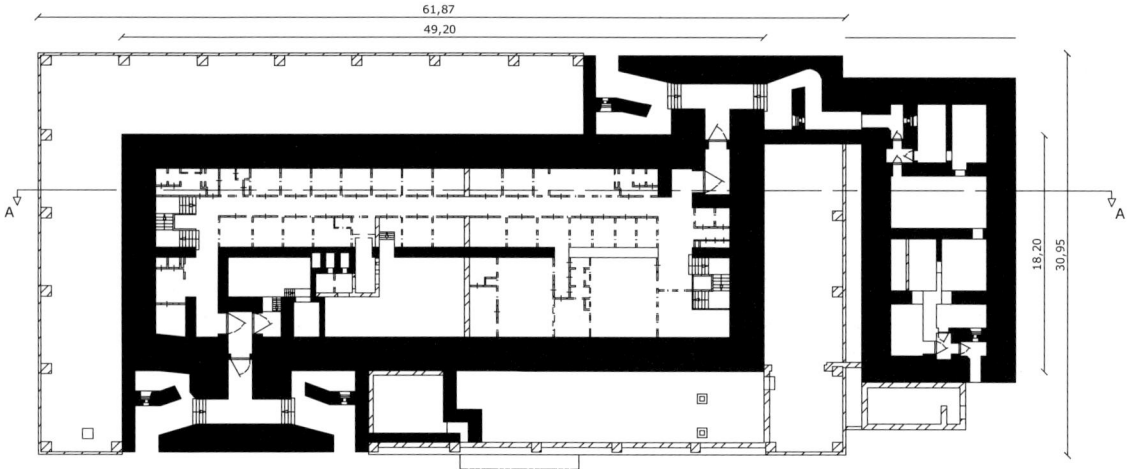

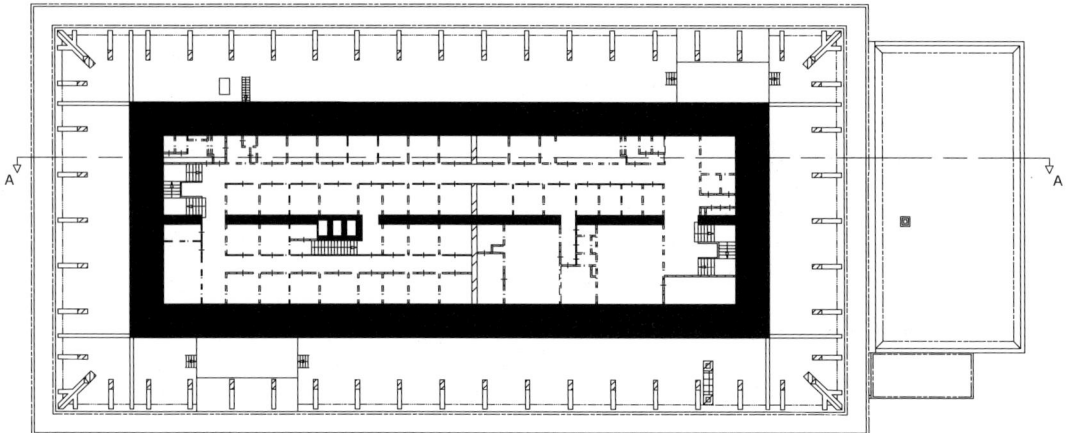

Top
269. Clingendaal, Elisabeth and Karl Gonser, camouflaged bunker for Seyss-Inquart and his staff (reconstructed drawing). Bunker in black, later-added kitchen bunker on right

Middle
270. Clingendaal, ground floor of camouflaged bunker for Seyss-Inquart and his staff; bunker in black, later-added kitchen bunker on right

Bottom
271. Clingendaal, upper floor of camouflaged bunker for Seyss-Inquart and his staff, bunker section in black

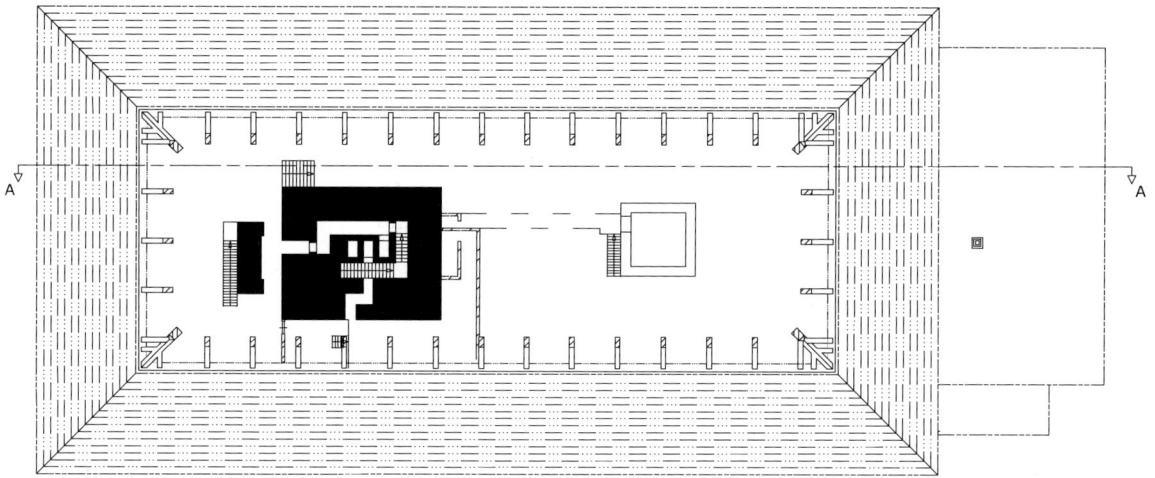

272. Clingendaal, attic storey of camouflaged bunker for Seyss-Inquart and his staff (reconstructed drawing), bunker section in black

Siedlung und Bauten's shelters varied from small bunkers in the form of camouflaged extensions for individual dwellings to long covered trenches, usually straight but sometimes with angular deflections according to the terrain. The trench type was a regular feature of schools requisitioned by the Germans, or other German-held buildings with a large number of occupants or visitors. The basic structure was a long corridor divided in two by a wall the same size as the exterior walls. The spaces were 2.2 metres high and wide, while the walls were 1.2 metres thick. The whole structure was built of tamped concrete and usually had two similar entrances each containing an airlock, shower and toilets. The shelter projected about two metres above ground level and was covered with earth. The length varied from 40-60 metres, and it was about 9 metres wide. There were benches along one side of the long corridors and wooden bunk beds on the opposite side. The drawings usually mention the number of people to be accommodated. These shelters were necessarily equipped with a telephone link to the emergency exchange in Seyss-Inquart's shelter. The base's order list also itemized underwear for men, women and children, "baby clothes and vests" and "baby's bottles with rubber teats".[50]

The bases of Scheveningen and Clingendaal built under the supervision of *Siedlung und Bauten* differed sharply from the rest of the Dutch section of the Atlantic Wall. The land front with bunkers for anti-tank artillery, the many bombproof bunkers for medical care, water storage and kitchen facilities, and the bunkered headquarters and well-protected civilian centre of Clingendaal cannot simply be explained in military terms; there were also civilian and political considerations. In

273. Clingendaal, front and side walls of camouflaged bunker for Seyss-Inquart and his staff (photo Anja de Jong, 2005)

274. Clingendaal, side wall (kitchen) of camouflaged bunker for Seyss-Inquart and his staff (photo Anja de Jong, 2005)

the Dutch context the protection of large groups of Germans in bunkers was clearly a new task, for which a new typology had to be designed which was unlike that of the conventional military bunkers in the Atlantic Wall but which drew on examples of civilian shelter programmes in Germany and on the specifications of the *Luftgaukommando* in Amsterdam.

FAREWELL TO SHELTER CITY

After September 1944 the process of evacuation ground to a halt. The "Hunger Winter" had begun, claiming 2,100 lives in the Hague alone. Thefts of combustible material and desperate excursions in search of food were a growing phenomenon. Dogs, cats and birds vanished from the street scene; they ended up in the pot. There was no soap to be had anywhere. Scabies was widespread, and people's hair and skin crawled with lice.

A lack of fuel to heat homes was an additional problem during the harsh winter of famine, and the Shelter City became an important asset for scavengers. Any available wood was burned, including 21 wooden air raid shelters, the bridge over the Schenk waterway, the stands in the sports grounds, 55 wood-lined trench shelters and 29 school buildings.[51] The strip of open land along the Atlantic wall, which cut across the city at an average width of 350 metres, was widened even more by the hordes who dug up an estimated 50,000-60,000 trees and shrubs for firewood. The empty houses on the coastal side of the defence line were also plundered. Electricity supplies broke down, and sewage systems ceased to function. The city suffered from serious pollution and became a shambles. The allied bombardment of the Bezuidenhout on 3 March 1945, one of the most disastrous mistaken strikes of the occupation, cost the lives of 520 Hague citizens and left 12,000 people homeless. The destruction was enormous: 3,300 homes were destroyed or suffered severe damage, as were 290 business premises, 64 offices, five churches, 15 schools and eight hospitals.[52]

By the end of the occupation, a large swathe of The Hague lay in ruins. The total demolition on behalf of the fortifications amounted to 28,000 homes. "On top of that, 64 schools and 43 other public buildings were damaged, and huge quantities of road surfacing disappeared – 28,000 square metres of cobblestones and 290,000 square metres of clinkers. Nine bridges were lost, and several kilometres of sewers were broken open (...). In addition to the destruction, there were military works that needed removing – 500 metres of steel barriers, 37 kilometres of concrete tank barricades (dragon's teeth) four to five rows deep, 130 concrete bunkers, four kilometres of armoured concrete walls, 66 kilometres of barbed wire and nine kilometres of tank ditches and 5,000 foxholes."[53] The task of reconstruction meant rehabilitating an immense area of public space: a hundred hectares of woodlands, 130 hectares of public squares, 130 hectares of plantation in parks and 240 kilometres of street greenery.

The Dutch had been allowed only very restricted admission to the bleak environment behind the wall and the barbed wire barriers, and even then they had to show their passes. It was like a vast army encampment with the large former parks dotted with pieces of military equipment. The seaside hotel rooms had been left in a decrepit condition by the German officers who occupied them. On the side towards the sea, the promenade was shielded by a four-metre high concrete wall topped with barbed wire. The streets had been broken open, and the beach was pricked everywhere with concrete posts. Scheveningen had become a desolate landscape, with huge heaps of rubble, bombed buildings and unpaved streets. The Oranje Hotel was disfigured, the Kurhaus Cabaret demolished, and the pier was a charred wreck.

"A deadly silence now overwhelmed the international bathing resort, inhabited only by a population the size of a village. It was a silence (...) that appealed mainly to birds that flew in great flocks to the barricaded land where once the woodlands of the Haagsche Bosch had stood, so that the springtime song of the nightingale could be heard as never before. It was lonely and strange enough to be the only resident in an empty street, but it gave a distinctly melancholy feeling to see the centre of beach life and sea-bathing so depopulated at the height of the season."[54] The Hague had been transformed in the space of a few years into a nether world and Scheveningen into a ghost town.

BEATING THE RETREAT

If Seyss-Inquart, whose ideology precluded him from fleeing The Hague and who had built a wide cordon around his residence in Clingendaal, had gone to ground, he could have held out for a long time. As it turned out, however, all the efforts to fortify The Hague against a seaborne invasion and to build an underground duplicate of city life proved to have little impact on the duration or outcome of the occupation. The fortification project had started with dazzling efficiency: Scheveningen was almost complete by December 1943, and the base at Clingendaal was ready even earlier. But by 1944, more and more German divisions were withdrawing from The Hague. Seyss-

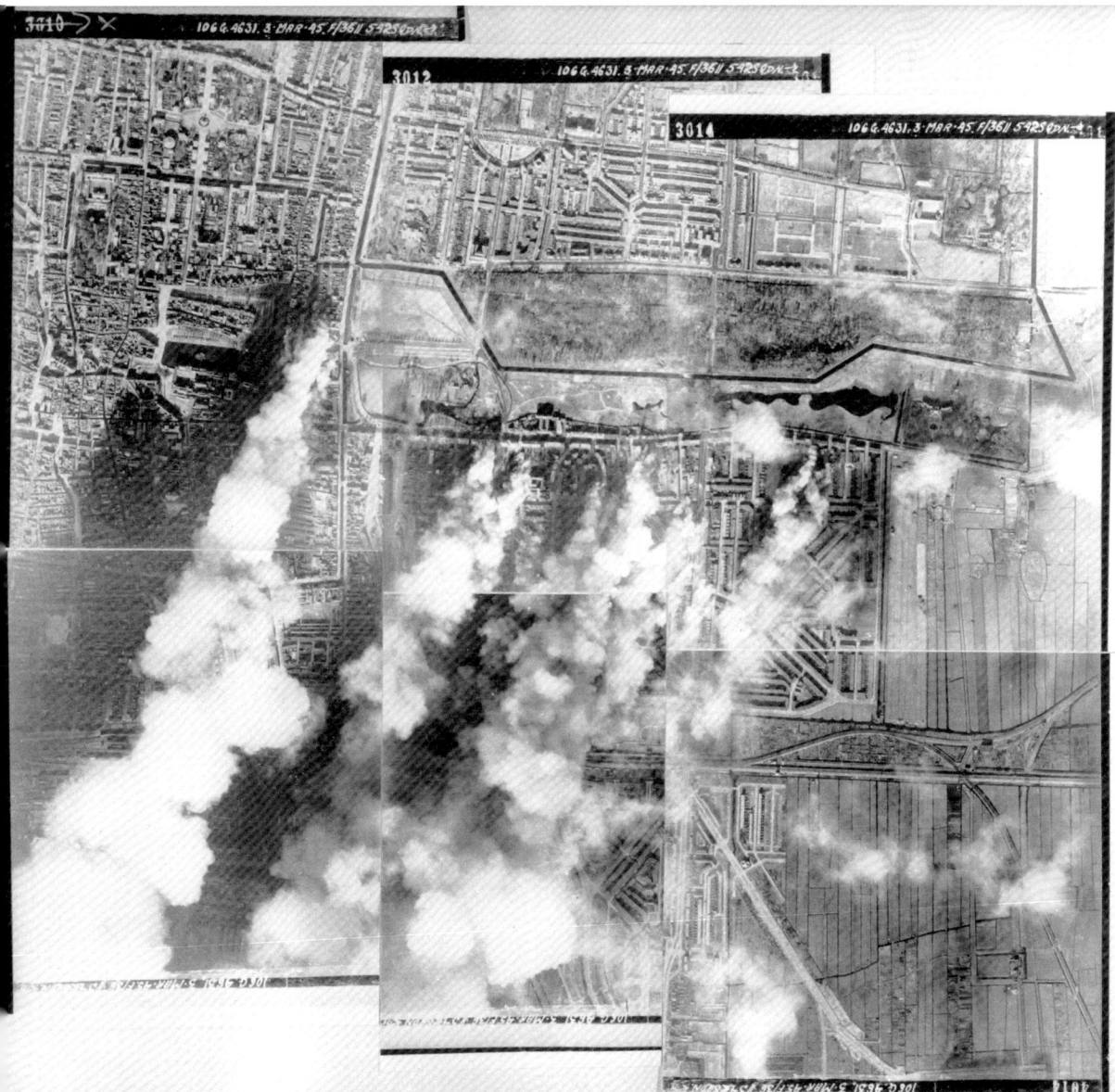

275. Aerial photomontage of bombing of Bezuidenhoutkwartier, 3
March 1945

276. Fire in Bezuidenhoutkwartier, 3 March 1945

Inquart's civilian headquarters was also drained of personnel. While operations on construction of the Atlantic Wall proceeded during 1943, the departments of General Commissioners Fischböck and Wimmer also left the city. They were dispersed to Arnhem, Delden, Deventer, Nijmegen and Utrecht, with Apeldoorn as the pivotal centre where Seyss-Inquart took up residence and Wimmer also lived part of the time. In order to accommodate the German civil servants in these towns, dwellings were requisitioned – initially, Jewish properties, but later other Dutch ones, too.[55] In September 1944 the Reichskommissar himself left for Apeldoorn, where bombproof shelters were already available for him and his staff, on the Loolaan. As for his private quarters, which he shared with the Wimmer family, the castle of Spelderholt in Beekbergen just outside Apeldoorn was put at his disposal.

Siedlung und Bauten designed air raid shelters in Amersfoort, Apeldoorn, Arnhem, Grave, Nijmegen and Utrecht (see Chapter 6, illustrations 187-190 and 198-209) to accommodate the many civilian organizations which had fled The Hague. In

277. Aerial photo of Bezuidenhout ruins

1943-1944 the office also worked vigorously to build shelters for the provincial representatives of the Reichskommissar, the commanding officers of several police divisions and the ss elite, along with bunkers for telecommunications centres. In the second half of 1944, *Siedlung und Bauten* acquired an extra task, that of "industrial relocation".[56] By then, however, the organization had itself left The Hague and was no longer working on the Atlantic Wall. That project, now pointless with everyone seeking safety in flight, was abandoned.

After the Liberation, Münster probably tried to pick up the strands of his former, less turbulent, profession in Austria. About 8 May 1945 Wimmer was captured and interned in The Hague, Hilversum, Scheveningen, Nuremberg and Dachau successively. After his provisional release, he returned to Austria and vanished from the official records. Efforts to trace him in 1948 and 1949 were in vain, and his dossier, then formally still open, was finally closed in 1957.[57] Seyss-Inquart was sentenced to death at the Nuremberg trials and executed by hanging.

278. Scheveningse Bosjes, 1945

279. Scheveningse Bosjes,
July 1945

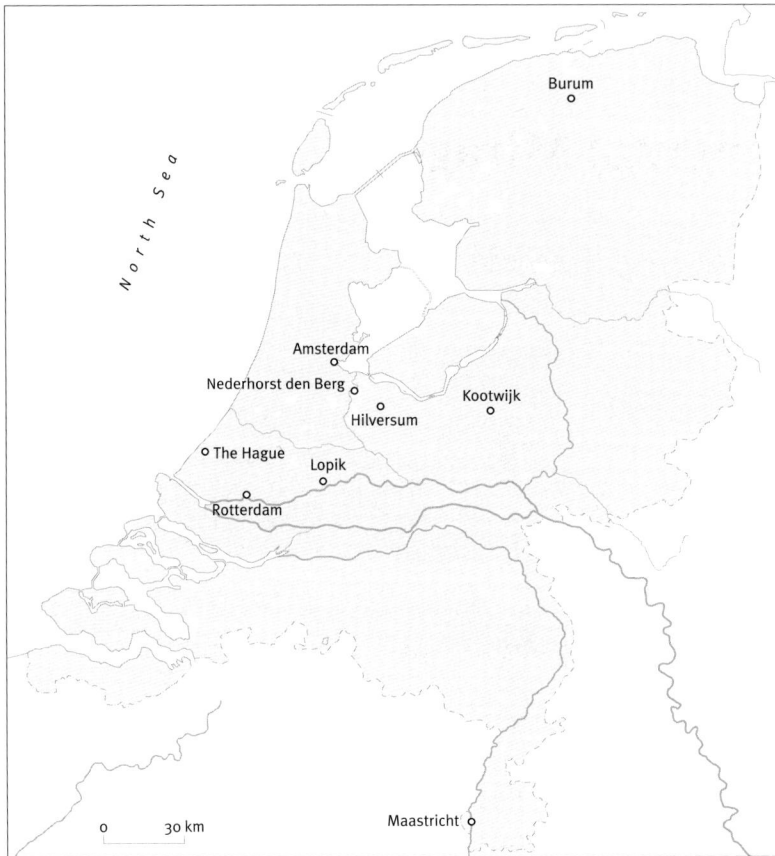

< *Page 326-327*
280. New pier in Scheveningen,
June 1964

CHAPTER 8

A Continental Mirage

Shelter City during the Cold War

URBAN PLANNING AND AERIAL THREATS FOLLOWING WWII

In December 1943, a committee of Dutch local government officials issued an internal memorandum evaluating the significance of the air raids on Rotterdam.[1] They concluded that the damage caused by high-explosive bombs was less severe than expected, but that the fires resulting from the concentrated bombing had been disastrous. This was partly due to the large windows in the buildings and the typically Dutch lightweight structural style. These observations motivated their recommendations to build house roofs and attic floors from fire-resistant materials, to promote concrete-framed building, to avoid unnecessarily large window openings and to create cellars or storage spaces in building basements.

More interesting than these architectural proposals were the disagreements on the consequences of the aerial threat for urban planning. The implications for the structure of existing and future cities split the committee down the middle. Some members argued for minimizing the hazard to civilians by reserving sites for public bomb shelters, as in Germany and Britain, during the future rebuilding and expansion of cities. The others opposed building more shelters on the grounds of advancing military technology; the enemy, they argued, would modify his tactics according to the situation on the ground. Existing cities, on the other hand, lacked the pliancy needed to adapt quickly. They supported this standpoint by citing the

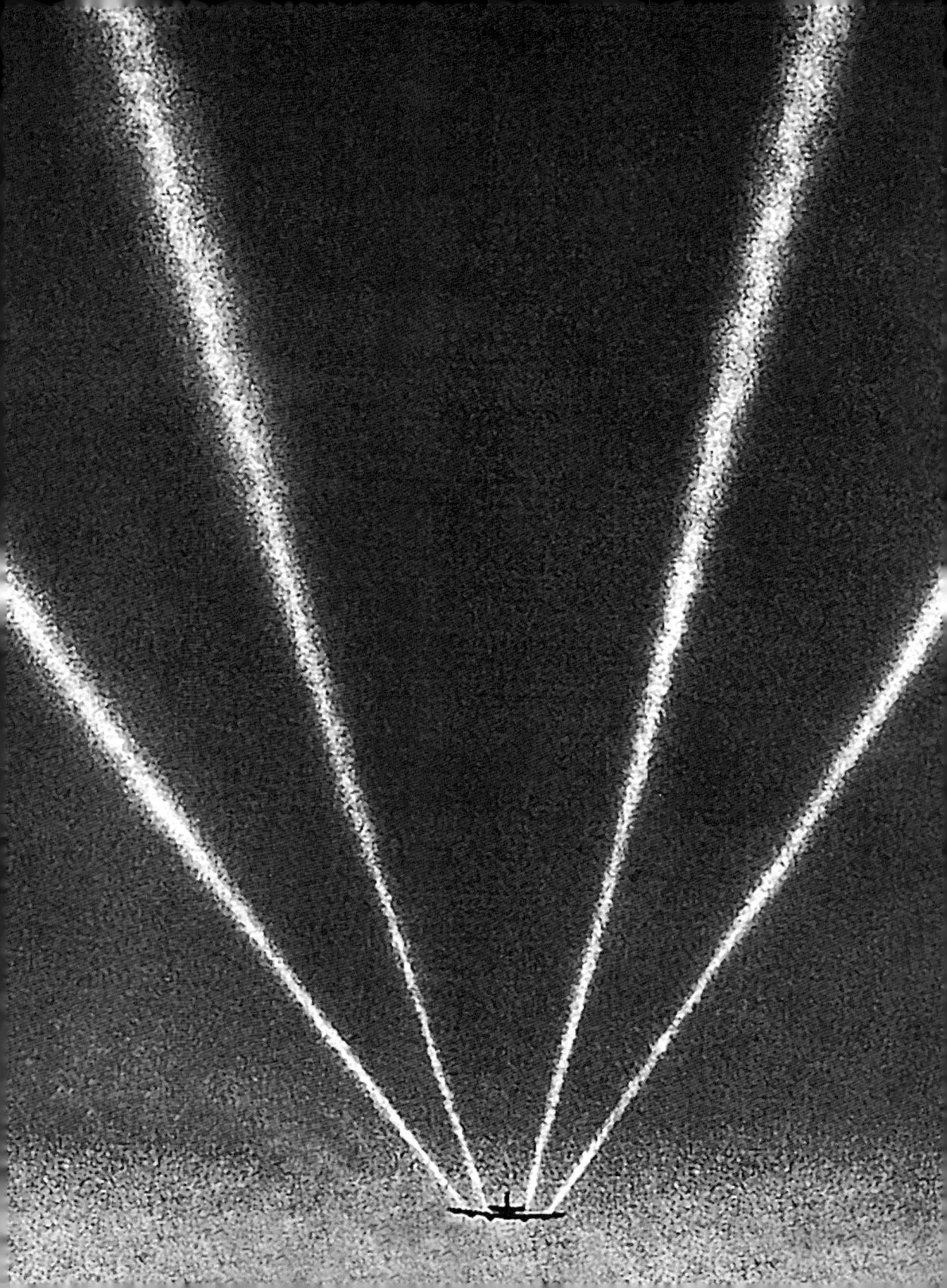

German building regulations, which in 1938 prescribed a distance of 500 metres between industry zones and residential areas, but by 1942 doubled the distance to 1,000 metres. The whole committee agreed nonetheless that the current urban design desiderata (low-density development and the separation of residential and industrial zones) were consistent with the demands of air raid protection.

When it came to the postwar reconstruction of the Netherlands, however, town planning and aerial defence requirements seemed at odds. Government policies aimed from the outset to give everyone a home to live in. All efforts and investments therefore concentrated on achieving quickly built, low-cost public housing. This implied a differently organized building industry, the use of industrial house-building methods and a higher level of standardization. Inner city redevelopment schemes and new suburbs were more spaciously designed than ever before, but air raid protection measures consistent with urban design criteria were nonexistent.

THE COLD WAR

The tone for the coming decades was set in 1945 when the term "cold war" was coined, followed two years later by Churchill's speech in which he described Europe being divided by an "iron curtain". The decisive moment at which the Dutch civil defence organization gained a status which was to remain fixed for the next 50 years was when the Netherlands joined NATO. The country's entry to the alliance was very half-hearted in nature, for the all-powerful Americans compelled the Dutch government to devote one-quarter of its national budget to defending against the putative Red Peril, indicating that they would otherwise withdraw Marshall Aid. The Dutch contribution to European defence consisted of reanimating the IJssel Defence Line and reinforcing it with a traditional water barrier – a system which would hamper invading armies by flooding a broad strip of countryside stretching from Nijmegen in the east to the Lauwerszee in the north.[2] The transatlantic solidarity was no more than a gesture, for the cabinet under Prime Minister Drees regarded the vast expenditures on national defence as squandered money. Efficient postwar reconstruction and boosting general prosperity would be a better way of keeping the masses satisfied and in line.[3]

The fears of what the future would bring were a product of the polarization of East and West and of the threat of nuclear war. The popular press began publishing portrayals of Hiroshima-like scenarios afflicting American cities – getting a taste of their own medicine, so to speak – as early as 1945. A headline in the *Chicago Tribune* of 26 October 1945 read "Just a wreck. That's Chicago under A-bombs". Imagined geographical transplantations of the horrors of atomic war featured regularly in American magazines such as *Life*, *Time*, and *Reader's Digest*. The November 1945 issue of *Life* published a detailed account of a 36-hour atomic blitz on Washington, followed by a "shower of enemy rockets" landing on twelve other big cities and an airborne invasion.[4] Philip Wylie's novel *Tomorrow!* (1954) was not only utopian in that it foresaw the earth purged of evils such as hypocrisy and Communism, and not just a lesson in civil defence, but a portrayal of complete immersion in collective fear. In the Soviet Union, too, people nurtured few illusions about the potential consequences of nuclear war.

The US government employed nuclear scientists, conscience-stricken or not,

282. Sheltering under the stairs with all the air-raid precautions near at hand. Illustration from public information booklet, 1950s

to inform and soothe the public. Their messages were drenched in moralizations, drama and cosmic metaphors.[5] One of the main pillars of American propaganda was to familiarize the public with the atom by using the tools of marketing to promote peaceful nuclear energy. Radioactivity became a popular topic. In the medical sector radioactivity was presented as nuclear healing: radiation saved lives.[6] General Electric funded a comic book titled *Inside the Atom* (1953), a colour animation film called *A is for Atom* (1952) and a Walt Disney film first shown on television, *Our Friend the Atom* (1957). The magical potency of radioactivity was also promoted in travelling exhibitions.

The immense American marketing effort did not go unnoticed in the Netherlands. The country's response to nuclear angst took the form of educational projects and public information films. In 1955, the country's first nuclear research reactor opened in the vicinity of Petten on the North Holland coast, and was followed two years later by the massively popular exhibition "The Atom" at Schiphol Airport. A government planning document for electricity generation, *Structuurschema Elektriciteitsvoorziening*, published in 1975, identified no fewer than eleven potential locations for building nuclear power stations. In the end two nuclear power plants were actually built: Dodewaard (decommissioned in 1997) and Borssele.

FIRST STRIKE

As in the 1930s, questions of whether measures should be taken to protect civilians and especially city dwellers from aerial threats, and if so what form these measures should take, became topics of widespread discussion. The issues debated seem in retrospect bizarre, even risible, but they were treated at the time as being of exceptional seriousness, as befitted the intense fear that prevailed. The rival power blocks aimed to deter each other from any thought of starting an atomic attack by building their own gigantic nuclear arsenals. The logic was not particularly sound or convincing, because the rationalization was coloured by blind faith in the effectiveness of nuclear deterrence. The governments and the intelligence services of the blocs on each side of the Iron Curtain had a distorted picture of the power relationships and public mood of the adversary. They therefore maintained a permanent state of alertness for a possible surprise attack. In 1960, the physicist Herman Kahn published a book *On Thermonuclear War*, which pointed out the logic of escalation towards a "doomsday machine"; a first strike with nuclear bombs on the territory of one bloc would set off an automated process which would end in planetary destruction. The likelihood of this happening in reality was not merely imaginary, as became clear in the Cuban Missile Crisis of 1962, when nuclear-armed missiles were ranged for attack on both sides. An American spy in Moscow, knowing he was about to be unmasked, transmitted a false report that the Russians were poised to launch a missile attack on the West; he seemed bent on dragging the whole world with him in his downfall.[7]

The worldwide audience sat aghast before one of the most expensive global theatre productions of the twentieth century. The precariousness of the nuclear balance became a popular topic in novels and films, such as the apocalyptic *On the Beach* (filmed in 1959) and the satirical *Dr. Strangelove or: How I Learned to Stop Worrying and Love the Bomb* (Stanley Kubrick, 1964; based on the book *Two Hours of Doom* by Peter George, 1958). It was clear how easily the world could be transformed into a charnel field by the impulsive, irrational or even deranged actions of politicians, generals and scientists.[8] A BBC television documentary-style drama by Peter Watkins, *The War Game* (1966), which portrayed the consequences of a nuclear attack on Kent, was considered so confrontational that it was not screened until twenty years later. Nuclear pessimism was a recurrent theme in popular music, too, as exemplified by Barry McGuire's protest song *Eve of Destruction*, an international hit in 1966. "The public had been bombarded again and again by war scenes and by hydrogen bomb stories, by warnings against fallout and by fantasies about monsters, by anti-bomb outcries and by shelter debates, with the Cuban shock only the last in a long series."[9]

MIRROR REACTION: DECENTRALIZE

The roots of America's defensive doctrine were to be found in the Strategic Bombing Survey, a series of reports that involved the participation of over a thousand researchers, including the elite of the social and physical science world.[10] They started in 1944 by studying the effects of the Allied bombing of German cities and factories and especially attacks on the infrastructure that sustained the economy and industry of the Third Reich. Of interest to us here is that the researchers' chilling account of the destruction in Hiroshima and Nagasaki marked a turning point in attitudes towards the atom bomb. It was the very mirror image of the Allied hubris that prevailed after the devastating first nuclear strike and the almost immediate collapse of Japanese resistance. From here on, the nightmare of atomic destruction crept into the attitudes and calculations of planners and scientists. They could not

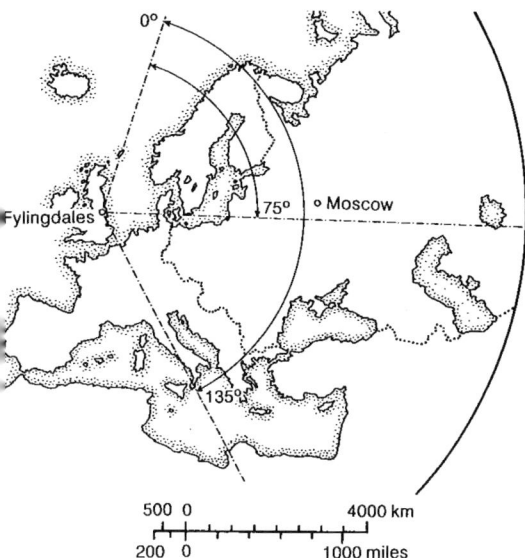

283. RAF Flyingdales (UK), early warning system showing reach of radar, 1950s. This system gave a warning time ranging from 2.5 to 17 minutes of incoming attacks

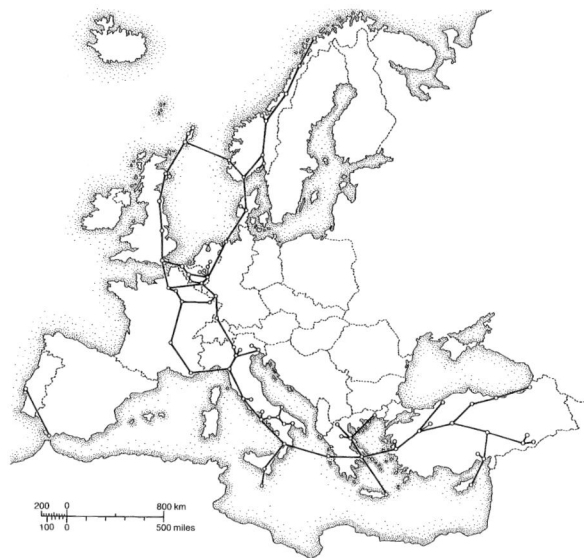

284. Ace High communication system for Allied Command Europe. This system functioned from 1960 to 1990 and had 48 locations (command centres, radar and communication stations)

avoid thinking what would happen if similarly destructive attacks were to take place on American soil. Would the nation's manufacturing centres and cities be able to protect themselves against the effects of heat, radiation and air pressure on human bodies and buildings?[11] While popular media depictions of the mass reaction, of a society paralysed by panic, gave little cause for optimism, sociological studies generally indicated that the fears could be overcome through training, self-control and the channelling of emotions.

Centralized cities were wide-open targets. This observation not only gave support to dispersal models but also to theoretical arguments for avoiding concentrations around intersections, bottlenecks and axes, and replacing them by grids and network patterns. "Space" seemed to be the only valid answer to the aerial threat. Now the garden city model, with a maximum of 50,000 inhabitants, resurfaced as the ideal. The concept of an irregular, stretched S-shape as a form of urban community also gained adherents. The interaction between scientists and planners resulted in a more scientific approach to urban space, which they analysed as a system that was not only vulnerable as a target but in some respects morally reprehensible, for example due to the unnatural extremes of city life such as the urban segregation of races and income classes. The only survival metaphor for the city was large-scale fortification. Their outlook could hardly have been more anti-urban. The cities were required not only to withstand atomic bombardment but to absorb it, clearly on the assumption that the surrounding countryside would be unaffected. US policy was now to decentralize not only industry but the family. A system of large public nuclear shelters would be impossibly expensive. In the shelter and evacuation programmes for middle-class families (some 60 percent of Americans in the 1950s) during the presidencies of Truman and Eisenhower, the ideals of safety, personal sovereignty and fortification were attuned to private car and detached house ownership, avoiding of course any form of urban concentration.[12] As consciousness of the nuclear threat developed in the early 1960s in step with the rising megatonnage of hydrogen bombs, the arguments favoured underground bunkers and mass evacuations.[13]

In early 1950s America, the mirror-image response was concretized as the national project *Is Your Plant a Target?* (1951) which asked urban communities to analyse and map the potential strategic and industrial targets and similar vulnerable spots within their own regions. Industrialists seeking a business location were exhorted to study the hazard maps and calculate the tax benefits of complying with official dispersal strategies. This entrepreneurial behaviour led in turn to reconsideration of the patterns of communication, administration and demography, and hence to development plans for satellite towns and villages, the avoidance of centres and an enhanced infrastructure of mains and cables and of interstate highways capable of meeting potential evacuation needs.

Here too lay the inception of cybernetics, not only the study of the human brain as a system but also of the functioning of the world as a geopolitical system against the background of a technical/abstract version of the Enemy.[14] This type of study, aimed at promoting the development of an aerial defence scenario tailored to each city and region, also made its inroads into Europe, starting with West Germany, the practice ground of the American armed forces. Bremen, Düsseldorf and Hannover were the first German cities to formulate a response plan to airborne nuclear attacks. Even if a nuclear war was unwinnable, the underlying thinking ran, it might be possible for civilians to shelter *en masse*. Illusions such as these evaporated in the course of the 1960s as the prospect of ballistic missiles became public knowledge and attempts to flee to safe locations were revealed to be utterly futile.

Physical preparations for a nuclear World War III went through three stages in Eastern and Western Europe.[15] In the first period, 1945-1955, atomic bombers powered by internal combustion engines were targeted at cities and industrial areas that enjoyed special aerial protection. The landscapes of West Germany (America's testing ground), Eastern Germany (the testing ground of the USSR), Britain and France were enriched with countless military typologies. Military airfields were enlarged and enhanced (for example, longer runways); the landscape was dotted with storage silos for ever more advanced nuclear stockpiles (but ever more maintenance-sensitive) which required a highly trained personnel for security, maintenance and the on-site assembly of weapons.

In the next decade, the focus shifted from defence against bombing raids to protection from the nuclear deterrent. The nuclear shield of the US had a frontline post in West Germany, but Britain and France had their own shields which depended on electronic detection systems to scan the national airspace and raise timely alarms.

The concept of a flexible response gained the upper hand from 1965 onwards. Defence against an attack from the air now included shooting down incoming rockets with anti-ballistic missiles in parallel with attacking a wide range of targets on enemy territory. The concept depended on the availability of warning systems for approaching missiles, a specific command structure, control by ground-based communication centres, mid-air interception by fighters and the bombardment of launch sites. In November 1967, for instance, the US Army chose locations near Boston, Chicago, Pittsburgh and Seattle as strategic missile-launching sites. These plans fell foul, however, of city residents who protested furiously against the siting of so many hydrogen bombs in their own backyards.[16]

Everyone knew, of course, that there could be no such thing as an impenetrable nuclear shield. Nationwide apathy was perhaps adjudged to be too passive, but some measure of apathy at least testified to common sense. While Kennedy was president, the US underwent a brief revival in its aspirations towards civil defence, with a fallout shelter programme as insurance against a possible war. But rather than initiating a civilian underground construction programme costing many millions, he encouraged individual citizens to build their own shelters. Tension rose steadily in the early 1960s and reached a climax in the Cuban Missile Crisis. Energized by fear, civil defence became a public obsession. The public was desperate for accurate information on how to act in the event of a nuclear emergency. Fear proved, as often before, a poor counsellor. Kennedy had promised to distribute a booklet of practical tips, and once it failed to materialize, eager entrepreneurs leapt to fill the gap. Swimming pool salesmen presented themselves as fallout shelter specialists, and biscuit manufacturers advertised survival packages. There was no shortage of credit available for private shelter builders.[17] Debates raged between the proponents and opponents of nuclear shelters. As of old, people wondered whether such shelters would ultimately just become tombs, and asked who would be admitted and at what price. A typically American slant on this question was the image of the gun-toting paterfamilias bravely defending the family fallout shelter against desperate strangers. By the time the government circulated the long-promised civil defence booklet[18], it was 1962, and the looming conflict precipitated by the construction of the Berlin Wall had just been averted. It was a nerve-racking time, nonetheless, culminating in the Cuban Missile Crisis in October that year. The booklet was in great demand. People began hoarding food supplies, and sales of shovels and sandbags reached unprecedented volumes. Some well-known Americans fled the country altogether. Yet the passion for nuclear shelters ebbed quickly after the denouement of the Cuban confrontation. Not a cent was now to be made from them, and the whole hype was soon forgotten.

THE BB: CIVIL DEFENCE IN THE NETHERLANDS

Most European countries established a civilian volunteer force to staff their own version of Shelter City. As in other countries, Dutch civil defence was a network whose nodes consisted of emergency communication centres, food stockpiles, production centres (such as plutonium factories) and technical/scientific research centres. Its commanders were provided with nuclear-hardened regional bunkers (surface or underground) and advanced communications systems. In the Netherlands, this network was no more than embryonic compared to that in surrounding countries. Its history has not yet been written, since not all relevant documents have been released from the archives. Nor do we have an international context that would allow comparison of the Dutch network with other countries, regarding differing military concepts, the bureaucratic and political systems, developments in military technology and their implications for urban planning, structural engineering and architecture.

The scale of the deterrent – nuclear attacks with the power to destroy not just cities but entire countries – was so great that no one still believed in the feasibility of national air defence. There was no prospect of anything more than a little post-traumatic care: "warnings and alarms, the construction of shelters, evacuation where appropriate, rapid firefighting action, rescuing and treating casualties, the accumulation of large stockpiles of food and fuel, the preparation of emergency harbours, emergency communication lines, emergency administrative measures, emergency hospitals, distribution of labour and food, emergency laws and regulations and so on"[19] would be merely a plaster on the wound. The idea of a duplicate Shelter Society remained improbable. In concrete terms that would mean all efforts would have to focus on a single aspect of civil defence: the protection of the civilian population against air raids. It should be added that the planners had no idea how to deal with the implications of the dizzying speed of the latest missiles or with the increasing power of nuclear bomb explosions, which cast doubt on the utility or necessity of public shelters.

The Dutch government, while compelled to increase the defence budget, was circumspect in its approach to civilian protection. It was already clear in the 1950s that a nuclear attack from the east would plunge all sectors of society into chaos

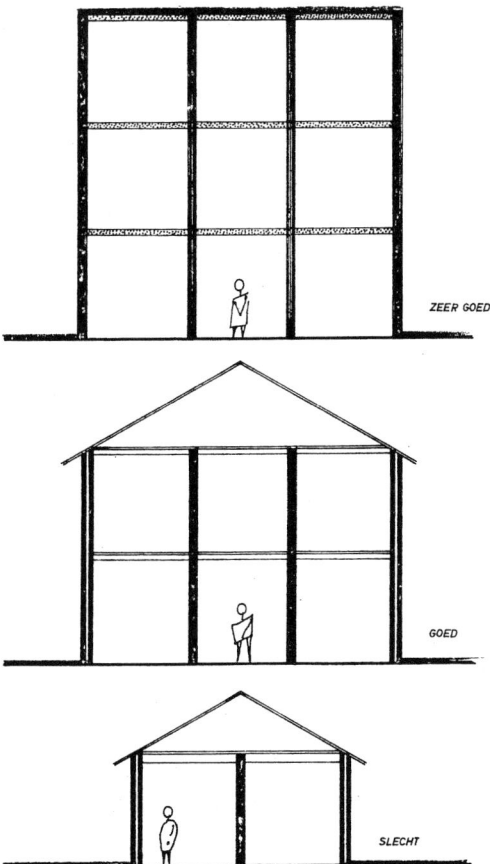

ZEER GOED

GOED

SLECHT

Left
285. Illustration material for lectures given by air raid protection staff of Dutch Ministry of Home Affairs; technical assessment of reinforced buildings for fallout protection, 1960

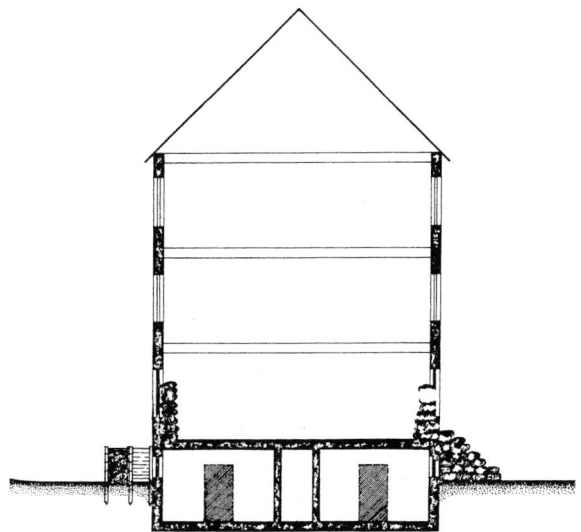

Right
286. Illustration material for lectures given by air raid protection staff of Dutch Ministry of Home Affairs; securing multi-storey buildings with reinforced cellars and sandbags before doors and windows, 1960

and that defensive measures against air attacks could be no more than ritualistic in nature. The most visible of these measures was a system of 276 watchtowers spaced at 16-km intervals over the territory of the Netherlands.[20] Half of the towers were erected on top of existing buildings, and the rest were built from scratch as frameworks of prefabricated concrete sections which were typologically cognate to hunting lodges. This type of tower was transparent but stood on an opaque concrete plinth into which the watchmen could retreat in the event of a nuclear strike. The purpose of the tower system is self-evident: to warn of threatening aircraft approaching under the detection range of the radar.

The doctrine underlying the 1952 establishment of the Dutch civil defence organization, *Bescherming Bevolking* or BB, was that of a conventional war and in particular of a repetition of the air raids of World War II. Since urban bombing placed many civilians at risk, the BB's main principle was individual self-preservation. The organization saw its primary task as educating the public about sheltering and other actions to be taken in the event of war. Its secondary priorities were to minimize the number of civilian casualties resulting from air raids, for example by organizing evacuations, and to cope with the consequences of such attacks as far as possible. The BB recruited civilian volunteers who would be able to arrive quickly at the scene of an emergency with knowledge of how to react, and would therefore have to remain in a state of continual readiness. The emphasis was on local organization. The country was subdivided into 42 A municipalities and 70 B regions (called *kringen* or "circles"), depending on the presence of objects of civilian or military importance. The Minister of Home Affairs and the command of the national *Bescherming Bevolking en Mobiele Colonnes* (Civil Defence and Mobile Brigades) occupied the peak of the civil defence pyramid. In the tier below them were the Queen's Commissioners and the Provincial Commandants of the BB. The Commandant of a province was responsible for the next lower echelon of commandants, each of whom had control over a large region or *kring* of multiple municipalities. Cities with large populations and national importance, namely Amsterdam, The Hague and Rotterdam, had their own BB organizations which reported directly to the respective Provincial Commandants. Every region was in turn structured into "sectors" and "blocks". A block consisted of a number of adjacent streets with a total population of approximately 1,000 people, and a sector consisted of a variable of number of blocks, notionally 10. The block was the responsibility of a Block Marshal (*blokhoofd*) assisted by a deputy, six volunteer firemen, six rescue workers and two alarm-raisers. Above the Block Marshals, the Sector Commandant had his own command post with direct lines of communication to the Regional Commandant. The national BB organization took responsibility for equipping all the echelons and providing communication links between all the regional, provincial and national command posts (in the form of telephone lines, induction telephones, radiophones, telegraphy and walkie-talkies) and for command-post bunkers and public shelters. With its paramilitary structure, the BB bore a close resemblance to the assistance organization of the 1930s and shared all its weaknesses. A fair amount has been published about the BB, which survived until 1986,[21] but little is now known about the construction and vicissitudes of its bunker network.[22]

With its optimistic, almost unrealistic, belief in its ability to protect the civilian population against a nuclear holocaust, the BB shrugged off scepticism at all levels of government. Shelter City once again had its own personnel. Over 100,000 volunteers received training as firefighters, first-aid providers, rescue workers and debris clearance operators. As in the 1930s, the cities were subdivided into sectors of 10,000 and blocks of 1,000 inhabitants with their associated officials, of whom the Block Marshall was most familiar to the general public. The intention was that, following an air raid, the well-equipped civil defence squads would rush out under the direction of the Block Commandant to conduct rescue work and suppress plundering and panic. More specialized work would be delegated to the professional municipal services such as the fire brigade, the health department, and departments responsible for debris clearance, security, decontamination and reconstruction. Services such as these were never put to the test, owing to the lack of air raids. They could never have functioned well because they were severely underfunded. The BB moreover enjoyed little popular respect, as the cumulative outcome of successive simplifications by the government, the press, scientific commentators and the general public. An aura of hilarious amateurism hung incessantly around the equipment and personnel of the postwar Shelter City.[23]

A preventive measure that was not taken seriously in the Netherlands of the 1930s, mass evacuation, was considered in greater detail in the 1950s. Countries such as France, Norway and Sweden developed evacuation plans for zones around major military targets and for the largest cities. The scale of these plans kept pace with the growing nuclear stockpile of the Soviet Union. An impending attack on the Netherlands' largest cities would require, it was reckoned, the transportation of some four million city dwellers.[24] In abstract scenarios like these, the size of the BB force would have to be expanded to 200,000 people. The extra volunteers would take responsibility for matters such as evacuation tents, sleeping bags, field kitchens, camp beds, cutlery and (250,000) drinking mugs. The project had a secret mobilization code, "walking stick, walking stick" followed by the names of the cities to be evacuated.[25] The chalk caves (actually old mine tunnels) in Valkenburg reappeared in the plans; they could provide shelter for 300,000 troglodytes. Secret escape routes were devised for the Dutch Royal Family, and also for strategic sectors of industry.

By the 1960s, the responsible politicians, the media and the general public were taking the evacuation plans less and less seriously. Not only would a mass exodus spark off panic and chaos, it was held, but the exit roads of the city would soon be jammed, frustrating the efforts of the public aid and defence services. Politicians were aware that providing a government-sponsored system of public shelters for the whole population would be financially infeasible, both in the near future and in the long term. Attention therefore shifted during the 1960s towards the home as a survival unit. "Stay where you are", the new policy enjoined, for that was the least hazardous for civilians. Every urban householder was now expected to fortify his home into a fallout shelter as a contribution to Shelter City.

On 25 September 1961, an envelope from the BB landed on the doormats of households in the main cities. It contained a folding cardboard notice bearing the title "Tips for the protection of your family and yourself" (*Wenken voor de bescherming van uw gezin en uzelf*), published in an edition of 3.3 million.[26] Three weeks later, the postman delivered a small oblong book with a soft red cover providing explanatory details (*Toelichting*). The envelope that contained the notice was designed to store the booklet too and had a small hole punched at one corner so that it could be hung up in a strategic place in the home. Individual citizens had to learn to quench firebombs, give simple first aid, extinguish small fires and protect part of their home from shrapnel and debris. The booklet also provided information and advice on air raid warnings, such as preparing a suitcase of essentials for an emergency evacuation and extinguishing fires with sand, a garden hose and a fire mop (a bunch of rags on a broomstick). It was like an echo of the 1930s.

Similar national exercises took place in Belgium, Denmark, Germany and Sweden. City dwellers in the Netherlands greeted the cardboard notice and the booklet with derision or at least a shrug of indifference. The prevalent opinion was that it was pointless to seek shelter from a nuclear attack. Shelter City was useless, and its personnel were a mere fig leaf covering government incompetence. Publications issued by the BB damaged their own image by underestimating the intelligence of the Dutch populace. The booklet *Bescherm u zelf* ("Protect Yourself") by F.J.W. Boddens Hosang treated atomic warfare as a domestic inconvenience. The first chapters warn of the dangers of modern traffic, gas leaks, slippery floors and poorly lit cellar stairs. The booklet continues with further tips on surviving the outbreak of nuclear war. Beyond the fatal radius of 1,600 metres around the hypocentre of a nuclear explosion, much could be achieved by dint of customary Dutch cleanliness, namely the disinfectant power of soap and water. Besides, Boddens Hosang assured her readers, the BB would rush to everyone's aid. "The BB emergency services are trained and equipped to rescue people in such circumstances. Make sure you keep a whistle or a bell in your shelter to attract their attention."[27]

The BB's incipient downfall was marked by an ill-judged charm offensive of 1960 which reached a low point in COPEX, an exercise to simulate life in a fallout shelter. Nineteen men and six women shut themselves up for a week in the BB command post in Arnhem. "They had no communication with the outside world apart from simulated news reports on the progress of the nuclear war and commentaries by BB staff members. The team emerged at the end of the week (apart from one woman who had to be extracted on the second day due to acute appendicitis). Everything had functioned smoothly, the BB assured their audience at a press conference, and the bunker dwellers had stood up well to their psychological ordeal. "Everyone was on first name terms after a while, and nobody kept aloof," the Commandant said. A 25-year-old telephone operator spoke of her own experience: "We didn't know one another beforehand so there was plenty to talk about. When we got bored with talking we could read, play chess, model clay and do all kinds of other activities. We formed a choir with 'Uncle' Jan van Nukoop from the communications service as conductor; our favourite number was *Wij zijn niet bang* ['We're Not Afraid'], and it was a lot of fun."[28] The newspapers dismissed the experiment as "utterly fatuous" and as a "stupid, miserable anomaly in Dutch history". This epitome of the experience economy *avant la lettre* missed certain vital ingredients: tension, fear and despair. From here it was downhill all the way for the BB. After the tranquil 1970s in which the perceived likelihood of World War III waned, the Dutch political world agreed to dispense with the BB. National politicians cultivated the argument that it was costing money without delivering any significant value. In 1986, the BB regions were abolished, and the provincial command posts were decommissioned. The BB finally slunk quietly from the scene in 1990.

SHELTER CITY INTERNATIONAL

Numerous bunkers were reutilized as fallout shelters, especially in Germany. Like most European countries in the first years of the 1950s, the Federal Republic gained its own civil defence organization in which old comrades met again. Once West Germany joined the ranks of NATO in 1955, reuse of the old bunkers became a serious option. They were refurbished and hardened against a nuclear attack during the Korean War, construction of the Berlin Wall and the Cuban Missile Crisis. There was a tremendous choice among the approximately 650 existing bunkers of all sizes and types. A guideline (*Richtlinien für Schutzraumbauten*, issued on 27 July 1955) specified the technical requirements for the building and fitting out of shelters. The rules agreed in essentials with the orders of the *Sofortprogramm* of 1943 (see Chapter 3).[29] That was hardly surprising, since German experts claimed with undisguised pride that no other country had developed suitable examples. On the contrary, much of their aerial defence policy (including the formal specifications) were based on the German wartime experiences. The specifications were admittedly outdated because the impact of an air strike would now be vastly more severe and because missiles were developing to the extent that they could reach targets much more quickly than their World War II predecessors, making timely warnings problematic. After building of the Berlin Wall started in 1961, the West German government boosted efforts towards air defence, but results were in the end largely cosmetic because of limited budgets. The costly construction of a gigantic nuclear shelter for the government in Bonn was illustrative of the scope of German policy; in the event of a serious attack, the government might survive thirty days longer than any survivors outside the bunker. By the time the balance was drawn up in 1989, newly built and refurbished public shelters had the capacity to protect about 3.5 percent of the urban population of West Germany.[30]

The German Democratic Republic, which joined the Warsaw Pact in 1955, scored no better than its Western consort. The new nation had the disadvantage that the Soviet army blew up considerably more bunkers than the Allies did in the West. Practically nothing came of the ambitious intentions ventilated in their air defence legislation of 1958 owing to the shortage of building materials and manpower. The central command bunker of the Third Reich in Zossen was converted to a nuclear-hardened command post for the Russian occupying powers, however.[31]

This half-hearted pattern of physical defence applied to most countries in Europe, apart from Scandinavia and Switzerland. In Denmark, some 5 million city dwellers could seek protection in public and private shelters; in Sweden this figure was about 5.5 million, and in Norway approximately 40 percent of the population. Switzerland was far ahead of all others: an estimated 90 percent of the population could seek protection in private shelter space in that country where Shelter City was fully integrated with the existing society.

287. Diakonissen
Bunker, Bremen
(D), 1945

SHELTER CITY IN THE NETHERLANDS

If we allow the impression of these efforts to sink in, the conclusion remains that Dutch society was never willing to expend large amounts of money for Shelter City or the Shelter Society, mainly because of the lack of public confidence in the protection offered by the buildings of Shelter City or in the competence of its personnel. The air defence measures in both East and West Germany during the Cold War show a striking similarity to those in the Netherlands, and may be summed up as follows. "According to the plans of the 1950s and 1960s, all architecture clients should have been compelled to build underground shelters in their houses. Since that was politically infeasible, the obligation turned into a recommendation, which practically everyone ignored. The public bunkers, which were actually conceived only for passers-by, thus became the shelters for the entire population – a more than dubious kind of shelter, according to the critics."[32] The Netherlands had 185 public shelters by the 1980s, often combined with metro tunnels or underground car parks and scattered arbitrarily around the country. Their capacity was less than 2 percent of the Dutch population.[33] Shelter City was nonexistent. Depending on the criteria chosen to evaluate the size and the effectiveness of the Shelter Society and the Shel-

288. Open trench shelter, Croeselaan, Utrecht

289. Bunker type 608, Amersfoort, designed by *Siedlung und Bauten*,
ca. 1943 (photo Anja de Jong, 2004)

ter Cities, we may conclude either that little came of them, or that the illusion of protection was largely achieved despite the limited support.

Be that as it may, several specific shelters whose approximate character and size are known were built in the prosperous years between 1960 and 1989 in the Netherlands.[34] They included:

- Military bunkers. Every province had a command bunker with an antenna up to 100 metres tall. In the 1950s, four radar-equipped bunker complexes were built, and concrete hangars for the protection of aircraft were built on airfields. A bunker complex was built as late as 1982 on the Woensdrecht air base, with at its core four multistorey car parks (with 5-metre-thick roofs) usable for storage of American cruise missiles.
- Bunkers for military support by the Ministry of Transport Traffic Inspectorate (12 units), the Netherlands Railways (12), the Pipeline Defence Department of the Ministry of Defence (number unknown), the Ministry of Transport Roads & Waterways (29 bunkers with fuel dumps, mainly at locks and bridges) and the PTT (23 telephone bunkers; telecommunication bunkers in Burum, Kootwijk and Nederhorst den Berg); the broadcasting organizations had new bunkers in Hilversum and Lopik.
- Shelters for personnel of essential industries. Bunkers were built under five bank offices. Utility corporations had to finance their own bunkers.
- Shelters for various echelons of government. The Government Buildings Agency built 2-storey command/non-command bunkers under practically every ministerial building and under the buildings of the Royal House. One bunker was built in each province to serve as a centre for civil defence. Between 1960 and 1980, 100 municipalities each built a command bunker for 15-100 people, often in combination with a new city hall (such as the City Hall/Opera House in Amsterdam; the City Hall of Rotterdam gained a link to the metro tunnel).
- The BB realized 47 bunkers for its own departments and regions.

The national shelter policy had all the traits of a paper tiger. Municipal councils parried the scenarios of The Hague with requests for bags of money, with procrastination or with an overt boycott of Shelter City. Large shelters were occasionally designed, but less often built. The designs with the best prospects of execution were combination projects such as tunnels, underground car parks and bicycle sheds (the quintessentially Dutch building type).[35] A new underground car park beneath

290. Demolition of oblong shelter in Wilheminapark, Utrecht, 1945

the Vrijthof square in Maastricht, for example, was conceived as a potential nuclear shelter. No less important was the recommissioning of 10 kilometres of tunnels under the historic city wall on the west of Maastricht; this project involved the provision of ventilation systems, steel airlocks, emergency water supplies, etc.

Structures such as these could, in times of crisis, be rapidly converted to shelters.[36] A characteristic example of the ups and downs of municipal shelter plans (whose urgency surfed on the waves of the international war threat) was the Amsterdam underground shelter plan. Of the 192 underground shelters planned in 1954, 21 had been completed six years later.[37] The prevailing opinion was that ground-level shelters would spoil the cityscape and hinder traffic, so they were banished to the foundations of new buildings and to underground car parks. In combination projects of this kind, the cost of the shelter component was chargeable to the Ministry of Home Affairs.

The banishment of Shelter City to the cellars of individual houses and the foundations of blocks of flats entailed unavoidable changes to the national building code and, more importantly, made it necessary to estimate the increased construction costs of buildings and – the ultimate question – to decide who would pay.[38] This hot potato passed back and forth between the responsible departments for decades and repeatedly ended up in that ephemeral space, the future. The 1955 building regulations stated that the floor slab between the ground floor and first floor of a block of flats had to be made somewhat thicker, although individual houses were not affected.[39] A new attempt was made to tighten up the building regulations when row houses with huge picture windows began sprouting up all over the Netherlands in the late 1950s, but expert obstruction by the building industry foiled this well-meaning effort, too. The last serious attempt, in the mid-1960s, landed similarly in the mire. Individual houses, quantitatively the major contributors to the Dutch urban fabric, held out against the imposition of building regulations for domestic fallout shelters until the end.

SANDBAGS BEFORE THE DOOR

By 1966 it was public knowledge that the government lacked any realistic policy for bomb shelters. The existing shelters could not be used in their present state. The general public did not know where they were, and in some cases they were full of stored materials. None of them was equipped with stocks of food and water. Following the attempts of the 1950s to establish a national air raid defence policy including public shelters, the accent now shifted to home shelters.[40] Here, too, it was obvious that this was an option for ostriches. The number of sandbags required to bolster weak points around the house (outside doors, toilet windows, cellar manholes, vulnerable facades, etc.) averaged 300 per dwelling, equivalent to about 400 million for the whole of the Netherlands. The output of jute sacks at the time was 3 million per annum. No one was prepared even to think about the work of filling all those sacks with sand.[41]

Considering how rapidly the government is able to gather knowledge about particular issues today, we may well recall with nostalgia the great national fallout survey conducted between 1966 and 1973. A small army of interviewers fanned out over the country to inspect Dutch households. Each researcher filled in 25 questionnaires daily on data relating to the resistance of Dutch homes to the dangers of nuclear fallout. They noted "construction type, room dimensions; window sizes; availability of toilets, emergency power supply, water and electricity in the intended shelter room; the shape of the roof; available ventilation; estimated costs of measures to be taken; and square metres of sandbag protection required."[42] After all the questionnaires had been fed into the computer system of the Government Mechanical Accounting Office and analysed, the results presented a cheerless prospect. Roughly one-quarter of the population could resort to a shelter at home, and a further quarter in a large building in the vicinity. The remaining 6.8 million Dutch citizens would be unreachable by simple protective measures. Even then, the horrific picture was far from complete. "What point was there in thinking about fallout protection for zones that ran a major risk of flooding in wartime? Or for the hundreds of thousands, if not millions, who would die through the direct effects of fire, radiation or collapsing buildings? Did it serve any useful purpose to devise partial solutions for a problem whose scope was unforeseeable and which was probably insoluble?"[43] Public confidence in the possibilities of Shelter City and the utility of extending it had reached rock bottom.

The results of the fallout survey never saw the light of day. Civil defence might be capable of many things, but it could do little against a full-scale nuclear war. "We would have to build a duplicate society under the ground, and then find a system by which we could hide ourselves away in it in the shortest possible time," Prime Minister Jo Cals said when addressing the Dutch Lower Chamber in 1965. "That would be impracticable, both financially and psychologically." Shelter City and, for certain, the Shelter Society was a continent-wide mirage and was now officially recognized as such. From the moment the government publicly placed question marks beside the feasibility of aerial defence, the incipient Shelter Society and its individual Shelter Cities entered a downward spiral, and heads shook pityingly behind the backs of their personnel, the BB. The BB realized that they were denied the resources to achieve what was expected of them, and limited their subsidies to combination projects and the refurbishment of existing shelters, including the buildings of the German-built Shelter City of World War II.[44]

In the medical arena, however, construction of underground shelters continued until late in the 1980s. Twelve emergency hospitals with 200 to 270 beds were built by dint of a special legal provision, and they were meant to function in some remarkable scenarios. Amsterdam's Academisch Medisch Centrum, a large teaching hospital built in 1975-1984, included for example an underground emergency hospital designed to protect 1,800 patients and 700 medical and nursing staff against nuclear fallout. The triage of patients for admission was to follow a multi-stage protocol. As one critical doctor characterized it: "On entering the first airlock you would meet a robot, which would pull the clothes of your body and assess how extensive and how deep your burns were. If they were bad enough, you would be given an euthanasia injection and guided out through the second airlock to the garbage heap. Anyone lucky enough to make it through to the second triage would get to meet a real doctor."[45]

GEOPOLITICAL CULTURE SINCE 1989

The dominant perception of the Cold War differed strongly from that of World Wars I and II; it was an ongoing transition from trench warfare, via dynamic, mechanized warfare, to a global theatre in which bluff and muscular posing kept the adversaries in a state of mutual terror. The potential conflagration points of the Cold War were localized on the periphery of the Western world. Closer to home, preventive measures against a nuclear war took place mainly on military grounds in remote areas. In the Cold War, a single bomb could eliminate a whole city and erase its function as a centre of political power or of industry. It was a technical advance in comparison to the city area bombing of World War II. Cities remained important targets on the military maps of NATO and the Warsaw Pact. The capacity of intercontinental ballistic missiles to destroy all the important urban centres simultaneously was emblematic of the degeneration of warfare. This was the ultimate Blitzkrieg, but what would be the point?

Today, more flexible concepts prevail, ones which are less expensive and considerably more effective owing to the application of increasingly advanced information technology. Mobile troops with lightweight auxiliary equipment can be flown rapidly into a field of action; they have disposal over intelligent weapons which seek their targets easily and precisely. War is waged in specific geographical zones where local interests are involved, and the scale on which the built environment is destroyed is much smaller than in the Cold War scenarios.[46]

The step-by-step renovation of air defence systems has followed a clear pattern during the last 50 years. Telecommunications and, in the more recent decades, information technology have come to dominate all fields of military planning. They were in effect the precursors of our contemporary global information era in which orbiting satellites play a key role.[47] America's Strategic Defence Initiative of the 1980s must be interpreted in this context – an advanced shield of orbiting satellites equipped with powerful lasers capable of destroying incoming nuclear warheads, intended to protect the entire population of the USA. Apart from its immense scale, this costly system is conceptually similar to the classic idea of the early aviation years in which the airspace above cities would be defended by continually circling planes. In the end, the SDI, or "Star Wars" as it was nicknamed, proved to be no more than a rhetorical Hollywood epic of battles in outer space fought with futuristic weapons.

Many people were affected by the preparations for civil defence – some were active in the manufacture and management of military and civil materiel, others in vehement protests against it. Everyone above a certain age retains memories of this era, although what they remember depends to some extent on their role – employed in the defence industry or marching in the mass protests.[48] Looking back over the technical equipment of the "nuclear age" – the communications centres, the missile silos, etc. – it is striking how static it all was, how heavily cast in concrete. The infrastructure of civil defence is nowadays largely redundant and fails to meet today's requirements. That era is over. It has become heritage.

Page 353 >
291. Ventilation shaft of the oblong shelter for Seyss-Inquart and his staff on Loolaan, Apeldoorn (photo Anja de Jong, 2004)

CHAPTER 9

The Ruin Value of Shelter City

THE CITY AS A TARGET

As a centre of commerce, pluralism, diversity and creativity, the city serves a vital purpose as the place where civilization is forged. Its buildings have an iconic function; they are signs and sites of power, prosperity and culture. Once at the service of kings, priests and divinities, cities were designed as walled citadels, strategic assets to withstand the envy and resentment of enemies. Today, the city is more vulnerable than ever – to the threats of urban guerrillas and to attack from the skies.

The modern, civilized excuse for urban destruction is that it is unavoidable collateral damage concomitant to the pursuit of military objectives. But annihilating the spirit of the city is more often the objective, and its public spaces, its idols, its symbols of urban vitality and its cultural heritage are the favoured targets. Destruction itself is nothing new: since time immemorial, the city and its inhabitants have been victims of natural disasters, of the untimely collapse of buildings, of ill-conceived urban developments and of strategic geopolitical assaults. They have been assailed from without and within, minorities have been expelled and repressed, and whole populations have been liquidated. The destruction of a cultural heritage, the representation of a shared set of values, is often part and parcel of a more general ethnic cleansing campaign.

In the nineteenth and twentieth centuries, cities boomed in both population and prosperity. At the same time their military significance changed, partly because city walls were no longer effective against the advancing technology of warfare. Industrial cities took on a new strategic significance, as the cogwheels of mechanized warfare. Military bases moved to the countryside, and the city was deemed a demilitarized zone. National armies fought their battles in open country.

In the Cold War, cities became the designated targets for atomic warheads, but they were not the place where wars were fought. The actual battles took place in the former colonial lands of Africa and Asia. The presence of citizens and of alert, critical media made cities rather inconvenient for military operations. Street-to-street fighting required exorbitant numbers of troops, and the so-called precision bombing made possible by new technologies proved ineffectual in densely populated regions where unintended conflagrations, explosions and sanitary or chemical hazards would be, to put it mildly, propaganda setbacks. So the cities were left blank on the military maps.

Whether cities are regarded as fortified dwellings, as concentrations of cultural heritage, as icons or as metaphors, they have become increasingly dependent since the twentieth century on the fragile infrastructure that supplies their inhabitants with victuals, water, fuel, energy and electronic communications. The obliteration of parts of this network by attacks from the air is an attractive strategic option for an enemy. The mere threat of such an attack is often enough to place governments and city dwellers under extreme pressure.

SECURITY GALORE

Complete protection of the population against aerial and terrorist attacks would be prohibitively expensive and unrealistic,[1] and by the 1960s governments were abandoning any pretence at providing it. Nonetheless, politicians still find electoral advantage in pandering to popular sentiment, so ensuring that public investments in security, surveillance, control systems and the monitoring of public space mount ever higher. The result is a level of security, surveillance and police preparedness that has been unprecedented since the mobilisation for World War II. The Shelter City concept is itself by no means a thing of the past. A new American embassy was recently opened in Baghdad, yet not a single photograph of the complex has been published despite the fact that with an area of 42 hectares, it is the largest embassy in the world. Its 21 buildings are organized as an autonomous mall, complete with a food court, cinemas and other amenities. The staff are housed in 619 bombproof apartments with slit windows (only 15% of the facade may consist of glazing). The hardened complex of buildings forms an impregnable fortress within the Green Zone, which itself is a parklike area measuring four square kilometres nestling in a bend of the River Tigris. This was the domicile of representatives of the former regime and the place where Saddam Hussein's neo-Babylonian palaces and his triumphant avenue were built. It is now the best guarded spot on the globe. Until the 1980s, American policy was to strew transparent embassies around the globe, buildings that emanated an aura of democracy, freedom and individual choice. In Baghdad, however, the opposite has been achieved – the embassy is an oversized bunker that cloaks its paranoia in the trappings of a consumer paradise. And what do we think about the defensible space of the Freedom Tower near Ground Zero in New York (design Daniel Libeskind and David Childs, 2006), the symbol of freedom and democracy when, for the sake of profitable rentability of floor space, the lower 60 metres above the lobby of the skyscraper had to be built in concrete without any windows?

EUROPE'S CIVIL DEFENCE THEME PARK

With the end of the Cold War, the military threat to Western Europe dwindled. The Netherlands refocused its capacities on NATO-related international peace missions, sending its forces out to restore law and order and to aid reconstruction in distant lands. While the military retained its classic task of bolstering internal security, the Dutch government decided to dissolve the national Civil Defence organization, the BB (see Chapter 8), in 1986. The Iron Curtain lifted not long afterwards, and the remains of Shelter City went up for sale. This phenomenon was an international one: suddenly, the military and civilian landscape of the Cold War changed into a transnational archaeological theme park, cluttered with silent witnesses to the advances in military technology and the new defensive strategies, building methods and location criteria that had emerged in the decades since World War II. The research behind the new technology had been narrow in its focus, concerned only with the defence of national borders and national airspaces. The nodes in the infrastructure of the defence communication network, cast in earth, iron or concrete, are sometimes still visible in the landscape as reminders of a bygone era, and sometimes still thrive behind the fences of military bases.

On 1 September 1990, most of the civilian bunkers in the Netherlands were decommissioned. Left empty, the monoliths raised a question with economic, cultural and moral dimensions: what next? From a defensive standpoint, both military and civilian, it was clear that the bunkers were now useless. With no prospect of shielding people from a nuclear holocaust, shelters suffice today if they have walls 30 cm thick, stay dry, and can be sealed against biological and chemical weapons. An anti-terrorist command centre is typically located not in a bunker but in a block of flats. The highly specific purpose for which the old bunkers were designed made them inflexible, at best still useful to house large installations of electronic hardware. Solidly built bicycle sheds and school classrooms, on the other hand, are more readily adaptable.

Although the bunkers have been on the market for quite a while, the story they tell of civilian hardships under aerial bombardment has only recently started attracting the attention of historians and conservationists. This is especially true in Germany, where a revived interest forms part of a passionately felt economy of experience. So far, there have been few publications on the subject.[2] The polemics become concrete when they address the visible remains of the Shelter City era – people regard them variously as blots on the landscape, as works of art, as reminders of atrocities or as clues left for historians. In Germany their ruin value is topical, because of the national collective sense of victimhood now emerging after being buried for over half a century, and the self-confidence of the newly reunited sovereign German state, eager to play a prominent role on the world stage.[3] The UK, on the other hand, regards the civil defence remnants of World War II and the Cold War as part of an archaeological continuum and is actively engaged in preserving them for posterity.[4]

Next to nothing is known about the German civilian shelter project in the Netherlands, and whatever knowledge we may have had of the structures built by the BB during the Cold War, whether or not put to new uses later, is quickly fading from memory. A national policy towards the physical remains of the Cold War is nonetheless gradually taking shape. Several ministries, including Defence, are co-operating with the provincial and municipal authorities to accord a new lease of life to redundant hardened ensembles such as former military airfields.[5] So far, these efforts have gone little beyond good intentions; the approach is less than bold. A project like that in Hombroich (North Rhine-Westphalia, Germany),[6] in which contemporary architecture, art and landscaping have helped give a new cultural purpose to a redundant cruise-missile launching site complete with its bunkers, storage facilities, etc., is still a distant dream in the Netherlands. Or storing the Wiki Leaks servers in a former nuclear shelter in Stockholm.

Bunkers and other shelters have long been put to new uses all over Europe.

However, it has been difficult to find new functions for the larger spaces and ensembles such as the Atlantic Wall. Once a city regained a sufficient stock of housing, offices, prisons, hotels, clubs and restaurants, the conversion and business exploitation of wartime bunkers came to look like an absurdly expensive option. So, except where the larger structures could be adapted to new military purposes, they were left empty.

A SECOND LEASE OF LIFE FOR THE BUNKERS

The image of Shelter City branded on the retinas of city dwellers in the period 1940-1945 quickly faded after the Liberation of the Netherlands. The authorities offered attractive bonuses – sometimes up to 90 per cent of the expenditure – for removing obstacles, mostly of German construction. The demolition of the physical relics of Shelter City at crossroads and in squares, parks, roadsides and gardens was accompanied by the sound of explosions, pneumatic drills and sledge hammers. Those engaged in the work could reckon on the enthusiastic approval of bystanders. The iconoclastic fury was directed at the lighter structures; thick-walled objects built by the German occupiers stubbornly remained because their demolition proved extraordinarily complicated and expensive. For a time, the surviving structures served as Boy Scout halls, mushroom farms, bars and even Civil Defence command centres. Creativity thus gave the German-built air raid shelters a new lease of life.

In Germany itself, the bunkers remained in use much longer than those in the Netherlands, and their applications were more varied. Amid the flattened ruins of bombed-out cities, the above-ground bunkers stood proudly like twentieth-century menhirs. Germany now had to convert them from the functions of Total War to the needs of Total Peace. They were intensively used, especially in the first three years after the end of the war. In the grim circumstances of postwar Berlin, the former bomb shelters provided rudimentary accommodation for bombed-out families, refugees and released POWs. Some served as emergency hospitals and remand prisons. During the war they had been used for only part of the day, but now that they provided semi-permanent lodgings, the wretched level of amenities and the lack of daylight and comfort became all too obvious.

In June 1948, when the Deutschmark was introduced and border checks were tightened up, the flood of refugees dwindled and with it the demand for bunkers as living quarters. Several of them were converted into hotels to stand in for those that had been wholly destroyed in many German cities. The allies wanted to blow up all the bunkers, but this led to fierce disputes with the municipal authorities who preferred to retain them as temporary accommodation. Eventually, a compromise emerged: until 1950, the allies were free to demolish all bunkers with a potential strategic or military significance, while the less threatening structures would remain for residential purposes. Building workers eliminated any possibility of their reuse for military applications by drilling large holes in the roofs and walls. Seven hundred of the thousand bunker shelters were retained in Hamburg, for example. From 1948 onwards, dining out and other pleasures gradually returned to the city scene, and the former bomb shelters proved their usefulness as restaurants, brothels, cinemas, workshops for small businesses, aquariums, cold stores and bicycle sheds, and as repositories for furniture, textiles, victuals, coal and archives.[7] Much later, some of them gained an ecological application as hibernation nests for bats and hedgehogs, and others came to serve new cultural functions such as rehearsal studios for insufferably loud rock bands.

In West Germany as a whole, some three hundred bunkers continued to provide living accommodation. As time passed, it was no longer bombed-out families and refugees who sought shelter there, but the misfits of the increasingly affluent society. Many of the former shelters degenerated into scenes of poverty, drug abuse, prostitution and crime, a situation which persisted well into the 1970s. In 1989, Schleswig-Holstein and Niedersachsen studied the feasibility of rehabilitating some former bunkers as housing for economic migrants from East Germany.

In the Netherlands the situation immediately after the war was not so different from that in Germany. The bunkers that *Siedlung und Bauten* had designed also found new uses, and their interiors were often stripped out to accommodate the new functions. After the occupying forces left, for instance, a bunker in Nijmegen provided accommodation first for refugees and then for delinquents. In 1948 it became a store for archived documents, and from 1956 to 1973 it was a BB command centre.

REMNANTS OF THE COLD WAR

One aspect that is common to everything that I have called Shelter City is the terror of destruction raining down from the skies. It is a phenomenon that I sum up as a "protectionist reflex", for although motivated by real threats, it has often gone well beyond the bounds of rational defensiveness. Following the real nuclear devastation at the end of World War II, the Cold War raised the level of fear to a new pitch.

Not only were life and property at stake, but the whole of civilization, if not all life on earth, seemed doomed by the threat of a nuclear holocaust and a nuclear winter. The prospect of cities turned into radioactive deserts was rehearsed over and over again in novels and films in the 1950s onwards, not to mention in the simulated nuclear attack exercises of civil defence organizations. Nations invested heavily in programmes of research in the social sciences and in military and civil defence. The physical space of a city under nuclear attack was scrutinized for its effect on crowd behaviour, risk awareness and the concepts of good and evil. The knowledge acquired this way has influenced the design of cities and buildings, but the effect of the Cold War protectionist reflex on today's urban culture is an area that has hitherto received little scholarly attention.

Now that the Cold War is beginning to fade from our collective memory, we must decide how to deal with the physical relics and the strategic and communications concepts from that period. This applies not only at the level of built structures, but to the wider rural and urban context and the even larger military remains that span national borders. We therefore need a European strategy for dealing with the Great Relics of the Cold War era. An important component of the necessary research would be to document these structures in heritage terms, to identify their significant sites of memory and potential exploration routes, and to document archive material and make it accessible through databases and websites. Another important aspect would be reception research; the study of how people appreciate the large defensive structures of European history, which include the *Limes* (the fortified border of the Roman Empire), the New Dutch Water Line, the Atlantic Wall and the physical remnants of the Iron Curtain. This entails cataloguing spatial visualizations of cross-border heritage structures for the whole of Europe, and developing new heritage concepts and a new ideology of heritage. For conventional defensive buildings, authenticity of use is not usually much of an issue, but this is less clear in the case of geographically diffuse structures.

It is crucial that this approach to heritage distances itself from the conventional political attitude to heritage sites in war zones. Today's international institutional context (UNESCO, the World Bank, the NATO alliance and numerous NGOs) apparently subscribes to a heritage concept of reconstructing lost or damaged monuments, and this is applied in response to every crisis or disaster, every violent onslaught and every war. We hear pious statements about the peacemaking function of heritage. They commonly portray conservation, restoration and even reconstruction as humanitarianism, under the banner of celebrating collective cultural identity and nostalgia for origins.[8]

COLONIAL HERITAGE

What standpoint should we adopt towards the eroding remains of military and civilian bomb shelters? How can we establish their significance for the present? The nuclear shelters of the Cold War era call for a very different approach from one that would be appropriate for the civilian air raid shelters of the German-occupied Netherlands. In the conclusion of this book, I would like to present an example of a heritage concept for that unwelcome gift to the Dutch people from the Germans: the civilian bomb shelters the occupiers built in the Netherlands.

It is easily forgotten that there are two sides to the human story of these physical remains. Many Dutch people see the World War II remnants as ugly reminders of a period of aggression and occupation, best quietly forgotten and left to decay. Others argue that the story of the aggressors and losers must not be swept under the carpet, for a reception history must not be tainted by political correctness. To the Germans, the bunkers are part of their own history of bunker construction, built for the same purpose and with the same techniques; a kind of colonial heritage from the years of occupation. But while these shelters played little part in the bombing that took place in the Netherlands, their place in German memory is one of deep trauma. The miserable existence in the now almost forgotten Shelter City was not simply Spartan; the bombing was itself a horrific assault on the nervous system. Those who survived the bombs and the firestorms in the vulnerable city centres and working-class districts emerged to find their familiar surroundings a smouldering ruin. Moreover, the Germans experienced the destruction of cities in their homeland as a collective humiliation, which was aggravated after the German capitulation by a cloak of silence drawn over the experience of the Nazi era. Many survivors struggled in silence for the rest of their lives with recurrent images of the air raids and their time in the shelters.

Still, the civilian bunkers offered some asylum. These concrete monoliths saved many lives, but life there was a parody of normal civil life.[9] The panoptical space of Shelter City reduced humans to cave dwellers – not as in literary and sociological thought experiments of the nineteenth century,[10] but as part of twentieth-century total war. A human narrative of this kind must always form part of a heritage concept.

THE RUIN VALUE OF NAZI ARCHITECTURE

Another part of our perception of historical remains is our understanding of the cultural and ideological context that gave rise to them. The physical strength of the German bunkers, including those built in the Netherlands, and their aspiration to defy the ages must be seen in the light of the ideology of the Third Reich – an epoch which was extraordinary fleeting in comparison to its overweening ambition. The great ages of history, Albert Speer held, are embodied in their monumental buildings, which form a permanent memorial and a heroic source of inspiration. This was the basis of his theory of Ruin Value, which drew on the nineteenth-century adulation of the ruined remains of antiquity. Even when made with modern engineering, buildings could provide a "bridge of tradition" for future generations if designed with traditional features (brick cladding, marble, sculptures, etc.). But the prestige buildings of the Third Reich were far greater in size than those of ancient Egypt, Greece and Rome, guaranteeing the perpetuity of the Great Dictator's fame. "By using special materials and by applying certain principles of statics," Speer wrote, "we should be able to build structures which even in a state of decay would more or less resemble Roman models after hundreds or (such were our reckonings) thousands of years. To illustrate my ideas, I had a romantic drawing prepared. It showed what the reviewing stand on the Zeppelin Field would look like after generations of neglect, overgrown with ivy, its columns fallen, the walls crumbling here and there, but the outlines still clearly recognizable. In Hitler's entourage this drawing was regarded as blasphemous. That I could even conceive of a period of decline for the newly founded Reich destined to last a thousand years seemed outrageous to many of Hitler's closest followers. But he himself accepted my ideas as logical and illuminating. He gave orders that in the future the important buildings of his Reich were to be erected in keeping with the principles of this 'law of ruins'."[11] Speer's designs for Hitler had spectacular axes like stage sets, streets broadened into boulevards and oversized buildings dressed in a hyperbolic Neoclassicism full of explicit quotations from Roman and Greek models. The engineering was far from Classical, though, as indicated by Speer's discussion with Hitler about the immense dome he designed as the climax of the 5-km-long boulevard which was to crown Berlin as the capital of the new German Empire. Given the dome's diameter of 250 metres, Hitler saw its vulnerability to bombs, necessitating a massive, steel-reinforced, concrete construction.[12]

The fall of the Thousand Year Reich occurred somewhat sooner than its name would suggest, and the surviving built heritage of that epoch has taken on a purpose and character inconsistent with the kind of building whose ruin value Speer advocated. The most prestigious of these projects never left the drawing board or were incomplete, and those that were built were severely damaged or destroyed in the war.

A HERITAGE CONCEPT FOR THE DUTCH SHELTER CITY

In the case of the German-built bunkers in the Netherlands, the notion of their value as heroic ruins of the distant future seems at best ironic, for there is no sign of the hyperbole that dominated the architectural ambitions of Hitler and Speer. It nonetheless forms an important context for our choices of how to deal with the remaining structures. The Nazi architectural rhetoric did not go unchallenged even in Germany, where one of the figureheads of the Stuttgarter Schule, the architect Paul Schmitthenner, had criticized Speer's designs and ideas in the late 1930s.[13] The designs for the new capitals of the Führer were overdimensioned in his view – that is, inflated parodies of Classical examples, with exaggerated proportions and a superabundance of neoclassical ornament. Instead, Schmitthenner advocated a reserved, but dignified style consistent with the building type and without frills. We may place the architecture of *Siedlung und Bauten*, especially the settlement in Heerlen and the police barracks in Clingendaal, in this category. The architects of both these ensembles, the husband-and-wife team Elisabeth and Karl Gonser, were Schmitthenner's pupils. The dark side of the architecture of *Siedlung und Bauten* – the shelters including their camouflage and earthen coverings – is its wholly inward-looking character. It effectively represents a world turned in on itself. The civilian shelters were no more than safe receptacles for city dwellers. The Gonsers made a considerable contribution to this part of Shelter City in the Netherlands, but the dualism of its architecture is unmistakable in the representative police barracks and in Seyss-Inquart's bunker in Clingendaal camouflaged as a farmhouse. The mousehole and the Crystal Palace stood shoulder to shoulder.

The bunkers were necessarily visually inconsistent with their surroundings, whether urban or rural, and there is no point in trying to integrate them now. The bunkers should be allowed to erode where they stand in the town or countryside. Let them achieve their ruin value, let them be overrun with greenery as silent witnesses to the metamorphosis of culture into nature. The bunker is both an empty shell and an emissary from a parallel universe driven by a tunnel-vision ideology. Oblivious to questions of exterior or interior, of clients or of social meanings, the bunkers seem only bent on flaunting the naked core of their purpose. Their obdurate physicality shrugs off changes in society and the issues of the day, while their slow decline is an enduring emblem of architectural *vanitas*. I must admit that this heritage concept would be at odds with the normal approach in the Netherlands, where heritage preservation almost automatically means exploiting the remaining structures for cultural or commercial purposes. It would need changes in national policy to bring it about. Many people think that heritage is something that is created today – that it is the spiritual property of today's consumer and that every attempt to appropriate it, mentally or physically, is justifiable. That is a misconception. We can only do justice to the Shelter City heritage through an almost superhuman abstinence, by renouncing an educational mission, walking tours, bicycle trips, treasure hunts and any other form of commercialization or dumbing-down. The bunkers should be left alone for a thousand years until they decay into a state of eternal beauty. Only in this way will the Netherland's unloved Shelter City get its just deserts.

Between a row of garages and a large 1980s housing estate on Loolaan in Apeldoorn is an unobtrusive strip of no-man's-land measuring 30 by 5 metres (see the illustration on page 353). It is one of the best concealed bomb shelters of all those built for Seyss-Inquart. Its location is an oasis of tranquillity. Hemmed in by new buildings, a car park, lock-ups, the wooden fences of back gardens and sheds which nestle against the flank of the shelter, an intimate little landscape has developed here, framed by the back sides of other things. The long, narrow, half-buried bunker does little to recall its former purpose. The entrances have been bricked up, and one of them has been replaced by a decorative flight of stone steps. This leads the dawdling visitor to the roof of the shelter, where there is a bright green lawn fringed by tall shrubs. Roughly in the middle of this greensward, an eroded concrete slab juts out above the grass. It is the cover of the ventilation shaft and is the only thing in this landscape that recalls its former function. It could be the smallest cemetery in the Netherlands – a level green lawn with a single horizontal tombstone.

Notes

FOREWORD

1. *Trouw*, 8 March, 2003.

2. For one of the best interpretations of the Atlantic Wall, see P. Virilio, *Bunker archéologie*, Paris 1991 (1975).

3. "als selbständige Bauten abseits von Gebäuden errichtet oder mit Gebäuden in Verbindung gebracht oder an solche angebaut werden." H. Schmal and T. Selke, *Bunker. Luftschutz und Luftschutzbau in Hamburg*, Hamburg 2001, 58.

4. The term "machine à survivre" is adopted from Virilio, 39.

5. E. Bowen, *The Heat of the Day*, London 1949, 89.

6. Information provided by Dan Cruickshank, May, 2004.

7. W.G. Sebald, *On the Natural History of Destruction*, London 2003. J. Friedrich, *Der Brand. Deutschland im Bombenkrieg 1940-1945*, Munich 2002. J. Friedrich, *Brandstätten. Der Anblick des Bombenkriegs*, Munich 2003. Exhibition, Stadtmuseum Karlsruhe: "Luftschutz und Luftkrieg in Karlsruhe 1933 bis 1945", with the new, updated edition of E. Lacker, *Zielort Karlsruhe. Die Luftangriffe im Zweiten Weltkrieg*, Heidelberg 2005. D. Suess, *Tod aus der Luft. Kriegsgesellschaft und Luftkrieg in Deutschland und England*, Munich 2011.

CHAPTER 1

1. F.M. Dostoyevski, *Aantekeningen uit de ondergrondse* (1864), in *Verzamelde werken*, Amsterdam 1957, 164.

2. D. Pick, *War Machine. The Rationalisation of Slaughter in the Modern Age*, New Haven and London 1993, 5.

3. L. Kennett, *A History of Strategic Bombing*, New York 1982, 39-57.

4. S. Lindqvist, *A History of Bombing*, New York 2001.

5. H.G. Wells, *The War in the Air*, Leipzig 1930 (first edition London 1908), 221-222.

6. Sandor Márai, *De opstandigen* [The Rebels], Amsterdam 2003 (1930), 29.

7. The idea of an attack on the environment was expressed by P. Virilio, *Bunker archéologie*, Paris 1991 (1975), 38: "Ce sont ensuite les conditions mêmes de l'habitat humain qui sont devenues l'objectif prioritaire de la destructuration-destruction; c'est l'ensemble des conditions de milieu." The topic was taken up by P. Sloterdijk in *Luftbeben. An den Quellen des Terrors*, Frankfurt am Main 2002.

8. On the development of civil airfields, see J. Zukowsky (ed.), *Building for Air Travel. Architecture and Design for Commercial Aviation*, Munich and New York 1995. K. Bosma, "In search for the perfect airport", in A. von Vegesack and J. Eisenbrand (eds.), *Airworld. Design and Architecture for Air Travel*, Weil am Rhein 2004, 36-64.

9. W. Voigt, "From the hippodrome to the aerodrome, from the air station to the terminal: European airports, 1909-1945", in Zukowsky, 32.

10. "La vitesse supérieure des divers moyens de communication et de destruction est, entre les mains du militaire, le moyen privilégié d'une transformation sociale permanente et secrète, un projectile pour la destruction du

continuum social, une arme, un *implosif*".
Virilio, 19.

11. Chr. Asendorf, *Super Constellation. Flugzeug und Raumrevolution. Die Wirkung der Luftfahrt auf Kunst und Kultur der Moderne*, Vienna/New York 1997, 261. On the international role of architects in WWII: J.L. Cohen, *Architecture in Uniform. Designing and Building for the Second World War*, Toronto 2011.

12. J.H. van Riesen, "Algemeene beginselen van luchtbescherming", *De Ingenieur*, (1937) 4, V1.

13. E.C.P. Monson, *Air Raid Damage in London Being A Record of the Effect of Air Craft Attack*, London 1923. A. Calder, *The People's War. Britain 1939-1945*, London 1969, 21. Monson counted a total of over 100 attacks throughout the country, resulting in 1,413 fatalities.

14. J. Ray, *The Battle of Britain. New Perspectives. Behind the Scenes of the Great Air War*, London 1994, 125. See also Kennett, 18-38. J.M. Spaight, *Air Power and the Cities*, London, etc. 1930, 179-191.

15. J. Friedrich, *Der Brand. Deutschland im Bombenkrieg 1940-1945*, Munich 2002, 281-282. See also K. Kranich, *Karlsruhe. Schicksalstage einer Stadt*, Karlsruhe 1973.

16. Description of bombing and quote from C. van der Heijden, *Rampen en plagen in Nederland 1400-1940. Pestbacillen, paalwormen en plunderende Moskovieters*, Zaltbommel 2004, 134-139.

17. Cited by L. Elfferich, *Eindelijk de waarheid nabij. Analyses en emoties naar aanleiding van het bombardement op Rotterdam*, The Hague 1983, 140.

18. W.S. Churchill, *Thoughts and Adventures*, London 1932, 248.

19. Churchill, 246-247.

20. G.J. Ashworth, *War and the City*, London and New York 1991, 137.

21. Cited in Kennett, 49.

22. Cited in W. Mitchell, *Skyways. A Book on Modern Aeronautics*, Philadelphia and London 1930, 261. See also Spaight and B.H. Liddell Hart, *The Remaking of Modern Armies*, London 1927.

23. Kennett, 54.

24. Translated into German in 1935 as *Luftherrschaft*. On the influence of Douhet's theory on the continent, see Kennett, 72-88.

25. G. Douhet, *Luftherrschaft*, Berlin 1935, 49.

26. Douhet, 16.

27. A more detailed description of this attack appears in P. Sloterdijk, *Luftbeben. An der Quellen des Terrors*, Frankfurt am Main 2002, 7-12.

28. J. Rudolfs, *De gevaren van luchtbescherming*, Utrecht (undated) (1939), 4.

29. Quoted in Sloterdijk, 100.

30. R.H. Whealey, *Hitler and Spain. The Nazi Role in the Spanish Civil War 1936-1939*, Kentucky 1989, 102.

31. See e.g. E.A. van Genderen Stort, "Een en ander over luchtbescherming", *Technisch Gemeenteblad*, (1939) 8, 160-161; 9, 179-184; 10, 196-198. Idem, "De weerstand van gebouwen bij luchtaanvallen", *Staal*, (1935) 10, 165-170.

32. A.P.J. Hoogeveen, "Chemische strijdmiddelen. Oorlogsgassen", *Luchtgevaar*, (1934) 4, 57-58; 5, 88-89; 6, 119-121; 7, 165-167; (1935) 1, 10-12; 2, 54-57. E.A. van Genderen Stort, "Luchtbescherming en bouwkunde", *Staal*, (1938) 1, 3-5.

33. For an illustrated discussion of flying formations, see E.H. Knipfer and E. Hampe (eds.), *Der zivile Luftschutz. Ein Sammelwerk über alle Fragen des Luftschutzes*, Berlin 1934, 70-75.

34. For a contemporary report on the attack, see *Guernica. La mainmise hitlérienne sur le Pays Basque*, Paris, undated. Also see J. Salas Larrazábal, *Air War Over Spain*, London 1969. S. Payne, *Politics and Military in Modern Spain*, Stanford 1967. G. Eisenwein and A. Shubert, *Spain At War. The Spanish Civil War in Context 1931-1939*, London and New York 1995. H.R.

Southworth, *Guernica! Guernica! A Study of Journalism, Diplomacy, Propaganda and History*, Berkeley 1977. K.A. Maier, *Guernica 26.4.1937: die deutsche Intervention in Spanien und der "Fall Guernica"*, Freiburg 1975. G. Thomas and M. Witts, *Guernica: the Crucible of World War II*, New York 1975. M. Richards, *A Time of Silence. Civil War and the Culture of Repression in Franco's Spain. The Nazi Role in the Spanish Civil War*, Cambridge 1998.

35. P. Hinrichs, "Test für den Terror", in S. Burgdorff and C. Habbe (eds.), *Als Feuer vom Himmel fiel. Der Bomberkrieg in Deutschland*, Munich 2003, 67.

36. Whealey, 106.

37. On the tradition of fortified cities, see G.J. Ashworth, *War and the City*, London and New York 1991.

38. H. Goering, "Vorwort", in Knipfer and Hampe, 5. This quote has also appeared in various Dutch publications, for example in A.H. van Leeuwen and H. Sangster, *Schuilplaatsen en beveiliging tegen luchtaanvallen*, Leiden 1936, 2.

39. Asendorf, 233-234. See also R. Bruge, *Faites sauter la ligne Maginot. Histoire de la ligne Maginot*, Verviers 1973 (1985). Ph. Truttmann, *La fortification française de 1940: sa place dans l'évolution des systèmes d'Europe Occidentale de 1880 à 1945*, Metz 1979. J.E. and H.W. Kauffmann, *The Maginot Line. None Shall Pass*, London 1997.

40. For a review of German radar and radio stations, see A. Korthals Altes, *Luchtgevaar. Luchtaanvallen op Nederland 1940-1945*, Amsterdam 1984, Appendix III.

41. For further detail, see H.R. Kroon, "De alarmering voor luchtaanvallen", *Technisch Gemeenteblad*, (1938) 2, 30-31; 3, 53-55; 4, 70-72; 5, 97-99.

42. See e.g. J.H. van Riesen, "De luchtaanval", *Luchtgevaar*, (1934) 1, 2-6.

43. A. Romani, "I ricoveri nella difesa aerea" and "L'avvistamento ed i collegamenti nella difesa aerea", *Rivista di Artiglieri e Genio*, (1927) 5, 817-832 and 11/12, 1901-1911.

44. H. Schmal and T. Selke, *Bunker. Luftschutz und Luftschutzbau in Hamburg*, Hamburg 2001, 28-31.

45. O.N. Arup, *Design, Cost, Construction, and Relative Safety of Trench, Surface, Bomb-proof and Other Air-raid Shelters*, Westminster 1939.

46. A. Saint, *Towards a Social Architecture. The Role of School Building on Post-War England*, New Haven and London 1987, 12-15. J. Allan, *Berthold Lubetkin. Architecture and the Tradition of Progress*, London 1992, 353-363.

47. Arup, 29.

48. H. Schoszberger, *Bautechnischer Luftschutz*, Berlin 1934.

49. For Plan Voisin and plans for Algiers, see *Le Corbusier. Une encyclopédie*, Paris 1987, 28-32, 470.

50. Paul Wolf, *Städtebau*, Dresden 1920.

51. On the linear city model, see G. Fehl and J. Rodríguez-Lores, "Die Stadt wird in der Landschaft sein und die Landschaft in der Stadt." *Bandstadt und Bandstruktur als Leitbilder des modernen Städtebaus*, Basle etc. 1997.

52. Schoszberger, 207-212.

53. The information on this bunker complex is from H.G. Kampe, *Deckname "Zeppelin". Die Bunker im Hauptquartier des Oberkommandos des Heeres in Zossen*, Berlin 1997. Part of the German intelligence bunker was converted into a nuclear war command centre by the Soviet occupying army in the 1960s. It was not until the fall of the Berlin Wall that the complex was accessible for historical research. See also F.W. Seidler and D. Zeigert, *Die Führerhauptquartiere. Anlagen und Planen im Zweiten Weltkrieg*, Munich 2000, 291-298.

54. Owing to the high rate of attack by armoured troops, the following communica-

tion facilities were standard equipment: "Betriebskompagnie zur Bedienung der Fernsprechvermittlungen, motorisierten Feldfernkabelbau-Kompanien. Die Stammleitung jeder Panzergruppe sollte also eine Feldfernkabellinie sein, die mittels tragbarer Trägerfrequenzgeräte mehrfach genutzt wurde." H.G. Kampe, *Nachrichtentruppe des Heeres und Deutsche Reichspost. Militärisches und staatliches Nachrichtenwesen in Deutschland – 1830 bis 1945*, Berlin 1999, 437.

55. A. Speer, *Inside the Third Reich*, London and New York 1970, 415. Original text: A. Speer, *Erinnerungen*, Berlin 1969, 317.

56. Seidler and Zeigert.

CHAPTER 2

1. J.H. van Riesen, "Algemeene beginselen van luchtbescherming", *De Ingenieur*, (1937) 4, V2.

2. A. Calder, *The People's War. Britain 1939-1945*, London 1969, 21-22. Ph. Ziegler, *London at War 1935-1945*, London 1995, 10-11.

3. T.H. O'Brien, *Civil Defence*, London 1955, 144.

4. Calder, 22.

5. O'Brien, 228. J. Mack and S. Humphries, *London at War. The Making of Modern London 1935-1945*, London 1985, 20. Ph. Ziegler, *London at war 1935-1945*, London 1995, 68-70.

6. *War Time Lighting Restrictions for Industrial and Commercial Premises*, May 1939.

7. For further information see R. Woolven, *Air Raid Precautions and London Government, 1935-1945*, London 1988.

8. O'Brian, 148.

9. "For householders and persons in charge of a business, shop, hotel, lodging house or tenements the first action this recommended (under the heading Things to Do Now) was choice of a refuge-room, to be protected against gas and furnished for habitation during a raid. This room would be the householder's or shopkeeper's 'first line of defence because a respirator cannot protect the other parts of your body from dangerous liquids such as "mustard gas"'. It should be in the cellar or basement, if this could be made reasonably gas-proof and secure against flooding; otherwise it might be any room on any floor below the top floor. 'Any room within solid walls,' the handbook urged, 'is safer than being out in the open.' If war broke out and air raids took place, the head of the household's first duty after hearing the warning would be to send all under his care, with their respirators, to the refuge-room; and he should keep them there until he heard the 'raiders passed' and had satisfied himself that the neighbourhood was free from gas." O'Brian, 150-151.

10. Calder, 25-26.

11. O'Brian, 148-152.

12. For the Munich Crisis, see O'Brian, 153-165. For extensive details on the evacuation, see R.M. Titmuss, *Problems of Social Policy*, London 1950.

13. O'Brian, 324-328.

14. C.M. Kohan, *Works and Buildings*, London 1952, 363-379.

15. Cited in Calder, 36. See also Mack and Humphries, 14-19. Bernard Kops described his experience of evacuation from Stepney Green in September 1939 in *The World is A Wedding*, London 1963, 51-60.

16. Calder, 38.

17. Calder, 39-50.

18. Kops, 54.

19. Kops, 55.

20. H.M. Stationery Office, *A.R.P. Handbook No. 5*, with Supplement No. 5A, *Bomb Resisting Shelters* which appeared in August. The other handbooks were No. 1, *Personal Protection Against Gas*; No. 2, *First Aid and Nursing for Gas Casualties*; No. 3, *Medical Treatment of Gas Casualties*; No. 4, *Decontamination of Materials*; No. 6, *Air Raid Precautions in Factories and Busi-*

ness Premises; No. 7, *Anti-Gas Precautions for Merchant Shipping*; No.8, *The Duties of Air Raid Wardens*; No. 9, *Incendiary Bombs and Fire Precautions*; No. 10, *The Training and Work of First Aid Parties*; No. 11, *Camouflage of Large Installations*; No. 12, *Air Raid Precautions for Animals*. The following Air Raid Precautions Memoranda were also published: No. 1, *Organisation of Air Raid Casualties Services*; No. 2, *Rescue Parties and Clearance of Debris*; No. 3, *Organisation of Decontamination Services*; No. 4, *Air Raid Wardens*; No. 5, *Anti-Gas Training*; No. 6, *Local Communications and Reporting of Air Raid Damage*; No. 7, *Personnel Requirements for Air Raid General and Fire Precautions Services and the Police Service*; No. 8, *The Air Raid Warning System*; No. 9, *Notes on Training and Exercises*; No. 10, *Provision of Air Raid Shelters in Basements*. Finally, there were several pamphlets of 3-4 pages: *The Protection of Foodstuffs Against Poison Gas*, *Garden Trenches*, *The Protection of Your Home Against Air Raids*, *An Atlas of Gas Poisoning*, *Specifications etc. in Regard to Permanent Lining of Trenches*, *The Training of Air Raid Wardens*, *Pamphlet on Shelter From Air Attack*, *Wartime Lighting Restrictions, Lights Carried by Road Vehicles*. The Home Office issued a further five pamphlets in 1939: *Some Things You Should Know If War Should Come*; No. 2, *Your Gas Mask. How to Keep It and How to Use It*; No. 3, *Evacuation. Why and How?*; No. 4, *Your Food in War-Time*; No.5, *Fire Precautions in War Time*.

21. O'Brian, 193-194 and 219-223.

22. A special handbook was issued for industry: *A.R.P. Handbook No. 6 (Air Raid Precautions in Factories and Business Premises)*.

23. O'Brian, 193-195.

24. O'Brian, 142.

25. C. Fox, "The Battle of the Railings", *AA Files* 29 (1995), 50-60.

26. J. Allan, *Berthold Lubetkin. Architecture and the Tradition of Progress*, London 1992, 352-363.

27. A. Saint, *Towards A Social Architecture. The Role of School Building in Post-war England*, New Haven and London 1987, 12.

28. Allan, 356.

29. O'Brian, 190-192.

30. Ziegler, 10-11 and 71.

31. See further O'Brian, 200.

32. The following quantities were distributed prior to the London Blitz of September 1940: 2,300,878, of which 1,661,275 were the standard six-person model, 507,688 for four people and 131,915 for eight.

33. Ziegler, 26-27 and 72-73.

34. O'Brian, 187. See also *Air Raid Shelter Policy*, December 1938.

35. Kohan, 355.

36. A.R.P. Department, Circular 204, 28 August 1939.

37. Kohan, 359.

38. Mack and Humphries, 12.

39. O'Brian, 139.

40. Ziegler, 74.

41. O'Brian, 331.

42. Calder, 63.

43. An interesting survey may be found in Frommhold, *Luftschutzraum-Bauweisen*, Berlin 1939.

44. Frommhold, 5.

45. H. Schmal and T. Selke, *Bunker. Luftschutz und Luftschutzbau in Hamburg*, Hamburg 2001, 24.

46. D. and I. Arnold, *Dunkle Welten. Bunker, Tunnel und Gewölbe unter Berlin*, Berlin 2002, 103.

47. Kg., "Luchtbescherming op 'Schaffendes Volk'", *Luchtgevaar*, (1937) 9, 137-140. P.J. Goes, "Een luchtbeschermingshuis in Duitschland", *Luchtgevaar*, (1937) 5, 76.

48. Schmal and Selke, 26.

49. The first serious plans for Paris were published in 1937: P.H. Rey, "Paris objectif important", *L'Architecture d'Aujourd'hui*, (1937) 12, 31-33.

50. "Het einde der groote steden in zicht?", *Luchtgevaar. Tijdschrift voor Luchtbescherming*, (1939) 1, 6-7. "Luchtbescherming en stedebouw", *Gemeentebestuur*, (1939) January-February, 17-31. See also G.C. Kools, "Luchtbescherming en stadsaanleg", *Luchtgevaar*, (1936) 8, 135-136. Regarding De Casseres, see K. Bosma, *J.M. de Casseres. De eerste planoloog*, Rotterdam 2003.

51. "Voor luchtbescherming open bebouwing aanbevolen", *Telegraaf*, evening edition, 6 March 1939. "Bouwtechnische luchtbescherming. In het bijzonder bij den bouw van arbeiderswoningen", *NRC*, 12 March 1939.

52. Chief Inspector of Public Health H. van der Kaa, "Bescherming tegen luchtaanvallen", *Publieke Werken*, (1937) 1, 9.

53. Letter from Chief Engineering Consultant J.F. Hoytema to Municipal Executive of The Hague, 15 April 1939. Haags Gemeentearchief, 610-1819.

54. A. Dros, "Perspectieven der luchtbescherming", *De Socialistische Gids*, (1936) 9, 585.

55. *Aanwijzingen Luchtbeschermingsdienst* (1927) and *Leidraad Luchtbeschermingsdienst* (1931).

56. Pamphlet 1, Nederlandsche Vereeniging voor Luchtbescherming, *Algemeene beginselen van de bescherming der burgerbevolking tegen aanvallen uit de lucht*, The Hague 1937, 1.

57. *Luchtgevaar* was published from 1934 to 1944. Also appearing from 1941 to 1944 was *Pro Cive* (studies on civilian air raid protection issues).

58. J.H. van Riesen, "Zelfbeschermingsmaatregelen voor de bevolking", *Luchtgevaar*, (1935) 8, 129-136. See also A. Burgdorffer, "Luchtbescherming in eigen huis", *Luchtgevaar*, (1938) 8, 120-125. Idem, "Bouwkundige en de luchtbescherming", *Luchtgevaar*, (1935) 2, 22-25. For a critical study, see J.A.H. Perey, "Luchtbescherming", *Publieke Werken*, (1935) 6, 76-78; 7, 87-89.

59. Nederlandsche Vereeniging voor Luchtbescherming, *Zelfbeschermingsmaatregelen (gezinsbescherming)*, The Hague 1938, 25. In fact, some people took this advice seriously. In the days preceeding the bombardment of Rotterdam, J.A.C. Tillema, the chief engineer of the building inspectorate, claims that while at home with his wife and son in their house on Noordereiland, which came under fire, they wore kitchen pans on their heads. J.A.C. Tillema, "We zouden voor een geweldige taak staan: het wederopbouwen van Rotterdam", in F. Baarda, *Uit het hart. Rotterdammers over het bombardement*, Amsterdam and The Hague 1990, 150.

60. "Een nood-uitgave der Nederlandsche Vereeniging voor Luchtbescherming", *Publieke Werken*, (1939) 10, 155.

61. In Paris, for example, the Préfecture de Police (Secrétariat Général Permanent de la Défense Passive) issued *Ce qu'il faut faire pour vous protéger en cas d'attaque aérienne*, Paris, not dated. For legislation and concrete measures in France, see the special edition of *L'Architecture d'Aujourd'hui*, (1937) 12. Home Office, *The Protection of Your Home Against Air Raids*, 1938 and *Your Home As An Air Raid Shelter*, London 1940.

62. See e.g. J.H. van Riesen, "Het luchtbeschermingsplan", *Luchtgevaar*, (1935) 3, 38-42; 4, 57-61; 5, 77-81.

63. H. van der Kaa, "Bescherming tegen luchtaanvallen", *Publieke Werken*, (1937) 1, 8.

64. J.H. van Riesen, "Algemeene beginselen van luchtbescherming", *De Ingenieur*, (1937) 4, V1-7. See also F.A. van Drimmelen, *Handboek voor luchtbescherming*, Aalten 1939.

65. H. Peeters, *De geneeskundige hulpverleening bij luchtaanvallen*, Amsterdam 1937.

66. The State Inspectorate for Civil Air Raid Protection published the following precautionary instructions in 1940: *Luchtbescherming.*

Aanwijzingen ten behoeve van de zelfbescherming (voorbeelden van lichtbescherming, ter voorkoming van lichtuitstraling uit gebouwen). See also J.J. van Vlokhoven, "Luchtbescherming en verlichting", *Technisch Gemeenteblad*, (1939) 8, 166-167; 9, 182-184.

67. The NVL and the State Inspectorate for Civil Air Raid Protection jointly issued a series of booklets in 1939: *Richtlijnen voor de luchtbescherming van de Nederlandse Spoorwegen* for the railways, and similarly titled booklets for agriculture and animal husbandry, inland shipping and schools.

68. C.J.F. Caljé, *Wet betreffende bescherming tegen luchtaanvallen*, Zwolle 1936.

69. A. Korthals Altes, *Luchtgevaar. Luchtaanvallen op Nederland 1940-1945*, Amsterdam 1984, 78.

70. Amersfoort Muncipal Archives BNR 002.1. Municipal proceedings (1811-1945) no. 4144. The plan was revised again in 1940: *Luchtbeschermingsplan en instructies van den Luchtbeschermingsdienst te Amersfoort*, 26 March 1940.

71. Van der Tak memorandum, 13 February 1937. Amersfoort Municipal Archives BNR 002.1. Muncipal proceedings (1811-1945), No. 4144. See also S. Schilderman, "Schuilloopgraven versus schuilkelders", *Luchtgevaar*, (1938) 8, 126-127.

72. J.H. van Riesen, "Schuilloopgraven", *Luchtgevaar*, (1934) 6, 86-88; 7, 100-102.

73. Pamplet 5 of the Nederlandsche Vereeniging voor Luchtbescherming, *Verblijf in schuilplaatsen*, The Hague 1937 and pamphlet 6, *Schuilloopgraven*, The Hague 1938.

74. See e.g. A. Burgdorffer, "Schuilloopgraven", *Luchtgevaar*, (1938) 9, 137-140.

75. See also J.H. van Riesen, "Schuilgelegenheid", *Luchtgevaar*, (1937) 6, 86-88.

76. For a detailed account of this by construction engineers and architects, see A.H. van Leeuwen and H. Sangster, *Schuilplaatsen en beveiliging tegen luchtaanvallen*, Leiden 1936. J.J. Meulenkamp, *Bouw en inrichting van schuilplaatsen tegen luchtaanvallen*, Amsterdam 1939. A.C. Verschoor, *School en luchtbescherming*, Alphen aan den Rijn 1940.

77. Gasmaskerbesluit 1937, *Staatsblad* No. 856. Reliable gas filters were marketed by German companies such as Auer and APO (Anton Piller K.G. Ostero in the Harz). The latter sold three types: type PWL 6 could provide fresh air for 30 people, type 12 for 60 people and type 24 for 120 people.

78. E.A. van Genderen Stort, "Stalen schuilplaatsen", *Staal*, (1940) 1, 3.

79. J. Gerber, "Technische luchtbeschermingsmaatregelen", *Publieke Werken*, (1939) 12, 176.

80. NA, BiZa 02.04.53.15, ds 30, 105; letter from the Director of The Hague Public Works Department to the Inspector for Civil Air Raid Protection, 15 January 1940. And ds 31, 107.

81. *Gemeenteblad* No. 270 "Luchtbescherming", 28 April 1939. Letter from the Municipality of Amsterdam to the Minister of Social Affairs, 26 September 1939. Amsterdam Municipal Archives, Public Works 2513 A, 2723.

82. NA, BiZa 02.04.53.15, ds 31, 107. The Amsterdam Air Raid Protection Agency arrived at a different tally: 40 concrete and 128 wooden shelters, 27 under bridges and 68 in buildings. See *Aan hen die vielen bij de uitoefening van hun dienst*, 1945. GAA, B, 1940-1945 No. 232.10. See also GAA, Public Works, 5213 (1922-1956), 2723, 2724 and 2725.

83. NA, BiZa 02.04.53.15, ds 31, 107.

84. Drawings of open and closed trench shelters are included in a promotional brochure of the Municipal Radio Broadcasting Company, *Wenken voor luchtbescherming* (February 1940).

85. NA, BiZa 02.04.53.15, ds 31, 107.

86. S. Schilderman, "Schuilloopgraven versus schuilkelders", *Luchtgevaar*, (1938) 8, 126-127.

J.J. Meulenkamp, "De schuilkelder van de Rotterdamsche Lloyd", *Luchtgevaar*, (1938) 10, 161-165.

87. "Kantoorgebouw der Philipsbedrijven, Eindhoven", *Vakblad voor de Bouwbedrijven*, (1939) 48, no page numbers.

88. Inspectie Luchtbeschermingsdienst PTT, "Luchtbeschermingsmaatregelen in de hoofd- en bijgebouwen van het hoofdbestuur der PTT te 's-Gravenhage", 13 April 1942. NA, 2.16.81.15, PTT archives, Luchtbeschermingsdienst 1938-1943, 32. See also State Inspector for Civil Air Raid Protection, *Richtlijnen voor het nemen van beschermingsmaatregelen tegen luchtaanvallen in bedrijven (bedrijfsluchtbescherming)*, The Hague 1937.

89. NA, 2.16.81.15, PTT archives, Luchtbeschermingsdienst 1938-1943. This gives an indication of the initiatives the PTT took to create shelters in its own offices and telephone exchanges.

90. As indicated by drawings by the Government Buildings Agency from 1941. NA, Luchtbeschermingsdienst PTT, 1938-1943, 27.

91. The drawings are in NA, 2.16.81.15, PTT archives, Luchtbeschermingsdienst 1938-1943, 38.

92. A. Burgdorffer, "De eerste Haagsche vluchtkelder tegen luchtaanvallen", *Luchtgevaar*, (1934) 12, 186-188. A.H. van Leeuwen and H. Sangster, *Schuilplaatsen en beveiliging tegen luchtaanvallen*, Leiden 1936, 53-54. E.E.T. Dulfer, "De eerste vluchtkelder tegen gasaanvallen in Nederland", *Mavors*, (1934) 11, 641-646.

93. *Luchtbeschermingsplan voor de gemeente 's-Gravenhage*, February 1938. The municipality had already taken the first summary measures, such as dividing the municipality into sectors: *Voorbereidende maatregelen ter bescherming van de bevolking tegen de gevolgen van aanvallen uit de lucht*, 30 October 1935. Haags Gemeentearchief, 666-619.

94. Municipal Executive decision, 23 December 1938. Collection 1938 No. 609. Luchtbeschermingsmaatregelen.

95. Letter from directors of Municipal Plantations, Public Works and Planning & Housing to the Municipal Executive, 28 July 1938. Haags Gemeentearchief, 666-689.

96. Municipal Executive decision, 10 July 1939. Collection 1939 No. 348. Haags Gemeentearchief, 487-1872.

97. Haags Gemeentearchief 666, Inspecteur van de Bouwpolitie, since 1906 Gemeentelijk Bouw- en Woningtoezicht, 623 and 624. The Openbare Bekendmaking Luchtbescherming of 2 June 1944 stated, "Everyone has the duty to inform the Local Air-Raid Protection Warden when a cellar has been furnished as a shelter."

98. Meeting of municipal engineering staff with Councillor Feber, 25 March 1939. Haags Gemeentearchief, 610-1818.

99. Haags Gemeentearchief, 610-1818 (containing situation drawings by Municipal Works Department, May 1939).

100. Municipal Executive decision, 21 August 1939. Collection 1939, No. 413. This refers to designs for 130 trench shelters, 40 of which would have to be fabricated immediately in concrete. Haags Gemeentearchief 487-1872 and 666-622.

101. "Afbraak en verwaarlozing (1940-1945)", in R. Vijfwinkel et al., *'s Haags werken en werkers. 350 jaar Gemeentewerken (1636-1986)*, The Hague 1986, 293-294.

102. Municipal Executive decision, 10 July 1939. Collection 1939, No. 348. Haags Gemeentearchief, 487-1872.

103. Haags Gemeentearchief, "Gemeentebestuur 1936-1952", No. 610, 1820. The material for the shelters was imported from the USA and was supplied by the United Steel Production Company in New York and the Jones

and Laughlin Steel Corporation in Pittsburgh. The Municipal Building and Housing Department wrote a Dutch-language instruction with 11 figures for erecting the shelters. Haags Gemeentearchief, 666-1457.

104. After the municipality sold 72 Anderson-type shelters to the German army in August 1940, sufficient material remained for 121 units. Letter from Director of Public Works to the Councillor for Public Works, 24 August 1940. Haags Gemeentearchief 666-623. In connection with construction of the Seghbroek-polder Airfield in September 1940, residents of the nearby district of Kijkduin were offered shelters for placing in their gardens. The 84 units were intended primarily for the residents, but in the event of an air raid they were also obliged to admit other members of the public who happened to be outdoors. Letter from The Hague Municipal Executive to the Van de Houwen brothers, 28 September 1940. Haags Gemeentearchief 666-623.

105. J. Gerber, "Technische luchtbeschermingsmaatregelen", *Publieke Werken*, (1939) 12, 175.

106. It was noted that the Rotterdam shelters were much lighter in construction than those of other cities.

107. NA, BiZa 02.04.53.15, ds 31, 107.

108. C.J. Oosterholt, "Openbare schuilplaatsen", *Luchtgevaar*, (1938) 2, 24.

109. Structural engineering committee of Nederlandsche Vereeniging Luchtbescherming, "Ter zake van schuilgelegenheden", *Luchtgevaar*, (1940) 4, 16-19. See also the drawings in A. Burgdorffer, "Schuilloopgraven", *Luchtgevaar*, (1938) 9, 139-140.

110. NA, 2.04.53.15. BiZa, Inspectie van de Bescherming Bevolking tegen Luchtaanvallen, ds 30, folder 104 and 105.

CHAPTER 3

1. M. Kohan, *Work and Buildings*, London 1952, 249.

2. This is not intended as a complete typology of aircraft. Plane spotters were generously supplied with handbooks, even in wartime. A Dutch example is *Duitsche, Italiaansche, Britsch-Amerikaansche en Sovjetrussische oorlogsvliegtuigen (stand zomer 1943)*, Amsterdam 1943.

3. The radar systems installed in fighter aircraft and bombers were renewed and refined in the course of the war. The four main systems were A.I. (airborne radar for night flyers), GEE (grid navigational system), OBOE (pinpoint radar finder, used primarily in the latter half of the war by low flying Mosquito bombers) and H2S (a "magic eye" that helped the pilot judge ground conditions at night and thereby supposedly enabled precision bombardment).

4. G. Burssens, *Dagboek*, Schoten 1988, 47-48.

5. E.R. Beck, *The German Home Front 1942-1945*, Kentucky 1986, 3.

6. T.H. O'Brien, *Civil Defence*, London 1955, 505.

7. M. Foedrowitz, *Bunkerwelten. Luftschutzanlagen in Norddeutschland*, Berlin 1998, 98.

8. For example, the McAlaster Army Ammunition Plant (Oklahoma), which opened 18 months after the Pearl Harbour attack, occupied 18,000 hectares. The area contained 600 bunkers spaced at 250-metre intervals and connected by a railway.

9. J. Friedrich, *Der Brand. Deutschland im Bombenkrieg 1940-1945*, Munich 2002, 28.

10. J.P. van den Hout, *Vijf jaar luchtfront. Het vliegveld Gilze-Rijen in de Tweede Wereldoorlog*, Gilze 1988.

11. See R. Swart, 'Vliegbasis Deelen als luchtvaartinfrastructuur-monument', *Cuypersbulletin. Nieuwsbrief van het Cuypersgenootschap*, (1997) 3, 13-16. M.E. Peters, *Lichtblauw op de Veluwe. Een geschiedenis van het vliegveld Deelen 1941-1945*, (n.p.) 1996.

12. J.M.G. Derix and H. Keulards, *Vliegveld Venlo: met een kroniek van de luchtoorlog in Zuid-Nederland 1941-1945*, Horst 1990.

13. Some information on modifications to and new construction of Dutch airfields is available in NIOD, WBN 990, 993, 997, 1007-1024. On the role of Dutch construction companies, see J. Meihuizen, *Noodzakelijk kwaad. De bestraffing van economische collaboratie in Nederland na de Tweede Wereldoorlog*, Amsterdam 2003, 133, 137, 144-145.

14. E. Agricola, 'Camouflagetechnieken. Duitse kazernebouw en herinrichting van vliegbases', in K. Bosma and C. Wagenaar (eds.), *Een geruisloze doorbraak. De geschiedenis van architectuur en stedebouw tijdens de bezetting en wederopbouw van Nederland*, Rotterdam 1995, 88. See also I. Finally, 'Kazernes onder vuur! Typologische kenmerken als basis voor instandhouding en herinrichting van kazernes', *Jaarboek Monumentenzorg 1999*, Zeist and Zwolle 2000, 128-136.

15. Agricola, 88.

16. On the extremely complex and changeable organization of the air defence, see a text by W.H. Tiemens at www.tiemens.nl.

17. For an overview of German radar and radio posts, see A. Korthals Altes, *Luchtgevaar. Luchtaanvallen op Nederland 1940-1945*, Amsterdam 1984, Appendix III.

18. "Salzhering" near Den Helder, "Zander" near Zandvoort, "Seeadler" near Diemen, "Hase" near Harderwijk and "Teerose I, II and III" near Terlet. A.A. Jansen, *Wespennest Leeuwarden*, Baarn 1976.

19. On the church tower of Den Briel, in the meadows just outside Den Briel ("Brennessel I en II"), near Franeker ("Löwenzahn I and II", serving the airfield of Leeuwarden) and near Schagen ("Schneeglöckchen"). Information obtained from Tiemens. Nineteen locations with radar detection facilities are noted in B.C.

de Pater and B. Schoenmaker, *Grote Atlas van Nederland 1930-1950*, Zierikzee 2005.

20. www.tiemens.nl

21. For further information on the development of the Kammhubersystem, see Korthals Altes, 98-100.

22. Korthals Altes, 100.

23. H. Schmal and T. Selke, *Bunker. Luftschutz und Luftschutzbau in Hamburg*, Hamburg 2001, 26-27.

24. Schmal and Selke, 35.

25. As an example of competition between Nazi organizations at a municipal level, see W. Nachtmann, *Karl Strölin. Stuttgarter Oberbürgermeister im 'Führerstaat'*, Tübingen 1995, 239-246.

26. G.W. Schramm, *Der zivile Luftschutz in Nürnberg 1933-1945*, Nürnberg 1983.

27. The document concerned may be found in M. Foedrowitz, *Bunkerwelten. Luftschutzanlagen in Norddeutschland*, Berlin 1998, 10-11.

28. Foedrowitz, 18.

29. Foedrowitz, 15. On the latter category, see Foedrowitz, 55-74.

30. S. Mattl, "Melancholische Giganten. Die Wiener Flaktürme", in S. Wenk (ed.), *Erinnerungsorte aus Beton. Bunker in Städten und Landschaften*, Berlin 2001, 74.

31. Foedrowitz, 19.

32. B. Hatton, "Strategische Architektur. Die unbeweglichen Objekte der Vorstellung", in S. Wenk (ed.), *Erinneringsorte aus Beton. Bunker in Städten und Landschaften*, Berlin 2001, 62.

33. Foedrowitz, 12.

34. M. Foedrowitz, *Luftschutztürme und ihre Bauarten 1934 bis heute*, Wölfersheim-Berstadt 1998. "Een torenschuilplaats", *Luchtgevaar* (1938) 2, 25.

35. D. Suess, *Managing the Catastrophe: Bavarian Cities in the Total War*, lecture to Seventh International Conference on Urban History, Athens 28 October 2004.

36. Foedrowitz, 33. Six of the eight sections have been published: Plan (I); Construction (II); Ventilation, heating and cooling (III); Water inlet and outlet (IV); Electric current (V); Marking and equipment (VI).

37. Foedrowitz, 51.

38. See e.g. D. Schubert, "... Ein neues Hamburg entsteht... Planungen in der 'Führerstadt' Hamburg zwischen 1933-1945", in H. Frank (ed.), *Faschistische Architekturen. Planen und Bauen in Europa 1930 bis 1945*, Hamburg 1985, 299-318.

39. Schmal and Selke, 28-31.

40. Der Reichsstatthalter in Hamburg, der Architekt des Elbufers, *Bombensichere Luftschutzbauten. Erste städtebaulich-architektonische Ausrichtung*, Hamburg, February 1941, 2.

41. *Wettbewerb Wohnungstypen 1940. Ausgeschrieben im Okt. 1940 von der Gemeindeverwaltung der Hansestadt Hamburg*.

42. Schmal and Selke, 41.

43. See e.g. H.A. Schäfer, *Berlin im Zweiten Weltkrieg. Der Untergang der Reichshauptstadt in Augenzeugenberichten*, Munich 1985.

44. D. and I. Arnold, *Dunkle Welten. Bunker, Tunnel und Gewölbe unter Berlin*, Berlin 2002, 104. E. Dittrich, *Ernst Sagebiel. Leben und Werk 1892-1970*, Berlin 2005.

45. On the sometimes controversial "representative duties" of corrupt prominent figures in the party, on whose behalf large houses, estates and castles were expropriated, refurbished and enhanced with bunkers, see A. Speer, *Erinnerungen*, Berlin 1969. Mention is made of Hitler's temporary headquarters in Ziegenberg, a spur of the Taunus mountains (184), Bruly le Peche (185), Rastenburg in East Prussia (207), the bunker complex in Obersalzberg (230, 546-547), Schloss Klessheim near Salzburg (231), Berchtesgaden (231), the castle in Posen (231), a bunker in Pallach near Munich (547), the "Riese" bunker complex near Bad Charlottenbrunn (547) and the scattered bunker settlement in Winniza (Ukraine, 250).

46. D. and I. Arnold, 113.

47. D. and I. Arnold, 115.

48. The Führerbunker in the "Wolfsschanze" near Rastenburg (with a roof of 8-metresthick reinforced concrete), the bunker in Führerhauptquartier 'Riese' near Bad Charlottenbrunn (Niedersachsen) or "Olga" in the Thüringer Ohrdruf were more complete than the one at the Reichs Chancellery.

49. D. and I. Arnold, 142-143.

50. Speer, ch. 8 and 9.

51. A. Speer, 315. See also S.F. Kellerhof, *Mythos Führerbunker*, Berlin 2003.

52. Kellerhof, 44.

53. Cited in F.W. Seidler and D. Zeigert, *Die Führerhauptquartiere. Anlagen und Planungen im Zweiten Weltkrieg*, Munich 2000, 66-67.

CHAPTER 4

1. Ch. Madge and T. Harrison, *Mass Observation*, London 1937.

2. See e.g. A. Calder and D. Sheridan, *Speak for Yourself. A Mass Observation Anthology 1937-1949*, London 1984.

3. J. Mack and S. Humphries, *London at War. The Making of Modern London 1939-1945*, London 1985, 13-14.

4. See T.H. O'Brien, *Civil Defence*, London 1955, 358-360.

5. See C. Dobinson, *Building Radar*, London 2003.

6. O'Brien, 385.

7. N. Nicolson (ed.), *Harold Nicolson. Diaries and Letters 1939-1945*, London 1967, 109 and 110.

8. Nicolson, 110.

9. B. Kops, *The World is a Wedding*, London 1963, 63.

10. O'Brien, 388.

11. A. Calder, *The People's War. Britain 1939-45*, London 1969, 168.

12. O'Brien, 407-408.

13. E. Bowen, *The Heat of the Day*, London 1949, 85.

14. A. Powers, "Plymouth. Reconstruction after World War II", in J. Ockman (ed.), *Out of Ground Zero. Case Studies in Urban Reinvention*, Munich 2002, 98-115. F. Wintle, *The Plymouth Blitz*, Bodmin 1981. B. Chalkley, D. Dunkerley and P. Gripaios (ed.), *Plymouth, Maritime City in Transition*, Newton Abbot, 1991. "Plymouth 1943", in W. Durth and N. Gutschow, *Träume in Trümmern. Planungen zum Wiederaufbau zerstörter Städte im Westen Deutschlands 1940-1950* (Part I), Braunschweig and Wiesbaden 1988, 306-307. G. Dix, "Patrick Abercrombie", in G. Cherry (ed.), *Pioneers in British Planning*, London 1981, 103-130. J. Paton Watson and P. Abercrombie, *A Plan for Plymouth. The Report Prepared for the City Council*, Plymouth 1943.

15. T. Mason and N. Tiratsoo, "People, Politics and Planning; the Reconstruction of Coventry's City Centre', in J.M. Diefendorf (ed.), *Rebuilding Europe's Bombed Cities*, London 1990, 94-113.

16. Calder, 204.

17. Quoted in Calder, 170.

18. Calder, 155.

19. Calder, 172.

20. Mack and Humphries, 40.

21. Calder, 223.

22. Quoted in Calder, 171.

23. J. Ray, *The Battle of Britain. New Perspectives. Behind the Scenes of the Great Air War*, London 1994, 125.

24. R. Hillary, *The Last Enemy*, London 1949 (1942), 155-156.

25. Calder, 193.

26. Quoted in Calder, 163. On the more or less official organization and procedures for rescue and firefighting in bombed zones, see Calder, 198-202.

27. Mack and Humphries, 55-59.

28. C.M. Kohan, *Works and Buildings*, London 1952, 361.

29. O'Brien, 400. B. Kops described the effect of an exploding landmine in the entrance to the Columbia Market Shelter (Stepney) in *The World is a Wedding*, London 1963, 88.

30. Calder and Sheridan, 86.

31. Kops, 87.

32. On the defects of the shelters, see P. Ziegler, *London at War 1935-1945*, London 1995, 116, 132-133.

33. O'Brien, 520.

34. Calder, 186.

35. O'Brien, 392.

36. See A. Saint, "What the Underground Means for London", *Rassegna*, 66 (1996), 24-33. Ziegler, 116-117, 135-136. Mack and Humphries, 59-61.

37. Calder, 185.

38. J. Andrews, *London's War. The Shelter Drawings of Henry Moore*, Aldershot 2002.

39. Kops, 69.

40. "The Tube Dwellers, 1943", in Calder and Sheridan, 101-107.

41. Calder, 187. See also O'Brien, 527 and 538. The shelter was accompanied by an instruction booklet, *How to Put Up your Morrison Shelter.*

42. O'Brien, 531.

43. O'Brien, 531-532. For tunnel plans elsewhere in Great Britain, see O'Brien, 539-540.

44. Quoted in Calder, 188.

45. Ziegler, 137. Mack and Humphries, 92-93.

46. O'Brien, 528.

47. Calder, 174. Mack and Humphries, 78-82.

48. O'Brien, 408-409.

49. On the night of 16-17 April, there followed an attack by 450 planes which discharged 446 tons of high-explosive bombs and 150 tons of incendiaries. The attack started 2,250 fires and claimed 1,180 deaths and 2,230 severe injuries.

Over 60 public buildings, including the Admiralty and the Law Courts were damaged. At least six churches were destroyed and thirteen others damaged. St. Paul's Cathedral took a direct hit. O'Brien, 416.

50. See Ziegler, 161 for a description of the raid.

51. O'Brien, 419.

52. Calder, 214.

53. Calder. N. Longmate, *How We Lived Then: A History of Everyday Life During the Second World War*, London 1971. J.H. Forshaw and P. Abercrombie, *County of London Plan*, London 1943. P. Abercrombie, *Greater London Plan 1944*, London 1945. "Der County of London Plan 1943", in W. Durth and N. Gutschow, *Träume in Trümmern. Planungen zum Wiederaufbau zerstörter Städte im Westen Deutschlands 1940-1950* (Part I), Braunschweig and Wiesbaden 1988, 301-305. J. Mack and S. Humphies, *London at War. The Making of Modern London 1939-45*, London 1985. P. Addison, *The Road to 1945. British Politics and the Second World War*, London 1975. N. Bullock, *Building the Post-War World. Modern Architecture and Reconstruction in Britain*, London and New York 2002, 3-22. N. Bullock and L. Verpoest (eds.), *Living with History, 1914-1964. Rebuilding Europe after the First and Second World Wars and the Role of Heritage Preservation*, Louvain 2011.

54. Nicolson, 136.

55. On the British aircraft industry, see Calder, 444-459.

56. J. Friedrich, *Der Brand. Deutschland im Bombenkrieg*, Munich 2002, 44-45.

57. See e.g. H. Probert, *Bomber Harris: His Life and Times*, Greenhill 2001. D. Richards, *RAF Bomber Command in the Second World War. The Hardest Victory*, London 1994.

58. The results of this iconoclasm are described in H. Beseler and N. Gutschow, *Kriegsschicksale deutscher Architektur*, Neumünster 1988.

59. E.R. Beck, *Under the Bombs. The German Home Front*, Kentucky 1986, 8.

60. Beck, 9.

61. Based on Friedrich, 491-505.

62. Beck, 61.

63. Quoted by M. Foedrowitz, *Bunkerwelten. Luftschutzanlagen in Norddeutschland*, Berlin 1998, 109.

64. Foedrowitz, 130-131. On Tempelhof, see F. Schmitz, *Flughafen Tempelhof. Berlins Tor zur Welt*, Berlin 1997. E. Dittrich, *Ernst Sagebiel. Leben und Werk 1892-1970*, Berlin 2005.

65. Friedrich, 422-423.

66. D. and I. Arnold, *Dunkle Welten. Bunker, Tunnel und Gewölbe unter Berlin*, Berlin 1999, 127.

67. D. and I. Arnold, 138.

68. On the raids on Stuttgart, see H. Bardua, *Stuttgart im Luftkrieg 1939-1945*, Stuttgart 1985. Idem, 'Stuttgart unterm Bombenhagel', in M.P. Miller, *Stuttgart im Zweiten Weltkrieg*, Gerlingen 1989, 389-396.

69. F. Taylor, *Dresden. Tuesday 13 February 1945*, London 2004. Fictional treatments of Dresden also existed: H. Mulisch, *Het stenen bruidsbed*, Amsterdam 1959 ("On the far bank of the Elbe, in the valley, lay what remained of the city – an endless surf of rubble heaps, wreathed with wisps and tatters of white mist; a bride who had torn her veil to shreds on the sight of her lover. Beyond, to the south east, where the surf tailed off, blue hills undulated deep into Czech Bohemia."). Kurt Vonnegut, *Slaughterhouse Five*, New York 1969. Martin Walser, *Die Verteidigung der Kindheit*, Frankfurt am Main 1997 ('Klaus Bringer wusste noch, daß Lux in der Inferno-Nacht im Luftschutzkeller in Cotta nach der ersten Bombendetonation angefangen habe, die Ilias vorzutragen, griechsch natürlich, und griechsch habe er rezitiert, bis nach der letzten Bombe des letzten Angriffs nur noch das Heulen des Feuersturms zu

hören gewesen sei und Dresden erledigt war
wie einst Ilion.').

70. E. Kästner, *Notabene 45: ein Tagebuch*,
Zurich 1961, 40-41.

71. Friedrich, 378.

72. C. Asendorf, *Super Constellation – Flugzeug
und Raumrevolution. Die Wirkung der Luftfahrt
auf Kunst und Kultur der Moderne*, Vienna and
New York 1997, 213.

73. Friedrich, 229.

74. Christabel Bielenberg, quoted in Beck, 87.

75. Friedrich, 465. See also *The United States
Strategic Bombing Survey*, New York and London 1976 (reprinted).

76. D. and I. Arnold, 114.

77. See K. Klee, *Im 'Luftschutzkeller des Reiches':
Evakuierte in Bayern 1939-1953. Politik, soziale
Lage, Erfahrungen*, London 2004, 134-147, 251-
273.

78. Beck, 24-25.

79. R. Bauer, *Fliegeralarm. Luftangriffe in
München 1940-1945*, Munich 1987. I. Peermoser,
*Der Luftkrieg über München 1942-1945. Bomben
auf die Hauptstadt der Bewegung*, Neuberg a.d.
Donau 1997.

80. See e.g. H. Brunswig, *Feuersturm über Hamburg*, Stuttgart 1981. O. Groehler, *Bombenkrieg
gegen Deutschland*, Berlin 1990. M. Middle-
brook, *Hamburg, Juli '43*, Berlin 1983. H.E. Nos-
sak, *Der Untergang. Hamburg 1943*, Frankfurt
am Main 1948. J. Düwel and N. Gutschow,
*Fortgewischt sind alle überflüssigen Zutaten.
Hamburg 1943: Zerstörung und Wiederaufbau*,
Berlin 2008.

81. Bochum (twice), Bremen, Dortmund
(twice), Duisburg, Düsseldorf (twice), Emden,
Essen, Gelsenkirchen, Keulen (twice), Kiel,
Krefeld, Mülheim, Oberhausen, Wuppertal.

82. Beck, 64.

83. 'Der Feuersturm von 1943 und seine
Lehren', *Nordwestdeutsche Bauhefte*, (1953)
September edition.

84. Foedrowitz, 91.

85. H. Schmal and T. Selke, *Bunker. Luftschutz
und Luftschutzbau in Hamburg*, Hamburg 2001,
44.

86. *The United States Strategic Bombing Survey*,
New York and London 1976 (reprinted). For a
more extensive treatment, see P. Galison, 'War
Against the Center', in A. Picon and A. Ponte
(eds.), *Architecture and the Sciences. Exchanging
Metaphors*, Princeton 2003, 196-227.

87. Friedrich.

CHAPTER 5

1. W. Bartoszewski, *Der Todesring um Warschau
1939-1944*, s.l, 1969. T. Szarota, *Warschau unter
dem Hakenkreuz. Leben und Alltag im besetzten
Warschau 1.10.1939 bis 31.7.1944*, Paderborn
1985. J. Böhler, *'Grösste Härte': Verbrechen der
Wehrmacht in Polen September/Oktober 1939*,
Osnabrück 2005. Idem, *Der Überfall: Deutschlands Krieg gegen Polen*, Frankfurt am Main
2009.

2. F. Gollert (ed.), *Warschau unter deutscher
Herrschaft. Deutsche Aufbauarbeit im Distrikt
Warschau*, Krakau 1942, 23-24. Cited in N.
Gutschow & B. Klain, *Vernichtung und Utopie.
Stadtplanung Warschau 1939-1945*, Hamburg
1994, 21.

3. J. Friedrich, *Der Brand. Deutschland im Bombenkrieg 1940-1945*, München 2002, 407.

4. H.G. Wells, *The War in the Air*, London 1909.
Other destruction fantasies are to be found
in M. Page, "New York. Creatively Destroying
New York: Fantasies, Premonitions, and Reali-
ties in the Provisional City", in J. Ockman (ed.),
*Out of Ground Zero. Case Studies in Urban Rein-
vention*, Munich, etc. 2002, 166-183.

5. A. Korthals Altes, *Luchtgevaar. Luchtaanvallen op Nederland 1940-1945*, Amsterdam 1984,
332-333. P. Grimm, E. van Loo, R. de Winter,
*Nederlandse vliegvelden tijdens de bezetting en
bevrijding, 1940-1945*, Amsterdam 2009.

6. H. Blix, "Area Bombardment: Rules and Reasons", in *The British Yearbook of International Law 1978*, Oxford 1979, 31-42.

7. P.W.M. Hasselton, *Het bombardement van Rotterdam 14 mei 1940. Incident of berekening?*, Amsterdam 1999.

8. A. Korthals Altes, *Luchtgevaar. Luchtaanvallen op Nederland 1940-1945*, Amsterdam 1984, 56.

9. Cited in S. Burgdorff & C. Habbe (eds.), *Als Feuer vom Himmel fiel. Der Bombenkrieg in Deutschland*, Munich 2003, 62.

10. Burgdorff & Habbe, 62. See also L. Besymenski, *Stalin und Hitler: Das Pokerspiel der Diktatoren*, Berlin 2002. M. Blank and P. Jahn (eds.), *Blockade Leningrad. Dossiers 1941-1944*, Berlin 2004.

11. Korthals Altes, 51. L. Elfferich, *Eindelijk de waarheid nabij. Analyses en emoties naar aanleiding van het bombardement op Rotterdam*, The Hague 1983.

12. Manuscript report of the bombing and emergency work, Rotterdam Municipal Archives 653-4.

13. L.J.M. Koremans, "Luchtbescherming", *Publieke Werken*, (1940) 9, 122-123.

14. On the functioning of the fire brigade, see Van den Burg, 49-78. J. Broekman, *Rotterdam brandt. Mei 1940*, Rotterdam 1990.

15. "Bespreking op Zaterdag 1 Juni 1940 met het waarnemend Hoofd van de Luchtbeschermingsdienst te Rotterdam", Gemeentearchief Utrecht, archief Gemeentebestuur, IV 1094.

16. Van den Burg, 60.

17. 'Verslag van een bezoek aan Rotterdam, na het bombardement van 14 Mei 1940' (3 July 1940), Gemeentearchief Utrecht, Gemeentebestuur, VI 1094.

18. F. Baarda, *Uit het hart. Rotterdammers over het bombardement*, Amsterdam and The Hague 1990, 136.

19. National Archives, 2.16.81.15, PTT Luchtbeschermingsdienst, folder 28.

20. 'Verslag van een bezoek aan Rotterdam, na het bombardement van 14 Mei 1940' (3 July 1940), Gemeentearchief Utrecht, Gemeentebestuur, VI 1094.

21. Koremans, 123.

22. 'Bespreking op Zaterdag 1 Juni 1940 met het waarnemend Hoofd van de Luchtbeschermingsdienst te Rotterdam', Gemeentearchief Utrecht, Gemeentebestuur, IV 1094.

23. K. Postema, *Het bombardement. Herinneringen van een Rotterdams gezin*, Baarn 1980, 18 & 20-21.

24. R.E. Hoebeke, *Slagveld Sloedam*, Nieuw en Sint Joosland 2002.

25. P. Sijnke (ed.), *Middelburg 17 mei 1940. Het vergeten bombardement*, Vlissingen 2010.

26. Koremans, 123.

27. Korthals Altes, 60-61.

28. Letter from the mayor of Middelburg to L.J.M. Koremans, 1 October 1940. Zeeuws Archief, Gemeente Middelburg, 1250 Luchtbeschermingsdienst, ds 7.

29. Annual Report 1940 of Vereeniging van Beambten der Brandweer te Middelburg. Zeeuws Archief, Gemeente Middelburg, 1250 Luchtbeschermingsdienst, ds. 9.

30. J.J. van der Weel, *Opeens was alles anders. Oorlogsjaren in Middelburg 1940-1944*, s.l. 2004, 23.

31. L. de Jong, *Het Koninkrijk der Nederlanden in de Tweede Wereldoorlog*, part 3, The Hague 1970, 441-442. On damage and reconstruction in Middelburg, see K. Bosma, *Architectuur en stedebouw in oorlogstijd. De wederopbouw van Middelburg 1940-1948*, Rotterdam 1988.

32. Middelburg archives mention 19 shelters with room for 630 people: Klein Vlaanderen (Noordplein and Seisplein), Dam facing Kolstraat, Dwarskaai at Prinsessebrug, Loskade at Kanaalbrug, Poelendaelesingel, Lange Delft alongside former Hotel Verseput, Londensche Kaai facing Segeerstraat, Bierkade at Bellink-

brug, Vischmarkt, Haringplaats, Molenwater at Verwerijstraat, Molenwater at Koepoort, Nederstraat, Groenmarkt, Langevielebinnen-brug, garden behind Arbeidsbeurs, Markt (2 shelters) and the Stadsschuur grounds. Zeeuws Archief, Gemeente Middelburg 18125. Dienst Gemeentewerken 1.782 Luchtbescherming tijdens WOII 1939-1948. For a drawing of the more or less standardized shelter, see H. Sakkers and J. den Hollander, *Schuilkelders in Middelburg 1939-1984*, Koudekerke 2005, 13.

33. Helders Gemeentearchief, 11479. A. Abbenes (ed.), *Opstellen betreffende de Rijkswerf Willemsoord*, Willemsoord 1960, 294-296. R. Schendelaar, *Den Helder in de Tweede Wereld-oorlog 1940-1945*, Den Helder 2004.

34. M.G. Vroom, *Schrik, angst en vrees. Een psy-chiatrische en phaenomenologische studie naar aanleiding van vliegtuigbombardementen*, Den Helder 1942, 71.

35. Vroom, 74.

36. Vroom, 11.

37. "Acute Stress Syndrome is described as comprising the following symptoms: *dissocia-tie*: emotional flatness ('numbness'), reduced perception of the surroundings, derealization (temporary hallucinations and/or illusions), depersonalization (sensation of separation of mind from body, amnesia of certain aspects of the trauma), *angst*: insomnia, concentration difficulties, restlessness, easily irritated; *reliv-ing the trauma*: dreams, flashbacks; *aversive behaviour*: in particular, avoidance of people or things that recall the trauma. 'Posttraumatic Stress Syndrome' comprises the following symptoms: *helplessness*; *intense anxiety, fear of death*; *compulsive thoughts*; *emotional flatness, hyperactivity, concentration difficulties, insomnia, agitation or lethargy*; *autonomous hyperactivity* (sweating), *muscle tension*; *sense of guilt, low self-esteem, aversive behaviour*. The most wide-spread manifestations of these psychological

traumas include obsession with the disaster, emotional flatness, insomnia, hyperactivity, agitation and hypersensitivity and concentra-tion difficulties. C.J. IJzermans et al., *Gezond-heidsklachten en de vliegramp Bijlmermeer. Een inventariserend onderzoek*, Nijkerk 1999.

38. H. Hellinga, 'Den Helder, marinestad', in K. Bosma & C. Wagenaar (eds.), *Een geruisloze doorbraak. De geschiedenis van architectuur en stedebouw tijdens de bezetting en de wederop-bouw van Nederland*, Rotterdam 1995, 343.

39. Korthals Altes, 12. G.J. Zwanenburg, *En nooit was het stil... Kroniek van een luchtoorlog. Deel 2: Luchtaanvallen op doelen in en om Neder-land*, s.l., undated.

40. During the Occupation, the Nederlandsche Vereeniging voor Luchtbescherming and the State Inspector for Civil Air Raid Protection issued a series of brochures giving instructions originating from orders of Reichskommissar Seyss-Inquart: *Voorschriften voor de openbare luchtbeschermingsverlichting*, ongedateerd. *Voorschriften voor electrische gloeilampen met beperkte lichtuitstraling voor binnenverlichting*, December 1940. *Voorschriften voor voetgangers-lantaarns (zak- of handlantaarns) met beperkte uitstraling*, 1940. *Aanwijzingen ten behoeve van de zelfbescherming*, 1940. *Voorschriften voor voet-gangerslantaarns met beperkte lichtuitstraling*, January 1941.

41. P. Virilio, *Bunker archéologie*, Paris 1991 (1975), 44.

42. Korthals Altes, 7.

43. State Inspector for Civil Air Raid Protec-tion, *Voorloopige aanwijzingen ten vervolge op de "Richtlijnen voor het bouwen en inrichten van schuilplaatsen tegen luchtgevaar"*, 27 June 1940, 1. See also "Voorloopige aanwijzingen ingevolge verkregen oorlogservaring", *Lucht-gevaar*, (1940) 5, 13.

44. Amersfoort Municipal Archives BNR 002.1 Gemeentebestuur (1811-1945), nr 4153.

45. Including the Wernink type, a type consisting of annular segments and a tunnel shelter of roundwood covered with reinforced concrete panels.

46. G. (J. Gerber), 'Luchtbescherming', *Publieke werken*, (1940) 8, 108.

47. Korthals Altes, Appendix II.

48. Korthals Altes, 78-79.

49. On 18 July 1943, SS-Obergruppenführer Rauter ordered the heads of the air raid protection services in Arnhem, The Hague, Eindhoven, Groningen, Haarlem, Rotterdam and Utrecht to be transferred to the police. The mayors of these cities remained responsible for the homeless, for the air raid protection of utility companies and for the cooperation of the municipal technical departments. Gemeentearchief Rotterdam, 0.40.2 Openbare Orde, Veiligheid, Brandweer, Rampenbestrijding, 653-1.

50. E.g. Letter dd. 21 August 1941, ordering the Germanization of the Air Raid Protection Service in Utrecht. Gemeentearchief Utrecht, Gemeentebestuur, VI 1090.

51. C.J.F. Caljé, *Wet betreffende bescherming tegen luchtaanvallen*, Zwolle 1941.

52. "Open loopgraven", *Pro Cive*, (1943-1944) 5, 41-54. The Inspectorate still argued in 1942 for the placing of shelters made to the national standard in the countryside, as illustrated by drawings by the architect J.R. Prent: "Eenvoudige schuilgelegenheid voor zelfbescherming ten platteland", *Pro Cive*, (1942) 12, 284-312.

53. Korthals Altes, 165.

54. Gemeentearchief Rotterdam 497 Centraal Secretarie Archief 48, Minutes and report of Nederlandse Luchtbeschermingsvereeniging Afd. Rotterdam, 10 April 1943.

55. A. Wagenaar (ed.), *Het vergeten bombardement. Rotterdam/Tusschendijken 31 maart 1943*, s.l., undated. A.J.A. Hermans, *Het bombardement op Rotterdam door de Amerikaanse luchtmacht op 31 maart 1943*, Breda 1988.

56. Gemeentearchief Rotterdam 497 Centrale Secretarie Archief 48, Report of Nederlandse Luchtbeschermingsvereeniging Afd. Rotterdam, 10 April 1943. See also Gemeentearchief Rotterdam 273 Verzameling Tweede Wereldoorlog 16, C.J. van der Nus, "De Luchtbeschermingsdienst te Rotterdam gedurende den bezettingstijd", undated, 10.

57. Gemeentearchief Rotterdam 497 Centrale Secretarie Archief 48, Report of Nederlandse Luchtbeschermingsvereeniging Afd. Rotterdam, 10 April 1943.

58. Van der Nus, 1.

59. Van der Nus, 9.

60. The air raid protection specialist C.A. Muller (Chief Inspector of Police and administrator at Rotterdam City Hall) was appointed to lead the Air Raid Protection Department on 1 November, and was able to fulfil this function until November 1943. C.A. Muller, "Algemeene beginselen betreffende de organisatie van den luchtbeschermingsdienst in gemeenten in de 3e gevarenklasse", *Weekblad voor Gemeentebelangen*, (1938) 2 December, 1-16. Gemeentearchief Rotterdam 273 Verzameling Tweede Wereldoorlog 857.

61. For organograms see *Herinneringsboek Luchtbescherming 1940-1945 Rotterdam vak 3a*, Rotterdam, undated (1945), 28-29.

62. For a summary of the dates and numbers of victims, see note 57. Before the Public Order Service (*Ordedienst*) was created, attempts were made to obtain manpower by contracting unemployment benefit recipients. Van der Nus, 3.

63. Van der Nus, 3.

64. Van der Nus, 10.

65. Van der Nus, 11.

66. At the time of the German invasion, Arnhem had several open trench shelters,

constructed under a work creation scheme. For information on the intention to build new shelters, see Gemeentearchief Arnhem, X07.55 vv 07.354 no. 7. Whether the new shelters were completed was not found in the archive. Letter from Arnhem Air Raid Protection Department to the Mayor of Arnhem, 4 December 1939. Gemeentearchief Arnhem, X07.55 vv 7.354 (9172), X07.55 vv 7.354 no. 8.

67. Groote Oord 15, corner of Varkensstraat 24-25 (75 people), Rijnstraat 71 (150-175 people), Kortestraat 10a (70-75 people), Bovenbeek-straat 28, corner of Ruiterstraat (90-100 people), Hommelscheweg 232/Onder de Linden 1 (140-150 people).

68. Drawing 17316. Letter from director of Muncipal Public Works Department to Mayor of Arnhem, 6 January 1943. Gemeentearchief Arnhem, X07.55 vv 7.354 no. 8.

69. Gemeentearchief Arnhem, X07.55 vv 7.354 no. 8.

70. Luftgaukommando, Luftschutzanordnung No. 39, 17 August 1943. NIOD, DDPN, 10 (974).

71. For drawing and annotations, see Gemeentearchief Arnhem, 1.86 (451. GW 1795).

72. Letter from Mayor of Utrecht to Rijksinspectie voor de Luchtbescherming, 24-12-1940. Gemeentearchief Utrecht, Openbare Werken (829), no. 294 and Gemeentebestuur, VI, 1134.1-10.

73. Gemeentearchief Utrecht, archief Gemeentebestuur, VI 1134.9.

74. Air Raid Protection Department of the Municipality of Amsterdam, *Aan hen die vielen bij de uitoefening van hun dienst*, 1945, 9. Gemeentearchief Amsterdam, B, 1940-1945 no. 232.10.

75. A. Querido, *Het Wilhelmina Gasthuis*, Lochem 1966, 179.

76. J.L. van de Pauw, *De bombardementen op Amsterdam-Noord. Juli 1943*, Amsterdam 2009.

77. Cited in P. Jacobs, *Het wel en wee van de Amsterdamsche Luchtbeschermingsdienst in het tijdperk 1924-1946*, Amsterdam 1972, 19. Gemeentearchief Amsterdam, K83.

78. Gemeentearchief Amsterdam, Publieke Werken, 5213 (1922-1956), 2728.

79. Gemeentearchief Amsterdam, Dienst Wederopbouw 5223, volumes 1942, 1943 and 1944.

80. Letter from Head of Air Raid Protection Department to Director of Public Works, 28 September 1944. Gemeentearchief Amsterdam, Publieke Werken, 5213 (1922-1956), 2728.

81. G. Thuring & J.A. Hey, *Operation 'Argument', 19-26 februari 1944. De luchtaanvallen op de nazivliegtuigindustrie in de 'Big Week'*, Groesbeek 2005.

82. Korthals Altes, 195. A. Brinkhuis, *De fatale aanval 22 februari 1944. De waarheid over de mysterieuze Amerikaanse bombardementen op Nijmegen, Arnhem, Enschede en Deventer*, Nijmegen 1984, 56-65.

83. Brinkhuis, 74-127. No incendiary bombs were dropped. For further information on the bombing, see A. Mooij, *Vooronderzoek bombardement op Nijmegen op 22 februari 1944*, Amsterdam 2005. W. Tromp (ed.), *Een zonnige voorjaarsdag. Nijmegen 22 februari 1944*, Nijmegen 2004. J. Rosendaal, *Nijmegen '44.Verwoesting, verdriet en verwerking*, Nijmegen 2009.

84. B. Janssen, *De pijn die blijft. Ooggetuigenverslagen van het bombardement van Nijmegen 22 februari 1944*, Amsterdam 2005, 479.

85. Korthals Altes, 197.

86. A. Lammerts van Bueren, *De verwoesting van een oude keizersstad. Oorlogsrampen over Nijmegen 1940-1945*, Nijmegen undated (1946), 67. G. Plantema, *Nijmegen '40-'45*, Nijmegen 1977.

87. Janssen, 267.

88. Janssen, 210.

89. Janssen, 259.

90. Lammerts van Bueren, 68.

91. Cited from report by the wagon master Van Mameren in Korthals Altes, 197.

92. Lammerts van Bueren, 73.

93. Numbers for 1946: 2,200 dead, 5,500 with permanent disabilities. Total buildings destroyed: 1,789 houses, 4 cinemas, 2 schools, 20 office buildings, 1 farm, historic section of City Hall, railway station, reading room, university library, 4 factories, 500 shops, 20 cafés, 7 hotels, 6 garages, main fire station and police headquarters. Buildings severely damaged: 2,461 houses, 5 churches, 15 schools, 75 office buildings, 4 farms, a reading room, 5 libraries, 2 hospitals, an old age home, 8 factories, 100 shops, 20 cafés, 5 hotels, 8 garages, telephone exchange. Lightly damaged buildings: 1,300 houses, 3 churches. Undamaged: 4,248 buildings. Lammerts van Bueren, 125-127. Janssen arrives at a list of 763 fatalities: Janssen, 13.

94. J. H. Eilander (ed.), *Met de dood in de schoenen. 64 ooggetuigenverhalen, brieven en dagboekfragmenten van Nijmeegse burgers in de mangel van Market Garden*, Nijmegen 1984. Gemeentearchief Nijmegen, no. 327 Oorlogs-documentatiecommissie.

95. Private cellar shelters: see Gemeentearchief Nijmegen, Inventaris van de Gemeentelijke Dienst Bouw- en Woningtoezicht te Nijmegen (1888) 1915-1951, 333-350.

96. P. Begheyn, "In de schuilkelders van het Canisiuscollege, september-november 1944", *Jaarboek Numaga*, (1994), 154-182.

97. Lammerts van Bueren, 140.

98. The basement under the pavilion of public rooms was adapted as a main shelter in 1944 with a capacity for 1,500 people. B.J.F. Siebenheller, *Het Sint Canisius ziekenhuis in oorlogstijd 1940-1945*, Nijmegen 2000, 47-49.

99. Incidental references to the use of shelters: F.M. Eliëns, *Nijmegen tussen bezetting en bevrijding*, Zaltbommel 1995. Eilander. Brinkhuis, 107-113.

100. Diary of Mrs. Boumans, 2 October 1944, cited in Eliëns, 101.

101. Lammerts van Bueren, 107. Janssen reported 96 deaths: Janssen, 27.

102. Diary of K. Faber, 22-29 October 1944, cited in Eliëns, 103.

103. "Five deaths in city centre. Since the burial ground in front of our church was full, J. Bregonje was transported directly from Garage Moll (where all corpses were initially brought) to Brakkenstein cemetery. All funeral cars except one were destroyed by fire, so the dead were transported on an open truck." Diary of Father Schots, 19 October 1944, cited in Eliëns, 102.

104. Gemeentearchief Nijmegen, Collectie Oorlogsdokumentatie 5193.

105. "Kloosterkeldergangers uit oorlog weer bijeen", *De Gelderlander*, 16 February 2002.

106. Dean J. Teulings in Lammerts van Bueren, 8.

CHAPTER 6

1. T. Pollmann, *Van Waterstaat tot wederopbouw. Het leven van dr.ir. J.A. Ringers (1885-1965)*, Amsterdam, 2006.

2. See J. Kalf, *Bescherming van kunstwerken tegen oorlogsgevaren*, The Hague, 1938 and especially H.P. Baard, *Kunst in schuilkelders. De odyssee der nationale kunstschatten gedurende de oorlogsjaren 1939-1945*, The Hague 1946.

3. For a description of these dune bunkers, see M. Maring, "Het Paaslo-Pantheon: monument van kunstbescherming", in *Monumenten en oorlogstijd. Jaarboek Monumentenzorg 1995*, Zwolle and Zeist 1995, 112-113.

4. On 22 July 1940 the art collection of the Kröller-Müller Museum was put into storage in the shelter. A. Ohmstede, "De schuilkelder", *De Schouw*, (1989)1, 52-53.

5. From The Hague, for instance: Mauritshuis, Mesdag Museum, Paleis Noordeinde, Huis ten

Bosch, Rijksbureau voor Kunsthistorische en Iconografische Documentatie, Eerste Kamer, Algemeen Rijksarchief and Koninklijke Bibliotheek. For more detail, see Maring, 122.

6. "Anno domini MCMXLII egregiis artis patriae monumentis ingentibus belli periculis deo juvante eripiendis firmissimum hoc refugium aedificandum curavit populus batavus." Maring, 118.

7. H.J. Neuman, *Arthur Seyss-Inquart. Het leven van een Duits onderkoning in Nederland*, Utrecht 1967. K. Kwiet, *Rijkscommissariaat Nederland: mislukte poging tot vestiging van een nationaal-socialistische orde*, Baarn 1969.

8. For Rauter, see A.E. Cohen, "Rauters positie en bevoegdheden", in J.C.H. Blom, et al., *A.E. Cohen als geschiedschrijver van zijn tijd*, Amsterdam 2005, 195-207.

9. For Wimmer, see A.E. Cohen, "Interview met Dr. Friedrich Wimmer op 28 en 29 augustus 1947", in Blom et al., 331-374.

10. For more detailed information about the complex chain of command, see K. Bosma and C. Wagenaar (eds.), *Een geruisloze doorbraak. De geschiedenis van architectuur en stedebouw tijdens de bezetting en de wederopbouw van Nederland*, Rotterdam 1995, 46-53. J. Meihuizen, *Noodzakelijk kwaad. De bestraffing van economische collaboratie in Nederland na de Tweede Wereldoorlog*, Amsterdam 2003.

11. H.A.M. Klemannn, *Nederland 1938-1948. Economie en samenleving in jaren van oorlog en bezetting*, Amsterdam 2002.

12. Zwei-Jahres Bericht van Werckshagen, June 1942. NIOD, FiWi, Bevollmächtigte für die Bauwirtschaft, ds 1.

13. Bosma and Wagenaar, 91-99.

14. NIOD, FiWi 2283.

15. Letter, Bevollmächtigte für die Bauwirtschaft in den besetzten niederländischen Gebieten to the head of the Utrecht Telephone District, 4 December 1942. NIOD, DDPN, 3a (957).

16. NIOD, FiWi, Bevollmächtigte für die Bauwirtschaft, folder 3.

17. Letter, Georg Lanya to Münster, 24 April 1941. NIOD, FiWi 2224.

18. NIOD, FiWi 2224 and 2225.

19. Fifteen existing barracks were given the treatment; this occurred prior to the *Abteilung Siedlung und Bauten*, but was typical of the policy pursued during the occupation period. A striking feature is that the architecture was not given any particularly military character but had a rustic exterior. The low-rise buildings had pitched or double-pitched roofs, were built in brick with simple decorative motifs: stone moulding and corner stones, cross-bar frames, eaves and brick mosaic work. The buildings were dispersed in green surroundings so that they are not noticeable from the air. There were exceptions however: the officers' mess on Kampweg in Soesterberg was clearly intended to have a striking appearance.

20. A predecessor was the conversion of the Koningsheide sanatorium in Schaarsbergen (1941), requisitioned by the Wehrmacht in April 1942 and used for military purposes. In compensation, two cloisters in Limburg were converted in September 1942 into NAPOLA, functioning as such till September 1944. Special SS schools for the indoctrination of the Dutch were accommodated in Avegoor, a country house in Ellecom. For a detailed account, see N.K.C.A. in 't Veld, *De SS en Nederland. Documenten uit SS-archieven 1935-1945*, The Hague 1976, 137-145, 282-284. NIOD, FiWi 2257. D. Barnouw, *Van NIVO tot Reichsschule. Nationaal-socialistische onderwijsinstellingen in Nederland*, The Hague 1989, 29-47. H.J.M. Keulen, "Van Jezuïetencollege tot Academie voor bewustzijnsontwikkeling", in *Historische en Heemkundige Studies in en rond het Geuldal. Jaarboek 1996*, 185-224. J.H.C. de Pater, *Die Reichsschule für Jungen te Valkenburg*, n.p. n.d.

(manuscript, NIOD, 1970). N P. van der Steen, *Keurkinderen. Hitlers elitescholen in Nederland*, Amsterdam 2009. *Reichsschule Valkenburg*, n.p. n.d (brochure, 1940s, NIOD).

21. See E. Agricola, "Een geheime prijsvraag voor Duitse architecten. Opleidingscentrum voor jonge Führers in Soestdijk", in Bosma and Wagenaar, 61-72. NIOD, FiWi 2257.

22. After a design by Karl Gonser; carried out by the Government Buildings Agency; sketches, early 1942, opened February 1943. Still in use as Prinses Julianakazerne. For more detail about this barracks: E. Agricola, "Camouflagetechnieken. Duitse kazernebouw en herinrichting van vliegbases", in Bosma and Wagenaar, 79-88.

23. Neuman, 224.

24. Neuman, 226. For the SS training school in Avegoor and Vught concentration camp, see In 't Veld, 1287. "Hauserlaß: Jüdenviertel in Amsterdam", 22 March 1941. NIOD, FiWi 2227.

25. NIOD, FiWi 2244.

26. See E. Agricola, 'Een modelwijk voor kinderrijke gezinnen. De Maria Christinawijk in Heerlen', in Bosma and Wagenaar, 74, note 9.

27. Münster corresponded with his German and Austrian colleagues, sending them plans, design charts and standard models. NIOD FiWi 2244. See also Agricola, p. 74, notes 10 and 11.

28. NIOD FiWi 2215, 2216. Karl Gonser (1902-1979), who took up a post with *Siedlung und Bauten* on 16 May, 1941, had previously worked for the German architects of the Stuttgart School, Paul Bonatz and Heinz Wetzel. For the Stuttgart School, see K. Bosma, "De Stuttgarter Schule. Alledaagse architectuur voor het nationaal-socialisme", in Bosma and Wagenaar, 54-61. For Gonser's career, see p. 60. W. Voigt and H. Frank, *Paul Schmitthenner 1884-1972*, Tübingen 2003.

29. For more detail, see E. Agricola, "Een modelwijk voor kinderrijke gezinnen. De Maria Christinawijk in Heerlen", in Bosma and Wagenaar, 72-79.

30. Land transactions after January, 1941 via the NSDAP. Land purchases went through the "Amtsbereich in den Niederlanden: Amt für Volkswohlfahrt", NIOD, 2224. Gemeentearchief, Heerlen. Heerlen city council, 1919-1981, no. 172.

31. See T. Harlander and G. Fehl (eds.), *Hitlers soziale Wohnungsbau 1940-1945. Wohnungspolitik, Baugestaltung und Siedlungsplanung*, Hamburg 1986. The types used in Heerlen were RE III 6 (105 homes), RE II 6 (43 homes) and RE I 5 (89 homes), while three homes were given an individual design. Letter, Schimke to Gonser, 18 June 1941. NIOD FiWi 2244.

32. "Niederschrift über eine Besprechung vom 27. Nov. 1941" in the presence of Münster, Böhmcker and Aus den Fünten. NIOD, FiWi 2234. See also 2233-2236. For the contacts between Seyss-Inquart and his Amsterdam representative Böhmcker, with the latter doing the actual organizational work, see B. Stigter, *De bezette stad. Plattegrond van Amsterdam 1940-1945*, Amsterdam 2005, 34-36.

33. For a detailed study, see M. van Tielhof, *Banken in bezettingstijd. De voorgangers van ABN AMRO tijdens de Tweede Wereldoorlog en de periode van rechtsherstel*, Amsterdam and Antwerp 2003. The "Niederländische Grundstückverwaltung" Foundation, which came under *Siedlung und Bauten*, gave the expropriation of Jewish possessions the cloak of legitimacy. NIOD, FiWi 2237-2243.

34. NIOD, FiWi 2233-2243.

35. The NIOD archive contains not only the organization charts of the construction works of the *Abteilung Siedlung und Bauten* in the Netherlands, but also details of the tension between the primary civil projects of the Department (such as youth centres, casinos

for officers, and police barracks) and military objects. Bosma and Wagenaar, 47-53.

36. NIOD, FiWi 2283.

37. Letters, Münster 27 August and 11 September 1942. NIOD, FiWi 2283.

38. Letter, Kammler to Münster, 20 May 1942. NIOD, FiWi 2224.

39. For an organogram of the SS, see K. Bosma and C. Wagenaar, "Rivaliserende instanties. Duitse planning in bezet Nederland", in Bosma and Wagenaar, 50-51.

40. Letter, Generalkommissar für Verwaltung und Justiz, 20 March 1942. NIOD-WBN 569. Also at the meeting were Roloff, the engineeers Fiebig and Garther, Oberpostrat Kühlewetter, Oberforstmeister Hageman and Forstmeister Grünewald.

41. The firms in Amsterdam and Utrecht essential to German production had a special telephone link with the Luftgaukommando and were warned in advance about possible air raids. Description of warning procedure in the minutes of a meeting in the Luftgaukommando building, Keizersgracht 428, 24 September 1942. NIOD, WBN 980.

42. Luftgaukommando Holland, "Bestimmungen über die behelfsmässige Herrichtung von Luftschutzräumen in bestehenden Gebäuden", 16 November 1942. NIOD, WBN 980.

43. Luftgaukommando Holland, "Merkblatt für durchzuführende Werkluftschutzmaßnahmen". Wehrmachtsbefehlhaber in de Niederlanden, "Tagesbefehl Nr. 46/41", 28 August 1941. NIOD, WBN 980.

44. A separate Anlage was issued for "Luftschutzdeckungsgräben" in March 1943: "Bestimmungen für den Bau von LS-Deckungsgräben", Bauwelt, (1943) 13-14, 112-113.

45. Luftgaukommando, LS-Merkblatt Nr. 1. "Führung und Organisation des Luftschutzes in den Niederlanden", 1 February 1943. LS-Merkblatt Nr. 2. "Luftschutz in Wehrmacht-anlagen", 1 February 1943. LS-Merkblatt Nr. 3. "Der Luftschutzwarndienst", 1 February 1943. NIOD, WBN 980. The Abteilung "Holland" air raid warning service was housed in Herengracht 505 and had branches in Nijmegen (not completed), Breda (originally 's Hertogenbosch), The Hague, Geleen, Groningen, Rotterdam and IJmuiden.

46. Luftgaukommando, LS-Merkblatt Nr. 1. "Führung und Organisation des Luftschutzes in den Niederlanden", 1 February 1943. These provincial representatives had offices in The Hague (Plein 1813, 4), Arnhem (in the house of Angerenstein on the Velperweg), Utrecht (Maliebaan 10) and so on, while the "Verbindungsoffiziere zum Generalstaatsanwalt" had them in Amsterdam (Vening Meineszkade 13), Arnhem (Velperweg 66), The Hague (Koningskade 21), Den Bosch (Hekellaan 6) and Leeuwarden (Eewall 75).

47. After a direct hit on the Carlton Hotel, the Luftgaukommando moved to Vijzelstraat (the Nederlandsche Handelsmaatschappij building). After February 1944, after the abolition of the Luftgaukommando "und seiner Aussenstelle in Rotterdam", it renamed itself "Feldluftkommando Belgien/Nordfrankreich" and had its quarters in Nijmegen (Sterreschansweg 77). Letter, Feldluftkommando Belg./Nordfr., 29 February 1944. NIOD, WBN 980. D. van Hilten, Van capitulatie tot capitulatie. Een beknopte historische en technische beschrijving van de militaire gebeurtenissen in Nederland tijdens de Duitse bezetting van mei 1940 tot mei 1945, Leiden 1949, 70.

48. G. Hoogesteeger and R.A. Korving, Bellen voor vrijheid. Illegale telefoonverbindingen in de Tweede Wereldoorlog, The Hague 1990, 28.

49. Hoogesteeger and Korving, 60.

50. Hoogesteeger and Korving, 36.

51. "Da die Philipswerke seit einiger Zeit nur für die Luftwaffe arbeiten...". Memorandum, 3

September 1942. NIOD, DDNP, 73a-c (1523).

52. "Aktenvermerk über eine Besprechung bei der Firma Philips in Eindhoven", 15 September 1942. NIOD, DDPN 7 a, b, c (1523).

53. H. Knap, *Forschungsstelle Langeveld. Duits afluisterstation in bezet Nederland*, Amsterdam 1998, 205.

54. Confidential letter, Reichspostminister to Oberkommando der Wehrmacht in Berlin, 12 August 1940. Letter, Funksachbearbeiter van het Deutsches Fernmeldeamt to the Funkeinsatzleiter, 15 October 1940. NIOD, DDPN 71f.

55. J.G. Visser, *PTT 1940-1945 Beleid en bezetting*, The Hague 1968, 57-60. For more general historical accounts of the PTT, see G. Hoogesteeger, *Van lopende band tot telematica. Geschiedenis van de PTT in Nederland*, Groningen 1989. E.A.B.J. ten Brink and C.W.L. Scheller, *Geschiedenis van de Rijkstelegraaf 1852-1952*, The Hague 1954.

56. PTT annual report, 1945/1946, 7.

57. NIOD, FiWi 2224.

58. Knap, 169.

59. C. de Haan-van der Meulen and L. Udo-van der Sloot (eds.), *Tussen zand en zenders. De geschiedenis van Radio Kootwijk*, The Hague 1988, 47. For a detailed description of the functions of the buildings, see B-F: N. Koomans, "Het zendstation Kootwijk-Radio", *De Ingenieur*, (1931) 46, E131-E137.

60. Transmitter building A: a long-wave Telefunken transmitter (5 outdoor masts, each 212 m in height and one indoor mast) and three long-wave "Röhrensenders" from the firms Lorenz (1927; PEM), Philips (PEW), and PTT (1927; PER), each with a 100 m antenna; transmitter building B: a long-wave radio transmitter (1935); transmitter building C: 4 Short-wave telephone transmitters for phone connections with the East Indies (PDV, PCK, PCV, PDK); Transmitter building D: 8 short-wave transmitters for telegrams, 4 fixed-wave transmitters, 4 transmitters adjustable to 2 fixed wavelengths for links with the Dutch East Indies, North America, South America and Japan; transmitter building E: 2 telegram transmitters, 2 telephone transmitters (one BDR, PGE and LTA; the other for phone and fax connections on 3 fixed wavelengths), and short-wave antennae (directional antennae with horizontal dipoles and reflectors). Report to the Fachamt für Funkwesen Berlin-Tempelhof, n.d. NIOD, DPPN, 72a-c (1522). There were also two types of antenna: the rhombic antennas connected by cables to eight masts and the curtain antenna hung from 4 tubular masts, each 70 m high.

61. Knap, 249.

62. This system had some advantages: it was less vulnerable to interference, a given energy input yielded a much stronger signal at the receiver's end, and it was possible to transmit a number of telephone conversations simultaneously from a single transmitter.

63. Letter, Einsatzleiter Kootwijk to Deutsche Fernmeldeamt, 29 January 1941. NIOD, DDPN, 72a-c (1522). The Siemens-Eisengleichrichter was moved to building E in April 1942 for transmitters 5 and 7. Letter, Einsatzleiter Kootwijk to Deutsche Fernmeldeamt, 2 April 1942. NIOD, DDPN, 72a-c (1522).

64. Letter, Deutsche Einsatzleiter to Leiter der Deutschen Dienstpost in den besetzten niederländischen Gebieten (Funksachgebiet) in The Hague, 23 August 1940. NIOD, DDPN, 72a-c (1522).

65. *Jaarboekje van den Nederlandschen Omroep 1943-1944*. S. Rutten, "De omroep tijdens de bezetting", in C.M. Abrahamse (ed.), *Hilversum en de omroep*, Hilversum 1995, 107-116. P. Aartsen Tuyn et al. (eds.), *Radio Nederland Wereldomroep 1947-1987*, Hilversum 1987. D. Verkijk, *Radio Hilversum 1940-1945. De omroep in de oorlog*, Amsterdam 1974.

66. Letter, Reichskommissar to Linnemeyer,

16 December 1940. NIOD, DDPN, 72a-c (1522). Letter, Board of the PTT to the Beauftragte für das Post- und Fernmeldewesen, 24 July 1941. NIOD, DDPN, 4e (961). At this stage the PDX was used with a directional antenna for the German East Asia service, the PFG and PGG for the DNB-Funknachrichtendienst, from which the short-wave transmissions were received in Kootwijk, sent to Amsterdam, decoded there and sent on to Zossen. Letter, Reichsminister to der Deutschen Dienstpost in den besetzten niederländischen Gebieten, 6 March 1941. NIOD, DDPN, 70c (1522).

67. Letter, Reichsminister to Leiter der Deutschen Dienstpost in den besetzten niederländischen Gebieten, 6 March 1941. NIOD, DDPN, 70c (1522). See also NIOD, DDPN 72 a-c.

68. Oberpostrat Muth to Deutsche Fernmeldeamt, 27 June 1941. NIOD, DDPN, 72a-c (1522).

69. Memorandum to the Reichskommissar, 18 May 1942. NIOD, DDPN, 73a-c (1523).

70. Letter, Einsatzleiter Kootwijk to Deutsche Fernmeldeamt, 29 October 1942. NIOD, DDPN, 7a-c (1522).

71. Letter, Reichspostminister to Deutsche Fernmeldeamt, 12 February 1942. NIOD, DDPN, 7a-c (1522).

72. Letter, PTT board to Beauftragte für das Post- und Fernmeldewesen, 20 November 1942. NIOD, DDPN, 7a-c (1522). Gemeentearchief Barneveld 1.7778.511 doss. 16.991 Building permits, 55A/1941: annex, civil servants' building.

73. De Haan-van der Meulen and L. Udo-van der Sloot (eds.), Tussen zand en zenders. De geschiedenis van Radio Kootwijk, The Hague 1988, 68.

74. Reisebericht des OTI Gilles über eine Dienstreise vom 20. und 21.1.43 zur Funkstelle Kootwijk, 23 January 1943. Einsatzleiter Kootwijk to Deutsche Fernmeldeamt in Utrecht, 16 March 1943. NIOD, DDPN, 7a-c (1522). NIOD, NDDP, 3a (957).

75. NIOD, NDDP, 3a (957). Barneveld council issued a building permit on 21 October 1941. G. Crebolder, et al., Kootwijk, een parel in het zand. De geschiedenis van een Veluws dorpje, Barneveld 2000, 128.

76. Ir. Kägeler, Reisebericht über die Dienstreise von 5-11.2 nach der Fust Kootwijk, 8 February 1942. NIOD, DDPN, 7a-c (1522).

77. Letter, Oberpostrat Kühlwetter to PTT director, 20 February 1942. NIOD, DDPN, 7a-c (1522).

78. Letter, Deutsche Nachrichtenbüro Berlin to Reichspostministerium, 2 December 1943. NIOD, DDPN, 7a-c (1522). After the Liberation the underground cables were found to be in a bad state of repair.

79. See 74.

80. Letter, DDNP Arnhem to Deutsche Fernmeldeamt, Utrecht, 30 March 1943. NIOD, DDPN, 7a-c (1522).

81. Barneveld council issued a building permit on 16 December 1942. Crebolder, 128.

82. Transmitter 21 and the Friesland transmitter were disabled. NIOD, DDPN 7a-c (1522).

83. Letter, Leiter DDPN to Bevollmächtigten für die Bauwirtschaft in den besetzten niederländischen Gebieten, 1 October 1943. NIOD, DDPN, 4e (961).

84. De Haan-van der Meulen and Udo-van der Sloot, 102.

85. Crebolder, 122.

86. Building permit: Gemeentearchief Barneveld 1.778.511 doss. 16.991 Building permits, 9A/1944: garage, June, 1944. On 14 June 1944, 90,000 roof tiles and 15,000 bricks were transported by train to Assel. NIOD, WBN 359.

87. De Haan-van der Meulen and Udo-van der Sloot, 102.

88. Knap, 182.

89. Knap, 168.

90. Knap, 253.

91. Auftrag 34 issued by Berlin-Tempelhof. NIOD, DDPN, 73d (1524).

92. Knap, 252.

93. NIOD, DDNP, 73d (1524).

94. In April 1942 Seyss-Inquart commissioned the conversion of Valkenhorst and the construction of a bombproof bunker, a project carried out by *Siedlung und Bauten*. "Anordnungen", 27 April and 1 June, and "Genehmigungsbescheid", 25 September 1942. NIOD, DDPN, 4e (1961). Evidence that the Birkenhof bunker was designed by *Siedlung und Bauten* can be found in the first sentence of a letter from Linnemeyer to *Siedlung und Bauten*, 25 March 1944: "Das von Ihnen für die Forschungsstelle Langeveld errichtete Dienstgebäude Birkenhof..." NIOD, DDPN, 4e (961).

95. NIOD, DDPN, 3e (1961).

96. Knap, 237.

97. NIOD, Bevollmächtigte für die Bauwirtschaft, 23a, folder 1.

98. NIOD, FiWi 2270.

99. A camouflaged, three-storey monitoring bunker: cellar 9.55 x 17.50 m. long wing (over the cellar) 9.55 x 49.20 m, short wing 30.90 x 22.90 m. Measurements taken from drawings for conversion of interior on a design of A.F. Heesakkers, February 1976, gemeentearchief Valkenswaard. NIOD, Groep Albrecht, 20 May 1943, 190A, ds 2b. NIOD, FiWi, 2270.

100. For more technical details, see H. Sakkers, *Duitse bunkerbouw vanuit het Rijkscommissariaat – Abteilung Siedlung und Bauten 1942-1945*, Koudekerke 2004, 15-20.

101. See letter of the Nederlandse Postschutz to the DDPN, 24 July 1943. NIOD, DDPN 3a (957).

102. Correspondence, April and May 1944. NIOD, DDPN, 4e (961). Initially, there were six sets of bunk beds, three beds high.

103. Knap, 273.

104. NIOD, Groep Albrecht 190, 4c, 4d, 4e and 5a.

105. Knap, 311. "Forschungsstelle Langeveld ist inzwischen ins Reich verlegt worden." (14-9-1944). NIOD, DDPN, 4a (959).

CHAPTER 7

1. B. van der Boom, *Den Haag in de Tweede Wereldoorlog*, The Hague 1995, 21. See also "Afbraak en verwaarlozing (1940-1945)", in R. Vijfwinkel et al., *'s Haags werken en werkers. 350 jaar Gemeentewerken (1636-1986)*, The Hague 1986, 297-298.

2. Haags Gemeentearchief, 432-2677.

3. Van der Boom, 219-223.

4. Th.J. de Jong, *Van Rudelsheimstichting tot Van Helsdingenkazerne*, The Hague, 1991.

5. In this connection, see N.K.C.A. in 't Veld, *De SS en Nederland. Documenten uit SS-archieven 1935-1945*, The Hague 1976, 870-871, 910-913, 930-931, 985-986.

6. "Die Linie ist ausgesteckt, die einzelnen Kampfanlagen sind festgelegt, ebenso ein Panzergraben. Die Durchführung der Bauten übernimmt mein Diplo.Ing. Münster, der auch schon den Bunker gebaut hat und dem alle Beteiligten die rasche und solide Durchführung zutrauen, er wird's auch bestimmt machen. Die Sache steht so, dass Oberst Pausinger gewisse Teile auch des Stützpunktes Scheveningen lieber durch Münster fertigstellen lassen möchte als über die militärischen Baustellen." In 't Veld, 911.

7. For a detailed account of the importance for The Hague of the construction of the Atlantic Wall, see H.F. Ambachtsheer, *Van verdediging naar bescherming. De Atlantikwall in Den Haag*, The Hague 1995. For the consequences for the population, see Van der Boom, 109-142. For the adjoining part of the Atlantic Wall in Wassenaar, see C.N.J. Neisingh, "De Atlantikwall in Wassenaar", in F.R. Hazenberg et al., *Wassenaar in de Tweede Wereldoorlog*, Wassenaar 1995, 436-457. For the cartography of the Atlantic Wall in the urban fabric of The Hague,

see B.C. de Pater and B. Schoenmaker, *Grote Atlas van Nederland 1930-1950*, Zierikzee 2005, 92-93.

8. Van der Boom, 113.

9. H.E. van Gelder, *'s-Gravenhage 1935-1945 hoe het was, werd en worden moge*, Amsterdam 1946, 47.

10. Van der Boom, 38. See also "Afbraak en verwaarlozing (1940-1945)", in Vijfwinkel et al., 305.

11. Broadly speaking, the demolition process went as follows: Daal en Berg and surroundings, starting in December 1942, the surroundings of Kruisplantsoen and Stadhoudersplantsoen, January 1943, Zorgvliet, spring 1943, Haagse Bos and the surroundings of Clingendaal, spring and summer of 1943 and finally Duindorp, autumn of 1943.

12. Van der Boom, 39.

13. "Afbraak en verwaarlozing (1940-1945)", in Vijfwinkel et al., 302.

14. The entire process (except for the evacuation) can be followed in Haags Gemeentearchief, 610-1373.

15. Van der Boom, 130.

16. NIOD, Reichskommissar 14, no. 334.

17. I. van Huik, "'Ingebed in het zo karakteristieke groen.' Dudok en Den Haag in de jaren 1930-1950", in V. Freijser (ed.), *Het veranderend stadsbeeld van Den Haag. Plannen en processen in de Haagse stedebouw 1890-1990*, Zwolle 1991, 110. On 15 January 1944, Münster gave instructions for the dismantling of all the premises, which had been evacuated but were not scheduled for demolition. The aim was to collect electric wiring, plumbing materials, heating equipment, scrap iron, doors and other timber, gas fittings, floor covering, blackout material and gas cookers. The dismantling continued till September 1944 and amounted to 2,650 lots in Kijkduin, on Sportlaan and Stadhoudersplein and in the Geuzenkwartier, the Statenkwartier and the Naussaukwartier. Van der Boom, 140-141. "Afbraak en verwaarlozing (1940-1945)", in Vijfwinkel, et al., 304.

18. See also J. Meihuizen, *Noodzakelijk kwaad. De bestraffing van economische collaboratie in Nederland na de Tweede Wereldoorlog*, Amsterdam 2003, 669-670.

19. Letter, 24 April 1942. Haags Gemeentearchief, 487-1870.

20. Gemeente 's-Gravenhage, *Handleiding ten dienste van de bij de evacuatie betrokken leiders en helpers*, n.d. (c. 1941). Haags Gemeentearchief 487-1870. An updated version of this manual was published in 1944.

21. Van der Boom, 123-124.

22. Van der Boom, 121-122.

23. Van der Boom, 131.

24. NIOD, Reichskommissar 14, no. 192.

25. Houtrust (Conradkade), Scheveningseweg (Hotel Promenade), Wittebrug, Javabrug, Dierentuin emergency bridge, Malieveld (Jozef Israëlslaan, named Thorn Prikkerlaan at the time) and Benoordenhoutseweg.

26. "PaK-Stände" ("Panzerabwehrkanone") and anti-tank walls in the dunes north of Scheveningen and on the Boulevard, "KwK-Stände" ("Küstwachekanone") in the port, six objects round the Scheveningen transmitter, five shelters for troops and munitions bunkers on Belvedere, a "PaK-Stand" and a "Doppelgruppenunterstand" in Kijkduin, "PaK-Stände" on Duinlaan, Sportlaan, Houtrustbrug and two "PaK-Stände" and two "Mannschaftsstände" on Stadhouderslaan. Kaftan, Aktenvermerk, 28 September 1943. NIOD, FiWi 170. It is likely that the technical drawings for these objects were produced by the Pionierstab Wassenaar.

27. NIOD, FiWi, 2271 and 2272.

28. Van der Boom, 12.

29. Van der Boom, 12.

30. For instance, a nursery school on the Jan

van Nassaustraat, an "Oberschule", a "Volks-schule" at Dreibholzstraat 2-4, a "Deutsche Volksschule" on the Waalsdorperweg and a school on the Wassenaarseweg, where the daughter of Seyss (Dorli) was a pupil.

31. Van der Boom, 138.

32. NIOD, Groep Albrecht 190 (2b).

33. In 't Veld, 1287.

34. Lagebericht Wehrmachtskommandantur Den Haag, 19 April 1943. NIOD, Washington Papers, 70058-70066.

35. B. Koopmans, *Over bossen, parken en plantsoenen. Historisch groen in Den Haag*, The Hague 2000, 25.

36. Sakkers gives a summary of the military construction programme of *Siedlung und Bauten* at around the turn of the year, 1943-1944: "5 Munibunker, 6 Unterkünfte für 12 Mann, 1 Verteiler, 1 Bunker für Batterieoffizier, 1 Küchenbunker + Quelle, 1 Verpflegungsbunker, 1 Entgiftungsbunker, 1 Sanitätsbunker, 1 Offiziers-Unterstand, 1 Maschinenbunker, 1 Schreibstube, 1 latrine, 1 Waffenmeisterei, 2 Garage, 1 Stand für Funkmessgerät." The latter and the *Schreibstube* were however not carried out. H. Sakkers, *Duitse bunkerbouw vanuit het Rijkscommissariaat – Abteilung Siedlung und Bauten – 1942-1945*, Koudekerke 2004, 26.

37. In the Haagse Bos at the level of the Laan van Nieuw Oost-Indië and at the northern end of the Ruychrocklaan-Van Ouwenlaan. Ambachtsheer, 97.

38. Ambachtsheer, 138.

39. In the Vrijzinnig Lyceum (liberal Christian high school) on Parkweg and a school in Van Nijenrodestraat.

40. On Van Ouwenlaan and in the woods of Zanen near the estate of Clingendaal and in the woodlands of the Scheveningse Bosjes between Haringkade and Kanaalweg.

41. A garage on Kanaalweg.

42. Th.M. van Koppen and A.B.C.M. op 't Hoog, *De Prinses Julianakazerne*, The Hague 1988, 7.

43. Behind the barracks a munitions bunker and three other bunkers ("Baupunkte" 18, 19 and 20) were still standing. On 14 November 1942, Seyss-Inquart wrote to Himmler about the conditions under which he was prepared to remain in The Hague, "eine entsprechende Sicherung vor allem gegen Fliegerangriffe und auch hiefür habe ich inzwischen vorgesorgt, in dem ich, wie Sie ja wissen, eine erstklassige Polizeikaserne im Bau habe und daneben einen Bunker, der sich sehen lassen kann und in dem ein ganzes Bataillon nötigenfalls Platz hat. Dieser Bunker wird im Ernstfall auch sozusagen mein Rückhalt sein und wird nunmehr nachrichtenmässig ausgerüstet." In 't Veld, 870-871.

44. "Stadtbaumeister" van Kettwig and "Bevollmächtigte für den technischen Durchführung von Luftschutzbauten", A. Kubitza. NIOD, FiWi 2227.

45. Letter, Seyss-Inquart to Albert Speer, 8 June 1942. NIOD, FiWi 2277. The drawings were sent to Speer on 29 June 1942. FiWi 2227.

46. In 't Veld, 871.

47. The corridor and shelter were demolished during the conversion of the Logement, except for some remains at the entrance. H. Ambachtsheer and N. de Boer (ed.), *Van Logement tot Parlement 1617-2004. Een nieuw gebruik van het Logement van Amsterdam en het Algemeen Rijksarchief*, The Hague 2004, 31-32.

48. NIOD, FiWi, 2261, 2262, 2263.

49. Ambachtsheer, 41.

50. NIOD, FiWi, 2261, 2262, 2263.

51. "Afbraak en verwaarlozing (1940-1945)", in Vijfwinkel, et al., 298.

52. Van der Boom, 235.

53. "Afbraak en verwaarlozing (1940-1945)", in Vijfwinkel, et al., 311.

54. Resident quoted by Van der Boom, 139.

55. NIOD, Reichskommissar 14, no. 190, 192, 198.

56. On 16 June, 1944 Münster was appointed *Bevollmächtigte für Industrielle Umsiedlung*. NIOD, SSHP 77-85, 6c.

57. J.C.H. Blom, et al., *A.E. Cohen als geschiedschrijver van zijn tijd*, Amsterdam 2005, 373-374.

CHAPTER 8

1. W. Valderpoort, A.F. Bakhoven, D.A. Budde, J.W.J. Moerman, P.H. de Jong, J.A.C. Tillema and C. van Traa, *Rapport stedebouwkundige en bouwtechnische richtlijnen in verband met de luchtbescherming*, Rotterdam 1943. This report with urban planning and architectural guidelines was issued in reaction to the bombings of 14 May 1940, 3 October 1941, 28 January 1942 and 31 March 1943. GAR, 0.40.2 Openbare Orde, Veiligheid, Brandweer, Rampenbestrijding, 653-655.

2. E.C. de Reijer, *De IJssellinie 1950-1968*, Zwolle 1997.

3. B. van der Boom, *Atoomgevaar? Dan zeker B.B. De geschiedenis van de Bescherming Bevolking*, The Hague 2000, 14-15.

4. M. Farish, "Another Anxious Urbanism: Simulating Defense and Disaster in Cold War America", in S. Graham (ed.), *Cities, War and Terrorism*, Malden etc. 2005, 97.

5. S.R. Weart, *Nuclear Fear. A History of Images*, Cambridge and London 1988, 113-114.

6. Weart, 168-169.

7. Weart, 230.

8. R. Leenders, *Als de hemel valt. Bescherming Bevolking tussen fantasie en werkelijkheid*, Tilburg 2001.

9. Weart, 263.

10. For a fuller treatment, see P. Galison, "War Against the Center", in A. Picon & A. Ponte (eds.), *Architecture and the Sciences. Exchanging Metaphors*, Princeton 2003, 196-227.

11. Weart, 113-114.

12. For a fuller treatment of the social sciences in the USA and the analysis of urban areas, see Farish, 100-108.

13. For information on civil defence in the USA, see Weart, 127-137, 253-262. D. Monteyne, *Fallout Shelter. Designing for Civil Defense in the Cold War*, Minneapolis/London 2011.

14. Galison, 223.

15. W.D. Cocroft and R.J.C. Thomas, *Cold War. Building for Nuclear Confrontation 1946-1989*, London 2003, 84. On nuclear energy programs in Belgium, England, France and the Netherlands, see *Erfgoed van Industrie en Techniek*, 19 (2010) 2/3.

16. Weart, 311.

17. Weart, 256.

18. *Fallout Protection: What to Know and Do About Nuclear Attack*, Washington 1962.

19. Van der Boom, 31.

20. K. Volkers, *Geheim landschap, 200 jaar militairen op de Heuvelrug*, Utrecht 2006, 134.

21. For information on legislation in 1951-1952 (Wet op de Bescherming Bevolking, Wet op de Noodwachten, Wet Verplaatsing Bevolking and Wet ter Verzekering van het Beschikbaar Blijven van Goederen) and the lack of suitable financing, see Van der Boom, 37.

22. T. van Merwijk (ed.), *Civiele verdediging in het tijdperk van de wederopbouw. Categoriaal onderzoek wederopbouw 1940-1965*, Zeist 2007. B. van der Boom & B. Sorgdrager, "Foto-essay civiele verdediging in Nederland (1949-1989)" in M. de Keizer & S.C. Roels (eds.), *Staat van veiligheid. De Nederlandse samenleving sinds 1900*, Amsterdam 2007, 118-128. K. Bosma & C.E. Conijn, *De commandopost bescherming bevolking Memlingstraat Amsterdam-Zuid*, Amsterdam 2008.

23. R. Leenders, *Als de hemel valt. Bescherming Bevolking tussen fantasie en werkelijkheid*, Tilburg 2001.

24. Van der Boom, 151.

25. Van der Boom, 153.

26. Van der Boom, 220.

27. Cited in Van der Boom, 219.

28. Van der Boom, 243.

29. M. Foedrowitz, *Bunkerwelten. Luftschutzan-lagen in Norddeutschland*, Berlin 1998, 174.

30. Foedrowitz, 176

31. See also S. Best, *Geheime Bunkeranlagen der DDR*, Stuttgart 2003.

32. Foedrowitz, 177.

33. These figures were obtained from G.J. Ashworth, *War and the city*, London/New York 1991, 150.

34. The following details were obtained from Erik de Reijer from Stichting Functioneel Bunkerbeheer.

35. According to De Reijer, some 85 combination projects were completed in the Netherlands, ranging from viaducts and bridge abutments to cellars under blocks of flats (100 to 500 people).

36. In 1955, the City of Stockholm completed a nuclear shelter for 20,000 people in the form of a tunnel which functioned in peacetime as a car park for 500 vehicles.

37. Van der Boom, 249.

38. "Schuilkelders verhogen bouwkosten met 8 à 10%", *Bouw*, (1960) 4, 114.

39. See also "Schuilplaatsen in de onderbouw. Koninklijk Besluit van 28 Juni '55", *Bouw*, (1955) 40, 810-811. A.O. Schuil, "Toelichtende beschouwing", *Bouw*, (1955) 40, 811-814.

40. Van der Boom, 159.

41. Van der Boom, 181.

42. Van der Boom, 161.

43. Van der Boom, 162.

44. The ups and downs of the BB may be followed in the national monthly periodical *Paladijn* which was published from 1961 to 1976.

45. *Een avontuurlijk leven. Herinneringen van Joost Meyboom 20 mei 1932-25 januari 2003*, Groningen 2004, 31.

46. See e.g. the "Cities Unbuilt" issue of *Volume*, (2007) 1.

47. W.D. Cocroft & R.J.C. Thomas, *Cold War. Building for Nuclear Confrontation 1946-1989*, London 2003, 3.

48. Cocroft & Thomas, 3.

CHAPTER 9

1. See also the NIOD publication (eds. M. de Keizer and S.C. Roels), *Staat van veiligheid. De Nederlandse samenleving sinds 1900*, Zutphen 2007.

2. H. Angerer, *Flakbunker. Betonierte Geschichte*, Hamburg 2000. D. and I. Arnold, *Dunkle Welten. Bunker, Tunnel und Gewölbe unter Berlin*, Berlin 1999. M. Foedrowitz, *Bunkerwelten. Luftschutzanlagen in Norddeutschland*, Berlin 1998. H. Sakkers, *Flaktürme, Berlin, Hamburg, Wien*, Nieuw-Weerdinge 1998. T. Selke, *Luftschutzmaßnahmen in Hamburg während des "Dritten Reiches"*, Hamburg 1998. H. Schmal and T. Selke, *Bunker. Luftschutz und Luftschutzbau in Hamburg*, Hamburg 2001.

3. Anonymous woman, *Eine Frau in Berlin*, Frankfurt am Main 2003. E. Bahr, *Der deutsche Weg. Selbstverständlich und normal*, Munich 2003. W. Bönitz, *Feindliche Bomberverbände im Anflug: Zivilbevölkerung im Luftkrieg*, Berlin 2003. S. Burgdorff and C. Habbe (ed.), *Als Feuer vom Himmel fiel. Der Bombenkrieg in Deutschland*, Munich 2003. P. Glotz, *Die Vertreibung. Böhmen als Lehrstück*, Berlin 2003. L. Kettenacker (ed.), *Ein Volk von Opfern? Die neue Debatten um den Bombenkrieg 1940-1945*, Berlin 2003. G. Schöllgen, *Der Auftritt. Deutschlands Rückkehr auf die Weltbühne*, Berlin 2003. U. Timm, *Am Beispiel meines Bruders*, Cologne 2003. E. Todd, *Après l'empire. Essai sur la décomposition du système Américain*, Paris 2002.

4. Cocroft and Thomas 2003. W. Cocroft, "The Cold War. What to preserve and why", *Conservation Bulletin. The Archeology of Conflict*, (2003) June, 40-42.

5. See K. Volkers, *Geheim landschap. 200 jaar militairen op de Heuvelrug*, Utrecht 2006, 83-97, 153-162.

6. H. Masselink, "Voormalig oord van afschrikking geeft nu ruimte aan verrassende kunst", *Trouw*, 2 August 2005.

7. Foedrowitz, 150.

8. L. Allais, "International Style Heritage", *Volume*, (2009) 2, 128.

9. B. Hatton, "Strategische Architektur. Die unbeweglichen Objekte der Vorstellung", in S. Wenk (ed.), *Erinneringsorte aus Beton. Bunker in Städten und Landschaften*, Berlin 2001, 63.

10. R. Williams, *Notes on the underground. An essay on technology, society and the imagination*, Cambridge (Mass.) and London 1990.

11. W. Voigt, "Zwischen Weißenhof-Streit und Pour le mérite: Paul Schmitthenner im Architekturstreit der zwanziger bis fünfziger Jahre", in W. Voigt and H. Frank (ed.), *Paul Schmitthenner 1884-1972*, Frankfurt am Main 2004, 67-99.

12. A. Speer, *Inside the Third Reich*, London 1970, 97-98 (German original: *Erinnerungen*, Berlin 1969.)

13. Speer, 169.

Sources

ARCHIVES

Centrale Archief Selectiedienst, Winschoten
Centrale Sector VROM, The Hague
Gelders Archief, Arnhem
Gemeentearchief van Amersfoort, Barneveld, Heerlen, Huizen, Rotterdam, Valkenswaard
Haags Gemeentearchief, The Hague
Helders Gemeentearchief, Den Helder
Het Archief Nijmegen, Nijmegen
Het Utrechts Archief, Utrecht
Kenniscentrum, Apeldoorn
London Metropolitan Archives, London
Nationaal Archief, The Hague
Archief Binnenlandse Zaken, Inspectie van de Bescherming Bevolking tegen Luchtgevaar
Archief PTT
Archief Rijksgebouwendienst
Centraal Archief Bijzondere Rechtspleging 1945-1992
Nederlands Architectuurinstituut, Rotterdam
Archief C.B. Posthumus Meyes jr.
Nederlands Instituut voor Oorlogsdocumentatie, Amsterdam
FiWi Abteilung Bauwirtschaft
FiWi Abteilung Siedlung und Bauten
FiWi Abteilung Industrielle Umsiedlung
FiWi Bevollmächtigte für die Bauwirtschaft
Deutsche Dienstpost Niederlande
Groep Albrecht
Reichskommissar archief 14-16A
Washington Papers
Wehrmachtsbefehlshaber in den Niederlanden
Stadsarchief, Amsterdam
Zeeuws Archief, Middelburg

PHOTOGRAPHY

Berlin Story Verlag, Berlin
Bildarchiv Denkmalschutzamt, Hamburg
Bildarchiv Landesmedienzentrum, Hamburg

Bildarchiv Preußischer Kulturbesitz, Berlin
Bundesarchiv, Koblenz
Collection Michael Foedrowitz, Berlin
Collection Niels Gutschow
Historisches Museum, Hannover
Hulton Getty Picture Collection, London
Imperial War Museum, London
London Metropolitan Archives, London
Museum voor Communicatie, The Hague
Nordrhein-Westfälisches Hauptstaatsarchiv, Stuttgart
Regionaal Historisch Centrum, Eindhoven (archief Maarheze)
Ruhrlandmuseum, Essen
Staatsarchiv Bremen
Staatsarchiv Hamburg
Stadtarchiv Kassel
Stadtarchiv Neurenberg
Stadtarchiv Stuttgart

About the Author

Professor dr. Koos Bosma, VU University Amsterdam, chair Architectural History and Heritage Studies.

Koos Bosma is researcher of 20th century architecture and city planning. He did extensive research of the planning and design of the Dutch IJsselmeerpolders and the reconstruction of the Netherlands and Europe after World War II. In 1993 his dissertation about regional planning in the Netherlands 1900-1945 was published. Since that time he mainly published on housing, city planning and infrastructural planning, such as the civil engineering works of the Ministry of Watermanagement, the Channel Tunnel, the High Speed Trains-programs in Europe and the large European airfields.

The issues that have focussed his interest over the years are Theory of Architecture, City Planning and Reconstruction of European Cities after World War II. More recently he started studying heritage topics like the Atlantic Wall and Cold War relics.

His main publications in English are:

Ed. with H. Hellinga, *Mastering the City: North-European City Planning 1900-2000*, Rotterdam 1997.

Ed.and co-author: *Housing for the Millions. John Habraken and the SAR (1960-2000)*, Rotterdam 2000 (with D. van Hoogstraten and M. Vos).

'European Airports, 1945-1995: Typology, Psychology and Infrastructure,' in J. Zukowsky (ed.), *Building for Air Travel. Architecture and Design for Commercial Aviation*, Munich/New York 1996, 51-65.

Credits for Illustrations and Photography

Between brackets the page numbers are mentioned and if necessary more precisely:
a= above
b=below
le=left
ri=right

NEW PHOTOGRAPHY
Anja de Jong (239, 253, 254, 255, 259, 260, 261, 307, 308, 313, 314, 318, 346b, 353)

DRAWINGS AND SCHEMES
Cyane Conijn (240, 252, 256, 257, 258, 272-273, 307, 309, 311, 312, 313, 316, 317)

CARTOGRAPHY
Bert Brouwenstijn (20, 48, 178, 220, 264, 267, 272-273, 275, 277ri, 280, 294, 328)

CHAPTER 1
Hampe, *Deckname: "Zeppelin". Die Bunker im Hauptquartier des Oberkommandos des Heeres in Zossen*
    (43, 44)
NIOD (30ri, 32, 34, 35)

CHAPTER 2
Bildarchiv Denkmalschutzamt, Hamburg (74)
Gemeentearchief Rotterdam (83, 84)
Het Archief Utrecht (85)
Imperial War Museum (51middle, 52, 53le, 56middle, 58le, 59ri, 63, 68le)
London Metropolitan Archive (56le)
Nationaal Archief (80,81)
NIOD (46-47, 50ri, 51ri, 64, 69b, 85, 89)
Staatsarchiv Hamburg (50le)
Stadsarchief Amsterdam (86)

CHAPTER 3
Collection Foedrowitz (118, 119)
Collection Gutschow (116, 117)
NIOD (104re, 106)
Stadtarchiv Stuttgart (108)

Geographical Index

Index of Names

LHS

LANDSCAPE AND HERITAGE SERIES

Landscape & Heritage Series (LHS) is a new English-language series about the history, heritage and transformation of the natural and cultural landscapes, and built environment. The series aims at the promotion of new directions as well as the rediscovery and exploration of lost tracks in landscape and heritage research. These two theoretically oriented approaches play an important part in the realization of this objective.

LHS welcomes monographs and edited volumes, theoretically oriented approaches and detailed case studies. For more information about the series, please visit www.aup.nl or www.clue.nu.

PUBLISHED IN THIS SERIES

Proceedings

The Cultural Landscape & Heritage Paradox:
Protection and Development of the Dutch
Archaeological-Historical Landscape and its
European Dimension
Edited by Tom Bloemers, Henk Kars &
Arnold van der Valk
ISBN 978 90 8964 155 7

Landscape Archaeology between Art and
Science: From a Multi- to an Interdisciplanary
Approach
Edited by Sjoerd Kluiving &
Erika Guttman-Bond
ISBN 978 90 8964 418 3

FORTHCOMING IN 2012

Textbooks

Reader in Landscape and Heritage
Edited by Jan Kolen & Rob van der Laarse